THE UNIVERSITY OF ILLINOIS MEMORIAL STADIUM

This book offers a rigorous but graphically compelling narrative historic analysis of one of the most important civic buildings not only of the University of Illinois Urbana-Champaign, or the State of Illinois, but arguably of the United States, Memorial Stadium.

Like all spatial products, the design and construction of the University of Illinois Memorial Stadium embodies the social, political, economic, aspiration, and aesthetic values of its time. This book will engage in critical analysis including documenting the civic discourse that led to the Stadium and thereafter explore the iterative nature of the Stadium in shaping civic discourse. In this vein, central topics include its role in embodying the state's economic growth; the changing nature of the sociocultural tendencies and its impact on campus life and the University's community; the Stadium's effects on UIUC sports and the campus' built environment; the rise of College sports as big business; and the impact on mass culture across the State and the country, like the use of stadiums as concert venues and place of public discourse. More than a simple study of the building's conceptualization, design, and construction, this book reveals why Illinois' Memorial Stadium is an iconic part of the American Midwest's built landscape and in many ways part of the American mythic landscape.

This will be interesting reading for all those familiar with the building, as well as all students and scholars of sports architecture.

Kevin J. Hinders is an Associate Professor of Architecture and director of the Chicago Studio at the University of Illinois, Urbana-Champaign.

Benjamin A. Bross is an Assistant Professor of Architecture at the University of Illinois, Urbana-Champaign.

THE UNIVERSITY OF ILLINOIS MEMORIAL STADIUM

The First 100 Years

Kevin J. Hinders and Benjamin A. Bross

Routledge
Taylor & Francis Group

LONDON AND NEW YORK

Designed cover image: Kevin J. Hinders and Benjamin A. Bross, image courtesy of the Division of Intercollegiate Athletics Archives.

First published 2025
by Routledge
4 Park Square, Milton Park, Abingdon, Oxon OX14 4RN

and by Routledge
605 Third Avenue, New York, NY 10158

Routledge is an imprint of the Taylor & Francis Group, an informa business

British Library Cataloguing-in-Publication Data
A catalogue record for this book is available from the British Library

Library of Congress Cataloging-in-Publication Data
A catalog record has been requested for this book

ISBN: 978-1-032-64384-7 (hbk)
ISBN: 978-1-032-64387-8 (pbk)
ISBN: 978-1-032-64388-5 (ebk)

DOI: 10.4324/9781032643885

Typeset in Times New Roman
by codeMantra

Kevin J. Hinders: To my wife, Mary Perona Hinders, who has always selflessly taken care of all the important things in life, and to our family.

Benjamin A. Bross: To my father, Eduardo Bross T., an architect and urban planner, who showed me that the built environment embodies the values of its makers and users.

Together, the authors dedicate this book to all who died serving the United States of America.

April 25, 2024.

Inset 1
Huff's Sketch of the Stadium Site Plan near Washington Park. Shows a stadium (noted 73,000) with a colonnade to the north extending towards Washington Park. Courtesy of University Archives.

Inset 2
Huff's Description on the back of his Stadium Sketch, submitted to James McLaren White. "Each bank of seats 542 ft. Long and 114 ft. High. Colonnade of Doric Columns forming a frieze. Columns 22 ½ ft. High and 4ft. Diam. At base. 52 free standing columns and as manymore engaged." Courtesy of University Archives.

Contents

Acknowledgments   xi
List of Figures   xiii
Foreword   xxiii

INTRODUCTION   **1**

Illinois Memorial Stadium Memories   1

1 FOUNDING THE UNIVERSITY OF ILLINOIS   **5**

Introduction   5
Situating the Stadium   7
Prelude to the University   10
Founding the University, Future Home of Memorial Stadium   14

2 ORIGINS OF MEMORIAL STADIUM   **23**

Introduction   23
An Evolving University   23
The Impetus for a Stadium   27
Initial Campus Land Acquisitions, 1867–1925 (*green*)   36
Land Acquisitions, 1900–1919 (*orange*)   37
Land Acquisitions, 1920–1925 (*blue*)   37

**3 MEMORIAL STADIUM'S DESIGN AND
   CONSTRUCTION**   **43**

Introduction   43
The Stadium's Design   43
Design as an Expression of Time and Place   59

4 BUILDING MEMORIAL STADIUM   **75**

Introduction   75
Construction Begins   75
The Soft Opening   104
October 17, 1924   124

5 MEMORIAL STADIUM, 1924–1941   139

Introduction   139
A Thrilling Inauguration   139
The Golden Age of Sport   147
From 1924 to Pearl Harbor   149
Memorial Stadium as Venue   152
The Stadium Continues to Evolve   154
The Stadium's Impact on Diversity   164

6 FROM WORLD WAR II TO 1960   171

Introduction   171
Memorial Stadium during World War II   171
Memorial Stadium After WWII   177
The Television Era Begins   180

7 THE TUMULTUOUS YEARS, 1960 TO 1975   193

Introduction   193
The 1960s   193
Stadium Changes through 1974   205
The Stadium as Backdrop of Activism   213

8 A NEW STADIUM ERA   219

Introduction   219
Memorial Stadium Evolves, 1974–1989   220
Track and Field Takes Center Stage   226
Illini Football, 1975–1990   229

9 THE NEW MILLENNIUM   245

Introduction   245
Memorial Stadium in the 1990s   247
New Decade, New Century, and New Millennium   263

10 THE POINT AFTER   293

One Hundred Years of Sports and Innovations   293
Illinois Memorial Stadium is a Community Anchor   296

Bibliography   299
Index   307

Inset 3
Red Grange with the football, Michigan vs. Illinois, Dedication Game. Courtesy of the University of Illinois Division of Intercollegiate Athletics Archives.

Acknowledgments

From the front cover to the back cover, *The University of Illinois Memorial Stadium: The First Hundred Years* is the result of an extensive collaboration that included two Illinois School of Architecture professors and the sustained support of various people throughout the University of Illinois Urbana-Champaign and wider community. First, we acknowledge that Memorial Stadium provides us with a richly historic and ongoing narrative. To tell the Stadium's story, we are grateful to the countless number of people who have shared with us their valuable time, effort, dedication, and guidance to make this book possible. We note the primary role that the University of Illinois Urbana-Champaign Research Board played in generously funding much of this endeavor.

From the University of Illinois' Department of Intercollegiate Athletics (DIA), we are indebted to Athletic Director Josh Whitman, who not only ensured that we had access to all DIA archives but also provided the book's Foreword. We also thank the following DIA people: Kent Brown, Brett Stillwell, Derrick Burson, Roger Denny, and Kevin Snyder. We express our gratitude to the University of Illinois Urbana-Champaign Archives, noting the crucial assistance provided by Joanne Kaczmarek, University Archivist, as well as Sammi Merritt and Jameatris Rimkus. Similarly, we thank Jenny Marie Johnson from the University of Illinois Urbana-Champaign Maps and Geography Library and Beth Leitz from the University of Illinois Urbana-Champaign Facilities and Engineering Services. Without their energetic support and institutional memory, this book would not be possible.

We acknowledge the leadership of Francisco J. Rodríguez-Suárez, Director of the Illinois School of Architecture, who encouraged us to write about Memorial Stadium as a clear example of the lasting impact the built environment has on its users. Thank you to John Paul, retired journalism instructor from the University of Illinois College of Media. We thank Stephen Ferroni, who toiled with the authors to produce many of the Stadium's architectural illustrations, and Becky Standard, who provided us with her editorial services. Likewise, we are grateful to the Routledge (UK) editorial team, who enthusiastically received and supported this project from the beginning and have demonstrated great patience.

Finally, besides noting that we surely missed mentioning several more people who were instrumental in our labors, we also take a moment to acknowledge and thank our friends and family members who patiently supported us throughout this writing process, and without whom we would not be complete. From the depths of our hearts, thank you to you all.

List of Figures

Inset

1   Huff's Sketch of the Stadium Site Plan near Washington Park. Shows a stadium (noted 73,000) with a colonnade to the north extending towards Washington Park. Courtesy of University Archives.   vi

2   Huff's Description on the back of his Stadium Sketch, submitted to James McLaren White. "Each bank of seats 542 ft. Long and 114 ft. High. Colonnade of Doric Columns forminga frieze. Columns 22 ½ ft. High and 4ft. Diam. At base. 52 free standing columns and as manymore engaged." Courtesy of University Archives.   vi

3   Red Grange with the football, Michigan vs. Illinois, Dedication Game. Courtesy of the University of Illinois Division of Intercollegiate Athletics Archives.   ix

4   One Hundred Years of Illinois Football Coaches. Images courtesy of the University of Illinois Division of Intercollegiate Athletics Archives.   291

Foreward

F.1   Tight end Josh Whitman celebrates scoring a touchdown as a Fighting Illini. Photograph courtesy of the Department of Intercollegiate Athletics Archive.   xxiii

F.2   Josh Whitman, Director of Athletics, in his office overlooking Memorial Stadium. Photograph courtesy of the Department of Intercollegiate Athletics Archives.   xxv

Introduction

I.1   Francisco and his wife, Rebecca, enjoying a football game. Photography by Francisco J. Rodríguez-Suárez.   3

Chapter 1

1.1   Red Grange (furthest to the right) running for a touchdown. Courtesy of the University of Illinois Division of Intercollegiate Athletics archives.   6

1.2   British Geological Survey time chart. Based on The Geologic Time Scale 2012. BGS © UKRI.   7

1.3   Wisconsin Glacial Episode Illinois moraines. Modified from Hansel and Johnson, *Wedron and Mason Groups*, plate 1.   8

1.4   Campus moraine diagram. Image by Kevin J. Hinders.   9

1.5   Population of Illinois. US Census Bureau, *Twelfth Census*, table 1.   12

1.6   Coal mines in Illinois. Modified from M. E. Hopkins, January 1975. Courtesy of the University of Illinois Map Library.   13

1.7   Railroad Map of Illinois. Illinois Central Railroad Company, 1865. Courtesy of the University of Illinois Map Library.   15

1.8   Early map of the Illinois Industrial University by A. C. Kennedy and J. W. Rhodes. Courtesy of the University of Illinois Archives.   20

Chapter 2

2.1 The University of Illinois' first football team, 1890. Courtesy of the University of Illinois Archives. 24

2.2 George Huff. Courtesy of the University of Illinois Department of Intercollegiate Athletics. 25

2.3 Robert "Zup" Zuppke. Courtesy of the University of Illinois Department of Intercollegiate Athletics. 26

2.4 Homecoming game, Illini Field, 1910. Courtesy of the University of Illinois Courtesy of the Department of Intercollegiate Athletics. 27

2.5 Grounds of the University of Illinois, 1906. Tilton and O'Donnell, History of the Growth, 41. Courtesy of the University of Illinois Archives. 30

2.6 Masterplan of the University, 1905 C.H. Blackall. Courtesy of the University Archives. 31

2.7 Holabird and Roche master plan, 1920. This plan shows the removal of the Mount Hope Cemetery, and it is unclear what happens to the Auditorium. Courtesy of the University of Illinois Archives. 33

2.8 The gym during the April 1921 pep rally soliciting students for donations. Story of the Stadium. 34

2.9 Land acquisition records, 1867–1925. Image by Kevin J. Hinders and Stephen Ferroni. 36

2.10 The three Memorial Stadium site proposals. Image by Kevin J. Hinders. 40

2.11 Map of campus. Memorial Stadium Notes 1, no. 1 (July 22, 1922): 3. 41

Chapter 3

3.1 Kallimarmaro Stadium, Athens, Greece. Photograph by George E. Koronaio. Courtesy of Wikimedia Commons. 44

3.2 Circus Maximus. Durand, *Recueil et parallèle des édifices*, 41. 45

3.3 The Flavian Amphitheater (Colosseum). Durand, *Recueil et parallèle des édifices*, 39. 46

3.4 Bay Elevation of the Colosseum, Rome from a drawing by Josef Durm (Karlsruhe 1837–1919), arquitecto. Ver [1]. 47

3.5 Wrigley Field. Photograph by Arvell Dorsey Jr., https://flic.kr/p/bUxLDv, CC BY 2.0, https://creativecommons.org/licenses/by/2.0/. 49

3.6 Faculty sketch for the proposed stadium, February 1921. This rendering shows a circus stadium, honor court, and campanile without balconies. The Illinois Stadium "For Fighting Illini." 51

3.7 Faculty rendering of the proposed honor court & Greek theater. Perspective pencil study of the court of honor, The Illinois Stadium "For Fighting Illini," March 25, 1921. 52

3.8 A carillon was included in the honor court composition. Faculty drawing, perspective pencil study for the tower, The Illinois Stadium "For Fighting Illini," March 25, 1921. 52

3.9 Competition drawing by Holabird and Roche for Grant Park Stadium (now Soldier Field). Bruegmann, *Holabird and Roche*, 2:143. 53

3.10 Soldier Field, in Chicago, Illinois, set up for the Dempsey Tunney fight on September 22, 1927. Photograph by Kaufmann and Fabry Co. Chicago Historical Museum. 54

3.11 Soldier Field colonnade. Photograph by Raymond Trowbridge. Chicago Historical Museum. 55

3.12 A Glimpse of the Chicago Skyline from Soldier Field, Grant Park, Chicago. Courtesy of the Curt Teich Postcard Archives Digital Collection, Newberry Library, Chicago. 56

3.13 Monument to Victor Emmanuelle II, also called the Altar of the Nation Photograph by Globe Trotter Company, Courtesy Wikimedia Commons.   57

3.14 Soldier Field and Memorial Stadium. Drawing by Stephen Ferroni.   58

3.15 Early depiction of Memorial Stadium. Annotated by the authors. Courtesy of the University of Illinois Archives.   60

3.16 Early drawing of Memorial Stadium by Holabird and Roche. From *Story of the Stadium.*   60

3.17 Early drawing of a three-tiered stadium from the field looking toward the south horseshoe by Holabird and Roche. From *Story of the Stadium.* Note the horseshoe's colonnade is similar to Soldier Field.   61

3.18 Section of Grant Park Stadium. Burt, "Stadium Design," 72.   62

3.19 Section of Memorial Stadium. Burt, "Stadium Design," 82.   62

3.20 Stadium ramp tower, interior. Courtesy of the University of Illinois Archives.   63

3.21 Colonnade shortly after completion. Photograph by Raymond Trowbridge. Courtesy of the University of Illinois Archives.   65

3.22 Circulation diagram. Image by Kevin J. Hinders and Stephen Ferroni.   66

3.23 Stair tower ramps to upper deck seating. Image by Kevin J. Hinders and Stephen Ferroni.   67

3.24 Stadium section diagram. Image by Kevin J. Hinders and Stephen Ferroni.   67

3.25 Stadium longitudinal section through upper ramps and elevation. Image by Kevin J. Hinders and Stephen Ferroni.   68

3.26 Cross-section and elevation drawings of a reconstruction of the Colosseum in Rome. Line engraving by Luigi Canina, 1851.   69

3.27 Harvard Stadium. Courtesy of Harvard University, Cambridge, MA.   70

3.28 Drawings of the School of Architecture overall. Image by Eliza Peng.   70

3.29 Facade diagram. Image by Kevin J. Hinders and Stephen Ferroni.   71

3.30 The bas-relief sculptures over the ramp tower entries. Photograph by Kevin J. Hinders.   71

3.31 The bas-relief sculptures on the north and south ends of the ramp towers depict war, athletics, and education. Photograph by Kevin J. Hinders.   72

3.32 Carved medallions on the ramp towers. Photograph by Kevin J. Hinders.   72

Chapter 4

4.1 George Huff turns the first spade at the Memorial Stadium's groundbreaking, September 11, 1922. Courtesy of the University of Illinois Department of Intercollegiate Athletics Archives.   76

4.2 Stadium fund flyer. Courtesy of the University of Illinois Archives.   79

4.3 *Memorial Stadium Notes* 1, no. 2 (September 1922): 1. Courtesy of the University of Illinois Archives.   80

4.4 Structural steel shop drawings showing markups, December 14, 1922. Courtesy of the University of Illinois Archives.   82

4.5 Early grading and foundation digging, October 27, 1922. Courtesy of the University of Illinois Department of Intercollegiate Athletics Archives.   83

4.6 Formworks for the great hall and ramp towers being set, October 27, 1922. Courtesy of the University of Illinois Department of Intercollegiate Athletics Archives.   84

4.7 Foundation work completed prior to 1923. Courtesy of the University of Illinois Department of Intercollegiate Athletics Archives.   85

4.8   Early steel work for the great hall, January 23, 1923. Courtesy of the Division of Intercollegiate Athletics Archives.   85

4.9   Great hall steel columns erected, February 7, 1923. Courtesy of the Division of Intercollegiate Athletics Archives.   86

4.10 East stands, February 7, 1923. Courtesy of the Division of Intercollegiate Athletics Archives.   87

4.11 Derricks erecting the steel frame, March 8, 1923. Courtesy of the Division of Intercollegiate Athletics Archives.   88

4.12 West stands, March 8, 1923. Courtesy of the Division of Intercollegiate Athletics Archives.   88

4.13 East stands, March 24, 1923. Courtesy of the Division of Intercollegiate Athletics Archives.   89

4.14 East balcony steel erection, April 13, 1923. Courtesy of the Division of Intercollegiate Athletics Archives.   90

4.15 East balcony steel erection, April 28, 1923. Courtesy of the Division of Intercollegiate Athletics Archives.   90

4.16 Field and east stands, May 19, 1923. Courtesy of the Division of Intercollegiate Athletics Archives.   91

4.17 West stands with steel and seating underway, May 19, 1923. Courtesy of the Division of Intercollegiate Athletics Archives.   91

4.18 West stands, June 2, 1923. Courtesy of the Division of Intercollegiate Athletics Archives.   92

4.19 East stands, June 2, 1923. Courtesy of the Division of Intercollegiate Athletics Archives.   92

4.20 West stands, July 2, 1923. Courtesy of the Division of Intercollegiate Athletics Archives.   92

4.21 East stands, July 2, 1923. Courtesy of the Division of Intercollegiate Athletics Archives.   93

4.22 Aerial photograph of stadium construction, July 6, 1923. Courtesy of the Division of Intercollegiate Athletics Archives.   93

4.23 West stands, July 18, 1923. Courtesy of the Division of Intercollegiate Athletics Archives.   94

4.24 West stands, August 2, 1923. Courtesy of the Division of Intercollegiate Athletics Archives.   94

4.25 East stands, August 30, 1923. Courtesy of the Division of Intercollegiate Athletics Archives.   95

4.26 West stands, August 30, 1923. Courtesy of the Division of Intercollegiate Athletics Archives.   95

4.27 Great Hall Ramps Under Construction. Courtesy of the Division of Intercollegiate Athletics.   96

4.28 Great west hall looking north. Courtesy of the Division of Intercollegiate Athletics Archives.   96

4.29 West stands casting balcony seating, September 1923. Courtesy of the Division of Intercollegiate Athletics Archives.   97

4.30 East stands, October 12, 1923. Courtesy of the Division of Intercollegiate Athletics Archives.   97

4.31 West stands, October 12, 1923. Courtesy of the Division of Intercollegiate Athletics Archives.   98

4.32 Homecoming game crowd photo, against the University of Chicago, November 3, 1923. Courtesy of the Division of Intercollegiate Athletics Archives.   98

4.33 Homecoming action photograph. Courtesy of the Division of Intercollegiate Athletics Archives.   99

4.34 Building toward homecoming, 1923. Courtesy of the Division of Intercollegiate Athletics Archives.   100

4.35 Stadium button, *MSN* 2, no. 10 (November 3, 1923). 3.   103

4.36 Stadium seating plan. *MSN* 2, no. 9 (October 1923): 5.   103

4.37 Homecoming game panorama, against the University of Chicago, November 3, 1923. Courtesy of the Division of Intercollegiate Athletics Archives. 105

4.38 West stands, January 30, 1924. Courtesy of the Division of Intercollegiate Athletics Archives. 108

4.39 West stands, January 31, 1924. Courtesy of the Division of Intercollegiate Athletics Archives. 108

4.40 East stands, exterior, January 30, 1924. Courtesy of the Division of Intercollegiate Athletics Archives. 109

4.41 East stands, January 31, 1924. Courtesy of the Division of Intercollegiate Athletics Archives. 109

4.42 East stands colonnade, March 8, 1924. Courtesy of the Division of Intercollegiate Athletics Archives. 110

4.43 West stands, March 8, 1924. Courtesy of the Division of Intercollegiate Athletics Archives. 110

4.44 West stands colonnade, April 10, 1924. Courtesy of the Division of Intercollegiate Athletics Archives. 111

4.45 West stands colonnade, April 29, 1924. Courtesy of the Division of Intercollegiate Athletics Archives. 111

4.46 East stands colonnade, April 29, 1924. Courtesy of the Division of Intercollegiate Athletics Archives. 112

4.47 West stands, May 16, 1924. Courtesy of the Division of Intercollegiate Athletics Archives. 112

4.48 West stands colonnade, May 1924. Courtesy of the Division of Intercollegiate Athletics Archives. 113

4.49 East stands colonnade, May 1924. Courtesy of the Division of Intercollegiate Athletics Archives. 113

4.50 East stands colonnade, July 1, 1924. Courtesy of the Division of Intercollegiate Athletics Archives. 114

4.51 West stands colonnade, July 14. Courtesy of the Division of Intercollegiate Athletics Archives. 114

4.52 East stands colonnade, July 14, 1924. Courtesy of the Division of Intercollegiate Athletics Archives. 115

4.53 East stands colonnade, July 14, 1924. Courtesy of the Division of Intercollegiate Athletics Archives. 115

4.54 East stands colonnade, late July 1924. Courtesy of the Division of Intercollegiate Athletics Archives. 116

4.55 East stands colonnade, August 12, 1924. Courtesy of the Division of Intercollegiate Athletics Archives. 116

4.56 East stands colonnade, August 12, 1924. Courtesy of the Division of Intercollegiate Athletics Archives. 117

4.57 West stands colonnade, August 1924. Courtesy of the Division of Intercollegiate Athletics Archives. 117

4.58 East stands colonnade, September 3, 1924. Courtesy of the Division of Intercollegiate Athletics Archives. 118

4.59 West stands colonnade, September 3, 1924. Courtesy of the Division of Intercollegiate Athletics Archives. 118

4.60 West stands colonnade, October 1, 1924. Courtesy of the Division of Intercollegiate Athletics Archives. 119

4.61 East stands colonnade, October 23, 1924. Courtesy of the Division of Intercollegiate Athletics Archives. 119

4.62 Stadium from the southeast, October 23, 1924. Courtesy of the Division of Intercollegiate Athletics Archives. 120

4.63 Engraved column inscription: Charles P. Anderson EX18, 1st LT 96 AER SQ. Photograph by Kevin J. Hinders. 121

4.64 Stadium button. *MSN* 3, no. 8 (August 1924): 3. 122

4.65 All Roads Lead to Champaign-Urbana, September 4, 1924. This map was created for the homecoming game to

assist those traveling by car. Courtesy of
the University Map Library. 123

4.66 Blueprint for train depot at Neil Street
and Stadium Drive. Illinois Central
Railroad Company Office of the
Engineer. Courtesy of the University of
Illinois Archives. 124

4.67 President Kinley speaking at the
Memorial Stadium dedication, October
17, 1924. Courtesy of the Department of
Intercollegiate Athletics Archives. 125

4.68 Memorial Stadium after 1924. Courtesy
of the University of Illinois Department
of Intercollegiate Athletics Photograph
Archives. 126

Centerfolds Part I

C-1.1 Entry Level Plan. Image by Stephen Ferroni. 130
C-1.2 Colonnade Level. Image by Stephen
Ferroni. Roof Level. Image by Stephen
Ferroni. 131
C-1.3 Entry Level Plan with Horseshoe, 1929.
Image by Stephen Ferroni. 132
C-1.4 Stadium Dedication, October 19,
1924. Courtesy of the Division of
Intercollegiate Athletics Archives. 133
C-1.5 Longitudinal Plan. Image by Stephen
Ferroni. 134
East Stand Elevation. Image by Stephen
Ferroni. 134
West Stand Section. Image by Stephen
Ferroni. 134
C-1.6 Ramp Tower Elevation. Image by Kevin
J. Hinders and Stephen Ferroni. 135
Ramp Tower Section. Image by Kevin J.
Hinders and Stephen Ferroni. 135
C-1.7 Elevation Detail. Image by Stephen Ferroni. 136
C-1.8 1924 Team Photograph. Courtesy of
the Division of Intercollegiate Athletics
Archives. 137
C-1.9 Panorama of the October 18, 1924,
Dedication Game. Courtesy of the
Division of Intercollegiate Athletics
Archives. 137

Chapter 5

5.1 "The crowds came early to
Homecoming. From all directions,
they came to witness the dedication
of Illinois' great war memorial."
Homecoming and stadium dedication,
October 18, 1924. 1926 *Illio*, 151.
Courtesy University of Illinois Archive. 140

5.2 "The streets were thronged with people
Saturday morning who gathered to
watch the procession of the annual hobo
parade. And hoboes there were, of all
descriptions." Homecoming and stadium
dedication, October 18, 1924. 1926 *Illio*,
152. Courtesy University of Illinois Archive. 141

5.3 "The vast crowds, restlessly
awaiting the approaching game,
milled about the streets in aimless
wanderings." Homecoming and stadium
dedication, October 18, 1924. 1926 *Illio*,
153. Courtesy University of Illinois Archive. 142

5.4 "The entire town was decorated for
the occasion. Unique arrangements
carried the significance of the dedication
homecoming." Homecoming and
stadium dedication, October 18, 1924.
1926 *Illio*, 154. Courtesy University of
Illinois Archive. 143

5.5 "Governor Small came and was met
by the military escort. Dr. Noble
accepted the Stadium in the name of
the University, the bands playing the
national anthem as Gladys Pennington
raised the flag, and stood silent while a
lone bugler blew taps." Homecoming
and stadium dedication, October
18, 1924. 1926 *Illio*, 155. Courtesy
University of Illinois Archive. 144

5.6 "Then the game began and as Grange
charged repeatedly down the field,
sixty-seven thousand people sent
up cheer after cheer and the stands
rocked and swayed with the sound."

Homecoming and stadium dedication, October 18, 1924. 1926 *Illio*, 156. Courtesy University of Illinois Archive.   145

5.7   "Telegraph instruments clicked out the progress of the battle, thousands of eager listeners followed the game by radio while those who were fortunate enough to be there kept one eye on the ball—and the other on Grange." Homecoming and stadium dedication, October 18, 1924. 1926 *Illio*, 157. Courtesy University of Illinois Archive.   146

5.8   First Chief performance, October 30, 1926. Courtesy of the University of Illinois Department of Intercollegiate Athletics Archives. V.V_N.1_P.1.   152

5.9   220 yards low hurdles, track meet versus Notre Dame, Memorial Stadium. Courtesy of the University of Illinois Department of Intercollegiate Athletics Archives.   153

5.10   Interscholastic Circus. 1930 *Illio*, 192. Courtesy of the University of Illinois Archives.   154

5.11   Aerial photograph showing the walks, elms, tennis courts, and seating in the south end zone. Courtesy of the University of Illinois Department of Intercollegiate Athletics Archives.   155

5.12   Interior image of the Great West Hall's proposed ice rink. The *MSN* caption reads: "Start 1926 with Your Stadium Payment!" (5, no. 1 [January 1926]: 1).   156

5.13   Aerial photograph showing end zone improvements. Courtesy of the University of Illinois Department of Intercollegiate Athletics Archives.   161

5.14   Construction document by Holabird and Root of the concrete horseshoe construction. Courtesy of the University of Illinois Archives.   162

5.15   Huff and Zuppke grave sites in Roselawn Cemetery. Photograph by Kevin J. Hinders.   164

Chapter 6

6.1   Memorial Stadium West Great Hall housing proposal, February 6, 1942. Courtesy of the University of Illinois Archives.   172

6.2   Naval Diesel School fit out, July 28, 1942. Courtesy of the University of Illinois Archives.   173

6.3   Unloading the prefabricated Stadium Terrace units. Courtesy of the University of Illinois Archives.   174

6.4   Stadium Terrace looking southeast toward Memorial Stadium. Courtesy of the University of Illinois Archives.   175

6.5   Parade Grounds Units west of the men's dormitories and north of Memorial Stadium with Stadium Terrace to the west. Courtesy of the University of Illinois Archives.   175

6.6   Post-war housing diagram. Diagram by Kevin J. Hinders.   175

6.7   Coach Ray Eliot with players, 1946. *Left to right:* Paul Patterson, William Huber, Claude "Buddy" Young, Eliot, and Robert Cunz. Courtesy of the University of Illinois Department of Intercollegiate Athletics Archives.   176

6.8   The bell cast for the *USS Illinois*. Courtesy of the University of Illinois Department of Intercollegiate Athletics Archives.   177

6.9   WILL broadcasting center at Memorial Stadium plan drawing. Courtesy of the University of Illinois Archives.   181

6.10   Initial site plan of fieldhouse proposal framing the Armory across from Huff Gym, February 1944. Courtesy of the University of Illinois Archives.   184

6.11   Site plan of fieldhouse proposal on an axis with the Armory south of the proposed military axis, December 1944. Note the dormitories to the west across Fourth Street and the proposed "New

Mall" on the military axis. Courtesy of the University of Illinois Archives. 185

6.12 Site plan for a new Health and Physical Education Building north of Memorial Stadium. The structures were to be connected underground via tunnels and above ground with terraces (*right*). Courtesy of the University of Illinois Archives. 186

6.13 Basement in the proposed Health and Physical Education Building, 1945. Courtesy of the University of Illinois Archives. 187

6.14 Rendering for a new Health and Physical Education Building. Courtesy of the University of Illinois Archives. 188

6.15 Assembly Hall west entrance. Photograph by Kevin J. Hinders. 189

6.16 Assembly Hall interior. Photograph by Kevin J. Hinders. 189

Chapter 7

7.1 Head Coach Pete Elliott. Courtesy of the University of Illinois Department of Intercollegiate Athletics Archives. 195

7.2 First Illinois touchdown at the 1964 Rose Bowl. Courtesy of the Division of Intercollegiate Archives. 199

7.3 Dick Butkus (#51) and Jim Grabowski (#33) when they played for the Chicago Bears. Courtesy of the Division of Intercollegiate Archives. 200

7.4 Zuppke Field's north wall and the scoreboard. Courtesy of the University of Illinois Archives. 201

7.5 Athlete Bill McKeown and Head Coach Leo T. Johnson. Courtesy of the Division of Intercollegiate Athletics Archives. 202

7.6 George Kerr. Courtesy of the Division of Intercollegiate Athletics Archives. 203

7.7 Head Coach Nell Jackson. Courtesy of the Division of Intercollegiate Athletics Archives. 204

7.8 1967 Press box. Image by Kevin J. Hinders from drawings in the University of Illinois Archives. 207

7.9 1967 Press box as seen from the field. Courtesy of the Division of Intercollegiate Athletics Archives. 208

7.10 1967 Press box photographer's floor. Courtesy of the Division of Intercollegiate Athletics Archives. 209

7.11 1967 Press box reporter's floor. Courtesy of the Division of Intercollegiate Athletics Archives. 210

7.12 1967 Section through the west stands and press box. Drawing by Stephen Feronni. 210

7.13 New scoreboard, Ohio State game, Oct. 5, 1985. Courtesy of the Division of Intercollegiate Athletics Archives. 211

7.14 Aerial view of the stadium with new press box, 1972. Courtesy of the Division of Intercollegiate Athletics Archives. 213

Chapter 8

8.1 Memorial Stadium with newly installed artificial turf and lighting. Courtesy of the Division of Intercollegiate Athletics Archive. 221

8.2 Head Coach Gary Wieneke. Courtesy of the Division of Intercollegiate Athletics Archives. 227

8.3 Big Ten champion men's track and field team. Courtesy of the Division of Intercollegiate Athletics Archive. 228

8.4 Program cover, 58th Annual NCAA Track and Field Championships. Courtesy of the Division of Intercollegiate Athletics Archive. 229

8.5 TailGREAT at Memorial Stadium. Courtesy of the Division of Intercollegiate Athletics Archive. 232

8.6 Farm Aid 1985, Looking toward the stage to the north. Courtesy of Memory

Lane Photography, Photograph by Scott
Christenson. 237

8.7 Farm Aid 1985, Looking south from
the stage. Courtesy of Memory Lane
Photography, Photograph by Scott
Christenson. 237

8.8 Rendering of the football offices.
Courtesy of the Division of
Intercollegiate Athletics Archive. 238

8.9 The Bubble exterior. Courtesy of the
Division of Intercollegiate Athletics
Archive. 239

8.10 The Bubble exterior. Courtesy of the
Division of Intercollegiate Athletics
Archive. 239

8.11 The Bubble interior. Courtesy of the
Division of Intercollegiate Athletics
Archive. 240

8.12 Fire damage to the artificial turf at
Memorial Stadium. Courtesy of the
Division of Intercollegiate Athletics Archive. 241

8.13 Fire damage to the artificial turf at
Memorial Stadium. Courtesy of the
Division of Intercollegiate Athletics Archive. 241

Chapter 9

9.1 Howard Griffith running against the
Southern Illinois Salukis. Courtesy of the
Division of Intercollegiate Athletics Archives 248

9.2 Grange Rock. Courtesy of the Division
of Intercollegiate Athletics Archives. 249

9.3 East Balcony Renovation. Courtesy of
the Division of Intercollegiate Athletics
Archives. 252

9.4 Memorial Stadium Campus Plan. Image
by Kevin J. Hinders. 254

9.5 Irwin Indoor Practice Facility under
construction. Courtesy of the Division of
Intercollegiate Athletics Archives. 255

9.6 Irwin Interior Practice Facility interior
looking southeast. Image by Kevin J.
Hinders. 256

9.7 Henry Dale and Betty Smith Football
Performance Center. Courtesy of the
Division of Intercollegiate Athletics
Archives. 257

9.8 Memorial Stadium 2008 addition
proposals study model. Courtesy of the
Division of Intercollegiate Athletics
Archives. 258

9.9 Christie Clinic Illinois Race Weekend,
2016 finish line heading south. Courtesy
Christie Clinic Illinois Race Weekend. 261

9.10 Red Grange Statue, Courtesy of the
Division of Intercollegiate Athletics
Archives. 262

9.11 Grange Grove Entry. Courtesy of the
Division of Intercollegiate Athletics
Archives. 262

9.12 Grange Grove. Courtesy of the Division
of Intercollegiate Athletics Archives. 263

9.13 HNTB proposed alterations to Memorial
Stadium. Courtesy of the Division of
Intercollegiate Athletics Archives. 265

9.14 Students and band section at the north
end of Memorial Stadium. Courtesy of
the Division of Intercollegiate Athletics
Archives. 266

9.15 Student Cheering Section. Courtesy of
the Division of Intercollegiate Athletics
Archives. 267

9.16 Weight room facility. Courtesy of the
Division of Intercollegiate Athletics
Archives. 268

9.17 Colonnade Club under construction,
April 2008. Courtesy of the Division of
Intercollegiate Athletics Archives. 269

9.18 North endzone following the Ball State
game, September 2, 2017. Photograph
by Kevin J. Hinders. 270

9.19 Florida Agriculture and Mining
University band, September 4,
2004. Courtesy of the Division of
Intercollegiate Athletics Archives. 270

9.20 Band halftime show October 6,
2023. Courtesy of the Division of

Intercollegiate Athletics Archives.
Photograph by Kevin Snyder.   272

9.21 West Stands with Colonnade
Club. Courtesy of the Division of
Intercollegiate Athletics Archives.   273

9.22 Scoreboard and end zone seating.
Courtesy of the Division of
Intercollegiate Athletics Archives   274

9.23 Social distancing and cutout images
in Memorial Stadium during the 2020
Covid-19 season.   275

Centerfolds Part II

C-2.1 Field Level Plan. Image by
Kevin J. Hinders.   280

C-2.2 Entry Level Plan. Image by Kevin J.
Hinders.   281

C-2.3 Upper level Plans. Image by Kevin J.
Hinders.   282

C-2.4 West Stadium at the 10 Yard Line. Image
by Kevin J. Hinders and Stephen Ferroni.   284

C-2.5 East Stadium Section: Image by Kevin J.
Hinders and Stephen Ferroni.   285

C-2.6 Longitudinal Section. Image by Stephen
Ferroni.   286

C-2.7 West Stadium image: Courtesy of the
Division of Intercollegiate Athletics
Archive.   286

C-2.8 North Endzone Section. Image by Kevin
J. Hinders.   287

C-2.9 and C-2.10 North Elevation and South
Elevation. Images by Kevin J. Hinders.   288

C-2.11 Photograph of the Stadium from the
south endzone. Courtesy of the Division
of Intercollegiate Athletics Archives.   288

C-2.12 Photograph of the West Colonnade
Club. Courtesy of the Division of
Intercollegiate Athletics Archives.   289

C-2.13 Stadium progression 1924-2014.
Image by Stephen Ferroni.   290

Chapter 10

10.1 Nebraska Game, Sept. 21, 2019.
Courtesy of the Division of
Intercollegiate Athletics Archives.
Photograph by Craig Pessman.   297

Foreword

The so-called "built environment," highlighted by buildings and landscapes, offers spatial settings that give meaning to our daily lives. The most powerful of these environments enables us to be part of something larger than ourselves, not only because they provide an opportunity to interact with others but also because they bind us to a past made tangible by the built form as we shape our shared future. This book, a rigorous examination of how the built environment can embody the values and stories of a community, celebrates the first century of the University of Illinois' Memorial Stadium. For more than 100 years, Memorial Stadium, the Colossus of the Prairie, has played a major role in the lives of students, student athletes, alumni, and faculty by informing and shaping a crucial part of our community's ever-evolving identity. Beginning with its conception, continuing with its cutting-edge design, innovative funding, breakneck fast-track construction, and progressing to its modern-day maintenance, advancement, and operation, the Stadium has generated some of the most iconic moments in college sports. The Stadium, in fact, has contributed meaningfully to the ongoing history of the region, the State of Illinois, and the United States of America. I know this first-hand because Memorial Stadium has been, and continues to be, a significant factor in shaping my life and my sense of responsibility toward our broader community.

The first time I experienced Memorial Stadium was during my initial recruiting visit to the University. I remember driving west toward campus with my parents, down Florida Avenue, when the street's treelined canopies fell away to reveal the Stadium, with its formidable brick façade and majestic limestone columns stretching toward the Heavens. I literally lost my breath. My sense of awe only grew during that visit when, later

that day, I walked on the very field where, on October 18, 1924, during the Homecoming game that celebrated Memorial Stadium's Grand Dedication, Harold "Red" Grange forever changed college football, providing the single greatest performance in the sport's history. I felt blessed to be invited to make my story one small part of that building's impressive legacy.

I knew how fortunate I was to play for the Orange and Blue. The game of football can be demanding, even exhausting, but my teammates and I never took for granted the privilege of preparing and playing in and around Memorial Stadium. We were part of the Fighting Illini football team, one of the most storied programs in the nation, and Memorial Stadium served as our home away from home. On fall Saturdays, surrounded by thousands of Illini faithful, we played home games on Zuppke Field—the heart of Memorial Stadium—which provided the backdrop for some of the nation's

Figure F.1
Tight end Josh Whitman celebrates scoring a touchdown as a Fighting Illini. Photograph courtesy of the Department of Intercollegiate Athletics Archive.

most legendary sports moments. We knew that with each game, we too were adding one more chapter to the Stadium's rich history.

Over my four years as a tight end for the University of Illinois, I experienced my share of thrilling plays, joyous victories, and heartbreaking losses. I enjoyed gathering with teammates in the locker room after a hard-fought win for rousing renditions of "Illinois Loyalty," sung amidst cascading water bottles and joyous celebration. Although it has been nearly 25 years since I played my last college football game, the intensity of those moments, those powerful experiences, conjures emotions that make the past feel like the present.

Before each game, I vividly recall standing with my teammates, tingling with energy and excitement, every hair on my neck raised, anxiously waiting for the doors to open so we could surge through the tunnel, to the field and our fans and the opportunity that awaited us. That environment offered the greatest high: throngs of people, sounds, and colors, all flooding my senses. To this day, my heart races when I remember the intoxicating mixture of anticipation, nerves, and preparation. Then the doors opened, and it was game time.

Decades later, I listened as University of Illinois alumnus and fellow football letterman Colonel Michael Hopkins described a similar memory during a talk with our football team. He discussed the unique feeling that lives at the intersection of uncertainty and training, at the moment where confidence meets chaos and calmness must prevail. The difference: Hopkins had become a renowned astronaut, and he shared with the team how these feelings, which he experienced moments before exiting the International Space Station for a spacewalk, paralleled those he felt just before exiting the tunnel at Memorial Stadium. Hopkins had trained countless hours for his mission, studying every detail and contingency, immersed in a secure environment, equipped with the latest technology, and surrounded by a supportive team. But in that moment, standing alone on the precipice of chaos and uncertainty, calmness prevailed because, as Hopkins described it, the feelings he was experiencing were eerily familiar from his

time in the Memorial Stadium tunnel. When the doors opened and he stepped into the abyss of outer space, it was game time.

Football, like all sports at the University of Illinois, is not just about winning and losing. College sports are about bringing people together, each with something to contribute to the wider community. My time as an athlete provided me with countless experiences that, to this day, instilled in me skills, confidence, and perspective that help me navigate my role as the Director of Athletics at the University of Illinois. Having the privilege to play on that field helped me understand that as a community, we need spaces where we can share together the moments that give our lives meaning.

As the Athletic Director, it is now my privilege to present to you this book, *The University of Illinois' Memorial Stadium: The First Hundred Years*. No other building on campus embodies the history and values of our community like Memorial Stadium. The University of Illinois is an academic institution founded in 1867, the direct result of the passage of the Morrill Act (1862), which was made possible by the State of Illinois' emergence as a global industrial and agricultural juggernaut. With the University of Illinois' athletic and sports programs increasingly dominating intercollegiate sports in the late part of the 1910s and into the early 1920s, my predecessor, the legendary George A. Huff, together with head football coach Robert Zuppke (for whom the field is now named), shared a vision for a grand stadium to honor those Illinoisians who served or died in the Great War (1914–1918), while at the same time embracing the present and preparing for a dynamic future.

From its inception, Huff and the Athletic Association (the predecessor to the modern-day Division of Intercollegiate Athletics) envisioned a stadium that lived large in the imagination, serving students, alumni, faculty, and the greater Illinois community by providing a festive venue for events like state-wide high school track and field meets, marching band gatherings, scouting jamborees, Fourth of July celebrations, and history-making concerts like Farm Aid. Memorial Stadium has also played its role in helping to bring about major societal change, having served as a vehicle that championed racial integration, the needs and rights of our differently abled community, and the indelible memory of loss, mourning, and protest.

Finally, as we must all confront the challenge of social, economic, and environmental sustainability, I am keenly aware that Memorial Stadium exemplifies our holistic, long-term sustainable future. The Stadium's value is not only as a sports venue but also as a landmark that guides the University of Illinois campus and surrounding community. Where other institutions of higher education have opted to demolish their older civic venues, we at the University of Illinois have chosen to increase our focus on holistic sustainability, honoring the heritage of our shared past while undertaking the necessary steps—and, yes, the expense—to maintain Memorial Stadium as one of the premier sports and civic facilities in the entire country. For members of the Fighting Illini community, the University of Illinois' Memorial Stadium has been, is, and will continue to be an anchor of our community's ongoing and ever-evolving history. Buoyed by a sense of security provided by the built environment, conscious of our ongoing efforts to honor our past and prepare for our future, and surrounded by our teammates—the University of Illinois and the broader State of Illinois community—please join me in celebrating the first 100 years of our storied Memorial Stadium.

I believe that the Stadium's best days, and the future we will enjoy with it, are still in front of us. It's game time.

I-L-L !!!

I-N-I !!!

Josh Whitman
Director of Athletics
Division of Intercollegiate Athletics
University of Illinois
Champaign, Illinois April 2024

Figure F.2
Josh Whitman, Director of Athletics, in his office overlooking Memorial Stadium. Photograph courtesy of the Department of Intercollegiate Athletics Archives.

Introduction

Illinois Memorial Stadium Memories

As Director of the Illinois School of Architecture (ISoA), it is my distinct honor to have witnessed the evolution of this important initiative from an idea to fruition in the form of this book. Our academic community, the University of Illinois Urbana-Champaign (UIUC), is fortunate to be located on one of the world's most beautiful campuses. Iconic images of the Quad, Alma Mater, and the buildings designed by Charles Platt, including the University's main library and the old architecture building, are engrained in the collective memories of every Illini. And yet, I felt that most of these architectural masterpieces have not been properly documented to preserve their legacy.

When I moved to Urbana, I remember looking for a book focused on Memorial Stadium and its history. At that time, I could not find one. During my search, however, I visited an antique store and stumbled upon a framed photograph that captured its Grand Dedication on October 18, 1924. The photograph revealed a packed Homecoming crowd enjoying a historic 39-14 victory over the University of Michigan. The smiling faces of the crowd hinted that they were spectators to one of the greatest college football performances ever when Harold "Red" Grange scored five touchdowns to help the Fighting Illini upset the Wolverines. I immediately acquired the unique memento, which now proudly hangs in my house, and serves to constantly remind me of the rich history of the Fighting Illini football program. Nevertheless, I still felt that there was a real need for a book and believed it would be an ideal initiative for the

ISoA, especially with Memorial Stadium approaching its first centennial anniversary.

I first glimpsed Memorial Stadium in the fall of 2019. It was Homecoming weekend in Champaign-Urbana, and I had been invited to interview for the directorship of the ISoA, the United States' oldest public school of architecture. My travels had started early in the morning the day before, when I flew out of my hometown of San Juan, Puerto Rico, and arrived in Chicago. The differences between each location were excitingly stark. I have visited, and even lived, in some of the most vibrant urban environments in the world, but the sharp contrast between places prompted me to compare through my mind's eye the tropical landscapes known to me since my youth with Chicago's mysterious low cast cloud-wrapped skyline. Then, I took the second and final leg of the trip, traveling in a relatively small Embraer plane. When on the final landing approach from west to east at Willard Airport (CMI) we suddenly broke through the thick clouds, and I was afforded a magnificent view of Illinois Memorial Stadium. Immediately, I perceived the Stadium not only as a sports venue, but just as importantly, an unforgettable landmark with its impressive double-tiered seating decks, south-side horseshoe bleachers, and colonnades visible across the vast Illinoian prairielands.

Aware that I had been a football coach at the Pee-Wee and High School levels, my hosts included in our agenda attending the Homecoming game as part of the visit's schedule. On the beautiful morning of October 19, I walked into Memorial Stadium alongside the Marching Illini, the nation's premier college marching

DOI: 10.4324/9781032643885-1

1

band. Once at the field level, we were all treated to a breathtaking flyover by two F-16 jetfighters streaking across the sky! I watched the entire contest from the northwest corner of the field, only a few yards away from our team. The University of Wisconsin's football team came to Memorial Stadium that day undefeated at 6-0, ranked #6 in the nation, and heavily favored to win the matchup. Illinois, a 30-point underdog, wore its gray uniforms and managed to stay close enough to the Badgers for the game's first three quarters. With time running out in the fourth quarter, the Illini drove down the field and positioned themselves to attempt a game-winning 39-yard field goal as time expired. The Stadium erupted in a frenzied celebration as James McCourt's kick split the uprights. A better ending could not have possibly been scripted for my first visit! I was standing directly between the North endzone and the Zuppke Field sign, when a massive crowd, mostly students, rushed the field. I was flooded with the kind of pure joyous energy that can only be experienced by attending a game at a Stadium filled with tens of thousands of electrified spectators, who, like me, had just watched a thrilling football game. Such is the power of the built environment, that it can bring so many people together in celebration; I felt the emotions overtake me as I joined the jubilant crowd on the field. I knew at that moment that I would accept the offer to become the next Director of the ISoA.

Since then, I have enjoyed Memorial Stadium as a fan and as an architect. The Stadium's aura transports me to my earlier memories of football stadiums at Georgia Tech and Harvard, where I received my undergraduate and graduate architecture degrees, respectively. As an avid sports fan I have also visited memorable athletic venues located at Auburn University and Notre Dame University; watched baseball games at Wrigley Field and Fenway Park; and have made the pilgrimage to soccer cathedrals, including Barcelona's Nou Camp and Real Madrid's Santiago Bernabéu in Spain. Four years after attending my first game in Champaign, I still feel awe and admiration every time I walk through Grange Grove toward the statue of the Galloping Ghost, Red Grange. As I walk toward the west entrance, compelled by the building's monumentality, I inevitably gaze upon the majestic columns and meditate on the 183 Illinoisans, most of which were alumni of the University of Illinois. Now, their names are inscribed on the columns, a timeless gesture of gratitude because of their ultimate sacrifice when they laid down their lives to preserve freedom. Then, as my excitement rises with each step that I get closer to the Stadium's entrance, I think about Illini football players, like Grange, Buddy Young, Dick Butkus, Tony Eason, and Simeon Rice, who left their mark on the field that rests between the Stadium's 200 columns. As I enter the Colossus of the Prairie, I wonder what new legendary player will I see emerge on that gameday.

I am proud that this beautiful book does justice to that venerable history, and grateful that my esteemed colleagues Kevin J. Hinders and Benjamin A. Bross led the project with rigor and immense enthusiasm. Bross is an urban historian who specializes in placemaking, while Hinders is an urbanist whose research concentrates on the built history of our campus, especially the master plan designed by New York architect Charles Platt. Though Holabird & Roche, a Chicago architectural firm, designed the Stadium, Platt's influence permeates throughout the development of Memorial Stadium. At that time, Platt, James White, the University of Illinois' campus architect, and Athletic Director, George Huff, played a significant role in locating the Stadium to ensure that it would be an anchor not only for the University's sports campus, but a landmark for the entire region. Moreover, Hinders and Bross are not just faculty, they are committed football fans as well: On any given home game football Saturday, you are likely to find them at the Stadium cheering on the Fighting Illini, and from 2017 to 2018, defensive lineman Kevin Michael Hinders, Prof. Hinders' son.

Since the image captured by the 1924 black and white photograph, Memorial Stadium has undergone a series of upgrades and renovations to maintain its place as one of the most important sports venues of the country. When a visitor enters the campus, it acts, together with the State Farm Center, as a welcoming monument. Every afternoon, their impressive silhouettes are framed by the orange tones of the endless prairie sunset, progressively giving way to the stunning nocturnal illumination. Beyond college football games, the Stadium has hosted state-wide high school track meets, a diesel engine school during World War II, the 1977 and 1979 NCAA Outdoor Track and Field Championships, the first FarmAid in 1985, the NFL's Chicago Bears during the 2002 season, graduations, marathon finish lines, and Fourth of July celebrations.

Perhaps a book on State Farm Center would be the next obvious collaboration. After all, Assembly Hall, as it was known previously, was designed by our own ISoA alumnus, Max Abramovitz. In the meantime, I sincerely hope that you will enjoy this beautiful collection of images and essays depicting a unique chapter of our Illini history. The pages of the next 100 years are still to be written. The Illinois Memorial Stadium is an embodied history, unfolding as an accumulation of present events built on the foundation of the past, now guiding us into the future: much like on a Saturday afternoon, the *USS Illinois'* bell rings across the Stadium.

Francisco J. Rodríguez-Suárez, FAIA
Director and Miers Professor
Illinois School of Architecture

Figure I.1
Francisco and his wife, Rebecca, enjoying a football game. Photography by Francisco J. Rodríguez-Suárez.

Founding the University of Illinois

Introduction

Societies produce built environments that embody an era's zeitgeist. In this sense, the history of the University of Illinois Memorial Stadium is a history of the United States of America. Its conceptualization, design, construction, and operation signaled the consolidation of a country that had been growing and evolving since its birth. By 1920, nearly 150 years had passed since the United States had achieved independence from Great Britain. In the years since much had occurred: the end of the Revolutionary War, the adoption of the Constitution by the thirteen former colonies, taking a role as a global leader when its entry into the Great Warr (World War I) in 1917 proved to be a crucial moment in world history. In the years between, the US had experienced western expansion, bloody wars with foreign countries and within its own borders, and the Industrial Revolution, which had helped transform the nation from an overwhelmingly agrarian country in 1790 to a more urban and rural one by 1920.[1]

In those 130 years, the territory that became the state of Illinois emerged as a locus of agricultural and industrial production, generating immense wealth. On the one hand, ancient geological forces had generated a region characterized by hydrological connectivity and agriculturally friendly fertile soils. To the region's east, the Great Lakes, especially Lake Michigan, played a pivotal role in American territorial and economic expansion. To the west, the Mississippi River provided a hydrological highway connecting regional agriculture and industry through the Great Lakes to the rest of the country and eventually the world. On the other hand, the same geological forces rendered the region rich in minerals, including energy-dense coal. With coal easily accessible and plentiful, Illinois' industry experienced exponential growth, which prompted an almost geometrical growth in the state's population.

By the time the US entered the Great War, Illinois had the third-largest congressional delegation, manifesting its political power. The decision to join the military action in 1917 was crucial in turning the course of the conflict and enabled the Allies to achieve victory in 1918. This participation signaled to the world the arrival of the US onto the world's geopolitical and economic scene. Two years later in 1920, with the United States entering a time of prosperity and rapid changes, the University of Illinois formally began a process that would not only produce a building expressive of the era's zeitgeist but also forever change the institution, its students and alumni, the surrounding community, the state of Illinois, and the nation as a whole.

The Stadium Is Conceived

When Robert F. Carr, president of the University of Illinois Board of Trustees (BOT) and an 1893 University graduate, called at 10:15 a.m. to order the Executive Committee's March 9, 1920, meeting, several topics were on the agenda, but one item in particular was central to the University's future.[2] In January of that same year, Acting President David Kinley, planning for the incoming post-WWI enrollment boom, made his forward-looking budget request to the board. Kinley was no stranger to the process, having sketched out the financial plans as vice president under his predecessor, Edmund J. James. However, the 1920 proposal was unlike any in the past: Kinley's plan to accommodate an ever-increasing student enrollment and compete with peer institutions called for twice the previous amount, an astronomical $12,000,000 (just under $187,500,685 in 2023 dollars).[3]

The funding's primary focus was the construction of over 40 new buildings, including a museum, an architecture building, dozens of world-class research laboratories, power houses, gymnasiums, and new student residence halls that would transform the physical campus.[4] Curiously, Kinley did not request funding for a new football stadium's design or construction in the January proposal. Yet when the full BOT met eleven days later in Chicago, Carr appointed George A. Huff, the athletic association (AA) director, along with Mrs. Busey, Mr. Abbott, Dean C. R Richards, and Mrs. Blake as chairman for a "Commission on following Campus Plans."[5] Huff was intent on making certain the student population balanced intellectual pursuits with physical activities. He used his appointment to ensure that physical education and the AA had a role in shaping campus planning. At the board's December 14, 1920, meeting Huff formally requested, and via unanimous vote received, "authority to undertake a campaign to raise funds for building a stadium."[6] The BOT instructed the Campus Plan Commission to "give consideration to the matter of plans and location of a stadium."[7]

With an AA-coordinated funding drive, $2,000,000 was secured through students, alumni, and community-wide donations and pledges. With the desire for a sports venue evidently popular, the commission was not only charged with placing board-approved buildings but now prioritized the Stadium's integration into the campus's overall growth.[8] Finally, based on the proposed siting of the architectural firm Holabird and Roche and the commission's recommendation, the board approved the final location on May 10, 1922. Over 100 years later, the southwest campus spot may seem inevitable if not obvious; yet, to comprehend why Memorial Stadium is situated where it is, it is important to explore how it, like all built environments, is the sum of time,

geography, and the history of sociocultural value systems embodied by the built form.

The Beginning of an Era

On October 18, 1924, over four years after BOT approval, the University of Illinois Fighting Illini took the field at 12:00 p.m. against the University of Michigan's Wolverines, officially dedicating Memorial Stadium. Coached by Robert "Zup" Zuppke and led by Harold Edward "Red" Grange's five touchdowns, the Illini would stun the Wolverines 39–14. At the end of the game, tens of thousands of students rushed onto the field, celebrated within the confines of the new colossus of the prairie, and confirmed Memorial Stadium as one of the major epicenters of American collegiate and university life (Figure 1.1).

While the much anticipated mid-October game had been planned nearly two years before, it marked just one milestone in a story that had started long before a single brick had been laid. The game's radio broadcast, one of college football's first, was heard by millions of people across the United States. That broadcast changed the landscape of higher education by thrusting college life into the center of American culture. Like those

Figure 1.1
Red Grange (furthest to the right) running for a touchdown. Courtesy of the University of Illinois Division of Intercollegiate Athletics archives.

radio waves propagating across time and space from an antenna, the effects of Memorial Stadium's conception, design, construction, and eventual operation would mark new highpoints as its story continued over the decades.

Situating the Stadium

Geographic Context

To better understand the Stadium's current location, it is necessary to understand its context on campus and in Champaign County. But to understand the University's location, it is necessary to go beyond the institution's founding, beyond the first human migration into the area, and into the distant past, to geological time, when what became the state of Illinois was first formed. A series of causal events continue to shape not only the Stadium's identity but also the people who attend the Stadium in the prairie.

The Stadium site's geography—that is, the sum of its specific geology, climate, and biome for a region on the Earth's surface—was forged during the Paleozoic era. After the Illinois Basin formed sometime between a billion and 600 million years ago (YA), it began to sink between the Cambrian and Mississippian periods (between 540 and 325 million YA).[9] With the basin depressed, what is today Illinois was covered by a shallow tropical ocean with "great thicknesses of sediment on the ocean bottom" and "great deposits of sand along the shore and offshore" that ultimately became sandstone layers.[10] At the same time, large calcium carbonate–rich shell concentrations were transformed into limestone, which, in combination with the sandstone layers, typify the Illinois Basin's lithic profile.[11] Crucially for the future state, these Mississippian-period limestone beds, over one kilometer thick in some places, would then "hold large amounts of oil and fluorspar"[12] (Figure 1.2).

At the end of the Paleozoic era, during the Pennsylvanian period, shifting and fractured tectonic plates eliminated the shallow ocean, transforming the landscape into a muddy, river-fed delta swampy forest. Over millions of years, this biome's tremendous concentration of tree, plant, animal, and insect organisms,

which were compressed under massive geologic pressure, transformed the Illinois Basin into one of the world's richest sources of coal. During the Mesozoic era (from 325 to 145 million YA), central Illinois' landscape was characterized by a dry climate, flower-covered hills, valleys, and reptiles.[13]

The Stadium site's current geographical characteristics, however, are the result of two major geological events. First was the Mississippi River's formation, nearly 70 million YA, at the beginning of the Cenozoic era.[14] Though the river's drainage basin, course, and discharge flow have changed over time, they molded the region's geographic identity. The river and its tributaries carved the landscape through erosive force, and its vast drainage basin and flows shaped the biome by providing life-supporting water.

The second event occurred during the Pleistocene epoch or Ice Age (circa 2.6 million to 11,700 YA), when massive glaciers advanced, retreated, and advanced

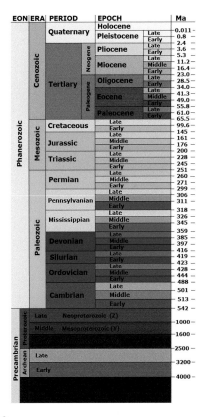

Figure 1.2
British Geological Survey time chart. Based on The Geologic Time Scale 2012. BGS © UKRI.

again before melting during warm spells.[15] At their maximum advance, much of the Earth's Southern and Northern Hemispheres were covered, and in North America glaciers reached what today is Nebraska. As the glaciers pushed southward, their massive size and weight crushed or reduced mountains and hills, filled valleys, and changed the flow of rivers, leaving relatively flat terrains in their wake. During warmer periods, "debris of all sizes was released by the melting ice and was carried forward by melt-water streams or deposited near the ice margin."[16] Those deposits became vast, deep, and fertile soil layers that in combination

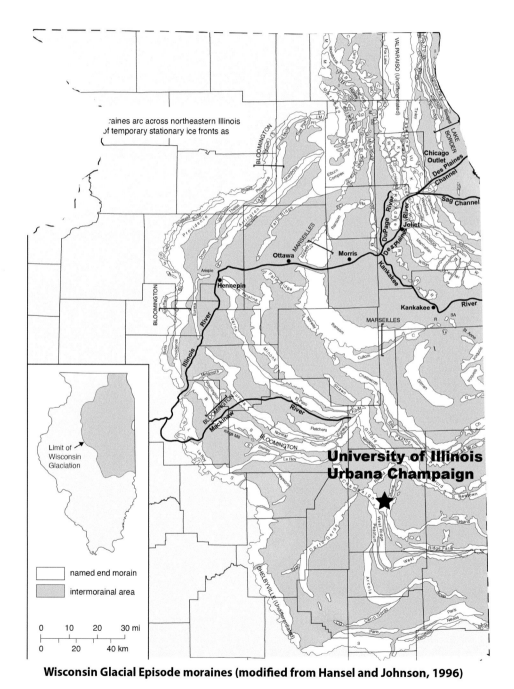

Wisconsin Glacial Episode moraines (modified from Hansel and Johnson, 1996)

Figure 1.3
Wisconsin Glacial Episode Illinois moraines. Modified from Hansel and Johnson, *Wedron and Mason Groups,* plate 1.

with the Mississippi River and its basin have enabled today's high-yield cyclical farming of Illinois' agricultural fields.

Champaign County

During the late Pleistocene epoch and into the early Holocene (the current epoch), Champaign County acquired much of its geologic, and hence geographic, characteristics. As the Ice Age ended (between 15,000 and 14,000 YA), glaciers retreated northward, leaving behind a relatively flat terrain interrupted by gentle slopes and water flows that form part of the greater Mississippi River watershed. One slope runs diagonally, northeast to southwest, generating the Upper Sangamon ridgeline that marks the eastern boundary of the Sangamon and Salt River watersheds: from Gibson City in Ford County through Champaign County and down to Mount Zion in Macon County. The glaciers' retreat left behind drift-free and rock-free fine-grained, thin layers of smooth textured mineral-rich materials called loess. Because of the minerals, these loess layers retain moisture, a soil characteristic very well suited for agriculture. They also are prone to flooding, frequently generating muddy swamps and marshlands. In contrast, in areas of Illinois not covered by glaciers, like those found near the town of Galena, the bedrock is nearer to the surface, which produces a less flat terrain that makes agriculture more difficult. Figure 1.3 shows the location of glaciers and where loess developed across the eastern part of the state. Note the absence of rocks, which would interfere with plowing.

Not surprisingly, Europeans and European Americans who settled in the southeastern part of the state in the early 1800s were amazed at the fertility of the prairie soil. John Woods, an English settler in the Albion area of southern Illinois between the Little Wabash and Wabash Rivers, wrote in 1819 that the "soil found in digging wells, is, first, a vegetable mold, next loamy clay, then sandstone, and lastly clay-slate, through which no one has penetrated."[17] He went on to speculate that coal lay under the clay because he had seen thin ribbons of the mineral near the prairie surface. Farther to the east, sometime between 25,000 and 14,000 YA,[18] a halt in the

Champaign ice sheet's retreat created the Champaign Moraine. Portions of this region of rocks and sediment are still visible such as at Mt. Hope Cemetery in the southern part of Champaign[19] (Figure 1.4).

The Upper Sangamon ridge (to the west) and the Champaign Moraine (to the south) acted as an earthen dam for the constant discharge of Boneyard Creek, a vascular watershed of the Salt Fork Vermilion River, and to the moraine's north an extensive wetland system developed. After heavy rains, portions of the Boneyard Creek watershed system would run to the moraine's south, feeding the headwaters of the Kaskaskia and Embarras Rivers. This connection would first be curtailed when the Illinois Central Railroad (ICR) line was built in 1855 and was finally severed with the construction of the Neil-Duncan US Route 45 corridor. Remnants of this hydrological system remain as picturesque detention ponds west of Fox Drive.

Throughout the mid-nineteenth century and into the twentieth century, much of the Midwest's wetlands were drained to produce valuable fertile agricultural land or speculative subdivisions. Historian Margaret Beattie Bogue noted that soon after the passage of the federal Swamp Land Act in 1850, the Illinois state legislature transferred its corresponding wetlands to the counties,

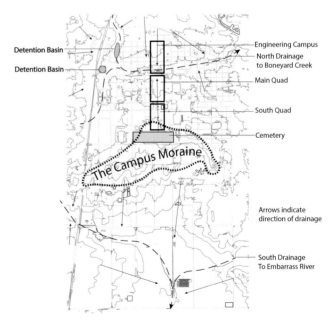

Figure 1.4
Campus moraine diagram. Image by Kevin J. Hinders.

which in turn sold large parcels to land speculators; by 1951 government and private sector initiatives resulted in "[m]ore than one-half of the crop producing land in Illinois, over 9,000,000 acres, [were] artificially drained."[20] Much of the draining was achieved through tiling, a method of burying ceramic-fired clay pipes 2 to 3 feet (60 to 90 centimeters) below the surface to carry water to adjacent creeks, canals, or rivers. In Champaign County, home of the Stadium, wetland drainage played an important role: portions of what became the University had been drained to enable farming and housing subdivisions, and Mathias L. Dunlap, who became wealthy using this technique, helped bring the University to the area.[21]

As the Ice Age came to an end and the Holocene began (circa 12,000 YA to now), the region's geology and topography settled into its current form. Moreover, despite humorous quips to the contrary, central Illinois' climate patterns became predictable—at least when viewed over long periods. Hot, humid summers, with often severe thunderstorms, are bookended by relatively cool, mostly dry, short springs, and falls; winters are usually cold and snowy. Generally, the average monthly highest temperature in Champaign County is 89°F (28.9°C) and occurs in July, while the lowest monthly average temperature is 16°F (−8.9°C) in January.[22] In terms of precipitation, it rains on average just over 41.28 inches (105 centimeters) a year, with May (4.88 inches or 12.4 centimeters) and July (4.69 inches or 11.9 centimeters) the wettest months, and most of the 23.2 inches (58.9 centimeters) of snowfall typically occurs between the end of November and the beginning of April.[23] This climate pattern is a key component of the region's habitability because it provides water not only to the various watershed systems and the animals and plants that depend on them but also for the region's farming activities over the last 200 years.

Prelude to the University

From the Archaic to First Nations

Humans first reached the area at the beginning of the North American Archaic period circa 12,000–10,000 YA, just as the Ice Age's land bridges disappeared.[24] Archeological evidence suggests that these humans followed big game such as mastodons, mammoths, bison, camels, and horses as they migrated across the Great Plains. Though most large mammals became extinct at the beginning of the Archaic, because of their geological evolution, rich soil, and plentiful water sources, these marshlands were a thriving ecosystem boasting enough water, animals, insects, plants, fruits, and vegetables to sustain humans through hunting, gathering, and insipient agricultural efforts. As the Archaic period ended, Paleo-Indian groups became larger and more organized during the Woodland period (circa 3,000–1,000 YA), eventually transforming into the pre-Columbian tribes that called the region home. Later during the Mississippian period, starting about 1,400 YA and until the arrival of Europeans, First Nations tribes established long-term agricultural practices, growing and regionally trading grains like little barley (*Hordeum pusillum*), squash, and maize.[25]

During the Mississippian period the Illiniwek (whose name was transformed by French settlers into "Illinois"), an informal confederation of twelve to thirteen Algonquian-speaking tribes that included the Cahokia, Peoria, Kaskaskia, and Michigamea, coalesced in central Illinois. While "[t]here are no signs that any American Indian permanent settlements or villages ever existed in what is now Champaign County," they probably "hunted game in Champaign County, setting up seasonal camps in the forested areas surrounding the prairies."[26] The Illiniwek were experts at selecting and hunting animals, not only as a food source but also for their pelts. Pelts were then made into clothing, including decorative and functional leathers and furs, and cladding materials for shelters. Significantly, it is in reference to this era that University of Illinois' students would create in the 1920s one of the University's most controversial symbols: Chief Illiniwek.

Europeans Arrive

From the beginning, Europeans who arrived in the late part of the sixteenth century found pelt trading with First Nations profitable. Throughout the seventeenth century, French fur traders, emboldened by lucrative royally sanctioned pelt-trading monopolies, pushed south from Canada, across the Great Lakes region, and down the Mississippi River Valley in search of new pelt sources. This push unleashed the so-called Beaver Wars, or French and Iroquois Wars, between the Iroquois Confederation, who were supported by the British and Dutch, and French-supported tribes including the Algonquian speakers.[27] It was in this context that the first Europeans made contact with central Illinois' tribes when French explorers Jacques Marquette (a Jesuit missionary) and Louis Jolliet traveled south on the Mississippi River down to present-day Arkansas in 1673. By 1699, the French had established the village of Cahokia, the region's first permanent European settlement, on what had once been the largest First Nations urban center north of Tenochtitlan (present-day Mexico).[28] From the early eighteenth century onward thousands of European settlers arrived to seek trading and farming opportunities. Before the end of the century, French explorer and trader René-Robert Cavelier, Sieur de La Salle, and Henry de Tonty had built Fort Crèvecoeur on the Illinois River near present-day Peoria to buttress a regional pelt-trading monopoly against potential Iroquois raids from the west.

While farming and pelt trading proved to be major sources of European and First Nations wealth, another highly profitable industry developed in the northwestern Illinois Basin. In a region near the border with Iowa and Wisconsin dubbed the Glacial Drift Zone because Pleistocene glaciers had missed the area as they retracted, the landscape was carved by the Mississippi River and its silt banks. The river's erosive action had deposited easily accessible galena deposits. Galena, an ore composed of lead and sulfur that could be separated through low-temperature smelting, was mainly used by First Nations like the Sac and Fox to glaze pottery and stabilize naturally occurring paints and dyes. When the French arrived, the First Nations peoples had already been harvesting surface galena for centuries. For their part, Europeans utilized galena to manufacture lead-based products including musket balls, paints, and metal alloys used in industrial processes and machines. Many explorers and traders, like Julien Dubuque, a Quebecois

native, shifted interests and began to successfully exploit galena deposits. Using the Mississippi River as a trade route, galena ore would be exported throughout North America and then sold across Europe.

Meanwhile, the British sought a larger share of the highly profitable pelt trade and fertile farmland and continued expanding westward. Although the Beaver Wars had ended in 1701, by the early 1750s French claims to the Ohio River Valley were matched by British colonial desires, which generated increasing friction between the two parties and their First Nations allies. In 1756, with tensions at full boil between the French and the British throughout the world, hostilities broke out. The British and their allies eventually prevailed in the French and Indian War, in 1763, and France ceded all territories east of the Mississippi River to the British, including what would become Illinois.

Whereas French settlers had been somewhat dispersed and few, the European population in the British-controlled Ohio Valley swelled. The Illiniwek—French allies—found themselves politically weak and unable to prevent the full onslaught of British colonialist expansion into central Illinois. By the last third of the eighteenth century, the Illiniwek were displaced, and their numbers had dwindled because of disease (especially smallpox), violent clashes, and land treaties (usually coerced). "Other tribes then moved into Illinois to take over land formerly occupied by the Illinois and Miami. Some of the newly arrived tribes included the Fox (Mesquakie), Ioway, Kickapoo, Mascouten, Piankashaw, Potawatomi, Sauk, Shawnee, Wea, and Winnebago."[29]

The British, however, did not enjoy for long the spoils of the French and Indian War. Just 13 years later, disgruntled British colonial subjects, unhappy with the burden of taxation to pay for that war, initiated their own war to gain independence. In the end, the British controlled the Illinois Country from the end of the French and Indian War until their defeat in 1778 by the Virginia Militia under the command of Brigadier General George Rogers Clark. As part of the Treaty of Paris that ended the Revolutionary War in 1783, Illinois Country was officially recognized as part of the United States of America and four years later was designated part of the newly formed Northwest Territory.

Coal, the Economy, and the University's Origins

Between 1800 and 1809, Illinois Country formed part of the western edge of the Indiana Territory. Unhappy with the vast distances they had to travel to attend the business of the territory, residents successfully achieved recognition of Illinois Territory in 1809, which paved the way for the eventual admission of the State of Illinois into the Union in 1818. The area quickly experienced population growth. According to the Twelfth Census of the United States, from just after Illinois was organized as a territory on March 1, 1809, to just after being admitted as a state on December 3, 1818, the population jumped from 12,282 to 55,162. By the end of the nineteenth century, the state's population had reached over 4,800,000 inhabitants, an increase of over 39,000%![30] This enormous population spurt fueled a self-supporting cycle of economic and population expansion: as the population grew, the economy became more robust, which attracted even more people to call Illinois home (Figure 1.5).

Meanwhile, as the country experienced its version of the Industrial Revolution, the combination of farmland, pelt trading, galena mining, and abundant water and timber made the state an attractive destination for internal and foreign migration. Because of the industrial appetite for large, cheap, and reliable energy sources, thousands sought their fortunes among the Pennsylvanian period coal deposits. Even though Illinois was officially a free

TABLE 1.—POPULATION OF ILLINOIS: 1810 TO 1900.

CENSUS YEARS.	Population.	INCREASE.	
		Number.	Per cent.
1900	4,821,550	995,199	26.0
1890	3,826,351	748,480	24.3
1880	3,077,871	537,980	21.1
1870	2,539,891	827,940	48.3
1860	1,711,951	860,481	101.0
1850	851,470	375,287	78.8
1840	476,183	318,738	202.4
1830	157,445	102,283	186.4
1820	55,162	42,880	349.1
1810	12,282		

Figure 1.5
Population of Illinois. US Census Bureau, *Twelfth Census*, table 1.

state, Black Africans, Black African descendants, and others were forcibly brought to the region as slave laborers for construction projects, farmland, and mining.[31]

Illinois coal, "a combustible black or brownish-black sedimentary rock with a high amount of carbon and hydrocarbons,"[32] was abundant, cheap, and readily accessible by mining, and it released a large amount of energy when burned. While coal had been used regularly by the First Nations peoples, the arrival of Europeans generated the first major jump in demand: blacksmiths produced iron-based tools like horseshoes, which required furnaces operating at high temperatures; homes built in new permanent settlements needed heat sources during the cold Illinois winters plus metal tools and appliances like potbellied stoves; pelt trappers and traders also required metal tools and weapons. By the late 1840s, the growing volume of foodstuffs shipped up and down the Mississippi River, and to the east through the Great Lakes, prompted the construction of the Illinois and Michigan Canals and waterway infrastructure, which also depended heavily on coal-based energy (Figure 1.6).

As the whole of the American economy burgeoned, so did the demand for goods, including coal, which necessitated fast, reliable, and efficient transportation systems like railroads and steamboats to ship these goods from extraction centers to manufacturing centers. As the historian David Maldwyn Ellis observed, the nascent nation, however, did not have the economic wherewithal to undertake a transcontinental rail project of privately developed systems.[33] So Illinois Senator Sydney Breeze and Stephen A. Douglas (of Lincoln-Douglas debate fame) secured funding through the Land Grant Act of 1850, which instructed the federal government to cede federal land to states that would then either cede the land to railroad companies for their rights of way or sell it to finance construction. In the first iteration of the Act, land was ceded to Illinois, Mississippi, and Alabama. Importantly, Ellis notes that the federal government often got a handsome return on its investment because operating railroad lines significantly increased the value of federally owned land adjacent to the railroad grants.[34]

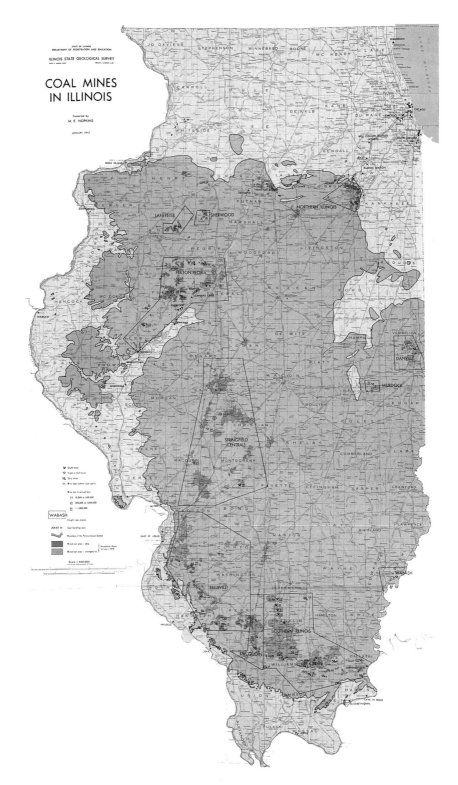

Figure 1.6
Coal mines in Illinois. Modified from M. E. Hopkins, January 1975. Courtesy of the University of Illinois Map Library.

Illinois wasted little time: it established the ICR and then quickly

selected a consortium of Eastern capitalists to construct and own the railroad. Federal land grants of nearly 2,600,000 acres [7% was within Illinois] provided the economic incentive; the initial investment of $27 million came largely from British and Dutch interests.[35]

The ICR executed an ambitious and expansive construction program throughout the 1850s. Kurt A. Carlson notes that ICR's network (Figure 1.7)

ran on a north-south line right up the middle of the state. Like ribs off the center spine, various east-west lines reached out to all parts of the state and beyond. The Illinois Central also had a direct track coming into Chicago from the south. From the southwest, the Rock Island Line and the St. Louis, Alton & Chicago entered Chicago through Joliet. The Chicago, Burlington & Quincy and two branches of the Galena & Chicago, met at Turner's Junction (now West Chicago), entering Chicago from the west.

The Rock Island made its way westward from Chicago, crossing the Mississippi in 1856 and opening up the prairies of Iowa and beyond. Our forbearers thought that it nothing short of remarkable that one could leave the shores of Lake Michigan in the morning and actually stand on the banks of the Mississippi River at nightfall.[36]

The railroad and canal systems' construction, productive farms, emerging industries, cheap energy sources, and political stability transformed Illinois into a major destination: the population skyrocketed from 850,000 in 1850 to 1,700,000 in 1860.[37]

Arguably the US Civil War (1861–1865) did much to establish Illinois as a major participant in the national economy. Already a vital contributor of grain, Illinois could put its exceptionally well-developed railroad and canal systems to use to transport food stuffs.[38] Moreover, since galena was a key component of munitions,

the region's deposits and industrial economy could meet the demands of a national conflict and support a burgeoning regional economy.[39]

Once the Civil War was over, railroad construction and use increased exponentially across the entire Northern Hemisphere. Illinois became a global agricultural, industrial, and financial powerhouse with Chicago as its most economically successful city. Like Rome centuries before, all *rail*roads seemingly led to Chicago; and whereas the antebellum South had coined "cotton is king," in Illinois coal was king. But industry and agriculture alone could not sustain a prospering region without new managerial leadership. Residents began to loudly call for a state university.

Founding the University, Future Home of Memorial Stadium

The Morrill Act

Even before the formation of the United States of America, the Congress of the Confederation of the United States had prioritized public university education. As part of the 1787 North West Ordinance, the confederation enacted legislation stating that "[r]eligion, morality, and knowledge, being necessary to good government and the happiness of mankind, schools and the means of education shall forever be encouraged."[40]

After the Constitution was ratified in 1788, an educational initiative was frequently proposed but found little traction among legislators despite the explicit requirement that each new state set aside land for a university. The Congressional Act of April 18, 1818, besides recognizing Illinois' entry into the Union, called for Congress to appropriate funding "for the encouragement of learning, of which one-sixth part shall be exclusively bestowed on a college or university."[41] However, with little federal appetite for enforcement and a lack of state financial support, the initiative languished.

After the Land Grant Act of 1850 had proven to be a useful tool for financing major infrastructure projects, its model of lot allotment was well understood and was eyed for education. Amid an agricultural, industrial, and transportation

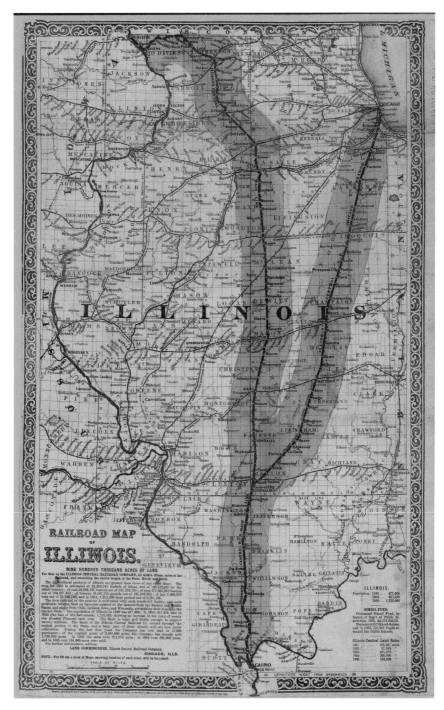

Figure 1.7

Railroad Map of Illinois. Illinois Central Railroad Company, 1865. Courtesy of the University of Illinois Map Library.

boom, groundswell support emerged throughout Illinois for an institution of higher learning that would produce graduates capable of quickly entering these fields. With the state in the ascendancy, Illinois politicians backed by industry and agricultural interests became a major force in national politics. The culmination of this political hegemony would be the election as president of a Republican senator from Illinois in 1860, Abraham Lincoln.

Unlike his predecessors, especially James Polk, Lincoln did favor passing legislation to fund public education through land grants. Lincoln's sympathetic view should not be a surprise, as he experienced the success of the land-grant program firsthand as the ICR's chief external legal counsel during the 1850s. When the Confederate states, which had traditionally killed this legislation in the past, seceded from the Union, the way was clear.

On July 2, 1862, Congress passed the Land-Grant College Act of 1862. Commonly known as the Morrill Act after its sponsor, Vermont senator Justin Morrill, it directed the federal government to cede land reserves to each state in accordance with its congressional delegation size (the sum of senators and representatives). In 1861, Illinois had sixteen representatives. Only New York (31), Pennsylvania (24), and Ohio (19) had more.[42] With 30,000 acres allotted per congressional representative, Illinois received 480,000 acres of land for

> the endowment, support, and maintenance of at least one college . . . where the leading object shall be, without excluding other scientific or classical studies, to teach such branches of learning as are related to agriculture and the mechanic arts . . . in order to promote the liberal and practical education of the industrial classes in the several pursuits and professions of life.[43]

As part of the Act's mandate, states had a finite time to accept the lands, sell them, and invest the monies. The investments then would support the development and ongoing operations of the schools. On February 14, 1863, Governor Richard Yates signed legislation to accept the land donation and form the committee entrusted to administer the acreage and establish a university.

Situating the University

With the funding a reality, determining an educational mission and location became the focus of a major struggle. As early as 1851, John Baldwin Turner, a Yale University graduate and former college professor at Illinois College in Jacksonville, had called for

the establishment of a major public state university. Baldwin garnered national attention on November 18, 1851, when he delivered an impassioned speech supporting a state university in front of a gathering of farmers in Granville, IL. The speech generated a full spectrum of reactions among its rural audience members, and its impact was soon felt across the country.[44] As evidenced by his influential pamphlet, *A Plan for an Industrial University for the State of Illinois,* known as the Granville plan, Turner recognized that Illinois' prosperity was heavily reliant on industry and agriculture.[45] As a representative of the industrial education movement, Turner believed Illinois needed a secular and pragmatic school that could continuously produce graduates who would participate in the "industrial classes."[46] While many newspapers were supportive of the initiative, others, like the *Illinois Weekly Journal* (Springfield), ran editorials highly critical of the proposal: for one writer identified only as J. T. S., this proposition was a call for "crusades against the religious denominations or sects of the state."[47]

Granville's plan was also met with strong opposition across the state. Some favored producing graduates in professional fields such as law, accounting, and medicine or strictly adhering to a traditional education focused on Greek, Latin, and philosophy. Other groups advocated for improving existing private or parochial colleges, like Illinois College, although some of these schools would close after only a few years of operation. A certain faction felt that it would be best to have no public monies dedicated to a college or university. In the end, however, Turner and his allies' vision of a primarily pragmatic education in industry and agriculture prevailed, but that was only the first step.

Even before state legislation for a public university had passed, competing camps, dubbed the "college men," lobbied the state legislature to fund their projects.[48] In his book, *The Movement for Industrial Education and the Establishment of the University, 1840–1870,* Burt E. Powell notes:

> As one might expect it was not the group of devoted men who had made the grant possible but it was a faction, or factions of the small college

men, who had striven hard from 1852 to 1857 to get possession of the college and seminary funds, who had called the plans of the industrial league and of Turner 'chimeras,' 'absurd,' and 'ungodly,' but who, now that the grant was within reach of the state, pushed forward in almost unseemly haste, to secure for their own institutions whatever part of the congressional bequest they possibly could.[49]

With the Civil War raging, the Illinois legislature tabled discussions about a university. This suspension, however, did not affect the furor of the debate between local and regional groups on the preferred location.

One faction represented by A. C. Mason, a state legislator, and G. I. Bergen, both from Knox County—home to Knox College—had begun lobbying for grant monies in February 1863. Legislation supporting this initiative would have passed early in 1863 if the state legislature had not recessed. Turner's group, including Jonathan Kennicott, a medical doctor and horticulturalist, promoted a convention in Springfield on June 9. John Reynolds, a state legislator and Turner ally, successfully postponed voting on legislation until after the convention was held. For Kennicott and twelve leaders from ten counties, the convention prioritized establishing the state university for the "greatest possible benefit to the industrial classes of the whole state."[50] In light of the more pressing Civil War, Turner successfully postponed further debate. Coincidentally, Governor Yates unilaterally delayed the discussion of university-centered initiatives on June 10.

Nevertheless, each group continued to refine its arguments through conventions, meetings, county fairs, and newspaper articles and editorials. At a convention on January 5, 1864, in Springfield, the Turner group finally approved a proposal:

there should be a single, new institution entirely separate from any existing college; the managing board of which should consist of five members residing in different parts of the state, no two in the same congressional district, who should be nominated by the executive board of the state agricultural society, approved by the governor,

and confirmed by the senate; the college should be established after considering the offers of such localities as chose to make them at the point which in the judgment of a locating board, offered the greatest facilities and inducements.[51]

The agriculturalists of the Turner group next began in earnest a statewide campaign to lobby their representatives. The college men responded by successfully persuading the governor to create a commission to study the possibility of dividing the grant monies between two new schools: one near the center of the state and the other near Chicago. That initiative would eventually fail but would lay the groundwork for the future University of Illinois Chicago. As the summer of 1864 gave way to the fall electoral season, both candidates pledged support for one centrally located engineering and agricultural university. With the Civil War winding down, the industrialists and agriculturalists jointly prepared to push the state legislature for a single grant for a single major university when it convened in January 1865.

On January 10, a bill was introduced to the House legislature,[52] and proposed amendments included language that called for two universities, one focused on agriculture to be located between Urbana and Champaign in Champaign County and one focused on "mechanic arts" to be near Chicago.[53] As the debate continued in Springfield, a legislative committee visited Champaign to verify the details of its proposal. Among multiple positive observations, the members noted that

Champaign county is located about the center of the State, North and South, and midway between Bloomington and the State Line on the east, it is remarkably healthy, and long celebrated for its fine cattle and abundant harvests. It is included in the great coal fields of the west, and at a depth of less than two hundred feet, as is shown by actual experiment, are found rich veins of the best bituminous coal.[54]

Despite the positive site report, several attempts to pass an amendment to support Champaign's bid failed; ultimately, the entire university legislation failed.

Thereafter, the same legislative committee produced a report proposing that all interested parties tender an incentivized location package and a governor-appointed, Senate-confirmed commission that would study and recommend the final location for a single school in the hope of generating statewide support for the school's final location.

The committee's new invitation for proposals was probably the result of House and Senate legislators affording their local constituents an opportunity to participate in the selection process. Even before January 1865, conventioneers had pitched their hometowns or counties' virtues. Powell notes that at a Springfield convention held in mid-December 1864,

> B. G. Roots on behalf of the Southern Illinois agricultural college at Irvington, offered a building already erected, a cash fund of $60,000, and considerable land if a state institution should be located there; Dr. Scroggs representing a company at Champaign, stated that it would tender to the state at the proper time a large building erected for college purposes, with ten acres of land, the whole valued at $100,000.[55]

Among the strongest criticisms of the Champaign submission was the apparent underlying desire to increase real estate values. One observer, who on the whole supported Champaign's bid, wrote in the *Illinois State Journal*:

> Indeed the only opposition to this feature of the House bill, so far as I can learn, has emanated from an effort at town lot speculation some years ago, on a naked tract of land lying between Champaign and Urbana, in the East part of the State. A certain company, it seems, undertook some years ago to lay that tract off in lots, and bring them into market by building on it a school or seminary of some sort. They have since, in some way, transferred their rights to Champaign County, and made that county the ostensible profferers [sic] of the donation. It is a quite respectable bid, for the first time. But it probably does not amount to one half the

amount of money which the location of the University there will give of additional value to their naked town lots, aside from all its other advantages to the place.[56]

Between 1865 and 1866, groups perfected their bids. In January 1866, Morgan County residents circulated a letter written by Turner and others to bolster their proposal and later that year attempted and failed to raise $300,000 through taxes to bring the school to Jacksonville. Ultimately, the lack of secured funding in combination with a persistent wish to unify the new institution with the existing Illinois College doomed Morgan County's bid.

Undeterred by the earlier legislative failure and critics, the Champaign County committee strengthened its proposal by agreeing to purchase the Urbana and Champaign Institute building (the first official home of the future Illinois Industrial University—the original name), committed additional agricultural lands, and resolved that the measure to raise

> one hundred thousand dollars be appropriated for the purpose of purchasing said building, a farm for the use of said Industrial University and for the purpose of bearing such other expenses necessarily involved in securing the location of the Illinois Industrial University in this county

be put on the ballot for approval on October 10, 1866.[57] Once the vote was taken, the initiative passed with 76% of voters (3,516) in favor.[58] That November when committee member Clark Robinson Griggs was elected to the Illinois House of Representatives, the committee members became confident they would be victorious.

When the state legislature convened on January 7, 1867, McLean County, home to several major institutions including a teaching college, entered one of the most promising bids and presented an attractive financial package. As the legislative session progressed, it became evident that the final competition would be between McLean County and Champaign County. Senator Tincher of Vermilion County introduced a bill in support of locating the new university in Champaign County; most other bills did not gain any traction.

This happened, in Griggs's words, because "[i]t was understood that the Senate would accede to whatever the House did."[59] Griggs could say this from firsthand knowledge: he had successfully negotiated his way to chairing the manufacturers and agriculture committee, where he routinely killed any potential threats to Champaign County's bid.

Empowered with a newly established taxation law, counties mounted new campaigns that promised ever-larger amounts of tax-financed support for the new university. From the session's onset and with Griggs's support, Champaign's committee mounted an intense, three-month "lavish" lobbying effort at Springfield's Leland Hotel to woo legislators that included "elaborate" meals, flowing alcohol, entertainment, and dubious overnight stays.[60] As these efforts gained ground, editorials in local and regional newspapers aligned with McLean and Morgan Counties, like Bloomington's *Pantagraph* and the *Jacksonville Journal,* began to openly criticize this pressure campaign.[61]

On February 8, the state legislature had official applications from Champaign, Logan, Morgan, and McLean Counties "including offers of money, bonds, and lands, to the two houses of the general assembly to secure the location of the industrial university in their respective localities."[62] Next, the House appointed a committee to visit each proposed site. Chair A. I. Enoch reported the committee's view that the value of McLean's bid and Morgan's bid—a combination of tax funds, land, and other assets—surpassed that of Champaign. The assessment sparked Champaign County's committee to note that it had undervalued the land and building assets and argued that McLean County's bid was untenable as the site had no water resources. McLean County's committee published a response agreeing with the valuation but decried the "absolutely and transparently false" claim about water availability.[63] Despite increasing financial offers from Morgan and McLean Counties and public dissension in Champaign County, key House and Senate members moved to support Champaign County's proposal and quashed attempts by other counties to form a governor-appointed commission that could stall the decision. On February 20, with sixty-seven votes in

favor and ten against, the House approved Champaign County as the location of the new university. The bill was introduced and passed in the Senate, 18 to 7, on February 25; on the last day of February, Governor Oglesby signed the legislation into law. Urbana-Champaign had officially become the home of the future University of Illinois (Figure 1.8).

Delivering on the Promise

Champaign County had until June 1, 1867, to fulfill its pledges or lose its hard-won victory to bring the school to its territory. The county and the new BOT immediately set to work acquiring land. It is clear that land speculation played a significant role for residents of Urbana and Champaign when the bid was assembled since over $100,000 was spent acquiring the promised property. For example, the Champaign County proposal included 400 acres from the holdings of Clark Robinson Griggs and Silvonia Griggs. They had purchased 520 acres from Delaware land speculators Merrit Carby and Eliza Carby for $13,000 in September 1864. On March 30, 1867, after the official awarding of the site, the Griggses sold 400 of these acres to the future University of Illinois for $22,000. Similar purchases for the promised property were consummated shortly after the award.

The county would pass the necessary bond measures and cobble together the land and resources to deliver to the State of Illinois its long sought-after university, one capable of supplying its industrial and agricultural entrepreneurs and companies with capable graduates. Coal, salt, lead, wheat, pork bellies, and other national and internationally distributed products had made Illinois an engine of economic development that drove population growth, and the University was conceived as the necessary next step to ensure prosperity.

Over the next year, the University, under the aegis of the governor, would incorporate its own BOT and set about transforming from an idea into a reality. With the arrival of an ICR line through Champaign in the mid-1850s, the agricultural and marshlands soared in value. As the state flourished, its population rose

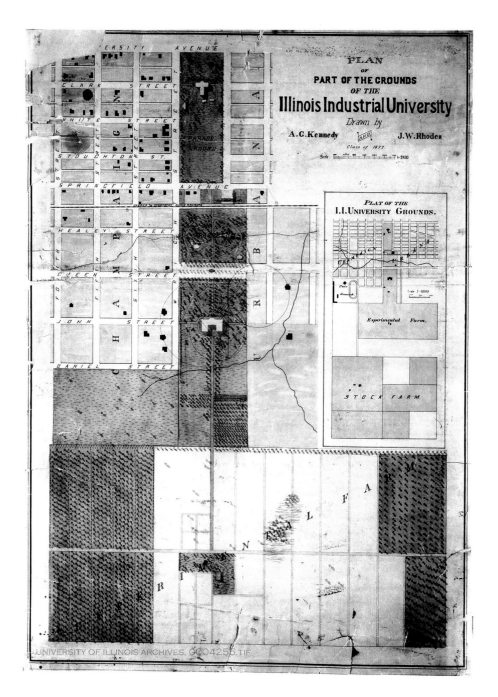

Figure 1.8
Early map of the Illinois Industrial University by A. C. Kennedy and J. W. Rhodes. Courtesy of the University of Illinois Archives.

and boosted University enrollment and the need for dormitories, classrooms, research labs, other buildings, and public spaces. In this context, a major catalyst in transfiguring the campus and its morphology was Memorial Stadium. Just as the University had proven to be a worthwhile struggle for those who championed an institution of higher learning as the embodiment of the promise of Illinois, so too did a world-class stadium prove valuable to anchor the next stage of development for the University and for state of Illinois.

Notes

1 Kennedy and Cohen, *American Pageant*, 540.
2 The capitalized term "University" refers specifically to the University of Illinois Urbana-Champaign.
3 See the Consumer Price Index Inflation Calculator, https://data.bls.gov/cgi-bin/cpicalc.pl.
4 Board of Trustees of the University of Illinois (BOT), meeting minutes, March 9, 1920, 699–700.
5 Ibid., 756.
6 BOT, meeting minutes, December 14, 1920, 155.
7 Ibid., 160.
8 The capitalized term is used to refer specifically to Memorial Stadium.
9 Whittaker, Elrick and Berg, "The Illinois Basin: The geologic Gift that Keeps Giving."
10 Vaiden, "Build Illinois."
11 Swann, "Summary Geologic History."
12 Frankie, "Building the Bedrock."
13 Vaiden, "Build Illinois."
14 Klinkenberg, "70 Million-Year-Old History."
15 Pester and Zimmermann, "Pleistocene Epoch."
16 Horseshoe Crab, "Pleistocene."
17 Illinois State Museum, "Why Are These Glacial Deposits So Good for Agriculture?"
18 Hansel, "End Moraines: The End of the Glacial Ride," 1.
19 Wickham, "Glacial Geology."
20 Bogue, "Swamp Land Act," 169.
21 Ibid., 178.
22 US Climate Data, "Climate Champaign – Illinois."
23 Angel, "Averages and Records."
24 Davis, *Frontier Illinois*.
25 Illinois State Museum, "Illinois Agriculture Begins."
26 Peterson, "Indigenous Illinois."
27 "Iroquois Wars," *Canadian Encyclopedia*, February 7, 2006; last edited July 31, 2019.
28 "Cahokia." *Encyclopedia Britannica*, last updated October 17, 2023, https://www.britannica.com/place/Cahokia.
29 Museum Link of Illinois, "American Indian Tribes of Illinois."
30 The population of 12,282 listed in the 1820 census almost certainly did not account for all of Illinois' inhabitants.
31 Illinois H.R. 0866, 101st General Assembly, 2021.
32 US Energy Information Administration, "Coal Explained."
33 Ellis, "Railroad Land Grant Rates," 208.
34 Ibid., 209.
35 Hankey, "Illinois Central Railroad."
36 Carlson, "Backing the Boys in the Civil War," 141–42.
37 Cole, *Era of the Civil War*, 8–13, 339.
38 VandeCreek, "Economic Development."
39 Carlson, "Backing the Boys in the Civil War."
40 Congress of the Confederation, "Northwest Ordinance."
41 Statute 1, chap. 67, sect. 6, 15th Congress, 1st session, in Library of Congress, "A Century of Lawmaking for a New Nation: U.S. Congressional Documents and Debates, 1774–1875," 430, http://rs6.loc.gov/cgi-bin/ampage?collId=llsl&fileName=003/llsl003.db&recNum=469.
42 US House of Representatives, "Representatives Apportioned to Each State."
43 Act of July 2, 1862 (First Morrill Act), 12 Stat. 503, chap. 130, 37th Congress, https://www.govinfo.gov/content/pkg/COMPS-10285/pdf/COMPS-10285.pdf.
44 Powell, *The Movement for Industrial Education*, 24.
45 Ibid., v.
46 Turner, *Industrial Universities for the People*, 16.
47 J. T. S., *Illinois Weekly Journal*, January 28, 1852.
48 Powell, *The Movement for Industrial Education*, 179.
49 Ibid.
50 Ibid., 180.
51 Ibid., 185.
52 Ibid., 193.
53 Ibid.
54 Ibid., 206.
55 Ibid., 191.
56 "A Looker On," *Illinois State Journal*, January 25, 1865.
57 Champaign County, Record of the Board of Supervisors, September 12, 1866, 111: 482.
58 Powell, *The Movement for Industrial Education*, 214.
59 Clark Robinson Griggs, interview, in Powell, *The Movement for Industrial Education*, 243.
60 Powell, *The Movement for Industrial Education*, 242.
61 Ibid., 248.
62 Ibid., 255.
63 The committee consisted of W. D. Somers, T. A. Cosgrove, and C. R. Morehouse. See documents in Turner manuscripts, Springfield; Powell, *The Movement for Industrial Education*, 485–86.

Origins of Memorial Stadium

Introduction

On one hand, the establishment in 1867 of the Illinois Industrial University, as the University of Illinois was called until 1885, was the culmination of nearly 20 years of constant efforts to establish an academic institution capable of meeting the demand for highly qualified graduates in the fields of engineering and agriculture. The school's first regent, John Milton Gregory, proudly declared that the school would be the "West Point for the working world."[1] On the other hand, it signaled the state's economic ascendancy as a national agricultural, industrial, and transportation hub. Four years later the 1871 Chicago Fire, though devastating, catalyzed Chicago's transformation from a regional power into a major international trade center, which further accelerated the state's population growth.[2] In 1870, the state's population was 2,539,891, an increase of more than 48.36% over the previous census.[3] By 1880, the number had jumped an additional 21.1% to 3,077,871, and by 1890 it was up to 3,826,351.[4] In that same period, Illinois went from the fourth most populous state of the republic to the third, surpassing Ohio. Because allotments to the federal government's House of Representatives are based on the census, Illinois consolidated its political might by sending to Washington D.C. the third largest congressional delegation.

Initially, the University of Illinois mirrored Illinois' economic growth and transformation, yet by the end of the nineteenth century, it was the University that invoked changes in the state, and it influenced schools across the country. By the early twentieth century, intercollegiate sports were dramatically affecting student and alumni culture across the nation, and the University of Illinois was a key leader. Moreover, in those early decades of the University's history, intercollegiate sports became a significant source of revenue. One effect of sports' rise in social and economic importance was the need to build major facilities.

An Evolving University

Expanding Boundaries

As the state of Illinois' population increased by nearly 1.3 million people from 1870 to 1890, the University's enrollment steadily swelled. The University opened its doors in spring 1868 with 77 students, all men.[5] Just a year and a half later, student enrollment had nearly tripled with 194 male and 14 female students. By 1880, enrollment again more than doubled to 329 male and 105 female students.[6] Slowly, the student body began to reflect the state's diversity. In 1884, Carlos Moctezuma became the first Native American University graduate; three years later, Jonathan Rogan enrolled, becoming the school's first Black African American student. By fall 1893, 15 years after its founding, enrollment had increased by 965% when the University welcomed 743 students, 109 of them women.[7] While enrollment drove demand for new and larger academic spaces, more students also meant bigger and more varied social activities, including singing, dancing, and sports.

During the nineteenth century, recreational, intramural, and institutional sports became integral to student life, but campus sports are almost as old as the University. In 1879, just 12 years after its founding, the University sponsored its first baseball team; in 1881, students had raised football goalposts on campus; and in 1890, the University fielded its first institutional football team (Figure 2.1).

That same year the baseball and football teams, together with the school's intercollegiate staff and student athletes who participated in the other University sponsored sports, formed a new organization:

The athletic program, the Athletic Association, began as a non-profit, separate corporation (articles of incorporation issued by the state of Illinois, February 21, 1890), which directed intercollegiate

athletics and was managed by an 11-member board of directors (6 faculty, 5 from membership of Alumni Association) appointed to the Board of Trustees.[8]

Once incorporated, the Athletic Association, or AA as it was known, had its own board of directors and budget, effectively operating as an independent entity nestled within the University. Athletic activities were expanding, and the AA sought space to host its sports. As one of its first efforts, the AA petitioned the University for land "to fence in and occupy exclusively a part of the north campus."[9] The property, located between present-day University and Springfield Avenues, included the site of the Old Main University Building, which had been demolished in 1880.[10] The "Elephant" as it was mockingly known, had been a major component of Champaign

Figure 2.1
The University of Illinois' first football team, 1890. Courtesy of the University of Illinois Archives.

County's winning bid to secure the University's location. In the ten years since its demolition, few site improvements had been carried out.

The AA submitted the request to the Buildings and Grounds Committee. By March 1891, still without a response, the AA amended its petition to include funding to regrade the area: "Some part of the expense will arise from the need of grading the grounds, especially in the part where the removal of the old building has left unsightly and troublesome cavities."[11] The University's Board of Trustees (BOT) agreed to a renewable three-year land lease and granted the AA $350 to regrade the area. Over the next 30 years, the site was transformed into baseball and football fields, which together with Kenney Gymnasium Annex, a drill hall until 1890, and Kenney Gymnasium (constructed in 1902), formed a vibrant sports complex on the north side of campus.[12] In 1896, the area was formally renamed Illinois Field, and an additional $250 was granted for site improvements.[13]

Thanks to full support from the BOT and the presidency, the AA would enjoy land leases and construct facilities without controversy or uncertainty for decades. On only one occasion was there a serious proposal to move the AA and its programs from Illinois Field. In 1917, the BOT studied the area as a potential future home for McKinley Hospital, a much needed medical facility to serve the University's growing student body. To this end, the BOT considered relocating the AA from its fields and building infrastructure on the north side of campus to an area currently defined by the Ikenberry Commons Residence (ICR) and Champaign's First Street, at an estimated cost of $50,000.[14]

Dawn of Organized Intercollegiate Sports

In early 1895, University presidents from across the country met at the Palmer House in Chicago to discuss the opportunities presented by intercollegiate athletics. At the meeting, attendees proposed and codified regulations and discussed how best to administrate these sports. Among them was newly appointed University of Illinois president Andrew Sloan Draper, who focused on forming an intercollegiate conference. Soon after, Draper wrote to alumnus George Huff (class of 1892) to

convince him to return to Illinois and take a leadership position. In his four years at the University, Huff had demonstrated remarkable athletic and leadership skills. In his freshmen year, the 16-year-old was captain of the baseball team, and in 1890 he joined the newly organized football team. Draper offered to Huff, now just 23, all coaching duties at Illinois in the fall of 1895. By June of that year, Draper submitted Huff's contract for BOT approval (Figure 2.2):

I also recommend the appointment of Mr. George A. Huff as assistant director of the gymnasium and coach of the athletic teams. Mr. Huff will come

Figure 2.2
George Huff. Courtesy of the University of Illinois Department of Intercollegiate Athletics.

to the service of the University for $1,000.00 during the next year and the athletic teams are willing to defray one-half of the expense involved. The department of physical culture and athletics has so developed as to make this step advisable, and I think we are fortunate in being able to secure the services of so good on [sic] assistant as Mr. Huff has shown himself to be.[15]

After Jacob Kinzer Schell's resignation as professor of physical training in 1901, Huff was appointed director of the Department of Physical Training, which raised his annual salary to $1,800.[16] Huff, however, relinquished direct football coaching duties and served instead as athletic director from 1901 to 1936. Huff's tenure was immensely fruitful as curricula-based, intramural, and intercollegiate sports flourished on campus.[17] As a result, he successfully lobbied the BOT for additional faculty and salary increases in the Physical Education Department. Moreover, under Huff's leadership, the University joined six other institutions to form the Intercollegiate Conference of Faculty Representatives, which was referred to as the Western Conference and later would become the Big Ten.[18] The seven original members of the conference were the University of Chicago, the University of Illinois, the University of Michigan, the University of Minnesota, Northwestern University, Purdue University, and the University of Wisconsin. The rise of intercollegiate sports necessitated an organization capable of coordinating sports across the nation, and under Huff's leadership, the AA was a founding member of the National Collegiate Athletics Association (NCAA) in 1906.[19]

In 1904, Huff hired alumnus and former Illinois football player Arthur Raymond Hall (class of 1902) to coach the football team. Initially, Hall coached with three other individuals, Justa Lindgren, Fred Lowenthal, and Clyde Matthews. However, from 1907 to 1912 Hall coached alone. His best season came in 1910 when the team achieved a 7–0 record, prompting some among the University of Illinois' faithful to claim that season as the school's first national championship. Most impressively, the 1910 team did not allow a single point to be scored against them. Hall, an Illinois lawyer, decided to give

up coaching football in 1912, dedicating himself instead full-time to his law practice, in nearby Danville, IL To replace Hall, Huff hired a promising young high school coach, Robert "Bob" or "Zup" Zuppke (Figure 2.3). Huff had become interested in Zuppke after his Oak Park and Forest City high school football teams won the 1911 and 1912 Illinois high school state championships. In 1914, in only his second year as Illini head coach, Zuppke's football team claimed the national championship. Between 1913 and 1941 Zuppke-coached teams achieved seven Big Ten Conference titles and claimed four national championships (1914, 1919, 1923, and 1927).[20] During Zuppke's heyday, teams gradually began to be identified in local, state, and national press first as the Illini, and then as the Fighting Illini.[21]

With each football team's success came increased national exposure, regional excitement, and new school

Figure 2.3
Robert "Zup" Zuppke. Courtesy of the University of Illinois Department of Intercollegiate Athletics.

rivalries. The tradition of homecoming emerged, when alumni were invited to attend festivities centered around a football game (Figure 2.4). At Illinois, "it was conceived in 1909 by students C.F. Williams and W. Elmer Ekblaw, members of the Shield and Trident senior society. They joined with another society, Phoenix, to organize the three-day event."[22] Now that they had associated traditions and had become prime social events, football games would increasingly serve as additional sites of camaraderie and competition. With game spectators a mix of students, alumni, faculty, and members of the wider community, it became clear that admission could be charged to view these competitions. Students and alumni from opposing schools might also travel hundreds of miles for away games and produce ticket and concession stand revenue. Initially, 300 wooden bleachers were installed at Illinois Field. As seating capacity

was added over time, the copious use of wood to build bleachers would earn Illinois Field its nickname, "the Lumberyard." Unsurprisingly, attendance quickly surpassed the stadium's sitting and standing capacity: "In 1914 when the enrollment at the University was 5,000, the seating capacity of Illinois Fields bleachers was 13,000. In 1920, when the attendance was 8,000 and our alumni numbered 42,000 the capacity of the field was 17,000, with standing room for 3,000."[23]

The Impetus for a Stadium

The Great War

The United States' entry into the Great War (1914–1918) helped Allies achieve a decisive victory. With the war

Figure 2.4
Homecoming game, Illini Field, 1910. Courtesy of the University of Illinois Courtesy of the Department of Intercollegiate Athletics.

winding down, President Woodrow Wilson introduced legislation for the Students' Army Training Corps (SATC) program, a precursor to the Reserved Officers Training Core (ROTC) program. While entry into the war initially depressed student enrollment at colleges and universities across the country, its end spurred enrollment. With the return after the Great War of nearly 5,000,000 men and women to civilian life, half of whom had served abroad, optimism and energy blossomed across the country.[24] At the start of the Roaring Twenties, and a new era of global power and hopefulness, people turned to leisure activities, including spectating organized sports like baseball and football.

Huff, the AA, and schools throughout the country seized the opportunity to charge admission to games. In 1915 after a seven-game season that included battles with Northwestern, Ohio State, and the University of Chicago, revenue from football games tallied $34,316.35 (equivalent to $1,045,360.96 in 2023).[25] Five years later, the 1920 season's total revenue jumped to $94,143.57 ($1,448,262.32). Though the home game against Ohio State is perhaps the most memorable of that season, it was an away game against the University of Chicago Maroons that produced the most revenue for the Illini: $25,953.33 in gate receipts.[26] From the onset, ticket prices were differentiated by the type of purchaser and interest in the opponent. By 1924, general admission tickets cost $2.50, whereas students and faculty could purchase coupon books for $10.00 that gave them access to home events at a cost of roughly 64¢ per game.[27]

Once the Illini claimed a national championship in 1914, Huff considered more seriously the need for a new stadium. After visiting peer institutions including Harvard, Princeton, and Yale to examine their facilities, he concluded that Illinois' football success warranted a similar investment. He wanted a stadium not only worthy of Illinois, a midwestern powerhouse, but also one that would maintain the football program competitive with other Big Ten teams. Thereafter, benchmarking Illinois' athletic facilities against peer institutions to remain competitive consistently drove the AA's, and later the Department of Intercollegiate Athletics' (DIA), long-term facility plans.

In spring 1919, under the guidance of the University's War Committee—which included Huff and Chairman L. H. Provine—letters soliciting suggestions for the University's war memorial were sent to organizations and people across Illinois including the University's Student Council, the Women's League, major donors, civic leaders, and important cultural figures.[28] Ideas ranged from memorial columns to annual lectures, but the most popular option by far was a vague "[p]ermanent, monument, useful."[29] A year later, Huff utilized the suggestion's ambiguity to push for a student-led vote to promote a stadium as the school's memorial monument.

However, the struggle to have a football stadium approved, much less financed, was still far from over. By the end of 1919, President Edmund J. James—instrumental in securing state funding for a graduate program, promoting primary research, and a massive building campaign—had ended his tenure, and David Kinley was confirmed by the BOT. Unlike his predecessor, Kinley was not enthusiastic about the AA or intercollegiate sports in general and eschewed asking for monies or approval for a stadium in his 1920 building and facilities' ten-year construction budget. Kinley's lack of support for college football was not unique. As John Sayle Watterson details in *College Football: History, Spectacle, Controversy,* during the last two decades of the nineteenth-century college football was embroiled in controversy about its violence. Pioneering football schools like Harvard argued for major reforms, if not an outright ban on the sport like the one it instituted, albeit temporarily, in 1885.[30] Harvard's president, Charles Eliot, found football antithetical to the mission of providing students with an education centered on "culture and a commitment to service."[31] In contrast Yale, under the leadership of "the father of football" Walter Camp, and Princeton often stifled or slowed reforms. For Yale this position may have been fueled by rivalry: after all, from 1876 to 1907, Yale would defeat or tie Harvard in all but three matches.

Eliot's influence did not wane, and the changes that came with the sport were bolstered by President Theodore Roosevelt (Harvard class of 1880), a longtime supporter. With Roosevelt's prodding, in 1903, colleges instituted football rules to reduce violence like giving teams a new set of downs when they advanced at least 10 yards; and in 1906, at his insistence, the Intercollegiate Athletic Association of the United States—what would later become the NCAA was established to regulate college sports.[32] For his part, Eliot wielded the power of his academic presidency and insisted that if Harvard was to play, regular season games would be held at one of the school's facilities and not at a neutral site. For much of college football's earliest years, where Harvard and Yale went, other schools followed. The Illini, like most other programs, would thereafter schedule home-and-home series in which each school hosted a game in alternating fashion.

In this unsympathetic climate and with Kinley in charge, Huff could not make headway on new facilities. One headline-grabbing game, however, gave Huff the opportunity to promote the necessity for a new stadium. On November 14, 1920, in the season's final game, the Illini played Ohio State University. Illinois had suffered only one loss (at Wisconsin) and was looking for a share of the Big Ten championship, while Ohio State was undefeated and hoping to win an outright conference championship. In anticipation, Ohio State's athletic department had requested more than its allotted number of tickets. Though at the time school enrollment at Illinois was 8,000 students, an estimated 50,000 people came to the game at the sold-out Lumberyard. Unable to accommodate the large than expected crowd, approximately 30,000 were told to watch from outside the venue.[33] In a dramatic end, the Buckeyes prevailed on a late touchdown pass, prompting the Ohio State faithful to storm the field. National press coverage of the game—a compelling tale of rivals battling to a thrilling conclusion—embodied the growing enthusiasm for intercollegiate sports, especially football. Soon, colleges and universities across the country began considering building major sports facilities. According to Leon Deming Tilton and Thomas Edward O'Donnell,

A great wave of football enthusiasm had swept the country in the fall of 1920, and this gave a further impetus to the stadium idea. Already, neighboring institutions were conducting drives for funds for the purpose of erecting memorial stadiums. Soon

there was a growing sentiment for such a memorial at Illinois, the movement being fostered by a large and enthusiastic following by the alumni, friends, and students at the university under the leadership of Mr. George Huff, director of athletics.[34]

The Ohio State game enabled Huff to seize the momentum provided by the popularity of campus sports. Just three weeks later, he collaborated with the University's newspaper, the *Daily Illini,* to get a student-focused vote on building a monument to memorialize those who had served in the Great War. Over the three-day period of December 8–10, 1920, students registered their preferences by casting ballots that featured several options for a memorial monument, including a football stadium. Fresh off the 1919 national championship season and the rush from the Ohio State game, students voted overwhelmingly for a stadium as the preferred way to honor those who had served or perished.[35] Armed with the student body's endorsement and snowballing ticket revenue, Huff approached the BOT:

A request from the Athletic Association, through Director G. A. Huff, for authority to undertake a campaign to raise funds for building a stadium.

On motion of Mr. Ward, it was voted that the Board hereby expresses its interest in and hearty approval of the movement to construct a stadium, and looks with favor on the proposal to have the matter pushed by the Athletic Association.[36]

While Huff did not yet have financial backing, he finally secured explicit support for the stadium. The next step was to present the BOT with a plan that addressed funding, location, design, and operation. At a March 1921 BOT meeting, the AA was authorized to raise funds, and at least the path for a new stadium was clear.

Planning for Memorial Stadium

Early on, Illinois Field was discarded as the future site of Memorial Stadium. Demolishing Illinois Field meant first locating an alternative site capable of hosting tens of thousands of spectators while construction was underway. One option was McKinley Field at a local high school that had recently hosted a professional football game between the Champaign Legion and the Decatur Staleys. Interestingly, the Staleys were two seasons away from becoming the Chicago Bears, who had as a player-coach University of Illinois alumnus and football player, George "Papa Bear" Halas. Though the November 11 game had approximately 500 people in attendance, the high school field's facilities were deemed insufficient to host major college football games whose spectator crowds were expected to often surpass the tens of thousands. Perhaps more important were the spatial constraints of Illinois Field. The site was too small to address current needs and could not be expanded to accommodate football's swelling crowds. It quickly

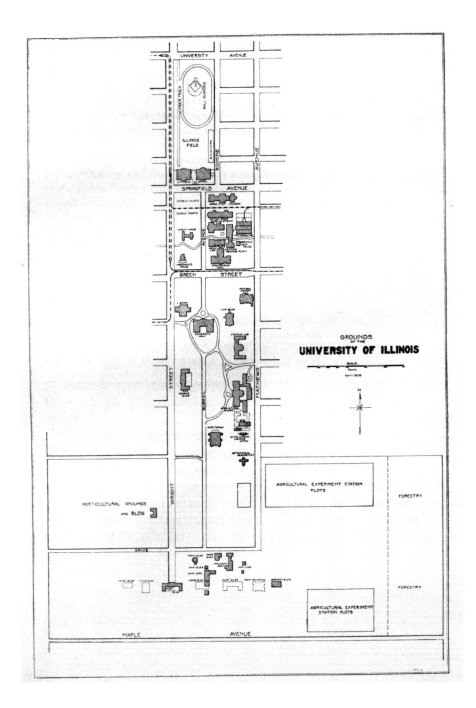

Figure 2.5
Grounds of the University of Illinois, 1906. Tilton and O'Donnell, History of the Growth, 41. Courtesy of the University of Illinois Archives.

became evident that the stadium would have to be built elsewhere.

From the beginning, the BOT took an active role in the stadium's siting and design. The Board had long been considering University expansion and growth, exploring a multitude of plans, and procuring land to facilitate expansion. By the time the BOT agreed to support the development of a new stadium, the campus had been steadily metamorphosizing from a haphazard arrangement of buildings on the original properties granted to the University into a coherent arrangement of structures that generated cohesive public spaces. One of the most significant buildings constructed during this phase was the Auditorium (now Foellinger Auditorium), designed in 1905 by architect and Illinois alumnus C. H. Blackall (class of 1877) (Figure 2.5).

Blackall proposed a master plan that organized campus buildings around a quadrangle. Originally, this quadrangle, or "quad," stretched along a north-south axis, bound to the north by Green Street and to the south by Foellinger Auditorium. Like the quad, it was understood that the stadium, would play a significant role in anchoring campus expansion and organizing space around it (Figure 2.6).

Over several years, the committee oversaw and submitted over a dozen master plans for consideration to the BOT. Each plan proposed new land acquisitions as a function of the University's expected student body and faculty's growth while maintaining a balance between collective open spaces, existing structures, and proposed buildings. This work reinforced an underlying order that could simultaneously enhance the campus' evolving aesthetics while providing a robust framework to guide future expansion. Any new stadium had to fit within this vision.

Not to be left out of the planning, the AA had been laying the groundwork for an enlarged athletic presence on campus for nearly a decade. As early as 1911, the AA purchased 20 acres of land west of First Street and east of the Illinois Central Railroad (ICR) tracks. Later that year Huff, in a letter to President James, mentioned this purchase and a need for additional space for physical education. Huff voiced his concern that the University was not providing exercise and physical health

instruction to the student body. Specifically, he outlined the need for "playgrounds" that would benefit all students but highlighted that the

> weak, frail, anemic ones, who are most in need of invigorating outdoor exercise, receive none.

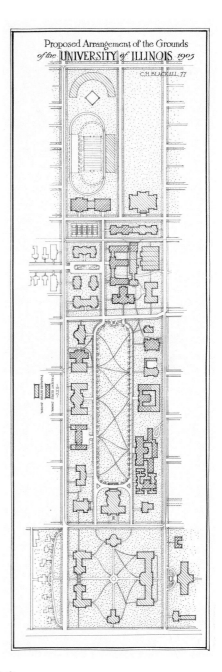

Figure 2.6
Masterplan of the University, 1905 C.H. Blackall.
Courtesy of the University Archives.

The latter are the ones that we desire to reach and interest, and we are doing so with our class games in football; class, fraternity, club, and departmental baseball games; tennis courts, and golf links.[37]

For Huff, the solution was not only more land but also multiple and larger facilities. He requested more baseball fields, handball courts, an ice-skating rink, fieldhouses, and a new gymnasium. To further his argument, Huff appealed to a shared vision of providing support for the adequate recreation and physical welfare of students: "you probably recognize some of your own arguments . . . because they are your ideas expressed to me many times."[38] To make his point, he compared the 35 acres of the University's current athletic facilities with those of peer institutions Cornell (60 acres), Harvard (50 acres), Wisconsin (42 acres), Michigan (38 acres), and Yale (29 acres). He portrayed the AA's land acquisitions as benevolent, even heroic:

I hold that the University, not the Athletic Association, is entirely responsible for this matter of a playground, but as the Association had a little surplus money. I could see no better way to spend it than for something which would help the whole student body.[39]

As he concluded the letter, Huff fired a broadside at the University and its failure to address the growing physical health needs of the student body: "every interest in the University is receiving attention in the comprehensive plans that are now being considered for the future development of the campus, except one, and that one is the recreation and physical welfare of the students."[40] After 1911, all campus plans showed westward expansion from the area south of Foellinger Auditorium, and the 160 acres that constituted 1867 University's land holdings. Thereafter, land acquisitions considered demands for not only academic and athletic facilities but also fields for recreational and military activities, including drills and parade grounds.

With Huff's continued pressure, by 1920 sports were integral to campus strategy and part of the vision for its future. Yet when the BOT commissioned a new master plan from the architectural firm Holabird and Roche, who at the time were designing several campus structures including a new library, a stadium was not a priority. This changed, however, because of two factors: first, the AA's success in producing revenue through intercollegiate sporting events, and second, student and alumni enthusiasm for football as evidenced by their committed financial support. Now, to avoid a confrontation, Huff and the AA sought approval merely to begin asking for donations toward a stadium (Figure 2.7).

In December 1920, the Athletic Board of Control (ABC) obtained permission from the BOT to solicit funds for a recreation field and stadium. One of the first money-raising mechanisms was to convince students to pledge monies toward the stadium's construction. After months of preparation, on April 25, 1921, Huff and the AA staff held pep rallies at the Old Annex Gym and the University's Auditorium. After a rousing speech at the gym, Huff introduced Zuppke, who before a raucous crowd publicly requested $1,000 in commitments from each student. According to Mike Pearson, a writer with the Fighting Illini,

[a] deep hush of expectancy filled the gymnasium. After a few seconds, a voice shouted, "I will give, sir!"

Bedlam ensued and "the youth was carried bodily over to the platform."

Zup announced his name as Ruy de Lima Cavalcanti of Bernabuco, Brazil.

Similar pledges followed in rapid succession from Princess Tirhata Kiram of The Philippines and J.C. Aquilar [sic] of Mexico. When the pledges were tallied, officials announced that their anticipated student quota of $350,000 had been doubled![41] On paper at least, the drive seemed overwhelmingly successful, raising over $700,000 ($12 million in 2023) in pledges.[42] But this hefty amount was still well short of the estimated total cost of $2,500,000 (Figure 2.8).

Therefore, a nationwide campaign designated some alumni (and some students) to be Stadium captains charged with meeting a donation quota and recruiting nine other people primarily from the AA's register of

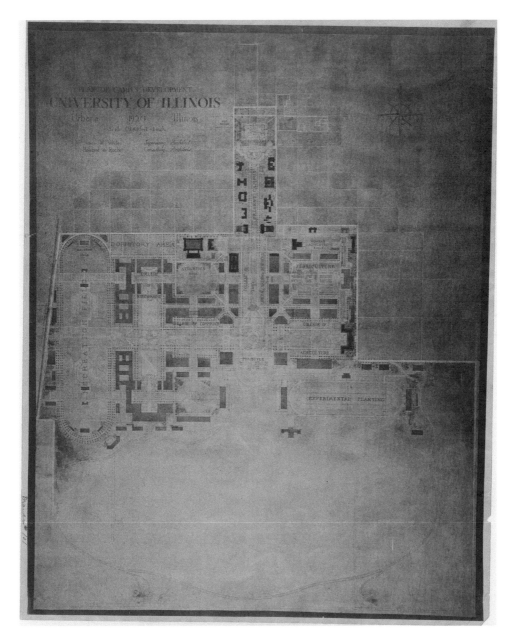

Figure 2.7
Holabird and Roche master plan, 1920. This plan shows the removal of the Mount Hope Cemetery, and it is unclear what happens to the Auditorium. Courtesy of the University of Illinois Archives.

"influential people," mostly alumni, to join the cause.[43] Even alumni with means were not guaranteed donors since they were often called on to fund competing projects simultaneously. For example, Illinois alumni were asked to contribute to the new Illinois Stadium at the same time many were contributing funds for Pasadena's Rose Bowl (1922), UC Berkeley's Memorial Stadium (1923) and the city of Los Angeles' own Memorial Coliseum (1923).

Another funding challenge derived from dissension within the state. Views among students, alumni, faculty, administrators, and Illinois residents fell into three categories. The first group opposed the project outright. The second favored construction and believed the University and the state had a responsibility to build it. The third contingent also supported construction but argued that its funding must emanate from students, alumni,

*"The gym annex looked like
the Chicago Coliseum during
the Republican Convention"*

Figure 2.8
The gym during the April 1921 pep rally soliciting students for donations. Story of the Stadium.

and state residents and not from University or state coffers. This last position, which ultimately carried the day, was based on two suppositions. Placing the burden on those interested would render any arguments against profligate state spending mute, and shifting the burden to people would generate genuine stakeholders, which would strengthen school spirit and loyalty.

A February 2, 1921, letter from major booster W. Elmer Ekblaw (1910), a former editor of the *Daily Illini*

and an organizer of one of the first college homecoming celebrations, to President Kinley makes this argument explicit:

As an alumnus of our University and observant of the activities in which the students and alumni engage, I have a very strong feeling that a deeper sense of responsibility and obligation must be developed among them. Until they recognise [sic] the heavy debt they owe their Alma Mater and the state that made their education and training possible, they will be neither loyal nor true. Until they sacrifice for Illinois, and serve her unselfishly, they will feel no keen interest in her welfare and progress.

It is my hope that the stadium movement will initiate a finer esprit du corps among our Illinois men and women everywhere, and organize them into a devoted, loyal, partisan body. To this end I earnestly hope that we can make this our irresistible argument —"You have never done anything directly for Illinois. You have made no sacrifice for her. Now you and all the rest of the Illini are called upon to respond to this appeal for direct services and support. We are going to raise every cent, every dollar, of the fund necessary to this project, without asking help of the Legislature or of the state funds. Now come across."[44]

On February 8, 1922, the BOT authorized the ABC to appoint the Stadium Executive Committee to act on behalf of the University to oversee the building campaign. On March 4, 1922, the committee was incorporated with the following members: Robert F. Carr (class of 1893), Chicago, chairman; George Huff (class of 1892), Urbana, vice-chairman; W. A. Heath (class of 1883), Chicago, treasurer; and Clarence J. Rosebery (class of 1905), Peoria, secretary and collection manager.[45]

At the end of 1922, the BOT sidelined Holabird and Roche and employed New Yorker Charles Platt to execute the newest campus master plan. He would spend the next dozen years designing eleven new buildings and constantly updating the school's master plan to accommodate expansion, and he was asked to weigh in on the placement and design of the proposed stadium. Overall, Platt favored a Georgian vocabulary, evident not only in his building designs but also at the master plan scale. Once the stadium became more than a planning exercise, the building's siting took on greater complexity.

The new structure would certainly be the single largest construction project on campus. Its scale would dwarf the existing buildings. And even more questions

arose about its function, such as the possibility of other uses for it, how intramural activities would relate to the building, and even whether intercollegiate activities would be viable in 25 or 50 years. Huff, however, had the clarity of vision to recognize that the stadium was more than a University sports venue. He knew that once the stadium was constructed, it would become a major center of activities for all of Illinois' residents. The University stated as much in *Complete That Stadium For Fighting Illini,* a booklet published during construction in November 1922,

> The memorial proposed then, will be more than a stadium, it will be the hub of an intense activity that will make the youth of our school able to meet fully the problems of life, a place where Illinois men and women can learn at first hand the principles for which Illinois men died five years ago.[46]

Assembling the Land

In the early part of the twentieth century, the University was in a fortuitous position compared with more urban educational institutions. Adjacent land was relatively inexpensive and available, and it began acquiring individual lots on the north side of campus and parcels of 20 or 40 acres on the south side. The July 23, 1913, BOT meeting minutes emphasized the intensity of purchasing:

> Mr. Moore, as Chairman of the Finance Committee, presented the following report and recommendation with reference to the purchase of land: The Finance Committee begs to report that they have not had sufficient time to examine all of the options and proposed tracts of land, nor to consult with the President of the University and the heads of departments. Your committee advises, however, that, in view of the liberal appropriation for buildings and land purchases, the board should set aside from the amount $400,000 for the biennium exclusively for land purchase, to provide for the present and partially for the future needs of the University.[47]

Empowered, the BOT went on to obtain over 400 acres of land contiguous with the campus.

Below is a summary of the land acquisitions.

Initial Campus Land Acquisitions, 1867–1925 (*green*)

1. 7.42 acres donated by Champaign County on May 8, 1867 (BOT, 35)
2. Miscellaneous properties bought from (block 41, lots 6, 7; block 42, lots 4–7; block 51, lots 4–7) or donated by (block 52, lots 1–6, 8–12; block 53, lots 1–2) the City of Urbana and individual lot owners (BOT, June 14, 1867, 139)
3. 40 acres (Wells tract between the Horse Railroad and the 160 acres to the immediate south); two lots purchased between the Horse Railroad and Springfield Avenue on June 14, 1867; two lots purchased by Regent Gregory and transferred to the University (BOT, 140; BOT, March 12, 1869, 88; BOT, March 12, 1869, 67)
4. 53.65 acres purchased from Johnathon and Amanda Stoughton and Elvia Babcock on May 10, 1867 (Land Acquisition Records, University of Illinois Archives)

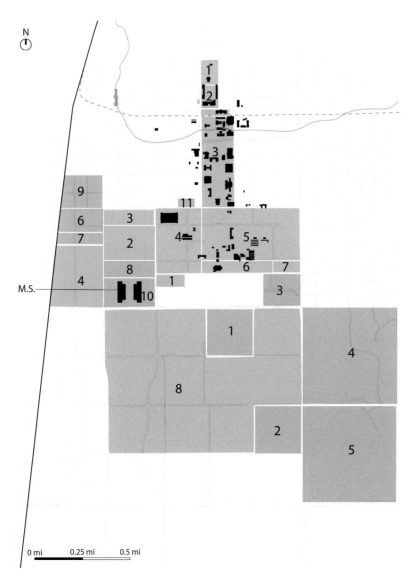

Figure 2.9
Land acquisition records, 1867–1925. Image by Kevin J. Hinders and Stephen Ferroni.

5. 80 acres purchased from Albert and Margaret Carle on May 10, 1867 (Land Acquisition Records, University of Illinois Archives)
6. 21 acres purchased from Jesse and Alina Burt on May 10, 1867 (Land Acquisition Records, University of Illinois Archives)
7. 7 acres purchased from Morris and Mary Burt on May 10, 1867 (Land Acquisition Records, University of Illinois Archives)
8. 405 acres purchased from Simeon Busey on March 30, 1867 (Land Acquisition Records, University of Illinois Archives)

Land Acquisitions, 1900–1919 (*orange*)

1. 40 acres purchased on June 28, 1907 (BOT, #24, 139)
2. 40 acres purchased on May 27, 1911 (BOT, #26, 140)
3. 27.8 acres purchased on July 13, 1912 (BOT, #27)
4. 160 acres purchased from the Busey family on July 23, 1913 (BOT, #27, 625)
5. 160 acres purchased on July 23, 1913 (BOT, #27, 625)
6. 20 acres purchased from the Scott tract purchased by the AA between 1911 and 1913 (BOT, #30, 639; BOT, #33, 220)
7. 10 acres from the Rhinehart tract purchased on September 6, 1913 (BOT, #27, 639)
8. 13 acres purchased on September 6, 1913 (BOT, #27, 639)
9. 21 acres purchased on July 11, 1914 (BOT, #31, 41)
10. 32.5 acres (Roland property) purchased on August 4, 1915 (BOT, #28, 220)
11. 402.5 linear feet of frontage on the Armory held by the Champaign Chamber of Commerce purchased by agreement Oct. 1, 1919. (BOT #29, 84). Purchase concluded on Lots 3, 4, 5, and 6, and Lots 8, 9, and 10 on Oct. 18, 1922 (BOT#30, 61)

Land Acquisitions, 1920–1925 (*blue*)

1. 6 acres (Nirider property) purchased November 9, 1921 (BOT, 126)
2. 20 acres (Stoolman property) purchased with the Stadium Fund May 10, 1922; bought on July 11, 1923, by the BOT (BOT, 210; BOT, 234)

3. Miscellaneous College Place properties acquired between 1922 and 1925
4. 47.6 acres (Hessel property) purchased December 28, 1925 (BOT, #33, 461)

The AA's Autonomy Questioned

During the century's teen years, Huff built up a formidable entity at the University. Gate receipts from athletic events made the AA a powerful and rather autonomous force within the University. However, it was sometimes unclear what roles and responsibilities were to be carried out by people under supervision and direction, be they coaches, instructors, or professors. Eventually, tensions over administrative duties and reporting came to a head. In a letter dated July 25, 1921, from President Kinley to Director Huff, it was clear that the former was not amused with Huff's creative bookkeeping, budgeting, and hodgepodge approach:

The more I study your budget and that of the College of Education the more convinced I am that the whole matter needs further discussion and the readjustment. Some of your sheets are marked "Physical Training" and some quote "Physical Education", and some other kinds. There are, I think, some recommendations for the department of Athletic Coaching, some for the Department of Physical Education, and some of other kinds. It seems to me that we need to differentiate more sharply between two or three things. Athletics belong to the Athletic Association. Physical training for men and women in the old sense in which we have used the term for many years, meaning thereby the gymnastic exercises prescribed for freshmen in order to keep them in good bodily condition, is a different thing and is not in any college. It has been assigned an independent department.

Physical education is still a third thing. I had supposed that all work done under this head was in the College of Education. I find that I am mistaken. I fear we are gradually getting sadly confused over these relationships and I shall be much obliged if you will bring the matter up in the fall with a view to having it thoroughly discussed and Senate action or administrative action taken making the necessary adjustments. In the meantime we shall have to leave matters pretty much as they are.[48]

The implications, and potentially negative impact, of an autonomous AA would not become evident until decades later. But, for the time being, Huff successfully maintained the AA separate from the rest of the University's administrative structure.

Property Values Dramatically Increase

This drive for land certainly expanded the campus, but just as situating the University in Champaign County had done nearly 60 years before, locating the Stadium generated tremendous land speculation sparking an escalation in property costs. Because the final location of the Stadium would affect the value of all surrounding properties, various prominent land-owning groups and families routinely lobbied the BOT to purchase land from them. Mary Elizabeth Bowen Busey, a BOT member since 1905 who would serve until 1930, made just such requests, as did campus architect James M. White.[49] Acting in his capacity as president of the Champaign Chamber of Commerce, he secured property the University could not afford and wrote to Kinley with a scheme:

DEAR SIR: The Champaign Chamber of Commerce has purchased lots 3, 4, 5 and 6, facing Armory Avenue just west of Fifth St., and lots 8, 9 and 10, facing Armory Avenue just east of Fifth St., believing that the University will someday want this property. One of the corner lots had been purchased with the view of putting a store upon it. It will be impossible to handle the large crowds which will ultimately go to the Armory on the ordinary width streets, and provision should be made for a large open area at the south end of Fifth Street. The improving of this property would have postponed the possibility of this development, and the Chamber of Commerce has therefore taken the chance of buying it and will be glad to hold it

until such time as the University can take title to it, but in the meantime would like to have sufficient returns to pay the carrying charges. The total frontage is 402.85 feet, and the cost to the Chamber of Commerce has been $18,539.16 which is $46.00 a front foot. To hold this property without cost the Chamber of Commerce should receive 6% on the investment plus taxes. The lots are available for tennis courts and it would be possible to put in eight courts as shown on the accompanying plan. To construct these and build suitable back stops will cost about $1,500.00. If the Chamber of Commerce should do this their investment in the property would be practically $20,000.00. If we build these courts can we rent the property to you, for 6% on our investment plus the taxes? If you desire the co-operation of the Chamber of Commerce in acquiring other property the University needs, we shall be very glad to discuss the matter with you.

In response, the BOT authorized the comptroller "to sign a long-term lease with privilege of purchase on the terms indicated." Years later, the Chamber of Commerce sold the land to the University (see Figure 2.9, Campus Land Acquisitions, 1867–1925, #11).[50]

The new property spurred internal competition primarily between the College of Agriculture and the Department of Physical Education. The College of Agriculture desired additional experimentation fields, and the Department of Physical Education coveted the land for ballfields, freshmen classes, training sites, and especially a new stadium that would become the centerpiece of its enterprise. Eventually, a détente formed, and Agriculture inherited parcels to the south, while Physical Education, and later Housing, picked up the majority of the land to the west.

Soon the search for an appropriate Stadium location was begun in earnest. The first site the BOT requested to be assessed was directly south of Mount Hope Cemetery and on an axis with the Stock Pavilion. However, this proposal would require building a grand processional promenade through the cemetery, which ultimately led to its rejection. In March 1922 the BOT again weighed in on a location:

1. That it be the unanimous voice of the Executive Committee of the University of Illinois Memorial Stadium that the Stadium shall be used in the broadest possible way not only for the staging of intercollegiate games and contests of every possible kind but also in the fullest possible development of intramural athletics in order that all of the men and women of the University, both students and faculty, may have opportunity for daily exercise and recreation;

2. That to carry out this purpose the Stadium should be located as close as possible to the center of the student population and activities in order to save time in going to and from the recreational fields;

3. That the location of the Stadium must give accessibility to the general public attending the so-called big games;

4. That it is the unanimous expression and request of this Committee that the location for the Stadium be selected as near to Armory Avenue as possible east of First Street and north of Maple Street [now Pennsylvania Avenue], Champaign, which runs south of the stock judging pavilion;

5. That funds be advanced from the Stadium collections, if the BOT shall find such advancement necessary in order to accomplish the purchase of a suitable site;

6. That a committee of three be appointed, with Mr. Huff and Mr. Zuppke available at such hearing, to present this resolution to the BOT and to urge our reasons upon such Board for prompt action accordingly.[51]

With the BOT's intentions clear, White wrote to J. A. Bradford, Ohio State University's architect, for advice on how planning for his new football stadium was proceeding. White clearly had misgivings about the construction and location of a 70,000-seat stadium. He told Bradford that the BOT and the AA wanted a multiuse building close to the campus center and outlined his concerns about the additional costs of necessary structural requirements. White preferred a separate building, worried that football might be a passing fad, and questioned the immense sunk costs of an enormous stadium.[52] But White also outlined the need for "a minimum of a couple hundred acres adjacent to the campus for intramurals, fieldhouses, stadium, military parade grounds and other related structures."[53]

Bradford's response was illuminating: "Do not under any considerations erect a stadium near your academic buildings, unless you wish to ruin the architecture of your campus. Our Athletic Association came very near persuading our Trustees to commit this blunder."[54] He also agreed "that we are in an abnormal athletic fever as far as intercollegiate sport" was concerned. He continued by "heartily" approving of intramural competition but offered "some misgivings as to the over development of intercollegiate athletics. I doubt the wisdom of erecting a stadium with seating capacity to exceed fifty thousand." Bradford concluded, "Don't let the present athletic enthusiasm wave spoil your academic campus."[55] White brought Bradford's advice to the attention of Holabird and Roche.

Controversy over the location began to brew. White and Platt, heeding Bradford's warning, prioritized addressing the Stadium's impact on the campus's urban design. Huff prioritized a sports-centered hub as close as possible to student residences. Perhaps sensing that the BOT was beginning to favor the architects' aesthetic considerations over his long-term vision, Huff changed tack and wrote a column for the *Daily Illini* arguing for his favored location. It was, for the former football coach, the perfect play. He was able to leverage his standing with the public, especially students and alumni, to push the BOT to accept his vision, while elegantly acknowledging the importance of White's and Platt's reasoning:

The site immediately west of the drill field, i.e., the land between First and Fourth streets and about one block south of Armory [A]venue is the one recommended by our Stadium committee since it is the best from the standpoint of accessibility and of elevation high enough to afford good drainage.

It has been our constant thought to make the Memorial Stadium and Field an all-year-round proposition and, to include under the Stadium, locker and shower rooms, basketball floors, hand ball courts, etc. In order to be useful from this standpoint it is necessary to have the Stadium as near as possible to the campus and to the student rooming district. For this reason, in addition to the matter of elevation and drainage, the Stadium committee has recommended the site mentioned above.

It is desirable, of course, that the Stadium should be located so that it will fit in with the general scheme of campus development, but unfortunately Professor White and Mr. Platt who have charge of this matter, feel that the location we favor is not the proper one from their standpoint. Meanwhile we are waiting for the board of trustees to decide.[56]

Though the *Daily Illini* declared that "[f]urther articles will be written by Prof. James M. White, supervising architect of the University, Charles A. Platt, consulting architect from New York and Coach Robert C. Zuppke" to generate "intelligent public opinion that may aid in reaching an agreement on the design and site," the counterarguments never materialized.[57]

Soon after Huff's column was published, chair William L. Abbott called a joint meeting of the Stadium Executive Committee, the Campus Plan Commission, and the University architects for April 21, 1922, at the Blackstone Hotel in Chicago. The day before, Holabird and Roche met with Platt and White to generate a report outlining the rationale for a site on 40 acres west of Fourth Street, east of First Street, and south of what is now Peabody Drive. Not insignificantly, this land was already owned by the University, while the stadium committee's favored site (including the Stoolman Tract and lots in College Place) would need to be purchased.

The six-member stadium committee, including Huff and Zuppke, resisted the architects' proposal, instead pushing for a spot closer to the campus core. However, President Kinley and BOT members began to support the architects' proposed site. The debate continued, and by late morning it was clear that the architects' proposal was winning. Before adjourning for lunch,

President Abbott inquired whether or not Mr. Huff would be satisfied if the stadium is located where the Architects recommended within a reasonable time there is provided a gymnasium and a fieldhouse. Mr. Huff said he would be, even though he is still of the opinion the Stadium should be placed on the Stoolman tract he hopes that the decision will be decided today.[58]

With this conciliation, the Stadium site was decided. Kinley and the BOT were careful to state that there could be no assurance of a gymnasium in the upcoming building budget request, but it was built—and would bear Huff's name.

Following a lunch break, the committee made the recommendation to the president of the BOT to accept the architects' proposal. Thereafter, "it was unanimously agreed to accept the opinion of the architects with a slight change moving the site about half a block east and placing the Stadium on the axis of the center of Washington Park."[59] Delay in the purchase of the land until July 1922, combined with land speculation, ended up costing $81,000—over 200% more than the original price of $40,000. Huff did not get the exact location he wanted—that was on land 20 acres south of Gregory and east of First Street known locally as the Stoolman property—but he did succeed in getting his massive sports complex and a prominent spot in Illinois history (Figure 2.10 and Figure 2.11).

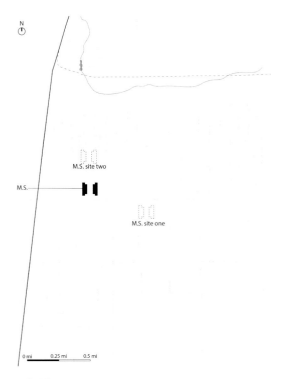

Figure 2.10
The three Memorial Stadium site proposals. Image by Kevin J. Hinders.

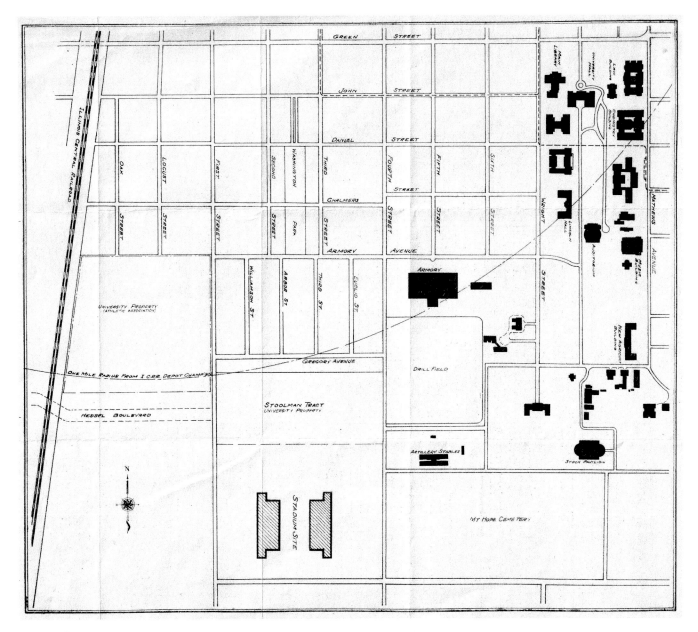

Figure 2.11
Map of campus. Memorial Stadium Notes 1, no. 1 (July 22, 1922): 3.

Notes

1 SmithGroup JJR, "The Impact of Place."

2 Miller, "The Great Fire," *Chicago History* 19, no. 1 (1990): 4.

3 Walker, "Report of the Superintendent," x.

4 Hunt, "Population of Illinois," 1.

5 Behle, "Educating the Sons of Toil."

6 Board of Trustees of the University of Illinois (BOT), *Third Annual Report*, viii; BOT, *Tenth Annual Report*, 9.

7 University of Illinois, "1892–93 Enrollment by Class and Sex," University Enrollment File, https://digital.library. illinois.edu/items/48dcd570-1469-0133-a7c8-005056960 1ca-7.

8 University of Illinois Division of Intercollegiate Athletics, "Historical Note."

9 BOT, meeting minutes, December 9, 1890, 38.

10 Grennan, "Life and Death of the Elephant."

11 BOT, meeting minutes, March 10, 1891, 67.

12 BOT, meeting minutes, March 13, 1917, 259.

13 BOT, meeting minutes, March 10, 1896, 235.

14 BOT, meeting minutes, March 13, 1917, 250.

15 BOT, meeting minutes, June 11, 1895, 95.

16 BOT, meeting minutes, June 11, 1901, 82.

17 Huff resigned to manage a professional baseball team in April 1907 but returned to the University after managing just eight games and was retroactively granted a "leave of absence." See BOT, meeting minutes, April 25, 1907, 101, and June 4, 1907, 110.

18 The original official conference name would remain until Big Ten was officially incorporated in 1987.

19 Big Ten Conference, "Big Ten Membership History."

20 Parks, "College Football National Champions."

21 "Fighting Illini FAQ," University of Illinois Archives.

22 Fighting Illini Football, "Illinois Homecoming History."

23 Baughman, "The Illinois Stadium," 2.

24 National WWI Museum and Memorial, "Coming Home."

25 1918–25 football season revenues, DIA, University of Illinois Archives. Calculation: US Bureau of Labor Statistics.

26 Ibid.

27 "Football Receipts," *Memorial Stadium Notes* 2, no. 2, December 1923, 3.

28 "Ideas for Memorial," *Daily Illini* 48, no.122, February 27, 1919, 4.

29 Ibid.

30 Watterson, *College Football*, 23.

31 Ibid., 27.

32 Watterson, "Political Football."

33 "Where We Stand," *Memorial Stadium Notes* 1, no. 1, July 1922, 1.

34 Tilton and O'Donnell, *History*, 101.

35 "Union Building Ballot is 637 in Plebiscite." *Daily Illini* 50, no. 69, December 10, 1920, 1.

36 BOT, meeting minutes, December 14, 1920, 155–56.

37 Tilton and O'Donnell, *History*, 204.

38 Ibid.

39 Ibid., 205.

40 Ibid., 206.

41 Pearson, "I Will Give, Sir."

42 "The Great Mass Meeting on April 25th 1921," in *Story of the Stadium*.

43 Handwritten notes, Alumni Association, Executive Director's Office Stadium Drive Records, 1921, Series No. 26/1/14 Box 1.

44 W. Elmer Ekblaw to Dr. David Kinley, February 2, 1921.

45 "Stadium Organization" *Memorial Stadium Notes* 1, no. 1, July 22, 1922, 2.

46 Complete That Stadium For Fighting Illini, *November* (date unknown), 2–3. University of Illinois Archives.

47 BOT, meeting minutes, July 23, 1913, 606.

48 Letter from David Kinley to G. Huff, March 28, 1920. University of Illinois Archives.

49 BOT, "Historical Leadership."

50 BOT, meeting minutes, October 4, 1919, 584.

51 BOT, meeting minutes, March 14, 1922, 173–74.

52 Letter from James White to Joseph N. Bradford, March 7, 1922, University of Illinois Archives.

53 Ibid.

54 Letter from Joseph N. Bradford to James White, March 21, 1922, University of Illinois Archives.

55 Ibid.

56 George Huff, "Huff Tells Opinion on Stadium Location; Define Controversy," *Daily Illini* 51, no. 155, April 1, 1922, 1.

57 Ibid, editorial note.

58 Minutes of a Joint Meeting of the Executive Committee of the University of Illinois Memorial Stadium and the Campus Plan Commission, University of Illinois Archives, April 28, 1922, 3.

59 BOT, meeting minutes, May 10, 1922, 209.

Memorial Stadium's Design and Construction

Introduction

By 1922, college football had become a big business across the United States, and since teams shared revenue from ticket sales, schools required larger facilities to remain competitive. No one wanted to be left behind, which prompted an explosive period of stadium construction, and with World War I still a fresh ordeal, many were designed to memorialize those who had served in the armed forces. Moreover, college football's popularity triggered the formation of sports conferences, whose mutually beneficial alliances and repeated contests capitalized on a loyal and enthusiastic fanbase and helped form enduring rivalries. As the popularity of football spread, attracting not only students and alumni but also a regional fan base, stadiums proved to be sound investments.

Indeed, the University of Illinois' Athletic Association (AA) recorded a steady rise in football ticket receipts from an annual total of just over $34,000 in 1915 to over $348,000 in 1925, a tenfold increase in ten years.[1] Not surprisingly, Big Ten universities constructed eight stadiums in the 1920s to meet attendance demands.[2] Most of these stadiums have continued to evolve and expand to accommodate new technologies and increase capacity; in some cases, older stadia were demolished and replaced by new facilities that addressed differing school needs and market demands. From its conception to its construction, Memorial Stadium was designed with the latest design philosophy, was imagined as an iconic structure, and was engineered to adapt as needed.

The Stadium's Design

The Stadium Is Conceived

The pledges of financial support from University students, alumni, and statewide organizations were not just important because they ensured the necessary monies to build Memorial Stadium; they were also an important indicator of overall support for the construction and the popularity of the Illini football program. Huff had successfully navigated the gauntlet of University politics to obtain BOT approval, and now he had to shift focus to ensure the new stadium would incorporate the spatial flexibility and innovative technology to address programming needs and provide a recurring income to sustain the sports programs. Logically, the first step in this process was to survey existing stadiums around the country to establish a comparative benchmark.

As head of the AA, Huff was always seeking ways to keep the Illini football program competitive. Over the previous 20 years, he had visited various peer institutions, particularly those with competitive college football programs. He examined their facilities, including stadiums that had recently been built and had taken tours of facilities at Harvard, Princeton, and Yale. Not surprisingly, *Memorial Stadium News*, a University newsletter focused on the Stadium's development and construction, frequently referenced these venues as benchmarks. Knowing these peers, the questions then became what program should be considered, what type of stadium should be built, and what historical design tradition should be used.

DOI: 10.4324/9781032643885-4

Stadium Typologies

Though stadiums dedicated to religious rituals, such as sacred rubber ball matches, had been erected in Meso-America as early as the Olmec civilization, (1500–800 BCE), the designers of Memorial Stadium considered historic forms built throughout the United States and Europe. The stadium as an architectural typology has existed in one form or another for 2,800 years. The word "stadium" is derived from the Greek *stádion*, a unit of measurement associated with competitive foot races run at Olympia in the Peloponnese. Archeological evidence suggests that starting with the first Olympic Games in 776 BCE, a proto-stadium environment was constructed to host athletic events honoring Zeus. It was composed of a flattened earth field nestled between gently sloping hills, measuring from stone marker to stone marker 191.78 meters long (equivalent to 600 Greek feet) and on average 32 meters wide from slope to slope. To the southwest, the track aligned with the altar for Zeus, signaling that the stadium and its events were part of a larger ritual. The gentle gradient provided a seating area for approximately 40,000 viewers (Figure 3.1).[3]

For the next 400 years, the popularity of sporting events spread beyond the Peloponnese, prompting the evolution of stadium design. By the fourth century BCE, stadiums across the Peloponnese ritual centers at Epidaurus, Dodona, and Delphi boasted seating made of limestone or other petrous material running parallel to the track on the long side. Dodona had a total of 21 or 22 seating rows. The stadium at Olympia and those at Epidaurus, Miletus, and Priene were U-shaped, with the seating area at right angles to the long sides. In 330 BCE,

Figure 3.1
Kallimarmaro Stadium, Athens, Greece. Photo by George E. Koronaio. Courtesy of Wikimedia Commons.

Athens built a new stadium named Kallimarmaro, directly over a 300-year-old racecourse, to host the Panathenaic games. As in Olympia, the stadium and its 850-foot-long track were nestled between two hills to take advantage of the slopes for seating. But this structure included long porous stone seating embedded into the hillside. The stadium was completely rebuilt in Petelic marble by a Greek-born Roman senator, Herodes Atticus, in 143 CE. Most importantly, the stadiums at Athens, like the one at Delphi, were U-shaped, but they had rounded turns from the long sides to the short side.[4]

Like the Greeks, the Romans developed and perfected their own stadium typology. Perhaps the two most famous Roman stadiums were the Circus Maximus and the Colosseum. Originally built in the sixth century BCE, the Circus Maximus was the site of the Ludi Romani (Roman Games) and intense horse-drawn chariot races. After a destructive fire in 64 CE, the Circus Maximus

was rebuilt to host nearly 250,000 spectators. Compared with contemporary Greek stadiums, the Circus Maximus's field dimensions were gargantuan: 540 meters long and 80 meters wide. The stands, 30 meters wide and 28 meters tall, ran parallel to the long sides and met at the southeast short side to form a continuous U-shape. The northwest side was bounded by a series of gates for grand entrances or race starts. The stands nearest to the track, originally covered in sand, were made of concrete and stone, while those more distant were made of wood. Spectators could walk from one area of the stadium to another, by egressing the stands through passages that connected to ambulatory corridors above grade. In these passageways, attendees could find food stands and other amenities.[5] Significantly, the outermost ring of the Circus Maximus was marked by a continuous arcade, which was used for circulating at the ground level around the venue.

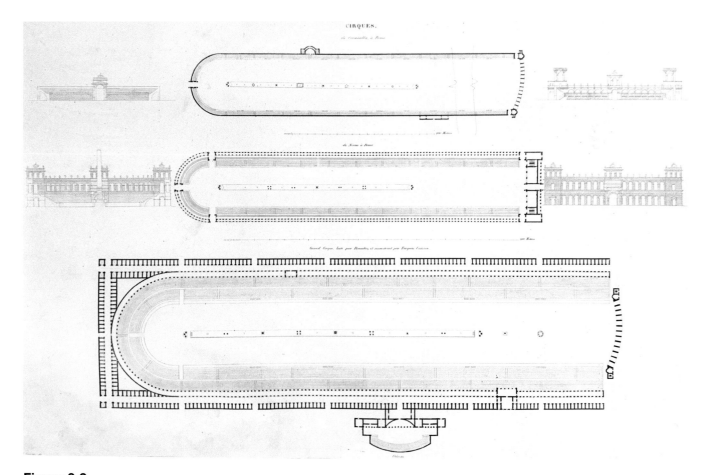

Figure 3.2
Circus Maximus. Durand, *Recueil et parallèle des édifices*, 41.

With its elliptical plan and continuous seating throughout the entirety of the perimeter, the Colosseum marked a significant typological variation from the Greek and Roman U-shaped stadiums and their long track stretches. Construction began in 70 or 72 CE during the reign of Emperor Vespasian, which led it to be referred to as the Flavian Amphitheater, and it was inaugurated by Emperor Titus in 80 CE. Two years later, Emperor Domitian added a second seating tier dramatically increasing the stadium's seating capacity (Figure 3.3).

The Colosseum would become an important design precedent for sports facilities. Unlike previous

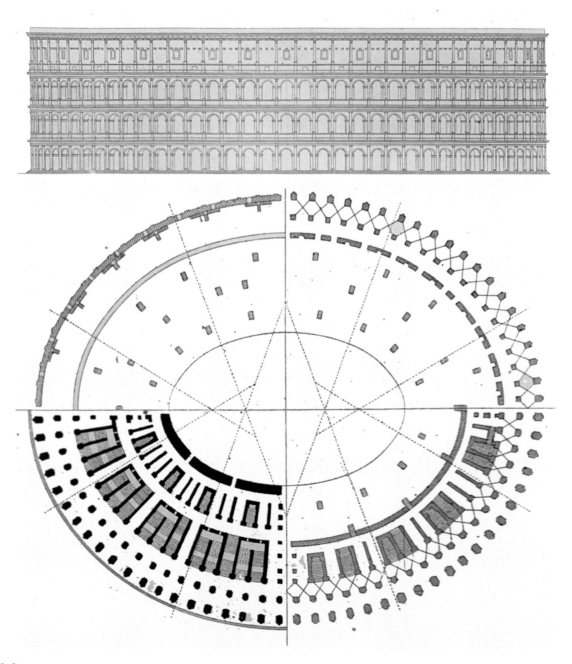

Figure 3.3
The Flavian Amphitheater (Colosseum). Durand, *Recueil et parallèle des édifices*, 39.

amphitheaters, the Colosseum did not have the benefit of a hillside for structural support, and therefore it was built as a freestanding structure. It was built using brick and concrete, which were then covered by a travertine stone veneer, that together produced "a complex system of barrel vaults and groin vaults measuring 620 by 513 feet (189 by 156 meters) overall."[6] Finally, three of its "stories are encircled by arcades framed on the exterior by engaged columns in the Doric, Ionic, and Corinthian orders; the structure's rising arrangement of columns became the basis of the Renaissance codification known as the assemblage of orders" (Figure 3.4).[7]

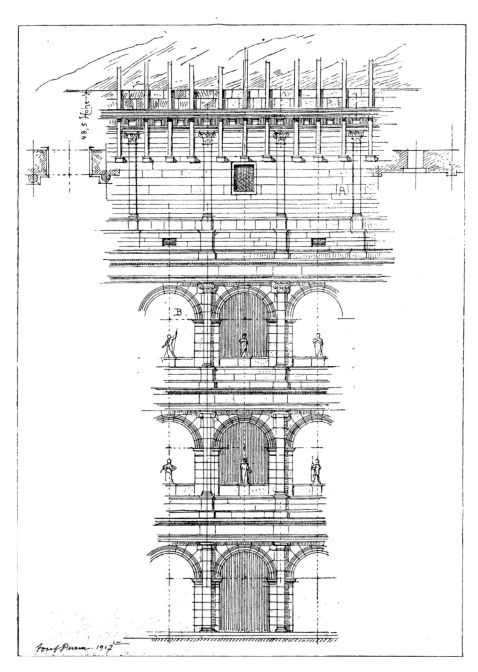

Figure 3.4
Bay Elevation of the Colosseum, Rome from a drawing by Josef Durm (Karlsruhe 1837–1919), arquitecto. Ver [1].

Contemporary Stadium Typologies

Over the next 2,000 years, stadium typologies would continue to evolve but retain spatial expressions found in these Greek and Roman forms. It is possible to examine the built environment much like one examines an organism to trace its current physiology and morphology to a distant biological ancestor. Moreover, just as it is useful to categorize living organisms into taxa to compare commonalities and variations, it is possible to examine contemporary stadiums, and their constituent spatial components, as belonging to one of four basic forms.

The first stadium type, and the simplest, consisted of seating or standing tiers—commonly referred to as bleachers because the platforms were exposed to the sun's bleaching action—located along one edge or all sides of a field. The platform section with the best views and most comfortable seating is often referred to as the grandstand. As Paul Goldberger notes in *Ballpark,* these seating types were developed long before college football and were commonly found in early twentieth-century baseball stadiums, circa 1909 to 1914.[8] Moreover, because the stands usually ran parallel to the long sides, like in the Circus Maximus, these arenas were commonly utilized for horseracing. Memorial Stadium's predecessor, Illinois Field, had this type of arrangement with a grandstand. Purdue's Ross Aide Stadium, built in 1924, was originally a grandstand, as was Iowa's Kinnick Stadium, which was completed in 1929. Examples of grandstand-style seating are ubiquitous in smaller venues, including most high school football fields.

The second contemporary type is best illustrated by Harvard's football stadium, built in 1903. Visited by Huff, it features U-shaped seating surrounding the field but is left open at the northeastern end. Today, it seats 25,884 people. Although it is modeled after Kallimarmaro, it is much wider because it accommodates the full width of the football field and a running track (since removed). By widening the central area, the stadium could field events, including football. Structurally designed by Harvard engineering alumnus Lewis Jerome Johnson, "Harvard Stadium remains the nation's oldest concrete stadium and the first architectural piece to use

vertical reinforced structural concrete."[9] This structural innovation would prove fundamental for the design of Illinois' Memorial Stadium. Like Harvard's circus-style stadium, Princeton's Palmer Stadium, which opened in 1914, also accommodated a track. Today, circus stadiums are also sometimes referred to as horseshoe stadiums. Other Big Ten horseshoe stadiums were built at Ohio State University (1922), the University of Minnesota (known as the "Brick House"; 1924), and the University of Indiana (1925).

Constructed in 1914, Yale's football stadium is a bowl typology and was the first of its kind in the United States.[10] As the name implies, bowl stadiums are oval or elliptical fields, like the Roman Colosseum, enclosed by seating or standing platforms on all sides. An advantage of bowl stadiums is that their centralized spaces are usually excavated, which places the field below the entry grade and means tall structural supports are not required. Compared with those in Harvard's U-shaped stadium, Yale's seating tiers have a relatively low-angled slope, which provides a deeper site to accommodate 61,446 people. Unlike Harvard's stadium, the Yale Bowl did not accommodate a track. Another trackless bowl stadium is the Rose Bowl, which was inaugurated in Pasadena, California, in October 1922 and designed by Myron Hunt. It started as a mix between an open horseshoe and a Colosseum-style stadium but underwent several modifications, including an aggressive expansion in 1928, to become a full bowl shape capable of seating 92,542.[11] New Year's Day postseason games have been hosted in the Pasadena arena since 1902, but the first game referred to as the Rose Bowl was held in January 1923. It is from this recurring game, "the granddaddy of them all," that college football would dub all postseason games bowl games.[12]

Just 13 miles to the southwest of the Rose Bowl is the aptly named Los Angeles Memorial Coliseum, designed in 1921 and inaugurated in 1923, which has a track for regional, national, and international track and field events that twice hosted the Olympic Games, in 1932 and 1984. Today, it seats 75,000 people and is the home stadium of the University of Southern California Trojan football team. Yet, of all the stadiums, the University of Michigan's "Big House" is the largest in the country with a seating capacity of over 107,000 people.[13] Located in Ann Arbor, it is home to the Michigan Wolverines, a founding member of the Big Ten Conference. In fact, the three largest stadiums by capacity in the United States are in the Big Ten Conference at Michigan, Ohio State, and Penn State.[14]

Finally, the last typology is the tiered or multiple-deck stadiums. Typically, seating tiers along the long sidelines are split into two or more levels to facilitate more seating closer to the field, which necessitates a higher structure. Professional baseball stadiums built between 1912 and 1914, such as Fenway Park in Boston, Wrigley Field (originally called Weigman Park) in Chicago (Figure 3.5), and Ebbets Field in New York are all tiered ballparks.[15] The tiered platforms were not just great for sightlines for most fans in attendance but served a pragmatic spatial purpose in their densely built urban areas. To accommodate sufficient seating, overlapping tiers were built horizontally into the surrounding urban fabric. Though few of these stadiums remain, their centralized locations and proximity to public transportation made them highly popular and the source of cherished collective memories across the United States. They would become a prototype for new venues for all sports.

Football did not have the limitations of baseball's infield and outfield requirements, which meant that multilevel seating could run along one or both sidelines, usually aligned with the end zones. Fans in even the most distant balcony could be closer to the field and had better views. In the 1920s, only two major double-decked football stadiums were built: the University of Illinois' Memorial Stadium and the University of Nebraska's Memorial Stadium in 1923.[16] Although Memorial Stadium at the University of Illinois was conceived as a pure tiered stadium, its design was modified to become a hybrid of the tiered and horseshow stadium types.

Figure 3.5
Wrigley Field. Photograph by Arvell Dorsey Jr., https://flic.kr/p/bUxLDv, CC BY 2.0, https://creativecommons.org/licenses/by/2.0/.

Since their beginning, stadiums were rarely pure typologies. One example of a combination stadium type is Dyche Stadium (now called Ryan Field), built in 1926 at Northwestern University. Tiered on one side with a single grandstand on the other, the arena has an overall horseshoe shape thanks to the curved seating at one end zone. Memorial Stadium was intended to have such a horseshoe located at the south end zone. Cost concerns led to the elimination of that horseshoe, and permanent end zone seating was added by the late 1920s.

Since their initial construction, many college stadiums have gone through such expansions and alterations. In 2000, a survey in Alva W. Stewart's *College Football Stadiums* shows that of the 114 stadiums used by Division I-A college football programs, 28 were categorized as grandstands, 15 were tiered, 12 were horseshoes, and 21 were bowls.[17] The remaining 38 stadiums have architectural features of two or more typologies, and the great majority of these were altered to accommodate changing needs. In the Big Ten, for example, Ohio State University's famous "Shoe" was originally constructed as a tiered horseshoe but grandstand seating was added to its south end zone. Illinois' Memorial Stadium would undergo several modifications that altered its typologies. Table 3.1 lists the typologies of the Big Ten stadiums constructed in the 1920s.

Illinois	Mixed: circus, tiered, and grandstand
Indiana	Circus
Iowa	Grandstand
Michigan	Bowl
Minnesota	Circus
Northwestern	Mixed: tier and circus
Ohio State	Mixed: circus with grandstand
Purdue	Grandstand

Table 3.1
Big Ten Stadium Typologies
Note: Includes Big Ten members through 1930. Michigan State built its stadium in 1923 but did not join the Big Ten until 1949. Nebraska built its stadium in 1923 but did not join the Big Ten until 2011. UCLA, USC Oregon and Washington joined the Big Ten in 2024.

The Design Commission

In the summer of 1921, with construction approved and funding drives well underway, two groups vied for the right to design Illinois' Memorial Stadium. Faculty members William M. Stanton, Lemuel C. Dillenback, and Stanley P. Stewart from the Illinois School of Architecture (ISoA) were unsurprising entrants. The ISoA had been established in 1873 by Nathan Ricker in part to address the growing demand for qualified design and building professionals during Chicago's post-fire construction boom and was the second oldest program in the nation. On July 6, 1921, L. H. Provine, who headed the ISoA, asked the BOT to seriously consider ISoA's team to design the stadium.[18] The team included Professors William Macey Stanton, L.C. Dillenback, and Stanley P. Stewart.

Granted an audience, the group produced exquisite hand-drawn and rendered drawings for a neoclassical circus typology stadium. Their drawings were widely circulated in newspapers across the state, used at student fund drives in spring 1921, and incorporated into *The Story of the Stadium,* a substantial promotional publication with short essays and opinion pieces. Their plan elaborated on details laid out by campus architect James White, who limited activities to football and track and field events and seating for 75,000 people on 65 parallel tiers, each 120 yards long. At the interior, between the seating and the football field, would be a quarter-mile track with a 220-yard straightaway (Figure 3.6).

The ISoA faculty's neoclassical design incorporated elements that students and colleagues had suggested as fitting for a memorial monument. The proposal included a campanile, a large bell tower (like that of Piazza San Marcos in Venice, Italy) that would be dedicated to Illinois ideals and commemorate soldiers and sailors who had died in service; it also featured captivating images of reflecting pools and fountains and an Italian garden landscape. A court of honor shaped like a Greek theater would have been bound on three sides by a colonnade; names of dead and wounded service members would be inscribed on the columns. Two smaller courts would be dedicated to soldiers, sailors, and marines. This aesthetic also mirrored President Kinley's championing of

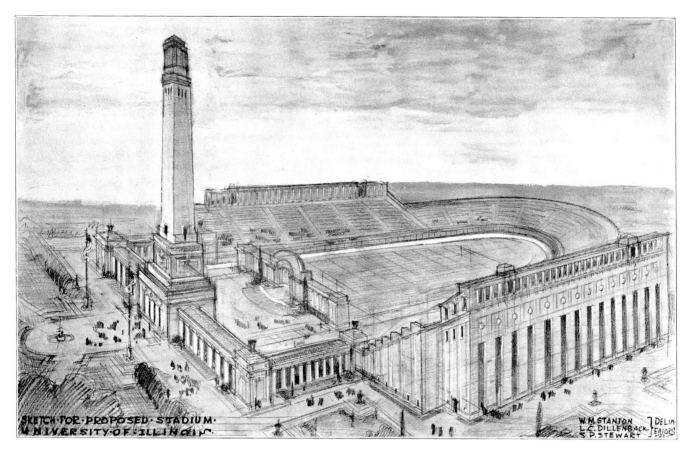

Figure 3.6
Faculty sketch for the proposed stadium, February 1921. This rendering shows a circus stadium, honor court, and campanile without balconies. The Illinois Stadium "For Fighting Illini."

Greek and Roman culture, which he believed would inspire in students the highest of intellectual, moral and ethical values (Figure 3.7):

Perhaps my greatest interest in the stadium is its cultural effect.

Our stadium will bring a touch of Greek glory to the Prairie.

Young men and women spending four years of their lives in the vicinity of such an edifice cannot help absorbing some of its lofty inspiration.

A still more practical cultural development will come from the Greek theater, seating 10,000 persons, which will stand in the honor court. It will be a setting for outdoor plays, pageants, May fetes and music festivals enriching the imagination of the participants and the beholders.

The setting, that of an old Italian garden, with the proscenium arch at one end, with the colonnades, archways and shining towers of the entrance, will bring an appreciation of old-world beauties, of fine and eternal traditions, which, blended with the ruggedness and shrewd intelligence of our people, will help us to realize the greatness which is our birthright.[19]

The Greek theater-like court of honor would have been bound on three sides by a colonnade; inscriptions on these columns would be that of the names of the dead and wounded. Two smaller courts, located outside of the court of honor, would also be dedicated, one to soldiers and the other to the sailors and marines (Figure 3.8).

The other group under consideration was the Chicago firm founded by William Holabird and

Figure 3.7
Faculty rendering of the proposed honor court &
Greek theater. Perspective pencil study of the court
of honor, The Illinois Stadium "For Fighting Illini,"
March 25, 1921.

Figure 3.8
A carillon was included in the honor court
composition. Faculty drawing, perspective pencil
study for the tower, The Illinois Stadium "For Fighting
Illini," March 25, 1921.

Martin Roche, known simply as Holabird and Roche (H&R). This firm had already been at work on the campus master plan and had been engaged by the BOT in October 1919 to produce designs for a hospital and a horticulture building.[20] Their campus plan proposed multiple east-west cross axes for the campus, including an axis that extended from Lincoln Avenue to the ICR tracks that would mark the then southern boundary of the campus. This plan also proposed extending the north-south axis further south by eliminating the Mt. Hope Cemetery, which today sits east, across Fourth Street from the stadium grounds (See Chapter 2).

Although the faculty proposal was endorsed by colleagues and students, H&R had the powerful Donor Committee (DC) on its side. Because the committee controlled all donations, it in effect controlled the

purse, and therefore its opinion weighed heavily in the BOT's decisions. And the committee members were powerhouses on campus: chair Robert F. Carr (who was also a member of the BOT), Huff, Zuppke, and Avery Brundage, an exceptionally influential alumnus. Outspoken and an unabashed supporter of intercollegiate and intramural sports, Brundage shared Huff's beliefs about physical fitness:

Someday physical training in its broadest sense will be as much and as important a part of our educational program as mental training. We have the best athletic department in the United States today at the University of Illinois—we must have the best athletic plant. As a monument to the past and an inspiration to present and future teams,

I am glad to contribute to the building of the most imposing Stadium in the country.[21]

Brundage had earned a civil engineering degree (1909) and was a decorated student athlete, playing varsity basketball and excelling in track and field, especially his senior year when he won a discus conference championship.[22] Years later, he became the head of the International Olympic Committee (1940–1962). Besides his athletic UIUC *bona fides*, Brundage also had ties to H&R, having worked for the firm as a construction superintendent from 1909 to 1912, when he resigned to compete for the US in the 1912 Olympics.

After the Olympics, Brundage founded a Chicago construction company that earned a reputation for innovation. Brundage reasoned that since H&R had been unanimously selected in a juried competition in December 1919 to design Municipal Grant Park Stadium (known today as Soldier Field; see Figure 3.8), it would be the best choice.[23] Five years later, Soldier Field was officially dedicated on October 9th, 1924, on the anniversary of the Great Chicago Fire. He championed the firm before the BOT, arguing that it not only had produced one of the country's most recent stadium projects but was uniquely qualified to address the multiple challenges of the new campus venue. Brundage, Carr, and the rest of the DC insisted on H&R (Figures 3.9–3.12).

After several meetings and working sessions, on August 1, 1921, the BOT made the selection official:

The matter of the architects for the Stadium was introduced. On motion of Mr. Abbott, seconded by Mr. Trimble, the following resolution was adopted:

Whereas the proposed Stadium is to be erected with money subscribed by alumni and other friends of the University and not with University money; and

Whereas a committee representing the donors, consisting of Mr. Avery Brundage, Mr. Robert F. Carr, Mr. Robert C. Zuppke, and Mr. George Huff have addressed a letter to the President of the University asking approval of the action of said committee in selecting as architects for the Stadium the firm of Holabird and Roche of Chicago; and

739. Grant Park Stadium. Competition plan, courtesy of Holabird & Root.

Figure 3.9
Competition drawing by Holabird and Roche for Grant Park Stadium (now Soldier Field). Bruegmann, *Holabird and Roche*, 2:143.

Whereas a letter was addressed to the Board of Trustees by Professor L. H. Provine, representing the Department of Architecture, urging that that department or members of it should be appointed architects for the Stadium; and

Whereas the Trustees are of the opinion that it is the right and privilege of the donors, through their representatives or committees, to select an architect for the Stadium, although it is also the opinion of the Board that their choice should not be objectionable to the Board. Therefore be it

Resolved, that the firm of architects selected by the committee in charge is acceptable to the Board of Trustees.[24]

Figure 3.10
Soldier Field, in Chicago, Illinois, set up for the Dempsey Tunney fight on September 22, 1927. Photograph by
Kaufmann and Fabry Co. Chicago Historical Museum.

With this resolution, the BOT sidestepped the ISoA's
proposal and allowed the donors' representatives to
select H&R.

Refining the Site Selection

Foreseeing an eventual student population of 30,000,
planners sought a site suitable to host various types of
sports and grow to accommodate an ever-increasing
level of student participation.[25] Campus architect James
White was keenly aware of how massive the new structure would be, possessing a completely different scale

than even the towering Armory. He and architect Charles
Platt argued for a spot on the less developed south side
on 40 acres between the Illinois Central Railway (ICR)
tracks and the Mount Hope Cemetery.[26] The width of
the playing field was 250 feet from stand to stand so that
football field and track and field track could be incorporated at grade. Because of the dual-tier seating parti, the
vast majority of spectators would sit between the field
endlines. Moreover, in preparation for future growth,
the Stadium was designed to eventually incorporate
permanent seating to the north and south sides, thereby
accommodating up to 92,000 spectators in the future.[27]

Figure 3.11
Soldier Field colonnade. Photograph by Raymond Trowbridge. Chicago Historical Museum.

A GLIMPSE OF SKYLINE FROM SOLDIER FIELD, GRANT PARK, CHICAGO   1079-31

Figure 3.12
A Glimpse of the Chicago Skyline from Soldier Field, Grant Park, Chicago. Courtesy of the Curt Teich Postcard Archives Digital Collection, Newberry Library, Chicago.

The design approved in May 1922 called for an

east and west stand with a total seating capacity of approximately 57,000. Each stand will consist of a main floor seating 18,657 and one balcony seating 9,986—a total seating capacity for each stand of 28,625.

Under each stand is a large hall 50 feet wide 415 feet long and 30 feet high. . . . The height of the top row of the balcony above the playing field is 114 feet.[28]

From the beginning, it was evident that officials and designers understood the site was prone to flooding. Because it was located between a moraine and the elevated ICR tracks that formed a natural dam, the architects would need to take extra precautions to ensure the field drained appropriately. Since the playing field would be 250 feet wide from stand to stand, it and the track could be incorporated at grade. For the east stands, the field would be depressed 16 feet below grade, which would still permit proper drainage, and the high point of the east stands would be 98 feet above grade.[29]

To understand the final design, it is useful to look at H&R's earlier buildings, especially Soldier Field. At

the time, the most noticeable feature for both was the extensive use of Greek-ordered colonnades. At Soldier Field, the Doric colonnades are set high above the field, marching along the long east and west sides, where spectators can overlook the stadium's interior, toward the city, and over Lake Michigan. Seen from South Lake Shore Drive, the colonnades were isolated architectural features that generated a striking contrast with Lake Michigan. The south end of these Doric colonnades marked the end of the stadium's straightaway and the beginning of the Roman-style circus seating area that bounds the stadium's south. Most remarkable was the designers' decision to locate the colonnades not at the building's base, where they could act as a ground-level arcade, but two stories above, which placed a greater emphasis on internal stadium circulation.

Soldier Field's neoclassical vocabulary and compositional scheme are perhaps indebted to two antecedents. The first is a civic monument nearly 4,800 miles (7,400 kilometers) away in Rome, Italy. The Monument to Victor Emmanuelle II (Figure 3.13) designed in 1885 by architect Giuseppe Sacconi (inaugurated in 1911 and then again in 1927) places its colonnade atop the last and highest (from the street-facing front to back) series of rising,

Figure 3.13
Monument to Victor Emmanuelle II, also called the Altar of the Nation Photograph by Globe Trotter Company,
Courtesy Wikimedia Commons.

massive platforms clad in Brescian marble and travertine. At 30 feet (70 meters) high and 459 feet (140 meters) wide, the Vittoriano (as it is called by locals) was built to announce a modern secular Italian state and act as a counterweight to the profound influence of Rome and the Roman Catholic Church. Like the Vittoriano, Soldier Field was meant to embody the aspirations of a population wishing to memorialize and celebrate the achievements of a city rebuilt, quite literally, from the ashes of a fire that had devastated the community 50 years before.).

A second influence on Soldier Field was the City Beautiful movement. Best exemplified by the overarching urban design approach to Chicago's 1893 Columbian Exposition, it strove to enhance cityscapes through neoclassical buildings, landscapes, and landmarks and highlight important civic spaces. Soldier Field's neoclassical Beaux-Arts vocabulary and landmark siting suggest H&R were cognizant of its role as a civic monument and were determined to make manifest the city's aspiration to transform Chicago into the "Paris on the Prairie."

In the same vein, the AA and the University looked to H&R to design a building and sports complex that, like its sports teams, would set the University apart from its peers. Memorial Stadium was more than a functional structure: it was conceived from its inception as an iconic edifice. Like Soldier Field's colonnades had modified the Chicago skyline, Memorial Stadium's colonnades would rise majestically above the central Illinois Prairie (Figure 3.14).

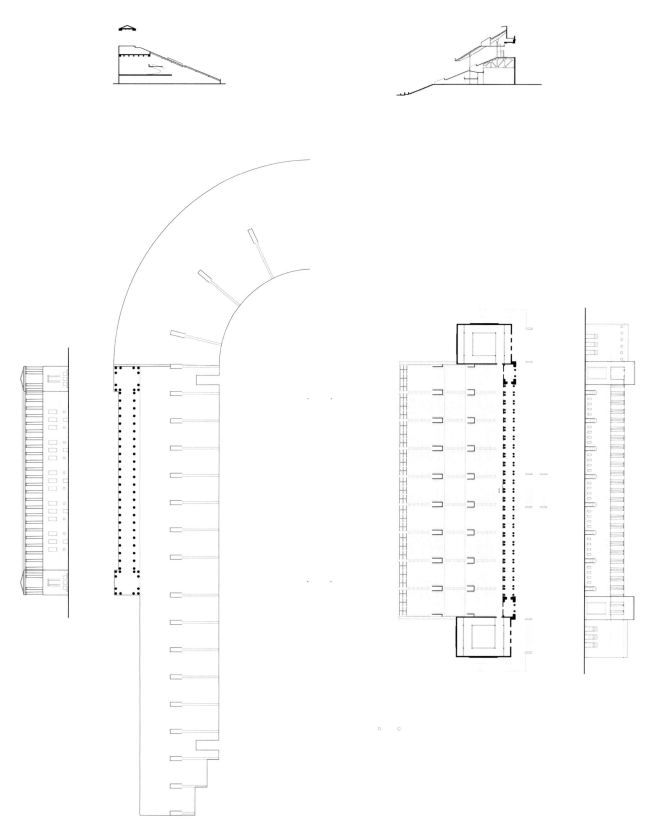

Figure 3.14
Soldier Field and Memorial Stadium. Drawing by Stephen Ferroni.

Design as an Expression of Time and Place

Design Considerations

Finally, on April 28, 1922, the BOT agreed to enter into a contract with H&R and would eventually pay the architecture firm $75,324.10. Below are the BOT's terms establishing the basis for their contract:

The Committee approved and affirmed the action of the Committee of the Athletic Board of Control in entering into contract with Holabird & Roche of Chicago for architectural work in connection with the Stadium upon the following terms:

Holabird & Roche are to furnish the usual architectural services necessary for the completion of the Stadium which shall include preparing reports and estimates for preliminary study of the project; working drawings and specifications to serve as a basis for taking bids and awarding contracts; large scale details and full size drawings; and superintending the construction of the work to assure that the materials and workmanship fully comply with the provisions of the plans and specifications. Their services embrace architectural, structural, mechanical, electrical, heating and sanitary portions of the structure.

It is understood that shop detail drawings shall be supplied by the contractor in accordance with the usual custom.

Architects' fees for the above services will be 5% of the entire cost of the work (as determined from the contract price), including the survey, borings if required, fixed or detached furnishings designed or installed under their superintendence.

Payments shall be made to the Architects as follows: $15,000 upon completion of the preliminary sketches; 2½% of the estimated cost of the work shall be paid, less the sum of $15,000 above stated, when the working drawings and specifications have been prepared, provided, however, that if the preparation of the plans extend over a period of more than two months, payments on account shall be made from time to time, such payments to be approximately proportioned to the progress of the work on the plans. After the contracts are let, payment of the balance (2½%) of the amount of certificates issued to the contractor or contractors shall be made at the respective times such certificates are issued, and the remainder of the 5% if there be any, shall be paid at the time of issuance of the final certificate, it being understood that the total of their fees shall be 5% of the total final cost of the work.

The contract further provides that should the work be abandoned after the preliminary sketches are prepared, the Architects shall be reimbursed to the extent of the actual cost to them.

The drawings and specifications are to remain the property of the Architects and to be returned to them upon the completion of the work, one complete set to be furnished to the Stadium Committee.

The Architects are to keep a complete record of all transactions and to render monthly statements of the condition of such contracts and transactions. No extras or credits are to be ordered except upon written approval of the Stadium Committee.

I note in the press proof of the minutes of the meeting of the Board of Trustees, on May 10th, last, that the purchase of the Stoolman property, so called, was reported to the Board and was given approval.

There has been no further meeting of the general Executive Committee of the Stadium. The Building Committee is still busy working out details in connection with the Architects and I understand that this Committee went to Columbus, Ohio, for the purpose of gaining first hand information in regard to the construction work of the Ohio Stadium, which may have a bearing upon the plans for our building.

Notices calling for the payment of the second installment, due July 1st, upon Stadium pledges, are now being prepared in the office of the Secretary and Collection Manager. It may be of interest to the Board to know that a small bulletin giving information regarding Stadium developments will be enclosed with these notices.

Respectfully submitted, C. J. ROSEBERY

On motion of Mrs. Grigsby, this report was received for record and the actions taken by the

Stadium Executive Committee as outlined in the report were approved.[30]

In the early planning stages, a variety of images were produced to help people visualize the future structure, increase interest, and encourage donations. One image shows the four main features initially considered: a field flanked by grandstand seating with a horseshoe end zone, an honor court, and a bell tower/campanile (Figure 3.15).

Memorial Stadium had been conceived as a three-tiered stadium, with the tiers bookended on each side with neoclassical flat-roofed towers that enclosed enormous poured on-site concrete ramps. However, it was constructed with two seating tiers on each side, which eliminated seating capacity, and reduced the height, but more importantly, provided significant construction cost savings. Both stadiums had colonnades three stories above the exterior grade level. However, unlike Soldier Field, Memorial Stadium had its Tuscan colonnades not as isolated arcades but framed as part

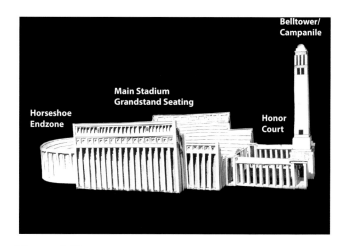

Figure 3.15
Early depiction of Memorial Stadium. Annotated by the authors. Courtesy of the University of Illinois Archives.

of a larger opening that integrated them into the overall facades. Each building also employed ramps to reach the midlevel vomitoria, the graphically named passageways located behind the tiered seating that enabled the fast exit of voluminous crowds. Both stadiums accommodated a

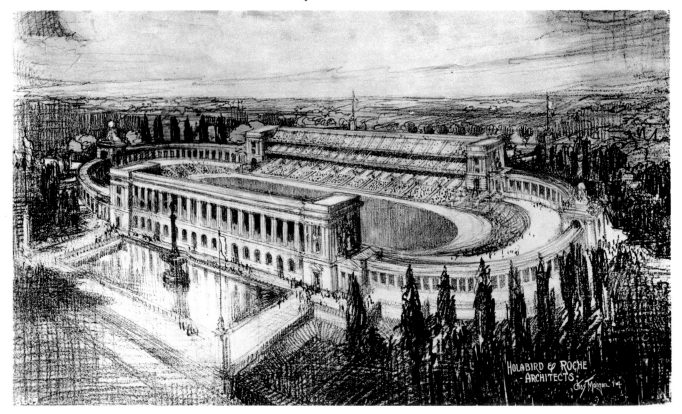

Figure 3.16
Early drawing of Memorial Stadium by Holabird and Roche. From *Story of the Stadium.*

track, curved seating to the south past the end zone, and an opening to the north. The Soldier Field track was a third of a mile with a 220-yard straight away, substantially larger than Memorial Stadium's quarter-mile track (Figure 3.16 and Figure 3.17).

For both stadiums, H&R utilized the buildings' long axes to generate long sweeping views to important local landmarks. The north side of Soldier Field opened to a vista featuring Grant Park and the Field Museum, which had been completed in 1921. Similarly, Memorial Stadium was sited to connect with a proposed quadrangle, Military Axis, and recreation fields that extended east to west from the South Quad to the railroad tracks. Similarly, early designs for both stadiums featured a monumental vertical element, like a campanile or obelisk,

that not only marked the north-south axes but visually drew the eye toward the sky. But because of a financial crunch, these elements, along with other decorative items such as fountains and ornamentation, were never completed at Memorial Stadium.

More emphasis was placed on practical and functional aspects such as structural stability and egress. Several tragedies in previous decades informed design strategies as architects and engineers sought to mitigate the inherent risks of crowds of more than 50,000 people. In 1900, a roof collapsed at the end of the California-Stanford game that caused the death of 20 people.[31] Just two years later, a seating area at Ibrox Park in Glasgow, Scotland, gave way and killed 26.[32] Closer to Illinois, in 1915 the Camp Randall bleachers crumpled

Figure 3.17
Early drawing of a three-tiered stadium from the field looking toward the south horseshoe by Holabird and Roche. From *Story of the Stadium.* Note the horseshoe's colonnade is similar to Soldier Field.

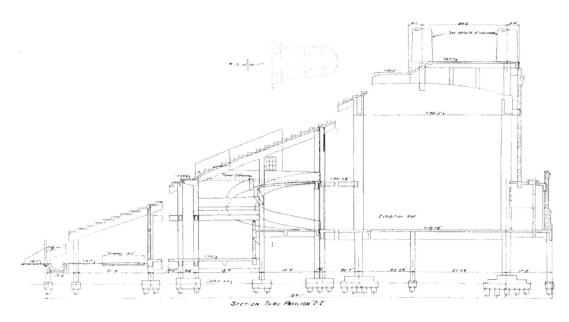

Figure 3.18
Section of Grant Park Stadium. Burt, "Stadium Design," 72.

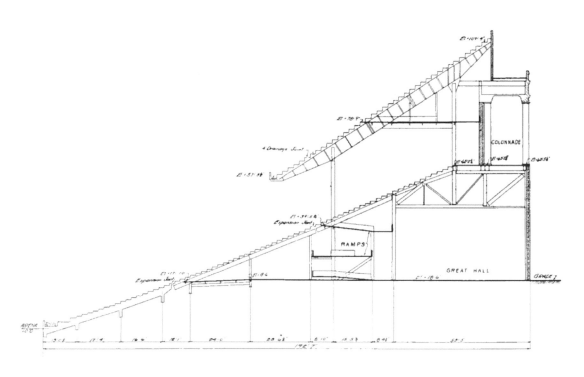

Figure 3.19
Section of Memorial Stadium. Burt, "Stadium Design," 82.

during a homecoming game between the University of Wisconsin at Madison and the University of Minnesota. Perhaps the most tragic scene at a sporting event, however, was the February 1918 fire at the Happy Valley Racecourse in which more than 500 died.[33] These catastrophes, some caused by structural failure, others by fires, weighed heavily on H&R. Structural criteria had to be developed and applied to safeguard lives, while ramp systems and the vomitoria had to manage panicked crowds rushing toward exits. Soldier Field (Figure 3.18) has a ramp from the exhibition hall to an interior hall balcony that allows access to the viewing seats through multiple vomitoria. Memorial Stadium (Figure 3.19) would feature an at-grade entry to enable access to the lowest-level vomitoria, while ramps from the great hall would allow access to the midlevel vomitoria. Ramps in the north and south towers would lead to the upper-tier seating, balconies, and the ceremonial perimeter colonnades (Figure 3.20).

Perhaps one of the most significant differences between the two stadiums can be found in Memorial Stadium's Tuscan colonnades, whose massing, rhythm, light, and shadow play make a poetic narrative. Platt likely had input on their design since he was frequently asked to comment on the work and advise the BOT. In one BOT meeting on June 13, 1922, Platt provided an overview of the plan, but instead of agreeing fully the BOT inserted a caveat that H&R was to further study the colonnades.[34] Eventually, the designers eschewed the subtle use of color common to the Beaux-Arts architecture that characterized Soldier Field. Instead, the Stadium took on a more Georgian character to match the architecture across the University. Focusing on the campus master plan, Platt had convinced the BOT that to generate a more unified campus, the new buildings had to exhibit a consistent vocabulary. The final facade also showed Platt's influence through its red brick and Bedford stone, which "was decided upon in order to make

Figure 3.20
Stadium ramp tower, interior. Courtesy of the University of Illinois Archives.

the structure as harmonious as possible with the present and contemplated buildings on campus."[35] Consistent with his proposed vision, Platt would eventually design eleven campus buildings, all in the Georgian style.

The Stadium as a Memorial

Over 350,000 persons from Illinois joined the armed services during World War I, and approximately 5,000 died. From the University of Illinois alone, 8,190 men and women had served, 1,159 in Europe, by the time the war ended. With one in ten eligible men drafted, the effect on student populations was profound. At the University of Illinois, the campus population dropped by almost a third. In the spring of 1917 alone, 1,262 students withdrew to join the war effort; for incoming freshmen, enrollment was down approximately 16.6% in fall 1917.[36]

To that point, the highest enrollment had come in October 1916, when 3,978 men and 1,236 women started classes. But registrar C. M. McConn was stunned by the results of a 1917 survey of Illinois high schools to estimate incoming freshmen numbers. He notified the BOT in July that only 486 freshmen were likely to enroll, not the anticipated 643. In the fall of 1917, 1,836 additional students enrolled, compared with 2,079 nonfreshmen for the same period in 1916. With 3,786 men and 1,290 women, the October 1918 total was not only a decrease from the high-water mark of 1916 but a precipitous drop considering that the University expected year-on-year growth of 10%. By October 1919, the student population stood at just 7,102. McConn calculated that between those who would not return and those who did not enter, the population was down 37%.[37] The implications were profound. The numbers represented a major shortfall in financing the aggressive building campaign. And they also pointed to mammoth war casualties, intense pain, and a need to memorialize the losses.

Jack Bell (class of 1923), a senior and chair of the Memorial Committee, summarized in the newsletter *Memorial Stadium Notes* the austere criteria for honoring the dead: "[o]n each column will be inscribed the military rank and military organization of an Illinois man who died in the service nothing more. The name

of the donor of the column will not appear upon it." Financial pledges by friends, family members, and even organizations like fraternities had been made in honor of the deceased. However, Bell made it clear that although many service members had no individual pledges, "they will have columns just the same" (Figure 3.21).[38]

Of the 200 limestone columns, each 22 feet tall, that make up the 15-foot-wide colonnades, 189 were inscribed with the names of those who died in World War I. Moreover, 184 columns have the names of Illini such as Gladys Gilpatrick, the only woman listed. The other 11 columns honor the memory of members of the Illinois community. One column memorializes the unknown Illini dead, while another set of columns is dedicated to those from the Students' Army and Navy Training Corps. One was supplied at the expense of Fielding Yost, the University of Michigan coach, who donated $1,000 to honor Curtis G. Redden, a Wolverine athlete and Illinois native. Another honors Laurens Corning "Spike" Shull, born in Sioux City in 1894, who earned varsity letters in football, basketball, and baseball at the University of Chicago. Shull was chosen as a first-team All-Western player and a second-team All-American in 1915. In 1917, he voluntarily enlisted, and having been commissioned as a second lieutenant in the infantry under the command of Theodore Roosevelt Jr. was mortally wounded at the Battle of Château-Thierry, France, on July 1918 and died August 5, 1918.[39]

Poems were written to be placed throughout the Stadium. In one, writer Bliss Seymour notes the mixed emotions of watching a sporting event after having experienced the horrors of war:

> The Stadium
> Like autumn leaves that flutter and grow still,
> The rooters hush and sink into their places,
> The gripping moment over. In their faces,
> [Young faces burning with the combat's thrill,
> And yet quite strangely old, and sober-eyed]—
> No thought dares enter of another game
> When killing and not scoring was their aim,
> And all of them fought on the selfsame side.
> Yet we remember them, and all those others
> Who lie in France. The stadium's grey stones

Figure 3.21
Colonnade shortly after completion. Photograph by Raymond Trowbridge. Courtesy of the University of Illinois Archives.

Forbid us to forget; the shadow tones
Across the field make, living and dead, brothers.
And in the shouting, we recall a day
When death came to the loser in the play.[40]

In another poem, written for the grand dedication ceremony by Lew Sarett, Illinois (class of '16) the text makes clear the Stadium's importance as a memorial:

Ode to Illinois
Know that the broken hosts
Of martial-moving ghosts,
Who gave to a warring world their last full breath,
And won to immortality in death,
Hovering in stadium shaft and tower height,
In memorial court and buttressed peak,
Shall watch for you, and speak
To you of Great Moments in a Greater Fight.
O Men of Illinois, in war and peace and play,
So may we live that when the crucial fight is won,
And the long race run,
These spirits of an elder day
Shall bend to each of us and say:

Well done! Well done!
Yours is the will to win.
Well done, my prairie son.

Composition and Function

Memorial Stadium, honoring those who served and commemorating them for the ages, was designed for spectacle, gathering, viewing, and movement. The main stands rise above the ground on a steel frame. The upper deck seating is carried by 27 trusses on each side. Virtually all vertical movement is handled by a series of ramps (see Figures 3.22–3.25).

H&R took a pragmatic approach and saw the design as a collection of functional pieces with each element serving a singular function. This strategy also permitted flexibility to accommodate an unfixed number of columns whose total would depend on donations. The main elements are

1. The track and field (spectacle);
2. The east and west great halls (gathering and distribution);

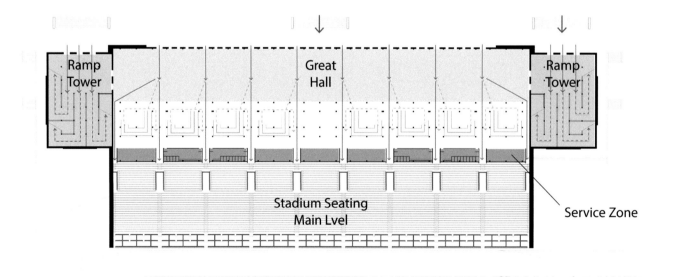

Figure 3.22
Circulation diagram. Image by Kevin J. Hinders and Stephen Ferroni.

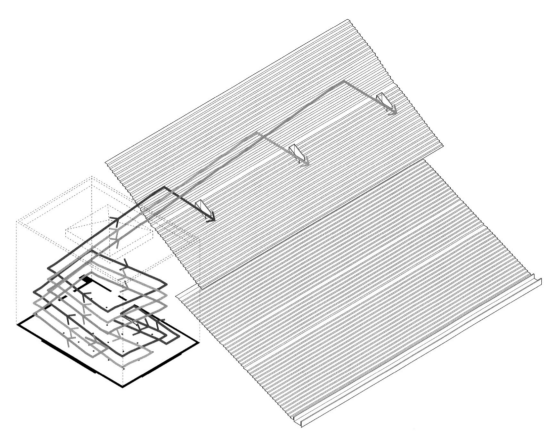

Figure 3.23
Stair tower ramps to upper deck seating. Image by Kevin J. Hinders and Stephen Ferroni.

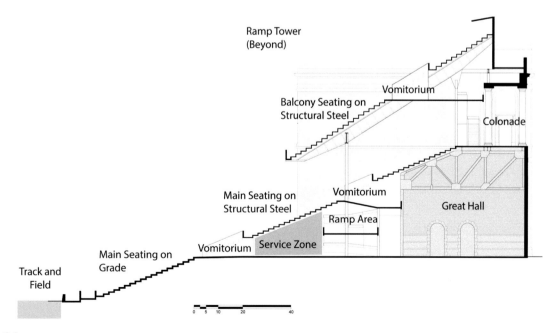

Figure 3.24
Stadium section diagram. Image by Kevin J. Hinders and Stephen Ferroni.

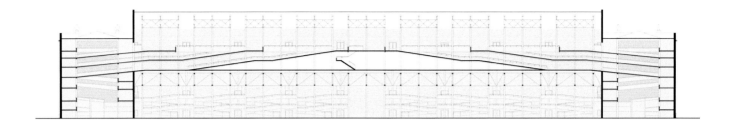

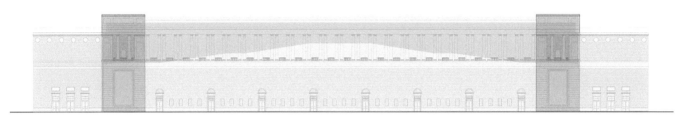

Figure 3.25
Stadium longitudinal section through upper ramps and elevation. Image by Kevin J. Hinders and Stephen Ferroni.

3. The stadium seating: the main seating on grade (ground), the main seating area on structural steel, and the balcony on structural steel (viewing);
4. The circulation through the ramps and ramp towers;
5. The colonnades (the memorial);
6. And the services, such as the bathrooms and concession areas.

Each element is either celebrated—such as the balcony seating—or is part of the structure's background—such as its services. Rather than tie the facade together with repetitive vertical bays, the major elements are arranged in a composition that calls attention to each element's function (see Figure 3.25). This style was a departure from campus buildings that had drawn inspiration from the Colosseum. Its structure consists of arches stacked on top of one another with decorative columns applied to the exterior surface. This stack is then repeated around the perimeter (see Figure 3.26). This strategy became common in Renaissance, Baroque, and neoclassical architecture. Indeed, Harvard's stadium is an austere version of the Colosseum stripped of its decorative columns but using a repetitive set of bays to create the exterior facade (see Figure 3.27). And the University

of Illinois has a multitude of examples, such as the Architecture Building, in which bays create the exterior facades (Figures 3.28).

Unlike the bay system, Memorial Stadium has a symmetrical composition around the 50-yard line running east-west and around the goalposts running north-south. The main facade's rhythm is established by eight arched portals leading to a great hall. Each great hall acts like the palm of a hand that then distributes spectators via fingers, or ramps and vomitoria, to seats. To either side of each great hall are the ramp towers. Each tower has its own symmetry about its entry. The towers contain three sets of stacked ramps that distribute spectators to the balcony seating. The colonnades above the great halls provide views away from the stadium to the surrounding grounds and campus and also mask the ramps. There is no formal correlation between the red brick of the great halls and the Bedford limestone colonnades. No discernable bays are repeated. Instead, a limestone and brick band separates the lower half from the upper half (Figure 3.29).

The exterior facade composition is held together with two large towers that serve as bookends. These limestone structures transition the center halls and colonnades to

Figure 3.26
Cross-section and elevation drawings of a reconstruction of the Colosseum in Rome. Line engraving by Luigi Canina, 1851.

the north and south ramp towers. The towers bear large panels with inscriptions. One reads:

May this stadium ever be a temple of sportsmanship inspiring the athletes of the University of Illinois and those who cheer them as they play

always to uphold the spirit and tradition of Illinois athletics and to play manfully and courageously to the last no matter what the odds. To play fairly within the spirit and the letter of the rules to win without boasting and to lose without excuses. May these ideals of manliness, courage and true

Figure 3.27
Harvard Stadium. Courtesy of Harvard University, Cambridge, MA.

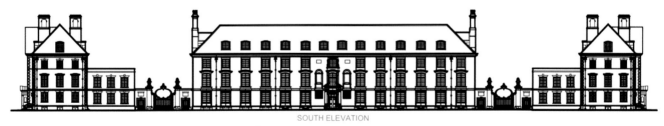

Figure 3.28
Drawings of the School of Architecture overall. Image by Eliza Peng.

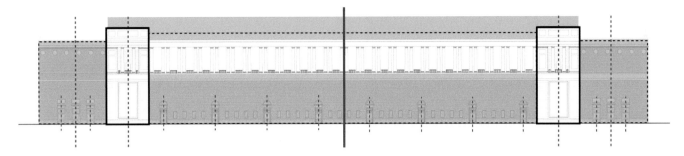

Figure 3.29
Facade diagram. Image by Kevin J. Hinders and Stephen Ferroni.

sportsmanship find expression not only within the stadium but throughout the life of the university. Above all may the stadium always be the symbol of a great united university drawing closer together in common bond and spirit all the men and women of Illinois.[41]

The ramp towers, in turn, help buttress the limestone towers and provide access to the colonnade and balcony seating. Each ramp tower has an elegant entry of three grouped doors with limestone bas-relief sculptural ornamentation above (Figure 3.30). The ramp towers feature bas-relief rectangular panels and round medallions. Three medallion carvings are repeated around the upper perimeter of each ramp tower (two facing the playing field, four facing the north-south axis, and six on the main facade of each ramp tower for 48 total). Like the colonnade column spacing above the great halls, these medallions are not arranged to correspond to the first-floor entries.

The central portal features the University's motto, Labor and Learning, along with founding date of 1867. The portal to the left features an athlete receiving a laurel wreath symbolizing victory. The portal to the right features soldiers shaking hands and an angel standing behind them.

Above this base, near the top of the ramp tower are the rectangular stone carvings depicting war, athletics, and education (Figure 3.31). The three repeated round medallions depict an owl with the University motto, a discus thrower with the Greek letters ΑΘΛΗΤΗΣ

Figure 3.30
The bas-relief sculptures over the ramp tower entries. Photograph by Kevin J. Hinders.

(athlete) and the head of a warrior (presumably Ares), presented in profile with the dates 1917 and 1919 to commemorate the US participation in the war (Figure 3.32).

Figure 3.31
The bas-relief sculptures on the north and south ends of the ramp towers depict war, athletics, and education. Photograph by Kevin J. Hinders.

Track Facilities

After all the wrangling about the vision for a sports complex and adjusting to a limited budget, plans for basketball courts, racket courts, and even a skating rink were shelved, and instead these areas became part of the concession row that supplied game attendees with food and refreshments. Ideas for a radio broadcasting center were also scrapped despite the allure of advertisement dollars. Only the track was retained, and its lanes ran parallel to the Stadium's long side and projected far past the end of the circulation towers toward the north side of the field. Seen from the football field, the ends of these running tracks were marked by four gate-like piers (two on each side). Temporary seating would be placed on the north side of the track field during football games.

Ready to Begin Construction

On April 28, 1922, the BOT formally agreed to enter into contract with H&R, and the lengthy process to build a memorial on the prairie would start:

> The Committee approved and affirmed the action of the Committee of the Athletic Board of Control in entering into contract with Holabird & Roche of Chicago for architectural work in connection with the Stadium upon the following terms:

Figure 3.32
Carved medallions on the ramp towers. Photograph by Kevin J. Hinders.

Holabird & Roche are to furnish the usual architectural services necessary for the completion of the Stadium which shall include preparing reports and estimates for preliminary study of the project; working drawings and specifications to serve as a basis for taking bids and awarding contracts; large scale details and full size drawings; and superintending the construction of the work to assure that the materials and workmanship fully comply with the provisions of the plans and specifications. Their services embrace architectural, structural, mechanical, electrical, heating and sanitary portions of the structure.

It is understood that shop detail drawings shall be supplied by the contractor in accordance with the usual custom.

Architects' fees for the above services will be 5% of the entire cost of the work (as determined from the contract price), including the survey, borings if required, fixed or detached furnishings designed or installed under their superintendence.

Payments shall be made to the Architects as follows: $15,000 upon completion of the preliminary sketches; 2½% of the estimated cost of the work shall be paid, less the sum of $15,000 above stated, when the working drawings and specifications have been prepared, provided, however, that if the preparation of the plans extend over a period of more than two months, payments on account shall be made from time to time, such payments to be approximately proportioned to the progress of the work on the plans. After the contracts are let, payment of the balance (2½%) of the amount of certificates issued to the contractor or contractors shall be made at the respective times such certificates are issued, and the remainder of the 5% if there be any, shall be paid at the time of issuance of the final certificate, it being understood that the total of their fees shall be 5% of the total final cost of the work.

The contract further provides that should the work be abandoned after the preliminary sketches are prepared, the Architects shall be reimbursed to the extent of the actual cost to them.

The drawings and specifications are to remain the property of the Architects and to be returned to them upon the completion of the work, one complete set to be furnished to the Stadium Committee.

The Architects are to keep a complete record of all transactions and to render monthly statements of the condition of such contracts and transactions. No extras or credits are to be ordered except upon written approval of the Stadium Committee.

I note in the press proof of the minutes of the meeting of the Board of Trustees, on May 10th, last, that the purchase of the Stoolman property, so called, was reported to the Board and was given approval.

There has been no further meeting of the general Executive Committee of the Stadium. The Building Committee is still busy working out details in connection with the Architects and I understand that this Committee went to Columbus, Ohio, for the purpose of gaining first hand information in regard to the construction work of the Ohio Stadium, which may have a bearing upon the plans for our building.

Notices calling for the payment of the second installment, due July 1st, upon Stadium pledges, are now being prepared in the office of the Secretary and Collection Manager. It may be of interest to the Board to know that a small bulletin giving information regarding Stadium developments will be enclosed with these notices.[42]

Notes

1 See Addenda # XX- excel spreadsheet on gate receipts from 1915 to 1925. Courtesy of DIA.

2 This count does not include universities that entered the Big Ten after 1930. Michigan State built its stadium in 1923 but did not join the Big Ten until 1949. Nebraska built its stadium in 1923 but did not join the Big Ten until 2011. The University of California, Los Angeles and the University of Southern California are scheduled to join the Big Ten in 2024.

3 Mee and Spawforth, *Greece*, 291.

4 Dinsmoor, *Architecture of Ancient Greece*, 250.

5 Rose, "Spectators and Spectator Comfort in Roman Entertainment Buildings: A Study in Functional Design," 106.

6 *Encyclopedia Britannica*, s.v. "Colosseum," January 5, 2023, https://www.britannica.com/topic/Colosseum.

7 Ibid.

8 Goldberger, *Ballpark*.

9 Mairead B. Baker, "Harvard's Colosseum: A History of Harvard Stadium," *Harvard Crimson*, November 18, 2022, https://www.thecrimson.com/article/2022/11/18/fb-2022-harvard-yale-stadium/.

10 "Yale Bowl," National Historic Landmark summary listing. National Park Service.

11 Stadiumguide.com, "Rose Bowl Stadium."

12 Williams, "How the Rose Bowl."

13 University of Michigan Facilities, "Michigan Stadium."

14 Penn State football joined the Big Ten in 1993.

15 Goldberger, *Ballpark*, 77.

16 Kenny, "Illinois Memorial Stadium."

17 Stewart, *College Football Stadiums*.

18 BOT, meeting minutes, July 6, 1921, 9.

19 "'Greek Glory on the Prairie,' Says President Kinley," in *Story of the Stadium*.

20 BOT, meeting minutes, October 16, 1919, 598.

21 "'As a Monument to Past and Future Teams,' Avery Brundage Subscribes $1000," in *Story of the Stadium*.

22 "Avery Brundage," Olympedia. https://www.olympedia.org/athletes/78168.

23 Chicago Public Library, "1924 Grant Park Stadium."

24 BOT, meeting minutes, August 1, 1921, 18.

25 "Plan Monster Athletic Field Near Stadium," *Daily Illini* 51, no. 175, April 30, 1922, 1.

26 "Trustees Fix Stadium Site," *Memorial Stadium Notes* 1, no. 1, July 1922, 1.

27 Ibid.

28 Ibid.

29 Ibid.

30 BOT June 13, 1922, P283.

31 Scott, "Big Game Disaster."

32 Newsroom, "On This Day 1902: First Ibrox Disaster," *Scotsman*, April 5, 2017, https://www.scotsman.com/sport/football/day-1902-first-ibrox-disaster-1452411.

33 Antiquities and Monument Office, "Three Historic Buildings Declared Monuments."

34 BOT, meeting minutes, June 13, 1922, 287–88.

35 "Trustees Fix Stadium Site," 1.

36 BOT, Estimates of Attendance, July 17, 1917, 420.

37 BOT, meeting minutes, October 4, 1919, 560.

38 Jack Bell, "The Memorial," *Memorial Stadium Notes* 2, no. 1 (February 1923): 3.

39 University of Illinois Alumni Association, "Lauren Corning Shull."

40 Bliss Seymour, poem read at the Grand Dedication, October 18, 1924.

41 Inscription, University of Illinois Memorial Stadium.

42 BOT, meeting minutes, June 13, 1922, 283.

Building Memorial Stadium

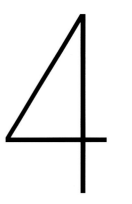

Introduction

In the early morning of Monday, September 11, 1922, a gentle drizzle of rain fell across Champaign County. By the afternoon the sun was shining, and temperatures hovered in the low sixties (°F), providing a near-perfect setting for the Memorial Stadium groundbreaking ceremony. *Spread Yo' Stuff* by Ethel Waters' Jazz Masters was the most played song by radio stations across the United States, while the Ottoman Empire was just weeks away from officially coming to an end. Hundreds of students, administrators, faculty, and community residents, including the local Rotarian Club, gathered at 1:00 p.m. to witness the event. After University of Illinois President Kinley spoke glowing words about George Huff, the director of the Athletic Association (AA), he described the future Stadium's role in shaping University life and exhorted all those present to see the construction through to its end. Huff then presented Robert F. Carr, chair of the Stadium Executive Committee, with a "life ticket" granting him access to all games at the Stadium in appreciation for his work. Then, Huff leaped from the grandstand and onto the empty field.[1] Reporters recorded that after "the first spade of earth was turned by George Huff,"[2] other dignitaries in attendance did the same, including Kinley, Board of Trustees (BOT) members Laura B. Evans and Edward E. Barrett, booster W. Elmer Ekblaw, alumnus and committee member Clarence J. Rosebery, Emma Manspeaker (a Gold Star mother),[3] and campus architect James S. White (Figure 4.1).[4]

Construction Begins

Fast Track Design and Construction

Reaching this groundbreaking moment had been a long and complicated process. It had been almost four years since the first discussions focused on the need to build a new stadium that would enable the University of Illinois to remain competitive in college football; a sport that would dominate the radio waves and provide a growing source of revenue for the AA. While enough money had been collected to initiate construction, the full amount needed to finish construction was still a distant goal and a constant source of anxiety for the University and the AA. Adding to the complexity and challenge was that the Stadium was being built fast-track. While preliminary drawings were delivered on June 13, 1922, much of the project was still being designed when construction began. Even more pressing was that the AA—and therefore the stadium's architectural firm, Holabird and Roche (H&R), and its contractor, English Brothers—had a real deadline. Opening day was already scheduled for what was hoped to be a monumental game against the Wolverines, the longtime rivals from the University of Michigan.

The final building site had only been definitely set on May 10, 1922—just four months before the groundbreaking ceremony. The Stadium would anchor the campus' southwestern side just south of Gregory Avenue and east of the Illinois Central Railway (ICR tracks between First Street and Fourth Street. Directly north

DOI: 10.4324/9781032643885-5

75

Figure 4.1
George Huff turns the first spade at the Memorial Stadium's groundbreaking, September 11, 1922. Courtesy of the University of Illinois Department of Intercollegiate Athletics Archives.

of the Stadium was the newly named Stadium Drive, and further north of that was the Parade Grounds (today the site of student housing). Local landowning families, some who in the past had contributed land to the University, now benefited from the increased property value generated by the Stadium's location.

To control all land surrounding the Stadium, the Stadium Executive Committee spent $81,079.75 on 18.5 acres, acquiring the Stoolman tract, within the William Williamson Subdivision, located directly to the north of the Stadium's site. Having acquired the Stoolman tract, the AA quickly sold it and property along the ICR to the University for $81,236.92.[5] The property along the ICR was no longer a part of the Campus Masterplan and the BOT decided to plot the property and sell it off as city lots.

PURCHASE OF STOOLMAN PROPERTY

It was reported that the Stadium Committee had ordered the purchase of the Stoolman tract of approximately 20 acres just south of College Place, in Champaign, at a price of $81,000.

On motion of Mrs. Evans, it was voted:

1. That the action of the Stadium Committee in purchasing with Stadium funds the Stoolman tract, legally described as being Lots seven (7) and eight (8) and the North 5.56 acres of Lot nine (9) and the North four (4) acres of Lot ten (10), all in William Williamson's subdivision, West half of Southwest quarter, city of Champaign, for the Memorial Stadium and Recreation Field, for the sum of $81,000, be and it is hereby approved.

2. That the President of the Board and the President of the University be and they are hereby instructed to make all necessary arrangements for payments and the transfer of the title.

3. That the sum of $81,000 or so much thereof as may be necessary to meet such cash payment as may be necessary, be and it is hereby appropriated from the Stadium fund for this purchase.[6] The appropriation was made by the following vote: Aye, Mr. Abbott, Mrs. Blake, Mrs. Busey, Mrs. Evans, Mrs. Grigsby, Mr. Hoit, Mr. Noble; no, none; absent, Mr. Blair, Mr. Herbert, Mr. Small, Mr. Trimble.

PURCHASE OF LAND FROM ATHLETIC ASSOCIATION

A recommendation that the Stoolman tract (18.51 acres) and the tract between First street and the Illinois Central right of way (20 acres) be purchased from the Athletic association for $81,236.92 and that $82,000, or so much thereof as may be needed, be appropriated from the Reserve and Contingent fund to meet the purchase price and the expense of the transfer.[7]

Kinley laid out a suggestion for the new acreage:

I have discussed with Mr. George Huff, President of the Athletic Association, the advisability of plotting and selling the twenty acres now held by the Athletic Association between First Street and the Illinois Central Railroad, and in addition the ten acres held by the University adjoining this property on the south. The removal of our north line, west of Wright Street, from Armory Avenue towards the south would make it possible for us to get on without this property. The Athletic Association is planning an independent storm-water Sewer from the Stadium recreation field, and drainage into this from these lots could be easily secured. I request authority to take this matter up and report to the Board at a later meeting on the advisability of plotting these tracts in city lots with a view to selling them off.[8]

The property along the ICR had been eliminated from the campus master plan, and eventually, the BOT achieved some success at selling it off as city lots.[9]

Farther north of the Stoolman tract was an area known as College Place. It had been subdivided, with some lots already sold to individuals. In some cases, homes had been built, but most were speculatively purchased, with buyers betting that the University would someday need these properties and would be willing to pay a premium. And they were right. Starting in 1917, the University began consolidating lots in Orchard Place, along Armory Avenue, between Third Street and Arbor Street, with the goal of building McKinley Hospital, a much-needed medical facility to serve the growing student body. To this end, the BOT considered relocating the AA from its fields and building infrastructure on the north side of campus (now the location of Ikenberry Commons Residence Halls) near Champaign's First Street at an estimated cost of $50,000.[10] Simultaneously the University began a longer process of buying over seventy lots extending up to what is now Gregory Drive.

LOTS IN COLLEGE PLACE

(9) A recommendation that the following lots in College Place be purchased:

From Miss Fanny B. Sherfy: Lots 1, 86, 94, 96, and 144; Consideration: $11,800; terms: $5,000 down, with interest on the balance at not to exceed 6 percent.

From Mr. A. W. Stoolman: Lots 4, 5, 59, 60, 61, 108, 111, 112, 113, 115, 119, 120, 145, 148, 149, 150, 153, 154, 157, and 158; Consideration: $29,900 and the six lots in the north half of College Place purchased as a site for the McKinley Hospital; terms: $10,000 down, with interest on the balance at not to exceed 6 percent, the University to assume the unpaid special assessments and Mr. Stoolman to pay the taxes for 1922.[11]

Huff and the AA could not have been happier with these land acquisitions, as consolidated property ownership around the Stadium signaled the University's willingness to "prepare for the development of an athletic plant large enough to take care of our rapidly growing student body."[12]

From a construction point of view, the Stadium's final location had two major advantages and one significant disadvantage. First, its location outside the cluster of existing campus buildings and on mostly unspoiled land made Stadium construction much easier and accessible with more flexible working hours. Second, the site's adjacency to the ICR tracks enabled the use of a rail spur to bring in heavy materials like structural and reinforcing steel, stone, and brick. But the flooding made the area's fine-scale hydrology brooks and streams swell and the clay soils saturate. This environment demanded extensive knowledge of proper foundation engineering to ensure that the Stadium would remain stable and not sink differentially. Moreover, employing that expertise would take substantial funding.

The Funding Challenge

Formal efforts to fund Memorial Stadium had begun with BOT approval in December 1920. From the outset, finances and construction were linked. After three student fundraising sessions raised over $700,000 in subscriptions, it was time to get to work on soliciting alumni and community members to accumulate the $2,500,000 total needed. The construction budget had been set at $1,600,000, with the remaining monies put aside for other necessary expenditures like loan repayment, debt service, and equipment purchases.[13]

To prepare their fundraising stadium captains, the AA produced the *Stadium Captain's Handbook,* a small booklet that outlined a pyramidal strategy: contact nine alumni from the more than 42,000 graduates and solicit a pledge. Although it is unclear how many captains came forward, they were trained to address donors' questions and concerns. On paper, the funding campaign thus far had been fruitful, with over 36,500 former students having pledged on average $24.60 each for a total of $897,900.[14] At the same time as the *Handbook* campaign was being implemented, the "Build that Stadium for Fighting Illini" campaign was rolled out during the spring of 1921. The two student directors, Anna Coolley, Class of 1921, and Reuben C. Carlson, also Class of 1921, worked tirelessly together to raise money for the Stadium. After falling in love during that spring, the couple wed in early 1922, writing a love story that would last over 70 years.[15]

Everyone—including current students—was solicited for funds, regardless of economic status. To make donating easier, the University proposed a payment schedule. Typically, students were encouraged to pledge $100, with $10 payable every six months for five years. Students with greater means were pushed to not only pledge more money but also pay in a shorter timeframe to help with construction cashflows. One fundraising poster stated: "If your folks have means and will help you subscribe to the Stadium, make your subscription as high as possible and pay it *all* on January 1, 1922" (Figure 4.2).[16]

Letters to the Building Committee, like one written by John A. O'Brien, chairman of the stadium campaign in the township of Champaign, make evident that collecting funds became increasingly difficult with each passing day. The lack of success, in turn, was having a discouraging effect on solicitors, who were mostly students. O'Brien's letter attempts to rally morale, appealing to the students to demonstrate "a corresponding increase in courage, patience and perseverance," adding that "[i]t will constitute a challenge worthy of the magnificent caliber of the men who are devoting themselves so generously to the successful completion of this great task."[17]

As part of a larger effort to keep the public informed — and of course to spur donations— in July 1922 the AA began circulating the newsletter *Memorial Stadium Notes* (*MSN*). Originally conceived as a quarterly publication, before long it was being mailed monthly and was distributed through 1926. In the first issue, the *MSN* staff noted that the University of Illinois had the fourth largest student body, with only the University of California, Columbia University, and the University of Michigan bigger; Minnesota, Ohio State, and the University of Pennsylvania were close behind.[18] This was not merely a report on a statistical curiosity but rather an attempt to rouse financial backers into action. Reading between the lines, this was meant as a warning that the Illini football team could become less competitive without full support (Figure 4.3).

By the time the first *MSN* issue was circulated in July 1922, it was evident that its focus on financing captured the concerns of everyone involved in the project As of June 1 of that year, a total of $1,853,868.85 in pledges—8,319 from students and 8,563 from alumni— were confirmed. Of the total amount, however, only

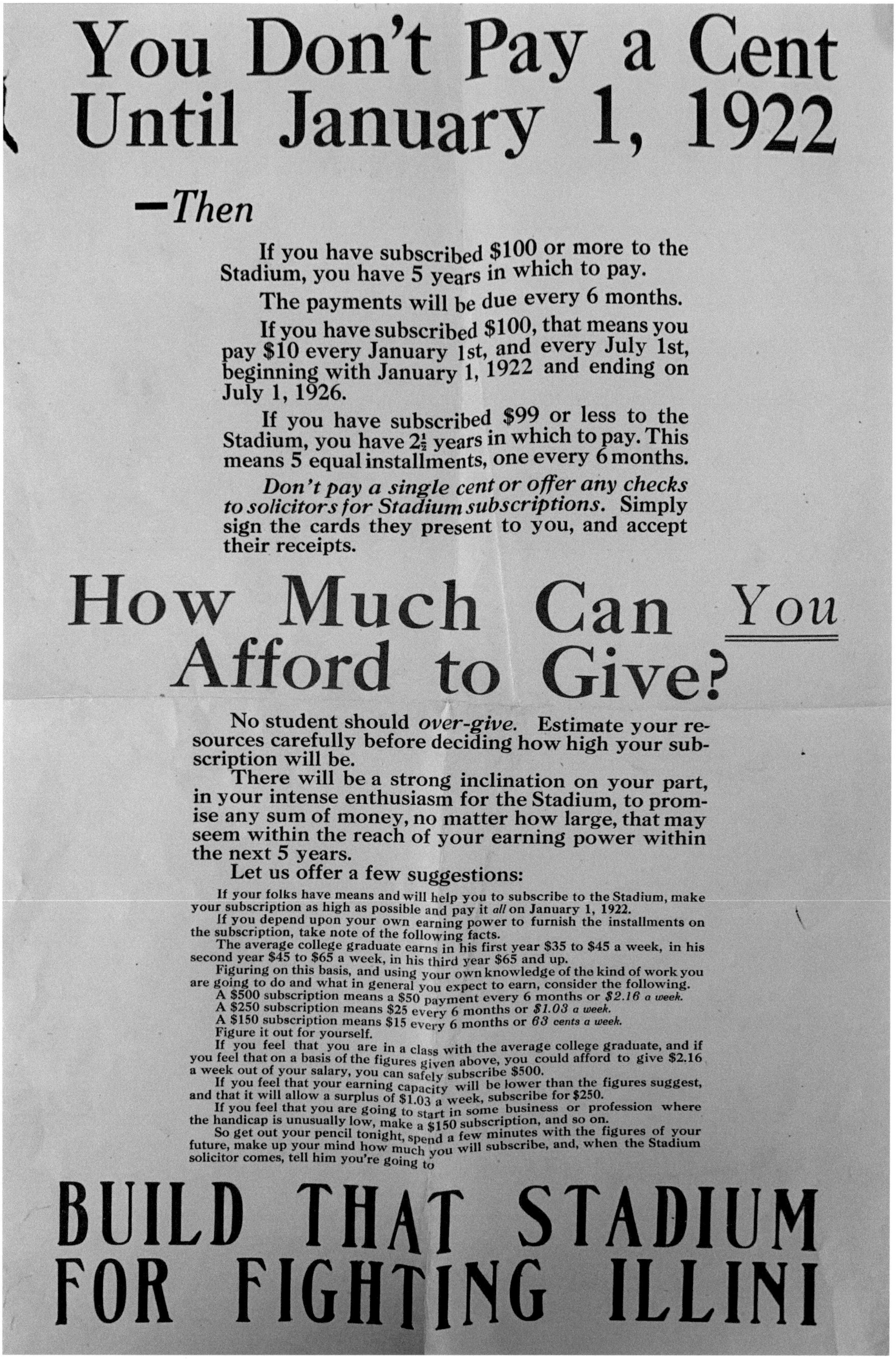

You Don't Pay a Cent Until January 1, 1922

—Then

If you have subscribed $100 or more to the Stadium, you have 5 years in which to pay.

The payments will be due every 6 months.

If you have subscribed $100, that means you pay $10 every January 1st, and every July 1st, beginning with January 1, 1922 and ending on July 1, 1926.

If you have subscribed $99 or less to the Stadium, you have 2½ years in which to pay. This means 5 equal installments, one every 6 months.

Don't pay a single cent or offer any checks to solicitors for Stadium subscriptions. Simply sign the cards they present to you, and accept their receipts.

How Much Can <u>You</u> Afford to Give?

No student should *over-give.* Estimate your resources carefully before deciding how high your subscription will be.

There will be a strong inclination on your part, in your intense enthusiasm for the Stadium, to promise any sum of money, no matter how large, that may seem within the reach of your earning power within the next 5 years.

Let us offer a few suggestions:

If your folks have means and will help you to subscribe to the Stadium, make your subscription as high as possible and pay it *all* on January 1, 1922.

If you depend upon your own earning power to furnish the installments on the subscription, take note of the following facts.

The average college graduate earns in his first year $35 to $45 a week, in his second year $45 to $65 a week, in his third year $65 and up.

Figuring on this basis, and using your own knowledge of the kind of work you are going to do and what in general you expect to earn, consider the following.

A $500 subscription means a $50 payment every 6 months or *$2.16 a week.*
A $250 subscription means $25 every 6 months or *$1.03 a week.*
A $150 subscription means $15 every 6 months or *63 cents a week.*

Figure it out for yourself.

If you feel that you are in a class with the average college graduate, and if you feel that on a basis of the figures given above, you could afford to give $2.16 a week out of your salary, you can safely subscribe $500.

If you feel that your earning capacity will be lower than the figures suggest, and that it will allow a surplus of $1.03 a week, subscribe for $250.

If you feel that you are going to start in some business or profession where the handicap is unusually low, make a $150 subscription, and so on.

So get out your pencil tonight, spend a few minutes with the figures of your future, make up your mind how much you will subscribe, and, when the Stadium solicitor comes, tell him you're going to

BUILD THAT STADIUM FOR FIGHTING ILLINI

Figure 4.2

Stadium fund flyer. Courtesy of the University of Illinois Archives.

UNIVERSITY OF ILLINOIS
MEMORIAL STADIUM NOTES

| Vol. 1 | URBANA, ILLINOIS, SEPTEMBER, 1922 | No. 2 |

Construction of Illinois Stadium Begins

ILLINI TO HAVE FIGHTING TEAM IN BIG TEN RACE

Football—those of you who are of the opinion that Illinois will be hopelessly out of the running this season are going to learn before the season is far gone that you are badly mistaken. Illinois is going to have a team to be proud of, one which is going to impress every opposing team with admiration and respect.

Illinois may not win the championship; to claim so much after losing the entire team is going pretty strong,

STADIUM FACTS

Subscriptions (Sept. 20th) $1,862,088.35
Collections (Sept. 20th) 394,084.66
Paid in full and cash donations (Sept. 20th) 81,767.61
Subscribers (Sept. 20th) 17,158
(Alumni and Citizens 8,797; Students 8,361)
Construction work begun September 5.
Time required for building 12 months.

WORKMEN MAKING RAPID PROGRESS IN EXCAVATING

Illinois Memorial Stadium is under construction. The long looked for structure which is to be a fitting place for Illinois teams and students as well as an everlasting honor to those Illini who gave their lives for their country is a reality. On September 5, English Brothers of Champaign, successful bidders on the general contract, staked out the site, just four days after the contract had been signed. On September 11, George

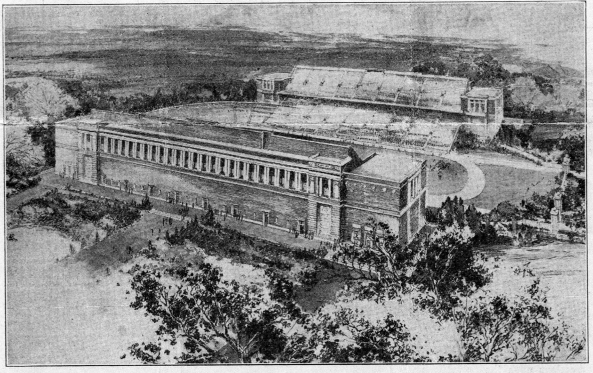

Showing the Illinois Memorial Stadium as it will be when work is finished in 1924. The photograph shows both stands with the upper and lower decks in view and also the memorial columns along one side. The south end of the Stadium will be terraced up many feet and a 12 foot wall of brick erected, taking away the open effect which some have objected to. The north end will also be enclosed by an artistic brick wall, leaving openings only for the two 220 yard straight-away tracks which will be constructed.

Figure 4.3
Memorial Stadium Notes 1, no. 2 (September 1922): 1. Courtesy of the University of Illinois Archives.

$269,594.75 had been collected. According to the *MSN*, 75% of all pledges were up-to-date with the agreed payment schedule.[19] Conversely, this meant that a rather large 25% of donors were in arrears. Three months later, pledged monies had increased slightly by $8,219.50 to $1,862,088.35. Collected monies saw a more dramatic increase of more than 46% to $394,084.66. This was the high point, as 1923 would see a precipitous decline.

With neither the University nor the state government funding the Stadium, Kinley seized the spotlight for sports and at the September 1922 BOT meeting obtained approval to request government funding of $60,000 to enlarge the women's swimming pool and $500,000 to put partially toward construction of a new men's gymnasium and additional space for the Engineering School.[20] Kinley, now firmly onboard the Stadium effort, lobbied for the new athletic facilities to be placed nearby. Slowly but surely Huff's grand vision of an athletic complex was coming to fruition.

As the end of 1922 approached, University freshmen had pledged an additional $102,300, while the upperclassmen added another $22,030 for a total of $1,993,598.35. Of these pledges, the University reported having collected $443,661.28.[21] By December 1922, the funding situation had so worsened that *MSN* authors openly declared, "Do not ask for cancellation or reduction of your pledge. That such a request cannot be granted, was decided by the Stadium Executive Committee one year ago. Death alone is accepted as a ground of cancellation."[22] Instead, the funding campaign announced that 7% interest would be applied to overdue payments.[23]

As the January 1, 1923, construction payment deadline approached, Huff grew deeply concerned and penned an open letter in the *MSN* that first congratulated those who had honored their pledges, called on others to speed up their payment schedules, and ended with an extraordinarily stinging reprimand:

TO THOSE OF YOU WHO ARE DELINQUENT

The carelessness of those of you who are delinquent has been a great disappointment to me. But I still have an abiding fate that encourages me to believe you will hasten to make your pledges good. I appeal to you to pay up immediately the amount you are behind, and also the installment which is due January 1.

I believe also there are many delinquents who are able not only to meet their obligations to date but to pay either all or part of their pledges in advance.

I appeal to you also to volunteer.[24]

Purchasing Construction Services and Materials

Because the project was built on a fast track, a steady and reliable supply of building materials with guaranteed prices was critical to the schedule and the budget. In what would be a prescient move, before a single shovel had been thrust into the ground a flurry of purchase orders to secure vast amounts of steel and concrete were sent out in spring 2022. At the June 13, 1922, meeting, months before the groundbreaking, the BOT approved

> the contract entered into on March 29, 1922, with the Corrugated Bar Company of Buffalo, New York, whereby it agrees to furnish approximately 1600 tons of reinforcing bars and spirals required for the construction of the University of Illinois Memorial Stadium according to plans and specifications of Holabird & Roche, Architects, such specifications to be in the hands of the Corrugated Bar Company by July 1, 1922, with the provision that Three Cents per cwt. from the base price herein named will be deducted where specifications are furnished by June 1, 1922.

> **PRICE:** BARS

> ONE DOLLAR SEVENTY CENTS per cwt. base, f.o.b. cars mill, with the present tariff rate of freight allowed from point of shipment to Champaign, Ill. Freight to be paid by you and credited by us on each invoice. . . .

> **PRICE:** SPIRALS

> Flat price of SIXTY-THREE ($63) DOLLARS per ton, completely shop fabricated, with the present tariff rate of freight allowed to Champaign, Illinois.

For field drawings and bending details $1.25 per ton of 2,000 pounds, figured on actual shipped weights of bars and spirals.

Final shipment to be made May 31, 1923, at option of Corrugated Co.

TERMS: All invoices to become due and payable thirty days from respective dates of shipment. Interest to be charged thereafter at 6% per annum. A discount of ½ of 1% to be allowed for payments made within ten days from date of shipment. Failure to make prompt payment is cause for deferring further shipment until delinquency is paid.[25]

From the total, the lion's share of the construction contract was awarded on September 1 to the locally based English Brothers, who as general contractors would earn $1,221,747 for their services. The company had been

established in Champaign in 1902 by Richard C. and Edward H. English, both of whom had graduated from the University in 1902. By the time of the bid for the Stadium, English Brothers had an impressive resume that included the Auditorium and the Stock Pavilion on campus (Figure 4.4).[26]

The second-largest construction contract of $189,950 was awarded to the Fort Pitt Bridge Co. and US Steel Company, both based in Pittsburgh, for the production, procurement, and installation of structural steel. Reinforcing steel to place in concrete load-bearing elements, e.g., columns, was purchased for $20,400 from the Corrugated Bar Company, which called home another major industrial city of the time, Buffalo, New York. The plumbing company Walsh and Slattery from Peoria was contracted for $59,000. Electric wiring was purchased from the A. H. Barth Electric Co. in nearby Springfield,

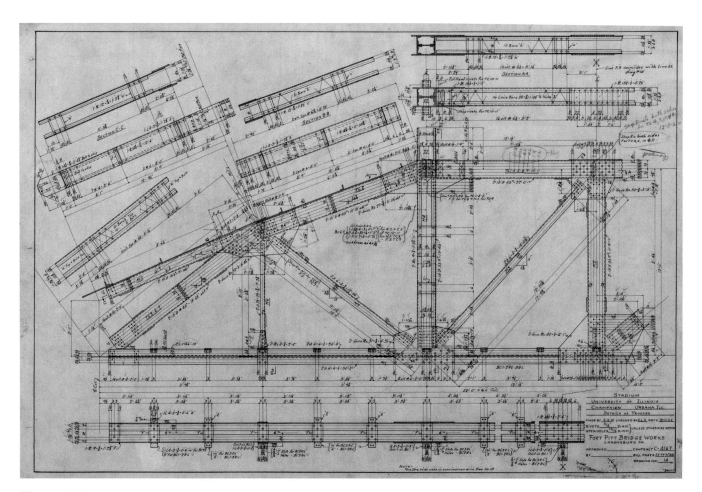

Figure 4.4
Structural steel shop drawings showing markups, December 14, 1922. Courtesy of the University of Illinois Archives.

Illinois. The heating and ventilating contract was awarded to St. Louis-based firm Sodemann Heating and Power Co. Finally, H&R's total fee for design services was $75,324.10. Without any cost overruns, the total was $1,566,421.10, about $33,579 shy of the estimated $1,600,000 initial design and construction budget.[27]

Construction Begins

On September 5, 1922, workers from English Brothers drove in wooden stakes to mark the major survey points of what would become Memorial Stadium. Once construction officially began on September 11, it proceeded at breakneck speed, which made cashflow even more critical in meeting the desired goals of a soft opening on November 3, 1923—a rehearsal of sorts—and a hard opening on October 18, 1924, to start the season against the Michigan Wolverines. By December 1922 with that first milepost less than a year away, major soil movement and terracing were well advanced, and foundation work, including column and wall footings, was nearing

completion. The December 1922 *MSN* reported that (Figure 4.5 and Figure 4.6)

[o]n December 15 all of the foundation footings, walls and piers for both stands to the 18 foot 6 inch grade had been completed. Within a few days the contractors expect to set all of the anchor bolts ready for the erection of the structural steel. The dirt fill necessary to form the floors of the great halls underneath both stands has also been completed. About 160,000 yards of excavation and fill have been handled leaving only about 25,000 yards yet to move. About 85 per cent of the excavation of the playing field has been made.

Provided deliveries of structural steel are made promptly and regularly, the contractors expect to complete the erection of the 2600 tons of structural steel in seven or eight weeks. It is the expectation that the seats in the main floors will be ready for use for the Chicago-Illinois game

Figure 4.5
Early grading and foundation digging, October 27, 1922. Courtesy of the University of Illinois Department of Intercollegiate Athletics Archives.

Figure 4.6
Formworks for the great hall and ramp towers being set, October 27, 1922. Courtesy of the University of Illinois Department of Intercollegiate Athletics Archives.

on November 3, 1923, which will be homecoming. English Bros. intend to bend every effort toward the completion of the seats in the main floor and to finish the ramps leading to the main floor seats from the ten entrances to each one of the main stands.

They will not make any effort to complete the ramp towers at each end of the stands unless delivery unless delivery of the structural steel for the balconies is made in ample time.[28]

This was a key juncture, as winter's bitter cold temperatures would make rupturing and moving soil much more difficult and energy intensive. Yet, the progress note ended with a dire warning (Figure 4.7):

The extent of the work to be completed by November 3 will depend first, upon the amount of subscription money collected and second, upon the promptness with which the structural steel is

delivered. The burden of responsibility is therefore as much upon subscribers as upon the contractors.[29]

The February 1923 issue of the *MSN* revealed that previous urgent alerts had not been heeded. According to another open letter penned by Huff, nearly 6,300 subscribers were delinquent to the tune of $138,943.[30] According to internal forecasts, this meant that by November 1923's soft opening, there would be a whopping deficit of $246,173.65.[31] To remedy the situation two steps were taken. To increase pledge collections, alumni were enlisted to visit delinquent subscribers. More drastic was a stopgap measure to temporarily reduce the scope by eliminating the southern curved seating area and reduce capacity to 54,612 seats. In contrast, the original plans with both southern and northern seating horseshoe curves would have boosted capacity to 120,000 people. Though this plan was never realized, it would have made Memorial Stadium the largest football stadium in the country (Figure 4.8).[32]

Figure 4.7
Foundation work completed prior to 1923. Courtesy of the University of Illinois Department of Intercollegiate Athletics Archives.

Figure 4.8
Early steel work for the great hall, January 23, 1923. Courtesy of the Division of Intercollegiate Athletics Archives.

Nevertheless, construction proceeded, and the seating and circulation spaces began to physically manifest themselves. The February 1923 issue of *MSN* documented the status (Figure 4.9 and Figure 4.10):

The main floor is 74 rows deep of which the first four are enclosed by railings to form boxes. There are 216 boxes. The main floor starts at an elevation of 1 foot, 6 inches above the playing field and rises to 62 feet, 2 ½ inches. The balcony starts at 57 feet, 372 inches and rises to 110 feet, 9 inches. The great halls are at an elevation of 18 feet, 6 inches.

Each stand is divided into 9 sections. The lower half of the main floor is reached by a series of 10 practically level tunnels from the great halls. Access to all other levels of the main floor and balcony is obtained by the use of ramps or inclined passages.

The use of stairways was not considered practical for a climb such as is necessary to reach the balcony tunnel, nor was any combination of stairs and ramps considered because whatever gain there is in time due to ramps would be lost by use of any steps either at the top or bottom of the inclined passage.

The upper half of the main floor is reached by a series of 8 ramps or inclined passages, leading up to portals at elevation of 39 feet, 6 inches. The balconies are reached by a triple ramp in each end tower. These ramps after encircling the towers lead off to 6 equal distant points of the balcony tunnel at elevation of 78 feet, 9 inches and from there lead out to ten portals half way up the balcony.[33]

Significantly, *MSN* pointed out the width of circulation spaces, indicating an awareness of the need for safe egress: "The main floor ramps are about 7 feet wide and balcony ramps are 11 feet, providing 8 feet, 4 inches exit for each hundred in the main floor and 8 feet, 8 inches for each hundred in the balcony."[34] The project's description continues:

Figure 4.9
Great hall steel columns erected, February 7, 1923. Courtesy of the Division of Intercollegiate Athletics Archives.

Figure 4.10
East stands, February 7, 1923. Courtesy of the Division of Intercollegiate Athletics Archives.

A Great Hall 50 wide by 414 feet long is provided in each stand. This has been made 38 feet high in the center allowing ample space for basketball courts or other indoor sports and for winter practice in outdoor sports. At some future date, swimming tanks, ice skating rinks, etc., may be provided in a part of these spaces.

A press box is provided in the center section of each section of each balcony. Each has accommodations for 144 persons seated at desks and for 30 seated without desks. Compared with other stadia, Illinois has a much greater number of seats at the sides of the field within the limits of the goal posts, there being 40,000 of the 54,672 seats so located and no seat is more than 54 feet beyond the goal line.

By February, all foundation work was complete and concrete columns had been poured. enabling the second phase of construction to begin. The concrete columns would support steel columns, which in turn supported the steel trusses that held up the sloped concrete slabs for the concrete seating. The first major shipment of steel tonnage had arrived in mid-January, and another 2,700 imperial tons were soon to be shipped from Pennsylvania steel mills. To lift up the massive steel columns and trusses, "two big derricks with 80-foot booms traveling on rolling platforms" were used.[35] Writers of February's *MSN* issue noted with a tone of trepidation that (Figures 4.11–4.13)

> [t]he arrival of the steel means the paying out of about $150,000, not to speak of $38,000, the cost of installing it. Here, then, is an expense of money mighty close to $200,000 that will have to be met very soon.[36]

Progress was relentless: "about sixty [train] cars came in from the east to be unloaded by the two huge derricks, with the 80-foot booms."[37] The visual effect of structural steel rising from the midwestern cornfields was a sight to behold, as its steep red ferric verticality starkly contrasted with the agricultural landscape. The *MSN* authors offered this evocative image to their readers:

The great steel skeleton of the Stadium is steadily pushing itself to the sky. Like silent sentinels keeping

Figure 4.11
Derricks erecting the steel frame, March 8, 1923. Courtesy of the Division of Intercollegiate Athletics Archives.

Figure 4.12
West stands, March 8, 1923. Courtesy of the Division of Intercollegiate Athletics Archives.

Figure 4.13
East stands, March 24, 1923.
Courtesy of the Division
of Intercollegiate Athletics
Archives.

a vigil on a snow-covered Plain, on either side stand the first four rows of columns, set back to where the great halls will begin (Figure 4.14 and Figure 4.15).[38]

In an optimistic, but incorrect, assessment, the article concluded by forecasting April 1 as the completion date for the steel structure. As if on cue, one month later the *MSN* reported the first major construction delay primarily from flooding that had created "a young lake" (see Figure 4.11 and Figure 4.12).[39] This was somewhat ironic, since Huff had argued that the location was better than other options precisely because of its drainage qualities—never mind that it was part of the Boneyard Creek discharge zone that fed the Vermilion River. The first in a series of short-lived strikes by construction workers had also slowed progress.[40]

Perhaps the most significant cause of the delays was insufficient structural steel. The *MSN* writers were not shy in suggesting that steel manufacturers had sold their product elsewhere at a higher profit: "Since the steel magnates can sell steel at a far higher price than their year-old contract calls for, perhaps there are

grounds for suspicion that they didn't hurry things just as much as they might have."[41] Historical evidence supports this indictment. From the end of the 1910s through the late 1920s, a building boom drove up the costs of structural steel, cement, and glass. In just one year from when the Stadium's steel was ordered in March 1922 to March 1923, the cost of structural steel had jumped a massive 49.7%, and overall construction materials had soared an average of 45.2%.[42] Implicit in this suggestion, however, was that the steel was diverted because of lack of payments. The *MSN* March issue noted with dismay that only 500 of the 3,300 completely truant pledges had new payments, which meant 2,800 people had paid nothing at all.[43] Concern was growing: internal discussions between the BOT and Huff soon focused on the likelihood of completing the project on schedule. It was only after the end of spring, in June of 1923, that the members of the Building Committee expressed some optimism that the Stadium would be ready for its soft opening in November (Figures 4.16–4.33).[44]

Figure 4.14
East balcony steel erection, April 13, 1923. Courtesy of the Division of Intercollegiate Athletics Archives.

Figure 4.15
East balcony steel erection, April 28, 1923. Courtesy of the Division of Intercollegiate Athletics Archives.

Figure 4.16
Field and east stands, May 19, 1923. Courtesy of the Division of Intercollegiate Athletics Archives.

Figure 4.17
West stands with steel and seating underway, May 19, 1923. Courtesy of the Division of Intercollegiate Athletics Archives.

Figure 4.18
West stands, June 2, 1923. Courtesy of the Division of Intercollegiate Athletics Archives.

Figure 4.19
East stands, June 2, 1923. Courtesy of the Division of Intercollegiate Athletics Archives.

Figure 4.20
West stands, July 2, 1923. Courtesy of the Division of Intercollegiate Athletics Archives.

Figure 4.21
East stands, July 2, 1923.
Courtesy of the Division
of Intercollegiate Athletics
Archives.

Photo by U. S. Army Air Service, July 6.

Figure 4.22
Aerial photograph of stadium construction, July 6, 1923. Courtesy of the Division of Intercollegiate Athletics
Archives.

Figure 4.23
West stands, July 18, 1923.
Courtesy of the Division
of Intercollegiate Athletics
Archives.

Figure 4.24
West stands, August 2, 1923.
Courtesy of the Division
of Intercollegiate Athletics
Archives.

Figure 4.25
East stands, August 30, 1923.
Courtesy of the Division
of Intercollegiate Athletics
Archives.

Figure 4.26
West stands, August 30,
1923. Courtesy of the Division
of Intercollegiate Athletics
Archives.

Figure 4.27
Great Hall Ramps Under Construction. Courtesy of the Division of Intercollegiate Athletics.

Figure 4.28
Great west hall looking north. Courtesy of the Division of Intercollegiate Athletics Archives.

Figure 4.29
West stands casting balcony seating, September 1923. Courtesy of the Division of Intercollegiate Athletics Archives.

Figure 4.30
East stands, October 12, 1923. Courtesy of the Division of Intercollegiate Athletics Archives.

Figure 4.31
West stands, October 12, 1923. Courtesy of the Division of Intercollegiate Athletics Archives.

Figure 4.32
Homecoming game crowd photo, against the University of Chicago, November 3, 1923. Courtesy of the Division of Intercollegiate Athletics Archives.

Figure 4.33
Homecoming action photograph. Courtesy of the Division of Intercollegiate Athletics Archives.

Fulfilling Pledges

A positive side effect of this financial crisis was the consolidation of the alumni network. By the spring of 1923, alumni were called upon to enforcepledge payments. Local chapters across the country, from Seattle to New York, became collection clearinghouses, as alumni leaders paid visits to donors late on pledge payments. This coordinated effort recognized that "[s]uccess rests upon the loyalty of the alumni who have agreed to visit delinquents. Theirs is not a pleasant assignment, but it is something that must be done if the Stadium is to be rendered secure."[45] Subsequently, Huff and the BOT's Clarence J. Rosebery began coordinating with alumni associations across the country in the hope that if members "organize collection campaigns in every locality where there are delinquents, it is predicted that they can bring the prodigals back in the fold in sufficient numbers to guarantee that financial distress will not threaten the Stadium."[46] Alumni were also periodically invited to pen letters or columns of encouragement for the *MSN*.

Despite making some headway on payments in February 1924, the University announced that those who had not fulfilled a single payment would face legal jeopardy.[47] Clearly, other strategies to generate revenue were needed. One attractive but expensive option was dedicating a column for $1,000 in the memory of a fallen Illini.[48] By April 1923, 187 of these columns had been privately donated. As another incentive, the AA began offering "seat options" to individuals who had paid their pledges in full.[49] These only secured seating, and a purchased ticket was still needed to attend a game. These were the precursor of the personal seat licenses that would become a mainstay of financing in the 1980s (Figure 4.34).[50]

Contracts allocated in May 1923 signaled that construction had entered a different phase. At the June meeting of the BOT, Rosebery reported that contracts had been extended on behalf of Huff for "finishing hardware," heating, and electrical systems. Costs for the hardware had risen so dramatically that the initial budget estimate required a change order from $6,000

Figure 4.34
Building toward homecoming, 1923. Courtesy of the Division of Intercollegiate Athletics Archives.

to $7,541, a jump of nearly 26%. The Building Committee changed boiler specifications, which added $834 to Sodemann Heating and Power's contract. The same report noted that the electrical contract would not proceed, as A. H. Barth Electrical had failed to meet bonding requirements. The new electrical contract to Freeman and Sweet of Chicago would result "in an increase of $5,258 in the cost of the Stadium."[51]

These financial outlays did nothing to improve the schedule. Though all structural steel had finally been delivered, construction was still slow. Rosebery noted in his report that

[c]onstruction work has been greatly delayed during the spring months by frequent rains and unfavorable working conditions as a result thereof. I am told that all of the structural steel is on the ground and that practically all of the reinforcing bars have been delivered; that English Brothers have a large amount of cement stored ready for use at the Stadium; that two-thirds of the lumber for the construction of the seats has arrived; that the rough grading of the playing field is now almost complete and that it will soon be ready for the

placing of the top soil and the placing of the drain tile under the playing field itself; that weather conditions permitting, the contractor will probably begin to pour by this weekend, the concrete for the first twenty-one rows of seats in the east stand.[52]

Rosebery, however, ended his report with optimism:

Members of the Building Committee are still of the opinion that the greater part of the Stadium seats can be finished within time for use for the Homecoming game on November 3. To accomplish this means that all of the contractors will have to work at high speed, under favorable conditions, between now and that time.[53]

From late April through the summer months, giant steel girders were being riveted to steel posts in preparation for the decking that made up the second seating tier. The vertical red steel structures, soil mounds, and waterlogged field would be humorously dubbed "Fort Oskeewowwow on Lake Zuppke."[54] By May 1, Lake Zuppke had been drained and would never appear again. Installing the field's drainage system was a high priority because the heavy rains of summer were approaching. Finally, in the early summer of 1923, the Stadium's field drainage system was laid and connected to the City of Champaign's drainage system. The system consisted "of two drains, each of 18-inch tile, which run the length of the field and are fed by laterals of 4-inch tiles."[55] With a dry field, Richard English expected "to have at least 300 men on the job in a short time but more carpenters and bricklayers" were needed.[56]

Like an ant colony hurrying to and fro, hundreds of steel and concrete construction workers attacked multiple Stadium fronts. Construction activity was so furious that writers at the *Atlanta Constitution* remarked:

> For the race to complete the seats in the stadium by November 3 can only be won by employing a huge force. Every carpenter who can be found is being added to the large gang on the job. As stadium construction goes into high speed, a better idea of the intensity of the task can be obtained. The carpenters are need to convert 404 miles of lumber six inches wide into the forms in which concrete will be poured. And the bricklayers will handle 4,800,000 bricks.

Significantly, the article concluded on an upbeat note, indicating that the AA was beginning to see financial daylight:

> It is going to take some hustling to have the seats ready for 55,000 people in November—but the job can be done unless unforeseen obstacles are encountered. All over the United States alumni are watching. There are 19,000 subscribers and as the time for the opening approaches, their interest shows by increased payments of subscriptions.[57]

Meanwhile, attention on the University's needs had also surged at the state level. In early February 1923, Lieutenant Governor Fred E. Sterling, and 200 state legislators—including Speaker of the House David Shanahan—observed firsthand the "overcrowded condition of the classrooms and library, the lack of dormitories," and "the need for new equipment."[58] Though

the visit was part of the state government's oversight obligations, it proved key in securing approval for Kinley's capital improvements. Three months later the legislature approved Kinley's request for $500,000 for the new men's gym. The *MSN* proclaimed, "When the Stadium, with its Great Halls and outdoor facilities, and the gym are completed, Illinois' athletic plant will lead 'em all."[59]

Construction finances had also stabilized. On the one hand, the reduction in project scope had proven an effective way to stay within budget. The May *MSN* issue noted that costs were being held steady at $1,603,502.85.[60] On the other hand, with the accrued interest and alumni outreach strategies in place, pledge fulfillment was significantly up. By the end of May, pledges had surpassed $2,000,000. Of those still delinquent, about 40%, or $103,629.27, was attributable to unfulfilled third and final payments. Writing in the June 1923 issue of the *MSN,* Huff felt assured enough to declare:

> I am glad to report that despite unexpected delays, Stadium construction is proceeding satisfactorily. It will be a close squeeze to complete the seats for Homecoming, November 3, but it is entirely possible barring unforeseen obstacles I believe it will be accomplished.[61]

Ironically, spring delays had had a positive, if temporary, effect on finances. Since construction estimates had slowed, the expected summer deficit had never materialized but was now calculated to occur sometime in the fall.[62] To ward off that crisis, July's *MSN* issue noted that "[o]ne big essential for Stadium success is a record-breaking payment for July. A fine start has been made—now for a splendid finish."[63]

Perhaps sufficiently confident in its timetable, the University officially publicized the November 3, 1923, homecoming game against the University of Chicago Maroons for the first time in the *MSN* that July.[64] There was further evidence of certainty in meeting deadlines when *MSN* readers were informed that Frank H. Beach, manager of ticket sales, would mail on or around September 1 blank ticket request forms to all those who were up-to-date with pledge payments.[65]

At $60,135.94, June pledge payments broke the previous single-month collection record.[66] This change in velocity matched the pace of building: the "first 23 rows of the lower deck on both sides were poured by July 1. This meant a total of more than 11,000 seats."[67] By August, fabrication of all four deck ramps was rapidly advancing, but the northeast deck ramps were furthest along. The four ramp towers, which allowed for point circulation independently from the deck ramps, would not begin construction until January 1924. Nonetheless, even without the buttressing ramp towers, the Stadium's overall appearance began to emerge as portions of the brick facades became visible. As concrete walls cured, bricklayers would begin to clad their surfaces. The burnt-umber bricks, selected by Platt, were supplied by the nearby Western Brick Company.

Located in Danville, near the border with Indiana, the Western Brick Company had become by 1911 the world's largest producer of bricks. Equipped with the region's extensive "[d]eposits of vitrifying clays, abundant coal reserves," and "excellent railroad transportation," the company would furnish at its height over 1,000,000 bricks per year.[68] Starting in the fall of 1922, the clay was extracted from the rich alluvial washes deposited by the Vermilion River and fired in beehive-shaped kilns. After cooling under controlled humidity and heat to ensure that surface fissures remained at a minimum, the bricks were then loaded onto train cars for the trip west.

As expected, this heady pace of construction was reflected in contractor bills. June invoices exceeded $102,000.[69] Fortunately at the close of June 1923, pledges crossed the $2,017,000 mark. Delinquent payments had dropped below 10%, with $195,000 in pledges still outstanding.[70] While descending to this lower level did not go unnoticed, *MSN* writers could not refrain from pointing out that nearby Purdue University had been so far more successful than the Illini in fulfilling pledges for its own stadium: "Purdue students in the university are delinquent only 9 per cent. Don't whisper it outside the family—but this intimates that the Boilermakers are meeting their obligations a little better than we are."[71]

As predicted by August's *MSN* issue, contractor payments reached a new high in July: just over $142,000 for the month. Another steep increase in invoices was expected for August since all steel had finally been placed. At the same time, delinquent payments were once again up, now over 15.7%. According to the *MSN*, 10,232 students along with 8,870 alumni and citizens had pledged a total of $2,017,887.35. From this amount, collected payments stood at $841,294.10, or slightly more than the expected hard construction costs. Whereas overall subscribed pledges did not increase, the missed fourth installment of $130,527.40 for July 1 represented nearly 50% of all pledge debts.[72]

Nonetheless, by the time the September 1923 *MSN* issue was published, over 37,150 seats had been poured in the east and west lower tiers. Memorial Stadium now had more than double the capacity of Illinois Field.[73] With all the structural steel in place, carpenters began erecting the necessary formwork to pour the concrete ramps that lay below. At the same time, carpenter crews located below and above the top tier continued building forms so that the concrete seating could be poured as fast as possible. Once the summer weather arrived, work on the playing field began in earnest, and the "[t]wo acres of fine blue grass were transplanted" in preparation "for the tread of the Illini and the Maroons."[74] As the construction pace continued to increase, so did the frequency and size of payments. Starting with the summer of 1923, outlays to contractors averaged $100,000 a month.[75] With finances temporarily under control and the Stadium poised to produce revenue from gate receipts, there were good reasons to be optimistic.

As the physical seats were being prepared, Beach announced a seating plan to accommodate as many students, alumni, and community members as possible in their preferred areas. On the southern half of the eastern tiers, students would sit together so as to generate a kind of cheering critical mass—key for home-field advantage; the north side would be for alumni. For the western tiers, only the northern half of the stands were reserved for subscribers, while the south side would be open to all.[76] The AA was particularly proud that it could boast that no stadium of its size had more seats between the goal posts—which at the time were set right on the goal line—in each end zone.[77] This meant that, when considering an additional total of 20 yards in depth, even more seats would have been located between today's goal posts.

The October *MSN* issue reported that with a little over a month left to go until the first game, only 10,000 of the 55,524 expected seats had yet to be poured. Sixteen concrete ramps leading to the lower decks were complete, and the drainage system was tested and functional. Such was the optimism of the moment that October's *MSN* issue declared: "There will be work to be done up to the last minute but—The Stadium will be ready for the opening!"[78]

However, the predicted fall financial crunch had arrived. With a balance of $44,890.28, pledge collections forecasted for $30,000, and pending invoices estimated at $135,000, the AA predicted that the total deficit would be over $37,000. With just weeks before the soft opening, the situation was grim.[79] Although subscriptions had risen another $14,000, collected payments had increased by only $25,000. Contractors' invoices for September totaled $103,725, marking the third month in a row that construction had cost over $100,000. Of the $296,482.50 recorded as unpaid pledges, $39,284.86, or 13.11%, was attributable to individuals who still had not made a single payment.[80]

Perhaps in an effort to stimulate action, in October's issue of the *MSN,* the AA announced that up-to-date subscribers would be mailed buttons to wear at the homecoming game (Figure 4.35). According to the *MSN* writers, these would "tell the populace that the wearer is all square with the Stadium" and would be "en régle at Homecoming."[81] It is unclear to what extent the pride of the full payer or the shame of the delinquent held greater influence in generating funds (Figure 4.35).

Finally, with the game less than four weeks away, the October *MSN* published the first seating plan (Figure 4.36):

Stadium Seats 55,524
The definite seating capacity of the bStadium is as follows:

Figure 4.35
Stadium button, *MSN* 2, no. 10 (November 3, 1923). 3.

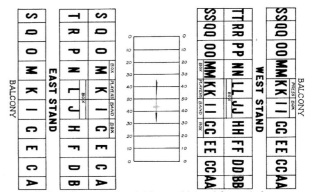

Figure 4.36
Stadium seating plan. *MSN* 2, no. 9 (October 1923): 5.

East stand: lower deck, 17,659; balcony [upper tier], 9643; boxes, 516; total, 27,818.
West stand: lower deck, 17,659; balcony [upper tier], 9411; boxes, 636; total 27,706.
This makes a grand total of 55,524.

In one of the more innovative approaches to the infrastructure—perhaps inspired by baseball's dugouts or hockey's team boxes—it was suggested that "[t]he boxes include provisions for the band and it is also George Huff's plan to seat both football squads in boxes, clearing the field entirely, except for cheerleaders, scoreboard workers and a few other necessary persons."[82]

In October, as promised, buttons were mailed to up-to-date subscribers, and Rosebery had agreed to meet with anyone in person to collect a payment and hand out a button. Even though the game was mere days away, collections had only marginally improved by a paltry $22,000. Those onerous invoices would nevertheless have to be paid.

Regardless of the impending financial cliff, *MSN* writer L. M. Tobin proclaimed with a sense of finality: "The great race against time is won. The Stadium is ready."[83] The Stadium, the AA, and the University had to greet the first incoming crowd, much was left to build out and finish in Memorial Stadium, and many more bills would need to be paid. The soft opening with its gate receipts could not have come at a better time. Without these cash injections, the Stadium would be—from a financial point of view at least—broke.

The Soft Opening

Working Toward the Soft Opening

Fall football training camp began on Saturday, September 15.[84] Though the "grafting operation on the playing field was a brilliant success and the blue grass which was transplanted from a nearby farm is flourishing," facility managers would not allow the athletes to trample underfoot the tender roots that were taking hold.[85] Practices were held in Illinois Field. By early September the *MSN* began reporting on the probable roster: future 1923 consensus All-American Team Captain J. W. McMillen at guard, halfback Harold "Red" Grange, and All-American Frank E. Rokusek. With an experienced team returning for the 1923 season, confidence should have been reasonably high. The

MSN authors, however, were somewhat more circumspect, commenting that "on paper it looks as if Illinois should be much better than last year."[86] Considering that 1922 had been a 2–5 season, this was not a tremendous endorsement. Most sportswriters, like Walter Eckersall at the *Chicago Tribune,* predicted that the University of Chicago would win the Big Ten Conference.[87]

The first game scheduled for November 3 was a deliberate choice for a soft opening. Although the Stadium would not be quite complete, operators could evaluate entry, seating, and exiting performance, and the overall usability of the facilities. The novelty of the game—and the excitement of homecoming—would increase enthusiasm for the new venue and produce more donations. And of course, the gate receipts would be indispensable. Ticket prices for this game had also been strategically raised. Whereas home games at Nebraska and Butler cost between $1.50 and $2.00, homecoming tickets would cost $2.50.

It was more than fortuitous that the soft opening featured a match against the formidable University of Chicago Maroons, coached by one of college football's formative figures, Amos A. Stagg. Stagg had helmed the Maroons since the cross-state rivalry's inception in 1892. Thirty years after the first game between the two schools, the Illini had lost to the Maroons 9–0, and the team was ready for a rematch. The University of Chicago versus Illinois games had also historically been the most lucrative for both schools. At that time, typically gate receipts were split 50–50, and the higher ticket prices would mean even more money for both teams. Having the soft opening against Chicago was also calculated to boost interest in the team and to advertise the new venue: Westinghouse station KYW Chicago would broadcast the game (Figure 4.37).

In preparation for the big day C. J. Rutherford, who presided over the Illini Student Union, in collaboration with Rosebery, who now chaired the alumni committee, developed a full slate of programs before the November 3 homecoming game. Held on the drill field south of the Armory and north of the Stadium were an intramural football game between freshmen and sophomores, tugs of war, wheelbarrow polo, boxing matches, and chariot

Figure 4.37
Homecoming game panorama, against the University of Chicago, November 3, 1923. Courtesy of the Division of Intercollegiate Athletics Archives.

races.[88] There was also a concert by the "w.g.b." (presumably the "world's greatest band"), a play put on by the thespian organization Mask and Bauble, and "perhaps an alumni-varsity baseball game."[89]

Before noon on Saturday's game day—in an inspiring gesture of acknowledging the past before celebrating the new—C. J. Moynihan, captain of the 1905 football team, led a rally at the Stadium that was capped off with the AA awarding varsity letters "to members of Illinois athletic teams before 1896, when there was no official award of the letter." Saturday festivities before kickoff featured the "famous" senior class hobo parade and a "parade of alumni 'I' men on the field before the game. After the game, students and alumni mingled at the Armory, participating in various meetings and progressive dances."[90]

On game day rain had created a muddy obstacle course on the trek to the Stadium. Although makeshift boardwalks were set down, hundreds of attendees left behind their mud-encrusted shoes, a testament to both the transcendent geological nature of the site and to the

energetic enthusiasm of these intrepid fans. The day's unfortunate interaction with less-than-ideal soil conditions did not go unnoticed; utilizing the "we are not the only ones with this problem" approach, writers of the February edition of the *MSN* felt compelled to report that the Harvard-Yale game at Harvard's Soldier Field had done "one better, according to all reports." Not only had "rubbers" (shoe covers) been left behind in the "quagmire," but

[c]ars parked in and around the field sank hub deep in mud. Husky loiterers appeared with planks from a nearby lumberyard and pried out mired cars at a dollar a pry. Illinois had manned parking places with horses with which to extricate cars and there was no charge.[91]

In a case of narrative mudslinging, the *MSN* article concluded by stating that whereas "Soldier field is old," Memorial Stadium was still under construction, and therefore "[w]hen the Stadium streets are paved and approaches constructed, discomfort will be reduced to a minimum even in the heaviest rain."[92] The implication was that Harvard's stadium, as far as the *MSN* writers were concerned, would still be *old* and *muddy*.

Sportswriter and newspaper editor Henry L. Farrell concurred. Having finished a trip to various venues and after sitting in the stands in Illinois, he declared:

> The Harvard stadium, the Yale bowl and the Princeton stadium. They are regarded in the east as the zenith of architectural skill and the maximum comfort for the spectators. Those in the east who think the football structures of the "Big Three" are the last word should take a look at the Ohio State stadium in Columbus, the Illinois memorial stadium in Urbana and the Nebraska stadium in Lincoln. Compared to these three big structures of the middle-west, the best in the east are antiquated and out of date.[93]

What would not feel out of date to his Illinois readers was loyalty to the concept of the Stadium as a place to commemorate World War I. Although the term "Fighting" had been used sporadically as far back as 1914, entry into the war had increased its usage, and students who attended Illinois began identifying themselves as "fighting." The nickname was formally added to team names around the construction period of Memorial Stadium in what was perhaps another acknowledgment of its origins and founding purpose.[94]

After the Soft Opening

Playing that homecoming game in an incomplete venue had been risky but worth it. More than 61,300 people had watched the Illini team in "blue jerseys and stockings" pull off a 7–0 victory,[95] with the lone touchdown scored by Red Grange. People from all over the state drove automobiles, flew, or rode special and regularly scheduled train cars to the game.[96] In preparation for the copious train travelers, the ICR had prepared a temporary whistle-stop just west of the Stadium. From there visitors could walk east on a makeshift boardwalk to

the grounds. So large was the game's attendance that the economic benefits spilled over to the general community. Consider that in 1923 the University of Illinois had a total of 8,407 enrolled students, while according to the 1920 census Champaign's population was 15,873 and Urbana's was 10,224.[97] This meant that on that fall day, visitors nearly doubled the population. Restaurants, bars, and other commercial establishments enjoyed an outstanding day, and hotel rooms and commercial boarding houses had shortages so acute that the Illini Student Union coordinated arrangements with Urbana-Champaign residents to rent or furnish rooms to visitors.[98]

Furthermore, whereas the first home game of the season at Illinois Field against Nebraska produced $13,620 in gate receipts, the soft opening's gate receipts totaled $132,239.42—a nearly tenfold increase. Upswings in profit margins were even more pronounced. Whereas the Nebraska game had produced a gross profit for the Illini of $2,759, the Chicago game generated an astronomical gross profit of $64,785—nearly 24 times more.[99]

The win marked the beginning of a successful three-game homestand in which the Illini defeated the Maroons, the University of Wisconsin Badgers (10–0), and the Mississippi State Bulldogs (27–0). The Illini would play their final game of the season at Ohio State, defeating the Buckeyes 10–0 to finish an undefeated season and outscore their final five opponents an astonishing 82–0. Despite their impressive record, the only postseason bowl game at the time was the Rose Bowl, which invited the University of Washington and the United States Naval Academy to play. The Illini, crowned national champions (along with the Michigan's Wolverines), would spend the winter at home.

The 1923 National Championship Season

By all accounts, the 1923 season had been a success on and off the field: the football program had generated $22,362.33 in operating expenses but produced $147,405.37 in revenue for a net gain of $104,190.12

from all sports.[100] In January 1924, the *MSN* reported that the AA had achieved a surplus for the first time in years. This success did not go unnoticed, and it wasn't long before questions arose about why the AA did not cover more of the Stadium's costs. Perhaps this is why *MSN* writers pointed out that the AA had in fact spent $196,863.79 and loaned another $50,000 to the Stadium project for a total nearing a quarter of a million dollars. Thereafter, as if to answer critics who questioned why the AA had not given the $50,000 outright or offered more loans, an *MSN* writer clarified:

> The answer is that this money and any other loans which the association may be able to make will be needed to complete the Stadium over and above the work provided for in the present contracts. It will be a tussle to pay the present contract out of the Stadium on account of delinquents.
>
> Completion of the Great Halls is not included in the contract. The architects have just furnished estimates of this cost. The lowest estimate is $170,000 and the highest $245,000. That is one big expense for which this and other loans must be repaid.[101]

After the Soft Opening

Despite the public cautionary calculations, financial stability followed the November 3 soft opening. In addition to the influx of monies from gate receipts, the arrival of winter prompted a slowdown in construction and thus smaller invoices. Though still insufficient, pledge collections crossed the $1,000,000 threshold on January 2, 1923. Perhaps most importantly, the AA not only continued to lend money to the project but also increased its leveraged position. As a result, from the end of the 1923 season onward, the AA would finish all pending construction tasks and iron out extant operational processes but face mounting debt. At no time was the looming deficit more visible than in the initial months of 1924. With the January 1 payment on the ledger, pledge delinquency climbed. By January 31, total pledges were tallied at $2,139,151.16, but only $1,053.881.52 had been collected.[102]

Since construction could not cease, the AA was compelled to take on additional debt to finish the project on time. Between January and May 1924, the ramp towers were finished, and the great halls' concrete walls were poured and then clad with Western brick. Once the towers were completed and the burnt-umber walls were visible, the Stadium began to take its final form.

That March, the MSN forecast that if all went as planned, it would take just over $605,000 to finish the work. The January balance sheet, however, showed the project had only $18,732.88 on hand but over $1,000,000 in pledge payments pending (Figures 4.38–4.62).[103]

These financial woes were no longer a secret even on the national stage. Lawrence Perry focused his February 12 sports column for the Washington Evening Star on the convoluted finances to illustrate the risks and incurred liabilities generated by construction loans. He first referenced Huff's concern about finishing the Stadium on time:

> If the stadium is to be completed this year, a few loyal alumni, who are members of the executive committee, must pledge their personal credit, sign their own names as security for the large amount that must be borrowed from the banks.
>
> This loan, according to Huff, will have to amount to a sum between $350,000 and $400,000 even granting a most favorable collection of pledges this year, with the athletic association stripping itself to aid the project.

Then he made his most poignant observation, which was a warning to other schools pursuing massive building campaigns:

> The situation may be useful in showing sister institutions what is liable to happen when great $2,000,000 amphitheaters are projected. After the music and the cheering and general hooray attendant upon launching of these stadiums subside, comes the long grind of collection from those

Figure 4.38
West stands, January 30, 1924. Courtesy of the Division of Intercollegiate Athletics Archives.

Figure 4.39
West stands, January 31, 1924. Courtesy of the Division of Intercollegiate Athletics Archives.

Figure 4.40
East stands, exterior, January 30, 1924. Courtesy of
the Division of Intercollegiate Athletics Archives.

Figure 4.41
East stands, January 31,
1924. Courtesy of the Division
of Intercollegiate Athletics
Archives.

Figure 4.42
East stands colonnade, March 8, 1924. Courtesy of the Division of Intercollegiate Athletics Archives.

Figure 4.43
West stands, March 8, 1924. Courtesy of the Division of Intercollegiate Athletics Archives.

Figure 4.44
West stands colonnade,
April 10, 1924. Courtesy of
the Division of Intercollegiate
Athletics Archives.

Figure 4.45
West stands colonnade,
April 29, 1924. Courtesy of
the Division of Intercollegiate
Athletics Archives.

Figure 4.46
East stands colonnade, April 29, 1924. Courtesy of the Division of Intercollegiate Athletics Archives.

Figure 4.47
West stands, May 16, 1924. Courtesy of the Division of Intercollegiate Athletics Archives.

Figure 4.48
West stands colonnade, May 1924. Courtesy of the Division of Intercollegiate Athletics Archives.

Figure 4.49
East stands colonnade, May 1924. Courtesy of the Division of Intercollegiate Athletics Archives.

Figure 4.50
East stands colonnade, July 1, 1924. Courtesy of the Division of Intercollegiate Athletics Archives.

Figure 4.51
West stands colonnade, July 14. Courtesy of the Division of Intercollegiate Athletics Archives.

Figure 4.52
East stands colonnade, July 14, 1924. Courtesy of the Division of Intercollegiate Athletics Archives.

Figure 4.53
East stands colonnade, July 14, 1924. Courtesy of the Division of Intercollegiate Athletics Archives.

Figure 4.54
East stands colonnade,
late July 1924. Courtesy of
the Division of Intercollegiate
Athletics Archives.

Figure 4.55
East stands colonnade,
August 12, 1924. Courtesy of
the Division of Intercollegiate
Athletics Archives.

Figure 4.56
East stands colonnade,
August 12, 1924. Courtesy of
the Division of Intercollegiate
Athletics Archives.

Figure 4.57
West stands colonnade,
August 1924. Courtesy of
the Division of Intercollegiate
Athletics Archives.

Figure 4.58
East stands colonnade,
September 3, 1924.
Courtesy of the Division
of Intercollegiate Athletics
Archives.

Figure 4.59
West stands colonnade,
September 3, 1924. Courtesy
of the Division of Intercollegiate
Athletics Archives.

Figure 4.60
West stands colonnade, October 1, 1924. Courtesy of the Division of Intercollegiate Athletics Archives.

Figure 4.61
East stands colonnade, October 23, 1924. Courtesy of the Division of Intercollegiate Athletics Archives.

Figure 4.62
Stadium from the southeast, October 23, 1924. Courtesy of the Division of Intercollegiate Athletics Archives.

who subscribed in the first flush of whipped-up enthusiasm and then found it difficult to meet their commitments.[104]

As if compelled to respond to Perry's public warnin, , in March 1924 *MSN* writers replied under the headline "This Article Hurt," "Let us give Lawrence Perry material for another story." Never ones to miss an opportunity to fundraise, they proceeded to write,

> Indignant alumni are sending clippings in from all points of the compass. They don't like it. Their own pride in Illinois is hurt. Supercilious alumni of other universities have razzed them. They want something done about it. . . .
>
> Now we cannot get very sore at this writer because his article merely reviewed the present situation. The best thing to do is to furnish him with the facts for another story to the effect that Illinois is going to complete the Stadium this year.
>
> Then the headlines will be something like this, "Illinois alumni and students rally to Stadium; It will be completed this year." Shall we tell Mr. Perry to write a new story?[105]

Completing the Stadium

On April 9, 1924, the Stadium Executive Committee gathered in Chicago, reviewed progress reports, and confirmed that the October 18, 1924, game against the University of Michigan Wolverines would be the Stadium's official inauguration "to the heroic dead of Illinois."[106] There was no turning back. The announcement in the *MSN* had its intended effect: April 1924's collected sum surpassed April 1923's total.[107] Significantly, the June *MSN* issue shared the momentous news that the columns were about to be hoisted up 80 feet in the air so that they could be placed in their final resting place above the great halls and below the second tier of seating decks, along the facade of loggias.[108] In the early days of June, the first column, dedicated to Corporal Alvin J. Adams, was put in place.

Made of Bedford stone (a variety of limestone), the columns had been manufactured in four sections: the base, two shafts, and the capital. Fabricating by sections enabled construction workers to better handle the immense weight of each component, while also maintaining control over the naturally produced pendulum

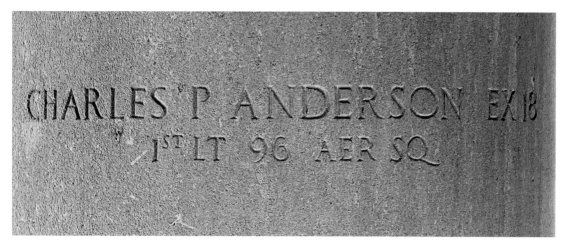

Figure 4.63
Engraved column inscription: Charles P. Anderson EX18, 1st LT 96 AER SQ. Photograph by Kevin J. Hinders.

during installation. The columns began as large volumes of stone quarried in Bedford, Indiana. After extraction, they were shaped on spinning stone lathes cooled by running water over the turning surfaces. Once a section was finished, it was loaded onto a train car, shipped to the site, secured by the derrick line, and lifted into place. A single train cargo car could ship "[f]ive columns, complete with caps and bases."[109] Each individual component was raised by the derrick into the loggia, where awaiting workers positioned the parts as they were lowered down to the loggia by the boom's end. The smaller sections meant less mass at the end of the boom and a lower possibility that the column section would swing wildly and hurt people or cause damage to the structure (Figure 4.63).

On the north side, the wall connecting the two towers was erected. At 12 feet and spanning across the field, it was pierced by two symmetrically located gates, each flanked by two 25-foot-tall imposing posts. The gates lined up with the racing track, providing each side of the track with the 220-yard straightaways necessary for track meets. The extended track straightaways ended a few yards shy of Stadium Avenue and turned into entry paths as they met the street to the north. Street-paving duties would be shared with the City of Champaign, which ensured that attendees would never have to trudge through muddy fields again.

By the end of June, both north ramp towers were completed, including all brick and stone cladding. When the skylights were finally placed a few days after finishing the exterior cladding, contractors tested the steam-based heating system that connected the two northern towers via a basement tunnel. Beneath the northwest tower was the main boiler room, which provided heat for the main athletic training facilities and locker rooms.[110]

While the Stadium approached completion, payments to contractors and suppliers had pushed April 30's deficit, the first recorded, from $17,792.66 to nearly $45,000.[111] Though still clamoring for students and alumni to fulfill their pledge commitments, the AA found itself once again injecting cash into the project. When June's finances were tallied, the AA had ponied up $264,281.90, but only $50,000 as a loan.[112] Once again, the AA turned to *MSN* to promote a campaign offering more lapel buttons that appealed to reader's sense of pride or guilt. These new pins were more poignant, announcing, "I HELPED BUILD THE STADIUM, PAID TO DATE OCT. 18, 1924" (Figure 4.64).[113]

By July, just over half of all the memorial columns had been placed. Next, iron grills 40 inches tall, designed to function as the guardrails spanning from column to column, were installed. Above the columns, the loggias' ceilings —"414 feet long and 14 feet wide and constructed of white cement plaster with

Figure 4.64
Stadium button. *MSN* 3, no. 8 (August 1924): 3.

large panels"—were also being built.[114] The great halls, untouched thus far, received temporary "cinder and clay floors" that would remain for several years.[115] Terrazzo was installed to serve as the floor surface in areas such as the bathrooms, and marble sinks and urinals were fixed to the interior plumbing in preparation for opening day.[116] Wishing to avoid the embarrassment of the November 3 mud festival, a concrete tennis court was constructed on the east side to connect to the street and act as a midway for game spectators, and nearby roads were paved.

In one of the clearest signs that the Stadium was nearing completion, the press stand went up atop the west-upper tier seating deck. Western Union Telegraph then lay "a conduit from Champaign and pulled a cable through to serve the country with the story of the Michigan game and other battles of the future."[117] Correspondents reporting on the games used the cable to send their dispatches, and the same conduit was used by Chicago radio company WGN to broadcast the play-by-play calls across the region.

Chicago's presence in Urbana-Champaign was notable. The student body was increasingly drawn

from Chicago, and alumni flocked to the city for jobs. Broadcasts by WGN not merely served alumni but kept families across the state connected and engaged the imaginations of future students. With so many devoted Illini so far north, transportation to and from Chicago became a major consideration in ensuring the Stadium's success. To this end, Highway 25 was extended during the summer of 1924 from the western edge of campus north to Kankakee and ran parallel with the ICR tracks.[118] This meant that Chicagoans could drive almost directly due south to campus instead of being forced to travel east toward Danville, on the border with Indiana, first before turning west toward Champaign County. Route 25 was built to parallel the Illinois Central Railroad's train tracks up to Chicago. Eventually, Highway 25 would become US State Route 45 (Figure 4.65).

Many others took the train to the game. To accommodate these travelers a new downtown depot was created in 1924. In addition, a whistle-stop by the Stadium at the intersection of Neil Street and Stadium Drive was set up to accommodate the loading and storage of 176 train cars, including coaches and Pullman cars. The University also constructed a boardwalk across the muddy plains to facilitate the movement of thousands of fans coming to the game by rail (Figure 4.66).

At the construction site, although some areas of the Stadium's ceiling still needed to be closed, plastered, and painted, the colonnades were finished by September 18. *MSN* writers stated with utmost certainty:

> For the purposes of the Dedication Homecoming, the Stadium is complete right now, although there are odds and ends which will occupy the workmen up to the last day. There is painting to complete and eight gangs are cleaning the walls and stone work. Both ramp towers on the south are completed. The surrounding fields are being graded.[119]

At that point, all that was left was to hang festive swags and banners throughout the seating decks, ramp towers, and wall surfaces. The jaunty atmosphere of course came at a steep price. Although the AA had already donated

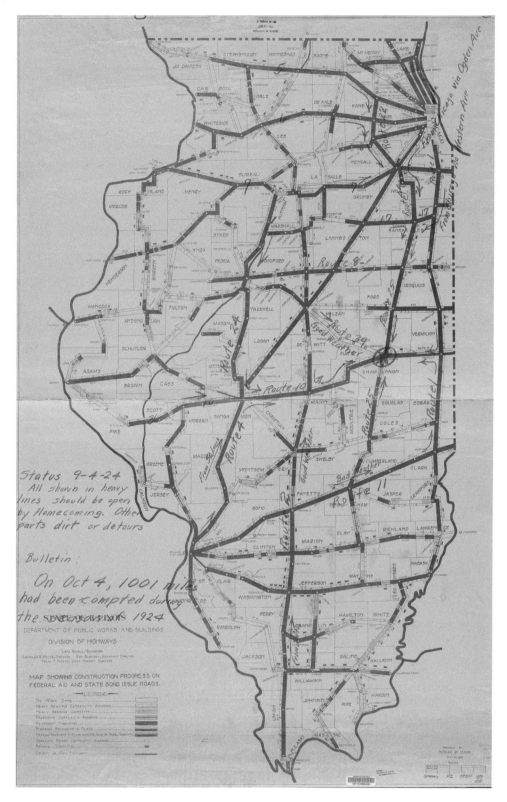

Figure 4.65
All Roads Lead to Champaign-Urbana, September 4, 1924. This map was created for the homecoming game to assist those traveling by car. Courtesy of the University Map Library.

Figure 4.66
Blueprint for train depot at Neil Street and Stadium Drive. Illinois Central Railroad Company Office of the Engineer. Courtesy of the University of Illinois Archives.

over $211,000, it officially loaned another $70,000 to the project for a total of $122,620.38. Even with this injection of cash, the Stadium was in the red. Despite carrying a total financial deficit of $148,731.06 by September 30, the Stadium was dedicated as planned.[120]

October 17, 1924

Dedication Ceremony

Having claimed a college football national championship in 1923, the Illini welcomed the 1924 season with deep enthusiasm. The fervor was felt throughout the Midwest. Writers for the *Chicago Tribune* declared that

> [f]rom the inaugural games two weeks hence until the close of the season, Nov. 22, the most spectacular outdoor sport for spectators will command the absorbing attention of those who take seriously to heart gridiron success or defeat of their alma maters.[121]

Illinois would play the first game away from home against Nebraska in Lincoln. The second game was with Butler, and it would be played in the new

Figure 4.67
President Kinley speaking at the Memorial Stadium dedication, October 17, 1924. Courtesy of the Department of Intercollegiate Athletics Archives.

arena as a last-minute dress rehearsal for the main dedication ceremony, grand inauguration, and homecoming match against the University of Michigan's Wolverines.

To mark the momentousness of the opening, all school offices were closed on October 17, and classes after 12:00 p.m. were suspended. Later that afternoon, University figures addressed the cheerful crowd at a dedication ceremony (Figure 4.67). For George Huff, it was the culmination of a decades-long effort. He had assembled a team of believers who preached the gospel of competitive intercollegiate sports programs, especially college football, and believed that a stadium was not only an athletic facility but a symbol of stature. Huff had successfully cobbled together enough support to build a colosseum on the prairie. At the ceremony, he addressed the celebratory crowd, reminding those in attendance for whom the Stadium was built: "Standing here in the shadow of this everlasting monument," Huff continued, "we can, and we will, resolve to keep alive that spirit which they so nobly exemplified in camp and on the field of battle."

The ceremony concluded when Lew Sarett (class of 1916) read a poem titled "Ode to Illinois." Sarett's voice rang through the crowd:

Know that the broken hosts
Of martial-moving ghosts,
Who gave to a warring world their last full breath,
And won to immortality in death,
Hovering in stadium shaft and tower height,
In memorial court and buttressed peak,
Shall watch for you, and speak
To you of Great Moments in a Greater Fight.
O Men of Illinois, in war and peace and play,
So may we live that when the crucial fight is won,
And the long race run,
These spirits of an elder day
Shall bend to each of us and say:
Well done! Well done!
Yours is the will to win. Well done, my prairie son.[122]

After reading the poem, it was time to bring the day's activities to an end. The next day, October 18, 1924, the Fighting Illini were ready to formally dedicate the University of Illinois Memorial Stadium (Figure 4.68).

Notes

1   "A Stadium for Fighting Illini," *Memorial Stadium Notes* (*MSN*) 1, no. 2, September 1922, 4.

2   "Workmen Making Rapid Progress in Excavation," *MSN* 1, no. 2, September 1922, 1.

3   Gold Star families have an immediate family member who died while serving the nation.

4   "A Stadium for Fighting Illini," 4.

5   BOT, meeting minutes, May 10, 1922, 210, and July 11, 1923, 234.

6   BOT, meeting minutes, May 10, 1922, 210.

7   BOT, meeting minutes, July 11, 1923, 234.

8   BOT, meeting minutes, July 12, 1922, 8.

9   Ibid.

10 BOT, meeting minutes, August 28, 1922, 510.

11 BOT, meeting minutes, March 13, 1923, 154.

12 "University Buys Land," *MSN* 1, no. 2, September 1922, 3.

13 "Fall Campaign Is Planned to Swell Pledges," *MSN* 1, no. 2, September 1922, 1.

Figure 4.68
Memorial Stadium after 1924. Courtesy of the University of Illinois Department of Intercollegiate Athletics
Photograph Archives.

14 "Stadium Campaign to Be Resumed in the Fall—$2,500,000 Will Be Objective," *MSN* 1, no. 1, July 1922, 4.

15 "Stadium Partners Decide to Remain Partners for Life," *Daily Illini* 51, no. 120, February 22, 1922, 1.

16 Fundraising poster, 1921. Courtesy of the University of Illinois Archives.

17 John A. O'Brien. Letter to All Stadium Workers from the Office of Champaign County Stadium Chairman, c. 1922.

18 "Where We Stand," *MSN* 1, no. 1, July 1922, 1.

19 "The Stadium Fund," *MSN* 1, no. 1, July 1922, 3.

20 "Kinley Approves New Gymnasium," *MSN* 1, no. 2, September 1922, 3.

21 "Stadium Facts," *MSN* 1, no. 3, December 1922, 2.

22 "Don't Ask for It," *MSN* 1, no. 3, December 1922, 4.

23 "Will Charge Interest," *MSN* 1, no. 3, December 1922, 2.

24 "George Huff Wants to Talk to You Builders of the Stadium," *MSN* 1, no. 3, December 1922, 1.

25 BOT, meeting minutes, June 13, 1922, 283.

26 English Brothers Company, "A History of Excellence."

27 "Work Progressing," *MSN* 1, no. 2, September 1922, 2.

28 "Stadium Facts," *MSN* 1, no. 3, December 1922, 2.

29 "Construction Progress," *MSN* 1, no. 3, December 1922, 2.

30 George Huff, "Many Are Loyal but Neglect by Others Imperils Stadium Completion," *MSN* 2, no. 1, February 1923, 1.

31 "Here's the Financial Situation in a Nutshell," *MSN* 2, no. 1, February 1923, 1.

32 "The Stadium," *MSN* 2, no. 1, February 1923, 2.

33 Ibid.

34 Ibid.

35 "Stadium Facts," *MSN* 2, no. 1, February 1923, 2.

36 Ibid.

37 "Steel Goes Up," *MSN* 2, no. 2, March 1923, 2.

38 Ibid.

39 "Stadium Facts," *MSN* 2, no. 3, April 1923, 2.

40 "They're Fighting Here—Fight, Too, Illini!" *MSN* 2, no. 4, May 1923, 1.

41 "Stadium Facts," April 1923, 2.

42 US Department of Labor, *Wholesale Prices*, 25.

43 "Stadium Facts," *MSN* 2, no. 2, March 1923, 2.

44 "Stadium Contracts," BOT, meeting notes, June 9, 1923, 202.

45 "Chicago Illini Collect Pledges; Need Alumni Aid Everywhere," *MSN* 2, no. 3, April 1923, 1.

46 Ibid.

47 "The End of the Rope," *MSN* 3, no. 2, February 1924, 2.

48 "Memorial Columns," *MSN* 2, no. 3, April 1923, 2.

49 "Seat Options," *MSN* 2, no.3, April 1923, 1.

50 Hill, "Personal Seat Licenses."

51 BOT, meeting notes, June 9, 1923, 202.

52 Ibid.

53 Ibid.

54 Photo caption, *MSN* 2, no. 4, May 1923, 1.

55 "Good-by Crew," *MSN* 2, no. 5, June 1923, 2.

56 "First Down—and Five Months to Go," *MSN* 2, no. 5, June 1923, 2.

57 "Rush Work on New Stadium, *Atlanta Constitution*, June 10, 1923.

58 "Legislators Pay Visit to U. of I., Learn Its Needs," *Chicago Daily Tribune*, February 9, 1923, https://www.proquest.com/historical-newspapers/legislators-pay-visit-u-i-learn-needs/docview/180501455/se-2.

59 "New Gym Near Armory," *MSN* 2, no. 6, July 1923, 3.

60 "Stadium Facts," *MSN* 2, no. 4, May 1923, 2.

61 "Help Stadium by Big Mid-year Payment," *MSN* 2, no. 5, June 1923, 1.

62 Ibid.

63 "Now for a Great Finish," *MSN* 2, no. 6, July 1923, 1.

64 "'Zup Is Eager," *MSN* 2, no. 6, July 1923, 2.

65 "Your Tickets," *MSN* 2, no. 6, July 1923, 2.

66 "Let's Make an Illinois' Finish!" *MSN* 2, no. 7, August 1923, 1.

67 "Pouring Our Seats," *MSN* 2, no. 7, August 1923, 1.

68 Don Richter, "Western Brick Helped Build Area," *Commercial-News*, February 15, 2015, https://www.commercial-news.com/community/western-brick-helped-build-area/article_6dbc4f88-b3c3-11e4-89a0-135d4179ae9d.html.

69 "$102,319," *MSN* 2, no. 7, August 1923, 2.

70 "Stadium Ledger," *MSN* 2, no. 7, August 1923, 2.

71 "Bully for Old Purdue!" *MSN* 2, no. 7, August 1923, 1.

72 "Stadium Ledger," *MSN* 2, no. 8, September 1923, 1.

73 "Nearly 40,000 Seats Poured," *MSN* 2, no. 8, September 1923, 2.

74 "Where Maroons Meet Orange and Blue," *Chicago Daily Tribune*, August 5, 1923, https://www.proquest.com/historical-newspapers/where-maroons-meet-orange-blue/docview/180513354/se-2.

75 Ibid.

76 "East Side Ours," *MSN* 2, no. 8, September 1923, 1.

77 Ibid.

78 "45,000 Seats Ready as Last Lap Begins," *MSN* 2, no. 9, October 1923, 1.

79 "The Cold Facts," *MSN* 2, no. 9, October 1923, 2.

80 "Stadium Broke Soon—Must Make Loan," *MSN* 2, no. 9, October 1923, 2.

81 "Wear a Button," *MSN* 2, no. 9, October 1923, 4.

82 "Stadium Seats," *MSN* 2, no. 9, October 1923, 6.

83 L. M. Tobin, "Mahomet Moves the Mountain," *MSN* 2, no. 10, November 1923, 1.

84 Walter Eckersall, "Many Big Grid Games on Big Ten Schedules," *Chicago Daily Tribune*, September 12, 1923.

85 "Transplanted Grass Does Well," *MSN* 2, no. 8, September 1923, 3.

86 "They'll Fight for Illinois—Back 'Em Up!" *MSN* 2, no. 8, September 1923, 4.

87 Walter Eckersall, "Football Fans to Get First Line on Teams Today, *Chicago Daily Tribune*, September 29, 1923.

88 "Tentative Homecoming Program Friday, November 2," *MSN* 2, no. 9, October 1923, 4.

89 "Come Home, Old Scouts!" *MSN* 2, no. 8, September 1923, 2.

90 Ibid.

91 "More Mud at Harvard," *MSN* 3, no. 2, February 1924, 2.

92 Ibid.

93 "Random Notes on Current Sports," *Toronto Daily Star*, October 31, 1924, 10, https://www.proquest.com/historical-newspapers/page-10/docview/1436768900/se-2.

94 Prom, "Fighting Illini Name."

95 "Back to the Blue!" *MSN* 2, no. 8, September 1923, 4.

96 "61,319 See Illinois Defeat Chicago, 7–0," *New York Times*, November 4, 1923, 2.

97 Oldrey, "Historical Census Data."

98 "61,319 See Illinois."

99 "1923 Grid Receipts," *MSN* 3, no. 1, January 1924, 2.

100 "A. A. Pours Money into Stadium," *MSN* 3, no. 1, January 1924, 2.

101 "Why Lend, Not Give?" *MSN* 3, no. 1, January 1924, 1.

102 "Stadium Ledger," *MSN* 3, no. 3, March 1924, 2.

103 Ibid.

104 Lawrence Perry, "Big Loan Will Be Necessary if Amphitheater Is to Be Finished by Next Fall, as Many Have Failed to Pay Pledges," *Washington Evening Star*, February 12, 1924, 22, https://chroniclingamerica.loc.gov/lccn/sn83045462/1924-02-12/ed-1/seq-22/.

105 "This Article Hurt," *MSN* 3, no. 3, March 1924, 3.

106 "It Will Be Completed This Year!" *MSN* 3, no. 5, May 1924, 1.

107 "You Broke April Record—Keep On!" *MSN* 3, no. 6, June 1924, 1.

108 "Now for the July Payment!" *MSN* 3, no. 6, June 1924, 1.

109 "Do Your Part for the Great Memorial!" *MSN* 3, no. 7, July 1924, 1.

110 "Stadium Progress," *MSN* 3, no. 7, July 1924, 4.

111 "Stadium Ledger," *MSN* 3, no. 7, July 1924, 2.

112 "See It Grow!" *MSN* 3, no. 7, July 1924, 4.

113 "Wear This Button," *MSN* 3 no. 8, August 1924, 3.

114 "Memorial Colonnades Grow in Beauty," *MSN* 3, no. 8, August 1924, 1.

115 "Prepare Training Quarters," *MSN* 3, no. 8, August 1924, 1.

116 Ibid.

117 "Stadium Is on the Last Lap!" *MSN* 3, no. 9, September 1924, 1.

118 "New Paved Road to Kankakee," *MSN* 3, no. 9, September 1924, 3.

119 "Stadium Is Completed," *MSN* 3, no. 10, October 1924, 1.

120 "Stadium Ledger," *MSN* 3, no. 11, November 1924, 4.

121 "In the Wake of the News: Football Season Here," *Chicago Daily Tribune*, September 14, 1924, https://www.proquest.com/historical-newspapers/wake-news/docview/180524824/se-2.

122 Maisel, "Living Memorials for Those Who Served."

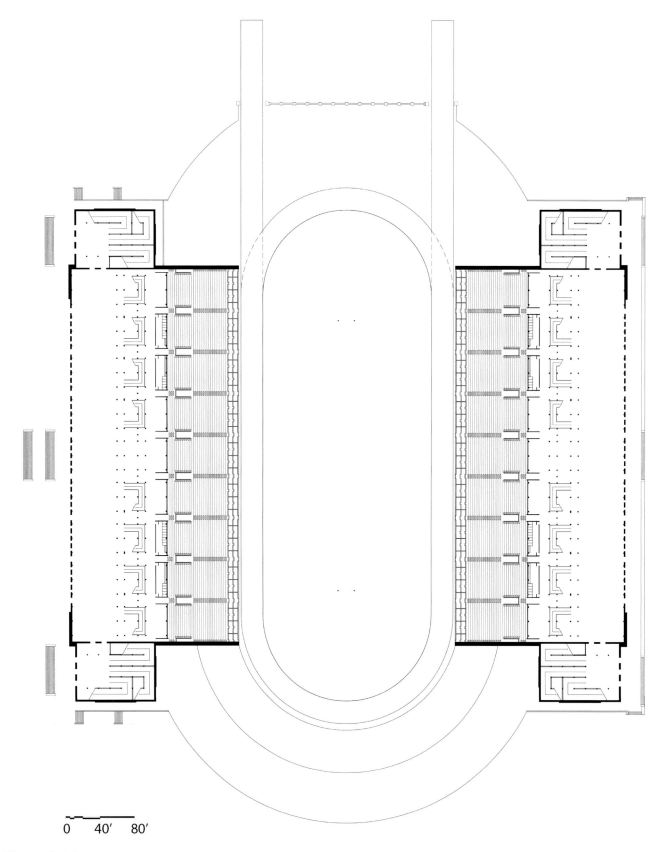

0   40′   80′

Figure C-1.1
Entry Level Plan. Image by Stephen Ferroni.

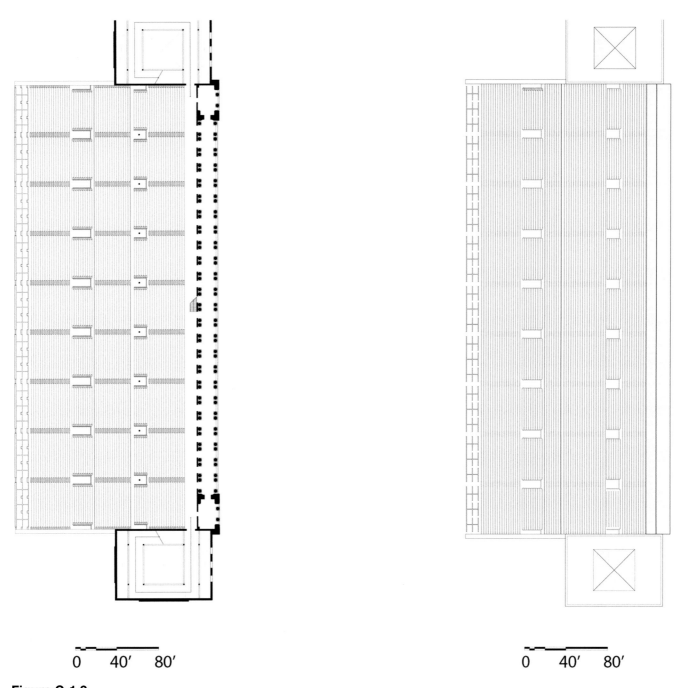

Figure C-1.2
Colonnade Level. Image by Stephen Ferroni. Roof Level. Image by Stephen Ferroni.

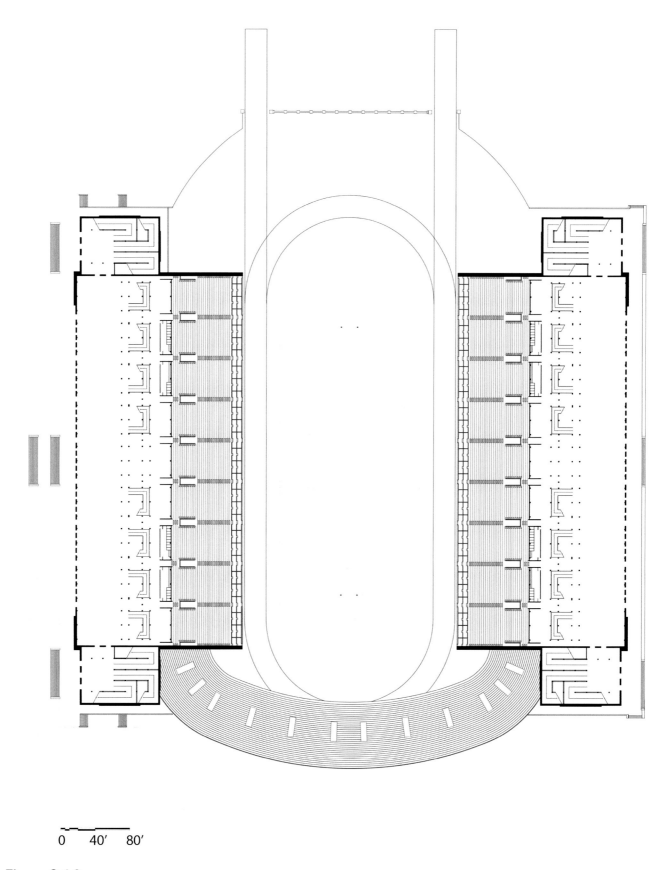

0   40′   80′

Figure C-1.3
Entry Level Plan with Horseshoe, 1929. Image by Stephen Ferroni.

Figure C-1.4
Stadium Dedication, October 19, 1924. Courtesy of the Division of Intercollegiate Athletics Archives.

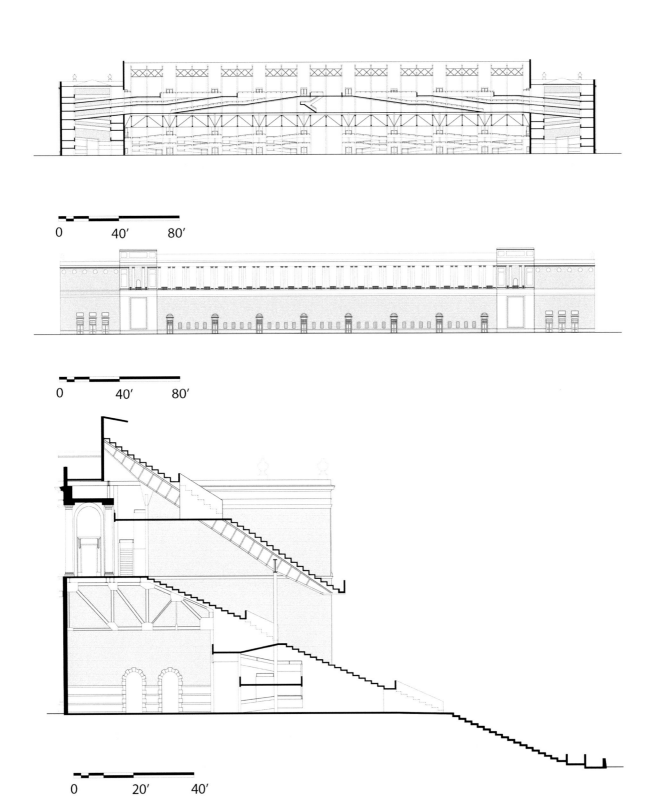

0   40'   80'

0   40'   80'

0   20'   40'

Figure C-1.5
Longitudinal Plan. Image by Stephen Ferroni.
East Stand Elevation. Image by Stephen Ferroni.
West Stand Section. Image by Stephen Ferroni.

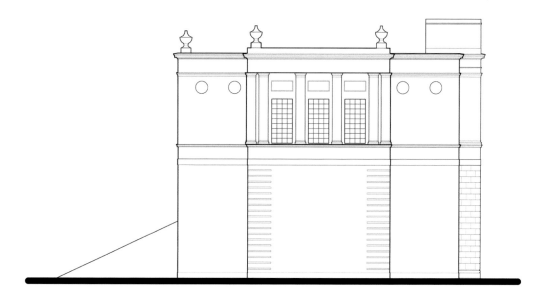

0   20'   40'

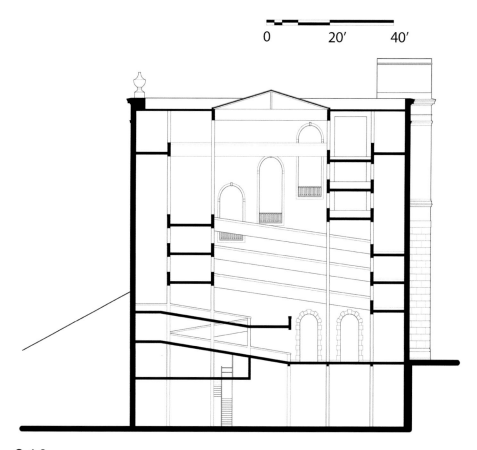

Figure C-1.6
Ramp Tower Elevation. Image by Kevin J. Hinders and Stephen Ferroni.
Ramp Tower Section. Image by Kevin J. Hinders and Stephen Ferroni.

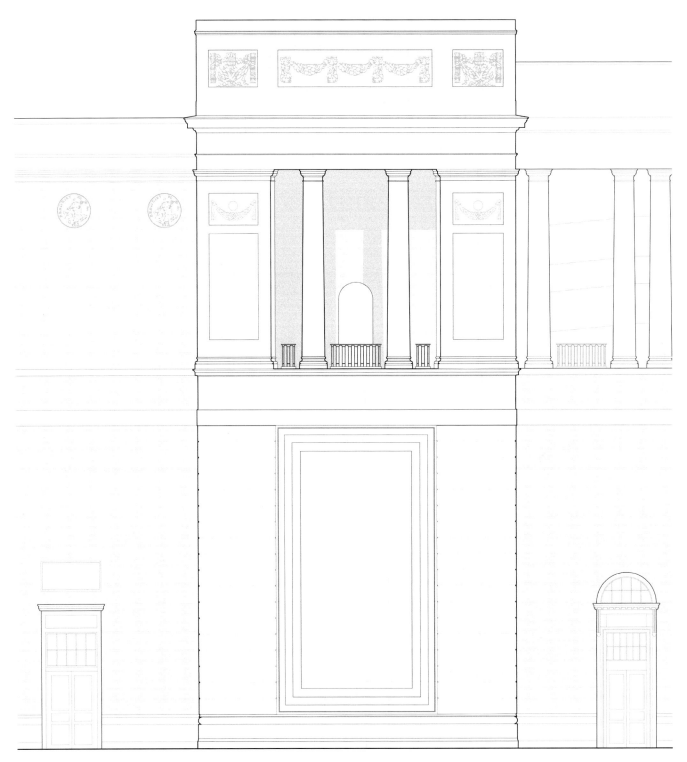

Figure C-1.7
Elevation Detail. Image by Stephen Ferroni.

Figure C-1.8
1924 Team Photograph. Courtesy of the Division of Intercollegiate Athletics Archives.

Figure C-1.9
Panorama of the October 18, 1924, Dedication Game. Courtesy of the Division of Intercollegiate Athletics Archives.

Memorial Stadium, 1924–1941

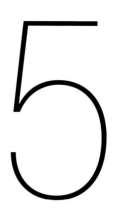

Introduction

The University of Illinois Memorial Stadium was officially dedicated on October 18, 1924. The Stadium successfully embodied an era identified as the Roaring Twenties, the Jazz Age, the Golden Age of Sport, and the especially aptly titled the Age of the Spectator. For the 1920s saw the successful marriage between sports stadiums and radio broadcasting, which produced exponential growth in the number of sports fans and attendance by people from all walks of life. In 1927, the Fighting Illini would earn their third national championship. The year after, in 1928, the Great West Hall was completed under the supervision of campus architect James White. Then in 1929, the same year as the stock market crash, the postponed southern horseshoe seating was finally finished, which brought the capacity to just over 67,000 spectators. The end of that initial construction cycle coincided with the end of the Roaring Twenties' ebullience and the start of the 1930s Great Depression. Like the economy, the Fighting Illini would also enter a down cycle that would eventually lead to Robert "Zup" Zuppke's retirement. The 1930s would end with Europe at war a conflict the United States entered on December 8, 1941. Like the University of Illinois' students, alumni, faculty, and staff, the Stadium played its part in World War II. While football was never abandoned, its great halls and adjacent areas were transformed into dormitories, training workshops, and staging grounds.

A Thrilling Inauguration

The Fighting Illini Upset the Wolverines

The 1923 college football season had ended with two schools from the same conference—the University of Illinois and the University of Michigan—recognized as college football national champions.[1] Each had finished the season with eight wins, but they had not played one another during the season. It was therefore more than fortuitous that the two schools would meet on homecoming on October 18, 1924, to officially open Memorial Stadium. With both teams starting the day with 2–0 records, the game would not only settle the debate over the true 1923 champion but also had significant implications for the Big Ten title that year.[2]

On game day, it was as if electricity ran through campus (Figures 5.1–5.7). The festivities began with the University of Illinois marching band "once said by Sousa to be the best college band in America," leading a parade to the stadium that included servicemen, for whom the Stadium had been built and was now dedicated.[3] With the southern circus seating still unbuilt, the Athletic Association (AA) put up temporary grandstands for 12,000 fans just beyond each end zone. The game was sold out, and 10,000 tickets were bought by fans who came to cheer on the Wolverines.[4] Not only were fans clamoring for tickets, but thanks to a snafu in the distribution of tickets to the Chicago-area offices, more tickets were sold than actual seats were available. In an example of finding silver linings, the AA decided to set up temporary bleachers to accommodate 2,000 more fans. That brought total attendance to a record 67,205 people.[5] The game was such a major draw that thousands more fans were unable to secure a ticket at all; the volume of visitors

DOI: 10.4324/9781032643885-6

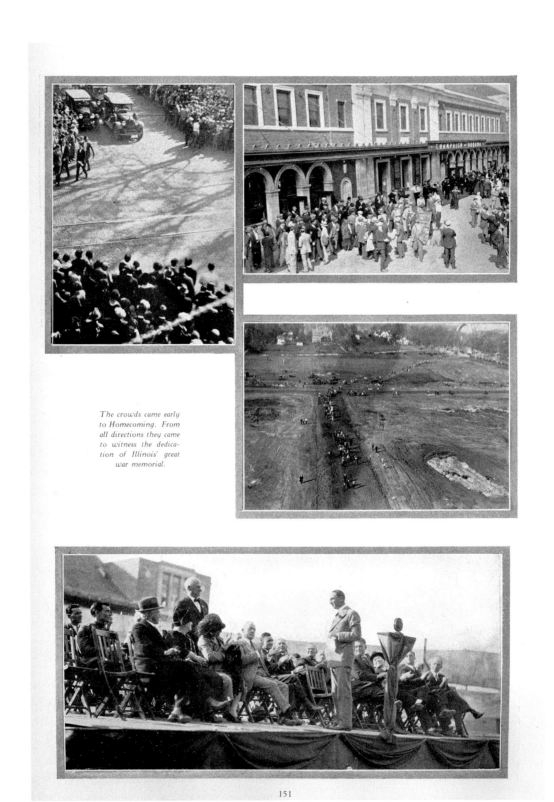

The crowds came early to Homecoming. From all directions they came to witness the dedication of Illinois' great war memorial.

151

Figure 5.1
"The crowds came early to Homecoming. From all directions, they came to witness the dedication of Illinois' great war memorial." Homecoming and stadium dedication, October 18, 1924. 1926 *Illio*, 151. Courtesy University of Illinois Archive.

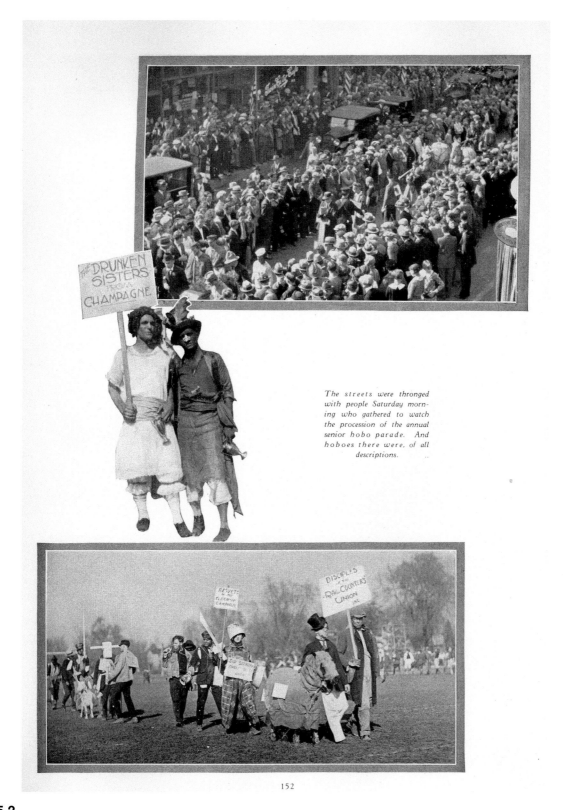

The streets were thronged with people Saturday morning who gathered to watch the procession of the annual senior hobo parade. And hoboes there were, of all descriptions.

Figure 5.2
"The streets were thronged with people Saturday morning who gathered to watch the procession of the annual hobo parade. And hoboes there were, of all descriptions." Homecoming and stadium dedication, October 18, 1924. 1926 *Illio*, 152. Courtesy University of Illinois Archive.

The vast crowds, restlessly awaiting the approaching game, milled about the streets in aimless wanderings.

153

Figure 5.3
"The vast crowds, restlessly awaiting the approaching game, milled about the streets in aimless wanderings." Homecoming and stadium dedication, October 18, 1924. 1926 *Illio*, 153. Courtesy University of Illinois Archive.

*The entire town was deco-
rated for the occasion.
Unique arrangements car-
ried the significance of the
dedication homecoming.*

154

Figure 5.4
"The entire town was decorated for the occasion. Unique arrangements carried the significance of the dedication homecoming." Homecoming and stadium dedication, October 18, 1924. 1926 *Illio*, 154. Courtesy University of Illinois Archive.

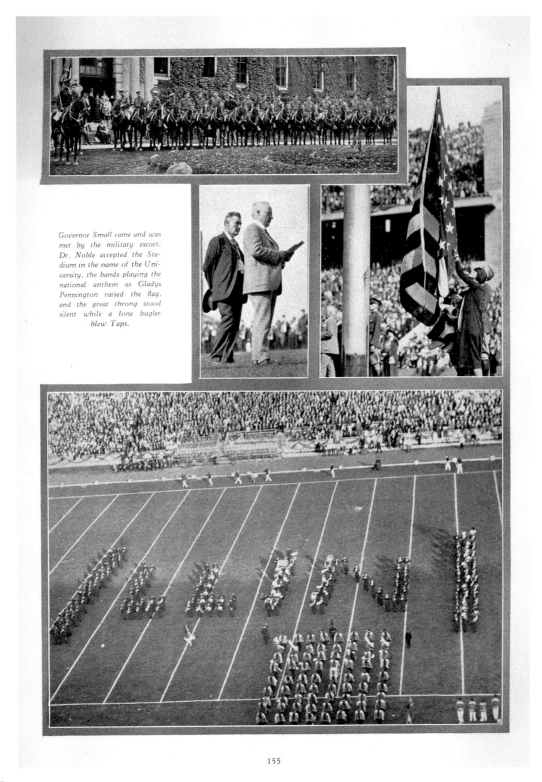

Governor Small came and was met by the military escort. Dr. Noble accepted the Stadium in the name of the University, the bands playing the national anthem as Gladys Pennington raised the flag, and the great throng stood silent while a lone bugler blew Taps.

155

Figure 5.5
"Governor Small came and was met by the military escort. Dr. Noble accepted the Stadium in the name of the University, the bands playing the national anthem as Gladys Pennington raised the flag, and stood silent while a lone bugler blew taps." Homecoming and stadium dedication, October 18, 1924. 1926 *Illio*, 155. Courtesy University of Illinois Archive.

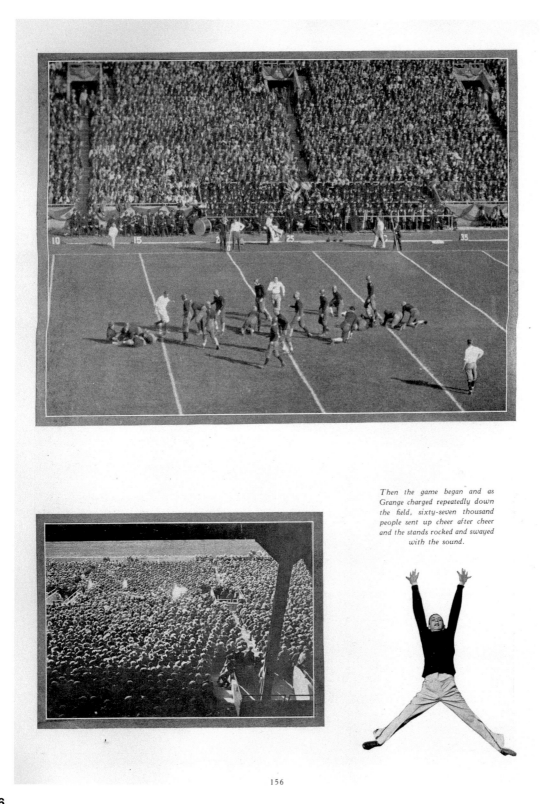

Then the game began and as Grange charged repeatedly down the field, sixty-seven thousand people sent up cheer after cheer and the stands rocked and swayed with the sound.

156

Figure 5.6
"Then the game began and as Grange charged repeatedly down the field, sixty-seven thousand people sent up cheer after cheer and the stands rocked and swayed with the sound." Homecoming and stadium dedication, October 18, 1924. 1926 *Illio*, 156. Courtesy University of Illinois Archive.

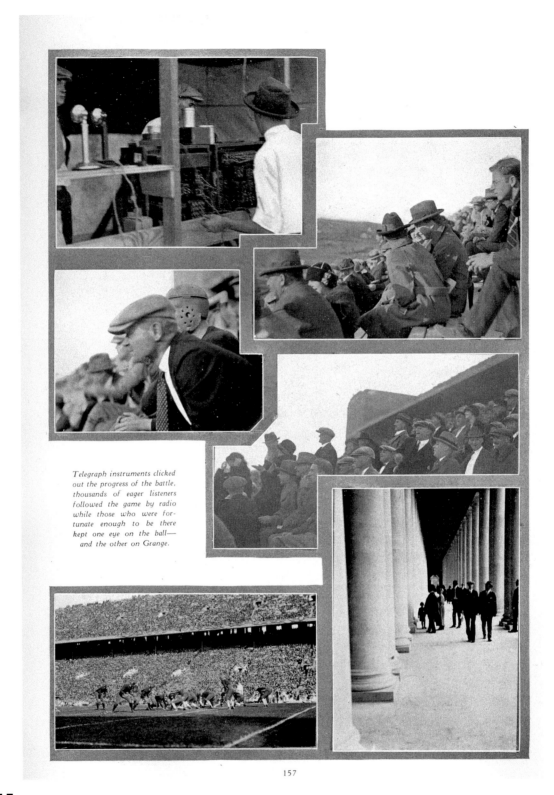

Telegraph instruments clicked out the progress of the battle, thousands of eager listeners followed the game by radio while those who were fortunate enough to be there kept one eye on the ball— and the other on Grange.

157

Figure 5.7
"Telegraph instruments clicked out the progress of the battle, thousands of eager listeners followed the game by radio while those who were fortunate enough to be there kept one eye on the ball—and the other on Grange." Homecoming and stadium dedication, October 18, 1924. 1926 *Illio*, 157. Courtesy University of Illinois Archive.

to Urbana-Champaign was so large that the Illinois Central Railroad (ICR), arranged for forty specials," train cars from Chicago to the whistle-stop directly to the Stadium's west.[6]

More than an hour before kickoff the gathering crowds had already filled half the Stadium. Raucous crowds in the east and west bleachers were festively decorated "equally [in] Illinois orange and blue, and Michigan's maize and blue."[7] At 1:30 p.m., drum major William M. Liscom (class of 1924) led the 175-strong Illini marching band— also in orange and blue—through the "Three-in-One" formations, which ended in the now-familiar "block I."[8] Shortly thereafter, 75 Michigan marching band members, sporting short maize-colored capes, joined the Illini musicians. Once on the field and under the joint direction of Michigan's band director, Captain Wilfred Wilson, the two bands together played *The Star Spangled Banner*. During the music, the team's captains gathered at the center of the football field for the coin toss to determine who would kick off. Illinois' team captain, Frank E. Rokusek, a 1923 All-American, called the toss in the air. Illinois won the coin toss and elected to receive the ball first. Under the gaze of Illinois' Zuppke and Michigan's first-year coach George Little, the game officially started when the Wolverines' team captain, Herb Steger, kicked off. The football bounced near the Illinois' five-yard line, just in front of Harold "Red" Grange. That day Grange, a 1923 consensus All-American, would be immortalized by sportswriter Grantland Rice with the moniker "Galloping Ghost" because of his "electrified" performance.[9] Grange cemented his legendary status when he scooped up the bouncing ball and ran the kick back for a touchdown—all before ten seconds had elapsed in the game. As Grange ran up the field, the already spirited home crowd went into a veritable frenzy. Illinois would go on to win the game 39–14, with Grange alone producing five of the six Illini touchdowns.

The Golden Age of Sport

An Era's Zeitgeist

While the nationally broadcast game elevated Grange into a mythic figure, the excitement he generated

among sports fans from all over the United States helped increase college football's popularity and economic power. Grange was not the only football character to achieve national relevance that day. College football had arrived with a sonic boom: the Army game versus Notre Dame would also grab attention from Grantland Rice, whose description of four Fighting Irish players as "the Four Horsemen" would help place college football at the center of the Golden Age of Sport.[10]

This era was forged by a confluence of major economic, social, and political forces. The United States was now nearly 150 years young and had begun to dominate the international stage. To be sure, it was an imperfect nation, especially in its long advance toward granting civil rights to all, but its citizens were also energetic, optimistic, and driven by a can-do attitude. This vantage point was born of hardship. Like Illinois, the country had been transformed over the last century. Its Union had survived a bloody Civil War to become an industrialized nation with an affluent and growing middle class whose ranks were swelled by immigrants and whose democratic principles left monarchies and empires as vestiges of an ossified past. It had sent 4,734,991 men and women to fight in the Great War across the Atlantic Ocean, buried 116,516 of them, and brought back over 200,000 wounded.[11] After the Great War, the country was further challenged when communities from rural villages to the largest metropolis lost another 675,000 lives because of the 1918–1919 influenza pandemic.[12] But by 1924, a resilient country was ready to take charge. It is in this context that Memorial Stadium was conceived and built and became a symbol of this time and the embodiment of a nation finding and embracing its self-confidence. As evidence of this newfound confidence, the Stadium had not been built by large corporate interests or through state contracts but by the people.

The Age of the Spectator

When Jim Sumner referred to the 1920s as the Age of the Spectator, he was pointing to both economics and time.[13] Consider the historic parallels with previous nation-states that reached the political and economic stability that allowed citizens not only the financial capacity but also the leisure time to engage in spectator activities. Not since the Roman Empire had so many stadiums been built for entertainment and sporting events by a society. And it was not just the industrial middle class but all Americans—from those in rural farm towns to large cities, from the working poor to the upper class living on Manhattan's posh Park Avenue—who demanded theater, cinema, dance clubs, and especially sporting events. With sports, audiences could engage in spirited rituals, seek thrills, and experience heartbreak.

Propelled by a burgeoning middle class that enjoyed economic prosperity and was unshackled from war and disease, the period felt as if a rubber band had been pulled back into full tension and then let go, which released an enormous amount of pent-up energy. Consider that before 1900, the United States was home to less than half a dozen stadiums with 20,000 or more seats. Of these, only Franklin Field in Philadelphia was home to a football team. By 1930, the number had exponentially jumped to over forty stadiums. Even more illustrative of sports' ascendancy, especially football, is that of the ten largest stadiums by capacity, nine—including the largest of them all, the University of Michigan's football stadium—were built between 1920 and 1930.[14] In December 1923, the Associated Press reported that total college football attendance had topped out at 5,000,000 spectators.[15] For a country with a population just shy of 112,000,000 at the time, this meant that nearly 4.5% of the population had attended a college football game. For comparison, in 2019 attendance was 47,537,702, which was less than 1.5% of the country's population.[16]

Widespread adoption of radio would also help usher in the Golden Age of Sports. Though rudimentary radio technology had been around since the turn of the twentieth century, station KDKA (Pittsburg) did not transmit the first scheduled broadcast until November 2, 1920, which was of a game in Pittsburgh's Forbes Field between the University of Pittsburgh and West Virginia

University.[17] Just under a year later, on October 8, 1921, KDKA was also the first to broadcast an advertisement during a college football game. When the contest between the visiting University of Chicago and Princeton University was transmitted coast-to-coast, the era of college football as a news-making sport on a national scale had officially begun. On November 4, 1922, WRM (which would become WILL) ran a telephone line from the campus radio lab to Illini Field and relayed the first play-by-play of a University of Illinois game.

Radio was not merely a source of entertainment that fueled the imaginations of those who someday hoped to attend their first game or sustained them until the next visit. For the poor in particular, radio generated collective memories and engendered neighborhood loyalties to amateur, college, and professional teams. By the mid-1920s, the "country was afire with radio fever."[18]

As radio technology improved, so did broadcasting range and quality, and that opened the way for profit. Using the model later adopted for television broadcasts, radio stations charged advertisers for airtime. Initially, companies ranging from local small businesses to national corporations sponsored college football broadcasts. Sports provided an excellent medium for intent listening: speed, excitement, and drama. Audiences would often remain close to their radios to not miss any important plays or color commentary. They were loyal and steadfast, and advertisers hoped to capitalize on their continued listenership. Not surprisingly, this made sports an attractive investment.

In another precedent-setting example in 1934—amid the Great Depression—the University of Michigan became the first school to sell exclusive broadcasting rights for $20,000 (approximately $452,875 in 2023). With attendance dramatically down, such a large sum of money did not go unnoticed. Just a year later, the Big Ten's governing board proposed selling all the conference teams' radio broadcast rights for $100,000, but in 1937 the University of Illinois vetoed the proposal and in 1939 sold exclusive rights to its football radio broadcasts.[19]

From 1924 to Pearl Harbor

Fighting Illini Succeed

After the game against the Wolverines, the Fighting Illini hosted two consecutive home games. The first was one week later against an out-of-conference team, DePauw University, and the Illini delivered a crushing 45–0 win. A week after that, in what was the first official Dad's Day celebrated at Memorial Stadium, the home team soundly beat the Iowa Hawkeyes 36–0. In what is the first known mention of the wind affecting sporting events at the Stadium, sportswriters noted the havoc it created for the punting units. A stiff burst caused one Iowa punt to travel out of bounds at the Iowa 25-yard line.[20] With a short field advantage, Illinois' Red Grange would rush on the third play from scrimmage for the game's first touchdown.

At that point, the Fighting Illini were considered favorites to win the Western Conference (later the Big Ten) once again. On November 8, they visited the University of Chicago Maroons at Stagg Field, where the teams battled to a 21–21 tie. The tied score meant that Illinois could at least capture a share of the conference title. One week later, however, the Illini would experience an upset at the hands of the University of Minnesota Golden Gophers (7–20). Their remarkable streak of fourteen straight wins had ended. Barring an unexpected loss to the University of Wisconsin's Badgers, the Maroons would nab another conference title. Though the Maroons finished with fewer wins than the Illini, they ended with a season record of four wins, one loss, and three ties, and their only loss was to an out-of-conference opponent. Moreover, the Maroons' schedule included one more in-conference game, which gave the team a slight percentage advantage of .750 to Illinois' .700 and the conference title. Nonetheless, the Fighting Illini were true to their moniker and finished the season by beating Ohio State at home 7–0.

Despite finishing the season 6–1–1 and in second place, the Illini would not be invited to a postseason bowl game. After the season, Grange was named the first unanimous consensus All-American in college football history.[21] The Illini had become a force. Energized by playing in a state-of-the-art venue and led by a proven coach, the Illini were one of the most dominant teams in all of college football.[22]

The Roaring Twenties Continue

The year 1925 was remarkable not only because the Stadium was finally in full operation, but also because the Stadium began to truly have an impact on the built environment, as various traditions—many still practiced today—began to take form and shape the campus and Illinois state residents' lives. The Stadium became more than a facility to host football games and other sporting events, it also became a locus of community and regional activity, drawing people from all places to experience the University and its offerings. With the Stadium now anchoring the southwest of the University's campus, in February of 1925, the Board of Trustees (BOT) voted to approve the use of the Ellis property, a parcel of land located between the Stadium and the ICR tracks, during the lull between seasons, the BOT approved converting Illinois Field, the previous home field of the Fighting Illini, into a "freshman varsity baseball diamond."[23] This redevelopment meant that all football practices would be moved to the Stadium. As September came to a close, the "New" Gym (later Huff Gym), as it was called to differentiate it from the north campus' Old Gym, was completed for $515,000. Designed by James M. White and Charles Platt and built by English Brothers,[24] it was devised to host intercollegiate basketball games, with a seating capacity of 8,000 people. Like Memorial Stadium, White and Platt clad the Georgian exterior with Western brick.[25] On the floors above, and surrounding the triple height needed for the basketball court, were new AA offices. Located on the east side of Fourth Street in Champaign, it followed Huff's vision for a vast sports complex on the southwestern edge of campus.

With the 1925 season about to begin, spirits were buoyant. Sportswriters across the country had been lobbying for more national contests. The impressive results of the Illinois, Notre Dame, Chicago, California, and Alabama football teams had generated discussion about teams from across the country playing one another. One Indiana newspaper would go so far as to categorically declare "Notre Dame–Illinois Game Would Be Best of Year."[26] Zuppke had announced that the Illini would indeed play Notre Dame during the upcoming season,[27] but it would not come to pass, and Illinois would meet Butler University at home instead. Despite this temporary setback for the Illini football team to break though to a wider national audience, the 1924 season had been an unqualified success for the Illini, and much of the starting lineup was returning. To meet fan demand, the ICR announced special fares not only for those traveling to Urbana-Champaign to watch home games but also for those traveling to away games. In this way, the Fighting Illini and the Stadium had a massive effect on the state's transportation network.[28] Regional newspapers such as the Bureau County Tribune (published in Princeton, Illinois) observed that the "[t]hree big games scheduled for the Memorial Stadium give indications that the 1925 University of Illinois football team will probably play before the largest football crowds in history."[29] But Zuppke's team struggled, losing three of the first four games, including the home opener against Nebraska and two of the first three games at the Stadium.

After a heart-wrenching loss at home to Michigan's Wolverines (0–3), the Illini would go on to win the last four games of the season, including a defeat of the University of Pennsylvania's Quakers 24–2 in an away game. The Quakers were no pushovers: just a year before, their record of 9–1–1 gave them a national title. Among the many game highlights, Grange introduced an innovative play Zuppke dubbed the "flea-flicker."[30] On November 21, the Illini finished the season strong by beating Ohio State at home, this time 14–9. Almost immediately after the win, and much to the chagrin of Huff and Zuppke, Grange left to play for the Chicago Bears. George "Papa Bear" Stanley Halas Sr., owner of the Bears and an Illini football alumnus (class of 1918), had finally convinced Grange to bring his talents, and fanbase, to professional football.

The Stadium as a Socializing Space

The 1925 season established the Stadium as central to student life. Student enrollment had swelled to 9,904, the largest in history.[31] From the beginning, Huff and the AA had identified athletic activities and sporting events as a social binder—even if true racial integration was well in the future. Therefore, it was vital to generate spaces and activities that would form commonalities between a large and increasingly diverse student body. The Stadium had become an effective anchor for social interaction. For example, an advertisement published in the Daily Illini by the G. C. Willis store focused on its role for women:

> There will be football games, afternoon functions, formal and informal dances. And to enjoy them to the fullest your wardrobe must be smart. . . . For fifty years we have catered to the college girl. We know her apparel wants and needs.[32]

An article in the *DeKalb Daily Chronicle* proudly listed the names of residents who had departed to start classes at the University. Tellingly, the article confirmed the importance of the Stadium as an element of social life:

> The state university will have a large number of students that are residents of this city and the surrounding community and DeKalb people who expect to attend some of the Illini football games will have little trouble in meeting friends while at the university city.[33]

One of the more unexpected effects generated by the Stadium was the result of its sheer size. While it had always been conceived as a venue open to fans, the jump in scale combined with a sense of anonymity produced increasingly rowdy, unruly, and vulgar jeering crowds. Whereas cheerleaders had been traditionally thought of as leading fans in chants supporting the home team, now there was a need to revisit their role. The *Daily Illini* writers noted that

> [t]he time has come to set forth another idea about cheer-leading. Because of the presence in the Stadium of so many people who were merely spectators,

the level of sportsmanship is much lower that it was for a number of years on old Illinois Field. The Stadium is so large, and it takes sound so long to travel from one side to the other that a cheer-leader can no longer hope to exercise intimate control over the crowd. The spectators who come for one or two games do not know the best traditions of Illinois. They often express their enthusiasm, therefore, in any way that comes to them. They boo, hiss, and ridicule; they shout unsportsmanlike remarks; they let their emotions run away with them.

With the challenge diagnosed, the *Daily Illini* writers suggested that

[t]he cheer-leader is not merely a semaphore; he is a strategist in the art of handling and controlling public opinion, crowd action and crowd thinking. The cheer-leader should be the director of a school in sportsmanship and high-minded enthusiasm. His pupils sit in the bleachers.[34]

For the *Daily Illini* writers, Stadium attendance was an opportunity to carry out social engineering focused on modifying and guiding public behaviors. The topic of fair conduct and respectable public behavior was so pressing for the University of Illinois and the AA that on the opening day of the 1925 season, Huff, writing as the "Director of Physical Welfare," published an article in the *Daily Illini* admonishing those who would attend the game later that day to "stand for sportsmanship, not only today but throughout the school year at every athletic contest." But perhaps most revealing was Huff's focus on taking the "lead in a movement to stamp out betting on intercollegiate contests." He concluded by reminding readers that "[i]n a way, we are on exhibition before the people of the state, and they will form their impression of the University from their personal contacts here."[35]

Alcohol on Campus

First as Illini coach and then as AA director, Huff used his position and reputation to promote reforms to establish good conduct and eschew betting. When the

NCAA's antecessor organization had formed in 1905, Huff was frequently sought to develop processes and rules for intercollegiate sports. One topic that occupied him was alcohol consumption on campus, especially at official University events.

Organized sports and the consumption of alcohol had emerged together in the late 1870s. In fact, one professional baseball league, the American Association, was born in 1882 when certain teams refused to abide by rules not to sell alcohol on Sunday. The association, or "Beer and Whiskey League," would disappear in 1891 but not before contributing at least four teams active today in Major League Baseball and demonstrating the profitability of selling alcohol to fans.[36] Despite the constraints of Prohibition that outlawed the manufacturing, selling, and transportation of alcohol beginning in 1920, its consumption remained popular in Illinois. The state's strong economy, coupled with its location on Lake Michigan and across from Canada where alcohol was never banned, made it a fertile market for the illicit distribution and sale of alcohol. Add to this atmosphere several college football programs, each with a growing fan base, and the clandestine consumption of alcohol would escalate. Mark Thornton observed that "[f]ootball fans are normally beer drinkers. However, they typically become brandy, bourbon, and rum smugglers at football games. It is easier to smuggle any given quantity of alcohol in the form of more potent beverages."[37]

By 1924, the alcohol problem on campus prompted student organizations to urge visiting Michigan fans to shun its consumption during homecoming celebrations at the Stadium's inaugural game.[38] By 1926, the problem of illicit consumption had become so serious that all ten directors of athletics of the Western Conference published a collectively signed letter objecting to "making big college football games the occasion for mass violation of the prohibition laws."[39] Not surprisingly, in 1927 "Huff helped shape a Carnegie Foundation study of college football excesses. Among other sins, the study sought to crack down on the alcohol abuse that pervaded campuses on football weekends."[40] Huff's anti-alcohol campaign was so successful, that neither beer nor any other alcoholic drink would be sold at the Stadium until 2002.

Memorial Stadium as Venue

Student Convocations

From the onset, Memorial Stadium was visualized as more than just a football field. Huff had imagined it as "an all-year-round proposition" filled with sports facilities like basketball and handball courts and holding activities that would support all students.[41] With major construction finished, new programmatic functions including convocation were introduced. Then called the Illini Pow-Wow, the first gathering on September 24, 1924, was an opportunity for officials and distinguished guests to address the entire student body.[42] This convocation at the start of the school year continued at the Stadium over the years—as long as the weather cooperated. Because President Kinley would be absent for the start of the 1925 fall semester, Huff was scheduled to accompany Provost and Dean Kendric C. Babcock to host the day's activities. Among the distinguished guests was Dorothy Mulberry (class of 1920), president of the Woman's League, who was slated to speak.[43] At the last minute, the convocation was postponed for a week so that Kinley could attend, but rain on September 30 caused another postponement, and the event was moved to October 1. At 4:00 p.m. that day, the marching band led students by class from the Quadrangle into the Stadium. Once there, Kinley invited the class of 1929 to make an "ephebic" pledge, which asked the freshmen to recognize their arrival at a life stage associated with maturity.[44]

In what would become a major tradition, in 1925 Huff invited Boy Scouts from all over Illinois and western Indiana to take part in the pregame pageantry. During the first game of the season and the Illini home opener against Nebraska on October 3, over 2,500 Boy Scouts sponsored by organizations like the Rotary Club and the Kiwanis paraded on the football field during halftime, finishing with a solemn flag ceremony.[45] Just over a year later, under the supervision of Assistant Director of Bands Ray Dvorak, two Eagle Scouts, Lester Leutwiler and Ralph Hubbard, introduced what would become the controversial figure of the Chief. On October 30, 1926, during halftime of a game between Illinois and the

University of Pennsylvania, the Chief, a student dressed in garments imitating First Nations ceremonial vestments, performed an interpretive dance at midfield. The routine ended when the Chief and the Penn drum major, dressed as the Quakers' mascot, met at midfield, shared a peace pipe, and "walked off the field arm in arm."[46] For the next 80 years, Chief Illiniwek, as the figure came to be called, would perform at many University sporting and institutional events, and his image appeared on businesses and products across the community (Figure 5.8).

Track and Field

Track and field events premiered at the Stadium when the freshman team held practices there on April 25, 1925.[47] Coached by Harry Gill, the full team inaugurated

Figure 5.8
First Chief performance, October 30, 1926.
Courtesy of the University of Illinois Department of Intercollegiate Athletics Archives. V.V_N.1_P.1.

its facilities on May 2, 1925, by beating Notre Dame in a dual meet 87–39.[48] H. E. "Bud" Evans tied the Illinois record for the 100-yard dash and then later tied the conference record for the 220-yard dash (21.2 seconds). Gill was no stranger to success. In 1921, he had organized "the very first NCAA championship in any sport, and his Illini won the inaugural event" (Figure 5.9).[49]

Two weeks later, between May 15 and 16, the Stadium hosted a state-wide high school track event for 34 Class A and 46 Class B teams (Figure 5.9). At the end of the meet, the Danville and Eldorado High School track teams had tied with 17 points each, sharing the Class A crown, while Hinsdale claimed the Class B championship with 28 points.[50] As a locus of state high school sports and activities, the Stadium became an iconic recruiting tool, attracting potential student athletes from the region and eventually from across the country, to attend the University of Illinois. In this sense the Stadium, and the University of Illinois, experienced tremendous success, prompting the 1929 Carnegie Report, to specifically mention the Stadium, and its cost, as part of a trend to build larger and more impressive facilities to actively recruit student athletes. Culturally, the Stadium as a civic venue had proven equally successful. Activities it hosted included concerts, speeches, a myriad of celebrations and traditions, incorporating state-wide high school events, many that continue to this day, e.g., every fall Memorial Stadium hosts marching bands from all over the state at the Illinois Marching Band Championships.

Figure 5.9
220 yards low hurdles, track meet versus Notre Dame, Memorial Stadium. Courtesy of the University of Illinois Department of Intercollegiate Athletics Archives.

Interscholastic Circus

More novel large-scale events also found new homes at the Stadium. In 1925 the Interscholastic Circus (IC)—a spring occasion when students were "trained as clowns and performers to put on a university circus show. There were awards presented to different categories focused on clownery, performance, and fraternity/sorority participation. Campus Greek life was integral to these performances every year."[51] Held every May since 1906 at the Old Gym and then at Illinois Field, the IC could enlarge thanks to the generous seating capacity and excellent vantage points of its new home. The IC perhaps served as an end-of-year pressure release valve, as audience members watched clowns, trapeze artists, and other performers executing daring feats. As C. O. Jackson related eloquently, the IC fit perfectly within Huff's Prohibition enforcement efforts:

> at the suggestion of the Athletic Association, it was decided to present it [IC] as part of the entertainment at Interscholastic Week-End in May. Strange as it may seem to us today, the chief reason for

staging the show at that particular time was as a substitute for other and less desirable attractions. In brief, the purpose of this early Circus was to keep interscholastic participants and friends away from downtown barrooms, and prevent, if possible, too much imbibing of strong liquor.[52]

In all, a record-breaking 10,000 attendees witnessed the IC at Memorial Stadium that Saturday.[53] The IC continued making its annual appearance until the event was discontinued in 1932 (Figure 5.10).

The Stadium Continues to Evolve

New Projects

With the football season over, in January 1925 the *MSN*, now published intermittently, revealed a BOT-approved landscape design that White would supervise throughout the spring and into the summer. By mid-April, White's "tree gang" had transplanted "young elm trees" on the "borders of the campus and the roads to the stadium." As

Figure 5.10
Interscholastic Circus. 1930 *Illio*, 192. Courtesy of the University of Illinois Archives.

INTERƧCHOLAƧTIC CIRCUƧ

called for in the design, trees lined "First and Fourth streets in Champaign, on the east and west terraces of the stadium and the four approaches on the north."[54] For its first decade in operation, each terrace was lined with twelve elm trees about 30 feet tall with trunks that varied between 10 and 14 inches in diameter.[55] The trees marched parallel to the main hall facades and entry doorways. In most cases, the trees were 20-year-old elms transplanted "from other parts of the campus with the utmost caution and success."[56]

After finishing with the trees, the tree gang proceeded to plant 600 shrubs "directly north and south of the Stadium."[57] To this day, most of the elms remain, and, as

designed, they provide generous shading canopies for those transiting through Champaign (Figure 5.11). The shrubs were located at varying distances from the Stadium, forming lines at 50, 80, and 100 feet away from walls and ramp towers.[58] By mid-June, the Stadium's surrounding softscape was nearly final.

Also underway was the construction of seven tennis courts from Fourth Street to the east stands, and eventually, the same number would be set up from First Street to the west stands.[59] Later that spring, a plan to convert the area just north of the Stadium into "playing fields, drill grounds for infantry and cavalry and rifle ranges"

Figure 5.11
Aerial photograph showing the walks, elms, tennis courts, and seating in the south end zone. Courtesy of the University of Illinois Department of Intercollegiate Athletics Archives.

was revealed.[60] By locating these activities north of the Stadium, the Military Axis was shifted south and away from the Armory building to the east.

New interior designs were also in development. In a June 1925 *Chicago Tribune* column, James O'Donnell Bennet shared the news that the Stadium would be "equipped for winter sports and will contain a gigantic skating rink and a freezing plant" (Figure 5.12).[61] Two months later, the *MSN* announced that the "ice-skating rink will be built in the west Great Hall of the Stadium at an estimated cost of $50,000, probably within a year and perhaps sooner," but then added the caveat that this could happen only "if University students demonstrate their interest by accelerating their payments on Stadium pledges."[62] This carrot approach was yet

another strategy for soliciting funds to erase the debt of $237,235.03. While on paper pledges amounted to just over $2,166,000, by July 1925 only a little more than $1,425,000 had been collected. The officially delinquent payments totaled $456,678.82, an amount more than enough to cover the outstanding bills and loans.[63]

The promised rink was to occupy the 410-foot long and 50-foot wide hall, and according to "[p]lans prepared by H. J. MacIntire, associate professor of refrigeration,"

60,000 linear feet of 1 1-4 inch pipe, placed four inches apart, will be laid on the earth floor and partly covered with sand. A calcium chloride brine at about 18 degrees Fahrenheit, will be pumped through these pipes upon which water will be

Figure 5.12
Interior image of the Great West Hall's proposed ice rink. The *MSN* caption reads: "Start 1926 with Your Stadium Payment!" (5, no. 1 [January 1926]: 1).

sprayed by means of a hose, building up an ice surface an inch thick. An ammonia compressor will be used to keep the brine cold, the capacity of which will be equal to about 80 tons, or the cooling effect obtained by the melting of ice at a rate of 80 tons each 24 hours.[64]

The article concluded by noting that despite the many innovative features of the proposed rink, Huff did not conceive of the hall as the future site for hockey games.

With the Stadium stands finished and excitement over the football season continuing to build, tickets for games, especially homecoming against Michigan, quickly sold out. In fact, at the conclusion of the 1925 season, the *MSN* proudly declared that "Illinois' football team played before approximately 379,639 people at home and abroad during the 1925 season, the greatest combined attendance in the history of American football."

In comparison, "Michigan's 1925 attendance, 353,000, was second." For Illinois, 198,262 went to home games for an average of just under 40,000 people. Nonetheless, with pledge payments still lagging, not only was the skating rink looking increasingly unrealistic but other planned elements like a basketball court, whose cost was estimated at around $100,000, seemed even more tenuous.[65] Of course, high attendance meant what should have been overflowing coffers, but as *MSN* writers pointed out in January 1926, the AA had to pay expenses like salaries, maintenance costs, and equipment, which in 1924 had tallied $67,135.[66] To quash the perception that monies on hand were excessive or were being wasted, Huff disclosed in a December 1925 interview the many possible uses for the revenue. He acknowledged the importance of the revenue the Stadium produced, observing that

[o]ne of the big arguments for the stadium was that football profits would supply funds for developments which could be obtained in no other way. The stadium is designed to be the center of a great system of athletes for all and we propose to carry out this plan.

Project costs ranged from a few thousand dollars—like a freshman baseball diamond at Illinois Field for $2,000—to higher-ticket items—like doubling the number of restrooms for $25,000 to finishing the east great hall's flooring and walls for $50,000. He also noted that the AA was interested in endowing academic chairs to conduct research into athletics. This was a logical evolution of a scholarly approach to the study of athletics that began with the founding of the Department of Physical Training in 1895. He added:

Some of the projects outlined are pressing—others must wait until they can be financed, and a few may never be reached, but the list is certainly sufficient to give the public an idea of how the profits will be spent usefully.

Huff then situated construction in terms of basic needs now versus future demands and continued:

But first we must complete the stadium. No one who has come here for a game in wet weather will question the necessity of making the approaches just as comfortable and mudless as possible. The number of rest rooms in the stadium should be doubled. Then should come the completion of the great halls.

Yet the largest Stadium improvement being considered was the construction of the south main stand, which would provide an additional 16,000 seats at a cost of approximately $320,000.[67] However, Huff conceded that there was

no immediate plan to add the south main stand to the stadium but it is something that will have to be kept in mind. As a profit-making proposition this extension would not pay for itself in years, but there are other considerations such as the beauty of the stadium which would undoubtedly be enhanced and our desire to accommodate our constantly increasing alumni and the people of the state.

Huff concluded that with the Stadium still in debt, much of the proposed improvements depended on fulfilling pledge payments. He placed that shared responsibility on alumni, students, and community members:

> The big thing that is needed now is for them to complete their payments to the stadium. The sooner the stadium is paid for, the sooner it will be possible to embark on this program. Let the subscribers to the stadium do their part.[68]

Stadium Improvements Continue

In February 1926, supervising architect James White disclosed at a talk to the Pan-Hellenic Council that the University had purchased a large swath of land east of the ICR tracks all the way to Lincoln Avenue. Curiously, White noted that in 50 to 100 years, the land occupied by Mount Hope Cemetery to the east would become a "driveway leading to the Stadium." Moreover, the University would build athletic fields and facilities directly west of the Stadium to the ICR tracks.[69]

A few months later in 1926, news spread that the stadium at Indiana University had suffered structural damage, and out of caution F. E. Richart from the University's Department of Theoretical and Applied Mechanics was dispatched to test the Stadium's quality and strength. Much to the relief of everyone, Richart determined that not only was the concrete working well but it would last longer than specified because the quality of the concrete exceeded the structural specifications by between 30% and 40%.[70] Precious funds would not be needed for repairs.

But improvements were needed, and time was of the essence to foil the weather. Late spring offered a window of mild weather—an end to icy days but weeks away from the fierce thunderstorms characteristic of central Illinois—and the exodus of students for the summer enabled the City of Champaign, in coordination with the University, to spend nearly $50,000 to build more concrete sidewalks and finish paving First and Fourth Streets south all the way to what is today Pennsylvania Avenue. These newly surfaced roads framed the approach to the site. And before the summer

rains could damage the new field, the AA invested in a tarpaulin-like cover that would be a first for a college stadium. At nearly $10,000, the "rubberized fabric" was manufactured in "four segments of 158 × 83 feet." Each section weighed about 4.5 tons (or just over 10,000 pounds).[71] Made by the Du Pont Fabrikoid company, this expensive raincoat bestowed necessary protection for a $1,700,000 investment.

Despite these outlays, by midsummer 1926 finances had significantly improved. After increasing its gifts to a total of $300,000, the AA reported that overall debt stood at just under $180,000.[72] Up to that point paying unfilled pledges had not been perceived as a priority, which had made it

> necessary for the Stadium Committee to borrow about $350,000 from the Continental and Commercial National Bank of Chicago, with which to pay the construction bills. This money was borrowed with the understanding that all unpaid subscriptions to the Stadium Fund would be held as collateral security for the payment of this loan, and that as collections were made the money would be turned over to the Continental Bank in reduction of the indebtedness. At this writing (July 1, 1926) about 11,000 subscriptions have been paid in full out of 21,100 pledges made to the Stadium Fund, and within thirty or sixty days probably another 500 to 1,000 subscribers will join the paid in full list.[73]

Pledge payments jumped nearly $100,000 for the year.[74] However, with the final scheduled pledge payment scheduled for July 1, the AA and the Stadium Executive Committee once again changed tactics and instituted a carrot-and-stick strategy. To incentivize subscription installments, purchasers were categorized by their payment status, number of desired tickets, and seating arrangements to determine an order for buying fall 1926 tickets.[75] Conversely, the novel stick approach involved making private information about subscribers public: June's *MSN* announced that

> within a few months a complete list of all subscribers to the Stadium with the status of their

subscriptions (amount paid and due, if any) will be published in a pamphlet which will be mailed to all of the 21,000 subscribers.[76]

With the new system in place, tickets to the major home contests quickly sold out. Though the Fighting Illini hosted six teams that fall, the Iowa, Pennsylvania, and Ohio State games sold out almost immediately. With excitement building, football practice got underway on September 15. In a column published in the *Urbana Daily Courier,* writers explicitly linked the state's working-class roots with the University, noting that the players were in good shape because "[s]teel mills, coal mines, factories, concrete gangs, and other forms of tiresome diversion have had their share of the Zupmen" during the summer break.[77]

Despite no longer having Red Grange, the Galloping Ghost, in the backfield, the team did not disappoint, compiling a 6–2 overall record. For the Illini, the season opener was at home against Coe College on October 2, which also served as the second annual Scout Day game. It was a relatively easy win with a final score of 27–0. The two losses came on an away game to the Michigan Wolverines (0–13) and to Ohio State in the season finale at home by a heart-wrenching score of 6–7. Curiously, though the Illini finished with a better record in 1926 than in 1925, total profits from football were expected to fall from over $305,000 to $220,000.[78]

Before the 1927 season, the AA demonstrated once again why Memorial Stadium was one of the leading sports and entertainment facilities in the United States. That summer it became the first in the Big Ten Conference to install a loudspeaker system and an electrically controlled scoreboard. The innovative scoreboard, which was wired directly to the press box, was designed by White's office. The new 63-foot-wide board was placed on the north end atop the 12-foot-tall north wall to loom 27 feet off the ground. Above the board hung the massive game clock measuring 6 feet, 6 inches in diameter. Other features included scores, football outlines to signal possession, penalties, and displays indicating downs and "yards to go."[79]

Perhaps these noticeable additions helped energize the discussions about how this new structure was not

benefiting the community. Arguments in favor of taxing the Stadium as a means to finance repairs on the urban infrastructure were made before the BOT. Champaign, Urbana, and Champaign County moved to recover some of the proportional costs of wear and tear by assessing the tax payment at $121,800. After deliberations, the BOT decided that because the Stadium was the property of the University and the University was a state institution, it was exempt from this kind of property taxation.[80] Notwithstanding the BOT's decision, arguments between the University and local governments would rage for decades.

Despite the political skirmishes outside the arena regarding taxation, excitement for the action to come inside it meant that tickets for homecoming and the anticipated tilt against the Maroons in 1926 sold out in a few days. The enthusiasm was warranted when the Fighting Illini went undefeated and with one tie, 7–0–1, to claim a share of the national championship.[81] The season opened against Bradley Polytechnic Institute (today Bradley University in Peoria), which had won twenty-four straight games. But after defeating Bradley 19–0, the Illini continued the home stand by drubbing Butler 58–0 and then played to a 12–12 tie against the Iowa State Cyclones. Next, the Illini traveled to Northwestern, edging out the Wildcats 7–6. This was the first time the teams had met since 1923 and marked the beginning of Illinois' longest-lasting rivalry. For homecoming on October 29, the Illini blanked the Wolverines 14–0. At Iowa City, the team proceeded to defeat the Hawkeyes by the same score. Illinois would finish the season by outscoring the University of Chicago Maroons 15–6 and securing the Big Ten Conference and national championships by beating Ohio State 13–0.

The summer before the 1927 national championship season, Huff and the AA decided to cease attempts at building a skating rink in the east hall, opting instead to finish the space for intramural sports, especially basketball.[82] According to the AA proposal, the entirety of the $48,000 cost to prepare the area would be covered by the AA itself. Not surprisingly, just over five weeks later, on September 27, the BOT approved the plan.[83] Yet, the desire to build a skating rink never disappeared. The successes of the 1927 season had enlarged AA revenue to over $306,000, which made it possible to finally make tangible one of Huff's dreams: an autonomous skating rink.[84] In March 1928, Huff requested Kinley's support in approving a plan for the AA to commission the rink and pay $225,000 from its own resources to build it near the corner of Fifth Street and Armory Avenue. By placing the skating rink as an independent venue north of the Stadium and across the street from the Armory, a grand athletic complex would dominate the southwestern campus. Almost exactly one month later, Kinley secured approval.[85] With the east hall now outfitted for intramural sports, particularly basketball, using AA funds of $48,000, the Stadium had become a nexus of diverse activities.[86]

The Peak of the Era

Just as the Illini football program steamrolled through the Big 10, the US economy showed no signs of slowing. The combination of football programs that attracted ever-larger home crowds and robust real per capita growth meant that not only were more students attending college than ever before, especially state schools like the University of Illinois, but also that more people had disposable income to spend on leisure activities like watching Illini football. Not surprisingly, Huff and the AA capitalized on this momentum to add programming and complete the original seating proposal—which of course would generate higher revenue. One of the first changes came before the opening home game against Bradley when the AA installed two medical emergency rooms.[87] Later that season Ben Crackle, the longtime supervisor of AA facilities, completed "basketball and hand ball courts under the west shelf."[88] The total cost for these improvements was $55,589, all paid from football revenue.[89]

Though Illinois would not win the national championship in 1928, it did have another outstanding year. The only loss was an away game in which the Michigan Wolverines edged out the Illini by one field goal. That final score was especially painful because the Wolverines had entered the game having lost four consecutive matches. Nevertheless, the Fighting Illini did win the Big Ten Conference with a 7–1 overall record and was ranked

seventh in the nation.[90] Another triumphant season may have assisted Kinley in securing BOT approval in January 1929 for replacing the south horseshoe temporary wooden bleachers with new concrete tiered seating. Holabird and Root (formerly Holabird and Roche), the original architectural firm for Memorial Stadium, were hired to produce a design that would wrap up the overwhelming majority of the original concept.[91] The firm was also commissioned to plan the long-postponed skating rink, which would be constructed on land acquired by the AA from $37,248 in football revenue (Figure 5.13 and Figure 5.14).[92]

The ongoing triumphs of the football program, along with a steady fulfillment of subscription payments, finally enabled the Stadium to turn the financial corner. By mid-September 1929, the *Daily Illini* announced that not only had debt been reduced to $32,000 but new subscriptions would no longer be accepted. An end had finally come to one of the most effervescent periods of student, alumni, and community energy and generosity.[93]

Just in time for the Illini to host Army in 1929, the south-side horseshoe seating for 9,771 fans went up. The sections cantilevered out and over the track, which meant that they did not interfere with the ground plane. For the highly anticipated Army game, wooden bleachers with an additional 1,500 seats were constructed from the ground plane up to the end of the south-side cantilever.[94] The 17–7 defeat of the Army team would draw the largest audience of the season and the second-largest crowd to that point: 68,798 in attendance.[95] The Illini winning streak continued with only a 7–0 loss coming in an away game at Northwestern University's Dyche Stadium and a 7–7 tie with the University of Iowa's Hawkeyes. The loss to Northwestern would also mark the beginning of a four-game losing streak in the rivalry.

The 1930s

The October 1929 stock market crash brought the remarkable Roaring Twenties to an end. Economist Gene Smiley summarizes the United States' robust economic growth during that decade: "Real GNP growth during the 1920s was relatively rapid, 4.2 percent a year from 1920 to 1929. . . . Real GNP per capita grew 2.7

Figure 5.13
Aerial photograph showing end zone improvements. Courtesy of the University of Illinois Department of Intercollegiate Athletics Archives.

percent per year between 1920 and 1929."[96] The early 1930s saw a deep contraction in the economy. In 1930, it contracted 8.5%; in 1931, it shrank another 6.4%, but in 1932 came the harshest reduction: a crushing 12.9%. The economy would rebound and then stabilize by the end of the decade. Then, because of the United States' entry into WWII, the economy would once again experience an explosive growth rate.[97]

In parallel with these financial struggles, the 1930s would prove to be a tumultuous time for the AA and the University of Illinois football program. Whereas the 1929 season had ended with a winning record of 6–1–1, in 1930 the Illini finished with their first losing

season since 1922 at 3–5. That season was also the end of another remarkable streak: from the start of the 1927 season until October 18, 1930, the Illini would either win or tie every single home game, a run of seventeen undefeated games. The only 1930 conference victory came against the Maroons, 28–0. The 1931 season, with an overall record of 2–6 and not a single conference victory, was the low-water mark of Zuppke's coaching tenure. One reason for this trend was the changing nature of college football, particularly the introduction of a controversial practice: student athlete recruitment.

Bringing in more talented athletes would be crucial. The Depression had not spared the University, and both

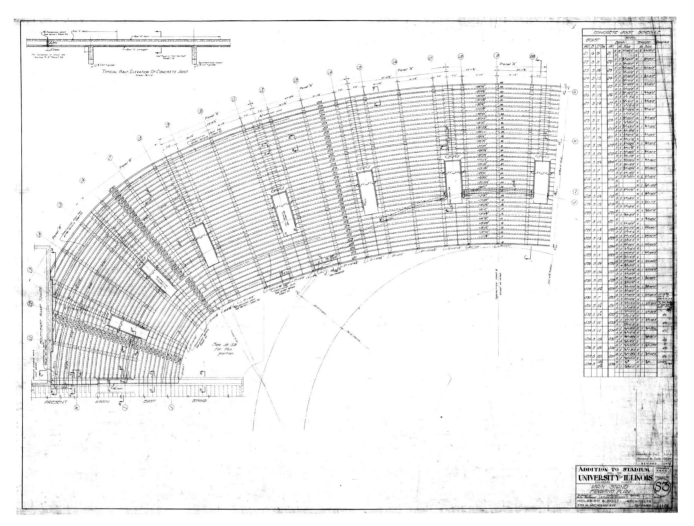

Figure 5.14
Construction document by Holabird and Root of the concrete horseshoe construction. Courtesy of the University of Illinois Archives.

tax receipts and enrollment were down. Whereas 13,467 students enrolled for the 1930 school year, by 1931 the number had shrunk to 12,814, a drop of 4.84%.[98] By the end of spring semester 1932, nearly 1,600 additional students had dropped out. For fall 1933, the downward trend continued and hit the lowest enrollment level at only 10,675 students—a whopping 20.7% decline.[99] Many students, including athletes, left school to seek work to support themselves and their families. This put sports programs at most schools at a disadvantage, because since the NCAA's founding in 1906, a scholarship or any other form of compensation was seen as tantamount to a salary—and therefore antithetical to the spirit of amateurism.[100] Educational institutions across the country

had deployed various tactics to recruit the best talent, often skirting NCAA rules or finding loopholes. This included finding students paid jobs during the semester or making covert under-the-table payments.

Under Huff's guidance and donor Avery Brundage's influence, Illinois adhered closely to the NCAA's rules. After all, Brundage had pushed for the Olympics to be an amateur-only sporting competition, deeming any form of remuneration cause for disqualification. Schools, however, began to experience a talent drain as the Depression continued. To reverse the trend, the Southeastern Conference (SEC) in 1935 "decided to allow athletes to receive normal student aid, including tuition, books, and room and board."[101] While the debate about compensating student athletes was ongoing, the Big Ten Conference under the leadership of John Griffiths led a large anti-scholarship faction that pushed the NCAA in 1935 to officially ban the practice. Because there was no way to enforce the ruling, the SEC could nevertheless fully employ this recruiting strategy.

With this disadvantage, the start of the decade had been rough for the Fighting Illini with two losing seasons in a row, but in 1932 the team course corrected and finished with a 5–4 record. Even so longtime coach Amos A. Stagg stepped down. Among the highlights of that season was when Northwestern's Ollie Olson set the still-standing record for the longest punt at Memorial Stadium with a booming kick that traveled 88 yards. Ultimately the Illini would lose the game with a disheartening score of 26–0. The next season showed more improvement with a 5–3 record and wins at home against the University of Wisconsin Badgers and the University of Chicago Maroons but a loss to Michigan's Wolverines. The 1934 season was the high point of the decade with only one loss (7–1), this time to the Wisconsin Badgers in an away game. Despite defeating the Ohio State Buckeyes at Memorial Stadium and possessing an identical overall record, Illinois would finish third in the Big Ten, behind Ohio State, because the Buckeyes had one more conference win than Illinois.

Perhaps feeling vindicated because the team's 1934 season had been so victorious, Huff and Zuppke continued to eschew the use of student scholarships or any other compensation to attract and retain talented student athletes. Then in 1935, amid the scholarship debate, Illinois tumbled down the rankings with a losing record of 3–5, but were at least victorious over a visiting Michigan is a low scoring game, 3-0. Even after the losing 1935 season, Huff and Zuppke held true to their position, refusing to recruit. The next year would be the last season Illinois achieved a winning record for some time; from 1937 to 1941 (Zuppke's last season), the Illini would at best log a .500 season record.

Huff's Death

On September 30, 1936, George Huff, longtime director of the AA, finally hung up his cleats when the BOT granted him a year's leave of absence. Since a trip to London in 1926, Huff's health had been steadily declining. Huff checked himself into Champaign's Carle Memorial Hospital, and at 10:27 a.m. on October 1, he died from complications from a surgery earlier in the week to remove part of his stomach in an effort to treat his ulcers.[102]

On the following Saturday, 9,000 Boy Scouts and 1,000 Girl Scouts from Illinois and western Indiana arrived at the Stadium for Scout Day, which Huff had organized ten years earlier. Before the kickoff, as had become tradition, the troops and Champaign and Urbana high school bands paraded from the Armory to the Stadium. The *Daily Illini* noted that

[s]couts taking part in this parade were admitted free to the Illinois-Washington game.

Marching, troop by troop and council by council, each troop and council bearing their colorful insignia, the scouts filed into the Stadium. Their numbers quite compactly filled the entire section allotted to them.

Another section of the scouts took part in a flag raising ceremony.[103]

As a testament to Huff's prominence, before the coin toss, all those in attendance stood in silence as troops lowered the US flag to half-mast.[104] Then the football team walked onto the field and, together with the audience, sang *Dear Illinois*.[105] In an apt conclusion to the day, the Fighting Illini beat Washington University 13–7.

Fittingly, Huff would be laid to rest in a grave in Mount Hope Cemetery across the street from the Stadium. As one way to acknowledge Huff's legacy, his headstone was situated to align with the 50-yard line of the Memorial Stadium's field. In the next months, discussions private and public were held about how to best honor his memory and legacy. As early as May 1921, while Huff was still alive, an opinion columnist in the *Daily Illini* called for Memorial Stadium's field to carry his name.[106] This naming proposal would be repeatedly denied by officials including campus architect James White, who made his feelings plain by noting he felt it "unwise to name anything for any living individual."[107] Eventually one of the grandest commendations for Huff would come on October 20, 1936, when the recently completed men's gymnasium was officially named after him (Figure 5.15).[108]

After Huff's death, some of his duties as director of the AA were given on an interim basis to Wendell S. "Weenie" Wilson, who soon found himself addressing a controversy inherited from Huff.[109] Since the beginning of the 1936 season, the role of scholarships—then called "subsidization" of student athletes—had ignited disputes among college athletic administrators. Huff "had fought so long against any hint of subsidization of athletes," and the new leaders had to determine the next course. At a Champaign Rotary dinner, Wilson deferred to Zuppke when asked about the recent push to allow

Figure 5.15
Huff and Zuppke grave sites in Roselawn Cemetery. Photograph by Kevin J. Hinders.

schools to use scholarships as a recruitment tool, noting with an exuberance that Illinois would "organize" itself and seek to maintain its high standards for student athletes.[110] Questions had erupted across the country not only about whether student athletes should be given scholarships but what the minimum academic standards should be for such students to be accepted to a college or university. Zuppke's unwillingness to dangle scholarships to recruit in the face of minimal enforcement of the ban set by the NCAA and the SEC's overt use of the tool, though not the only factor, played a significant role in the ensuing decline of the Fighting Illini.

With each losing season reducing fans' enthusiasm, attendance began to plummet. From 1924 to 1929, home game attendance had averaged 166,457 people for the entire season. The high points were 1925, with 192,165 ticket holders, and 1929, with 197,842. In contrast, from 1930 to 1941, the average season attendance for home games was just 112,658. This dramatic drop of just over 32% brought a devastating loss of revenue in already difficult times. During that period, 1933 had the lowest tally with 74,138 fans, which was the second-lowest (non-pandemic year) attendance ever recorded since 1924. The third lowest record was in 1941 when a mere 78,133 people went to Memorial Stadium all season long.[111]

Zuppke, renowned for his quick wit and pithy comments—known as Zuppkeisms—would demonstrate in the new decade the veracity of one of his most famous quips: "alumni are loyal if a coach wins all his games."[112] With game attendance continuing to slide and after compiling only three winning seasons in a span of twelve, Zuppke resigned and retired in 1941. Nearly two and a half decades later, in honor of his 29 years as head coach of the Fighting Illini, Memorial Stadium's playing field would be called Zuppke Field.

The Stadium's Impact on Diversity

Black Students

According to the 1870 census, Illinois' population of 2,539,891 included 28,762 African Americans, representing just over 1% of the total.[113] However, it was not until 1887 that Jonathan Rogan, the first African American student, enrolled at the University. Nine years later, in 1906, Maudelle Brown became the first African American woman registered as a student. Despite the growing African American population in Illinois, the number of African American students at the University remained significantly and disproportionately low through the 1930s, and this lack of diversity was reflected in the makeup of the athletic teams. Not until 1931, when Earl A. Jameson joined the team, did track and field have a Black athlete. For football, between 1900 and 1937 only two African Americans, Hiram Hannibal Wheeler and Roy Mercer Young, played, and although Alphonse Anders was the first Black player on a Zuppke-coached team, he did not take the field during a game.[114]

Perhaps the first Black athlete to get playing time for a Zuppke team was Isaiah "Ike" Hudson Owens. A defensive end, Owens enrolled for the fall 1940 semester but would not make the roster until 1941. When war broke out in December 1942, Owens enlisted, suspending his football career until his return in 1946. That year, Owens formed part of an Illini team that won the Big Ten Conference and beat the University of California, Los Angeles (UCLA) in the Rose Bowl. At the end of the season, Owens was voted by his teammates as the most valuable player. Across the state line, the *St. Louis Post-Dispatch* chided Missouri's segregationist universities with this detail:

> Ike Owens, hard tackling end, has been named by his fellow team mates, as 'the most valuable player' on the University of Illinois football squad this year. This fact should be more than a little interesting in Missouri. Under its new admission policy, St. Louis University would accept Ike Owens for academic study, but he could not get in at either Washington University or the University of Missouri. He is an American citizen yet his educational opportunities are restricted because of race. He does not have the approved color of skin.[115]

Three years after Zuppke stepped down from coaching in 1941, Claude Henry "Buddy" Young, another Black athlete, started at half back.[116] Like Owens, Young answered the call to serve his nation and returned after the war was over to play for the Illini. Part of that Rose Bowl team, Young led the offense and was named one of the most valuable players of the bowl game.

Jewish Students

About the same time that the first African American student enrolled at the University, Benjamin Bing, the first known Jewish student, graduated in the class of 1888. Even 20 years later, the University of Illinois was one of only a handful of higher learning institutions with a significant Jewish student population.[117] By 1913, the local chapter of the Menorah Society, a nonpartisan organization founded to provide Jewish students the resources to learn and transmit pride in their sociocultural and religious identity, was substantial enough to join with other chapters from across the country to found the Intercollegiate Menorah Society. Despite the presence of Jewish students on campus and greater awareness of their religious practices, antisemitism was still present. This stark truth was displayed in print when Samuel O. Shapiro wrote to the *Daily Illini* to request that athletic facilities, like tennis courts, be open to Jewish students on Sunday, as Jews observed the sabbath on Saturday. Thomas Arkle Clarke, the Dean of Men, replied, "This is a Christian country established upon Christian traditions and Christian principles . . . even when they may be opposed by foreigners or by those who would like to wipe out all our Christian traditions."[118]

One year later in 1918, B. Mittelman and G. Fleischman (both from the class of 1919) became the first known Jewish athletes and played on the basketball team.[119] With a growing Jewish population on campus, Rabbi Benjamin M. Frankel founded the first Hillel chapter in 1923. Hillel's mission is to generate a place where Jewish students, faculty, and alumni could openly embrace every aspect of Jewish life, and that welcoming space helped drive Jewish enrollment and increased numbers of Jewish student athletes. In 1924, Ralph Margolis became the first Jewish athlete to set foot on Memorial Stadium's gridiron for the Illini.

Margolis would go on to also letter in baseball in 1924, 1925, and 1926. In 1926, Chuck Kaufman earned a spot on the track and field team, helping the Fighting Illini earn what would have been a national championship had that year's intercollegiate meet been scored.[120]

Indirectly, the Stadium would play a major role in shaping not only Jewish student life at the University of Illinois but also the nation's built environment. In 1926, William "Bill" Pereira enrolled in the School of Architecture. A competitive intercollegiate fencer, he was also active in the Mask and Bauble drama club, directed theater works for the Hillel Players, and was a member of the Jewish fraternity Zeta Beta Tau.[121] Pereira, the son of Sephardic and Ashkenazi Jews who lived in Chicago, got involved with homecoming festivities in 1927 when the Homecoming Committee announced a competition in which eight cups would be awarded for the best-decorated fraternity and sorority houses. Pereira, also a drama club set designer, was a natural team leader for his fraternity.[122]

Pereira also joined Pierrot, a men's dramatic society, and made a surprising connection with another famed School of Architecture alumnus, Max Abramovitz (class of 1929). Abramovitz would later design Assembly Hall, currently known as State Farm Center, home of the Fighting Illini basketball teams. After Pereira graduated in 1930, he got his first job at Holabird and Root.[123] In still another twist, his experience in set design and familiarity with decoration that came at Illinois would prove to be invaluable in his career. Deep into the Great Depression, Pereira headed west to Los Angeles, where he started an impressive architectural career by decorating Paramount theater lobbies with a tight budget and then designing full theaters after the economy improved.

Clearly, the Stadium had begun to truly have an impact on the local, regional, and state-wide community. Traditions —many still practiced today— began to shape campus life and culture. The Stadium became more than a facility to host football games and other sporting events; it was a locus of community and regional activity, drawing people from all places to experience the University and its offerings. From hosting football games and state-wide high school marching band competitions to aiding the process of racial and religious integration, the Stadium was catalyzing major changes at the University of Illinois and across the state itself.

Notes

1 Illinois was selected by the College Football Researchers Association, Parke Davis (for *Spalding's Foot Ball Guide*), the Helms Athletic Foundation, and the National Championship Foundation (tie). Michigan was selected by only the National Championship Foundation (tie).

2 James Crusinberry, "67,000 to See Michigan and Illini Clash: Big Ten Title May Be the Prize to Victor," *Chicago Daily Tribune,* October 18, 1924, 17, https://www.proquest.com/historical-newspapers/67-000-see-michigan-illini-clash/docview/180639878/se-2.

3 Maureen M'Kernan, "New Illinois Stadium Riot of Color and Noise as Grange Runs over Wolverines," *Chicago Daily Tribune,* October 19, 1924, https://www.proquest.com/historical-newspapers/new-illinois-stadium-riot-color-noise-as-grange/docview/180622231/se-2.

4 M'Kernan, "New Illinois Stadium."

5 "67,205 Saw the Big Game," *MSN* 4, no. 11, November 2024, 1.

6 Crusinberry, "67,000 to See Michigan and Illini Clash."

7 M'Kernan, "New Illinois Stadium."

8 Marching Illini, "History & Tradition." Historical Timeline. https://www.marchingillini.com/history-tradition/timeline

9 LeBar and Paul, *College Sports on the Brink of Disaster*, 22.

10 Ibid, 23.

11 Blum and DeBruyne, *American War*, 2.

12 National Center for Immunization and Respiratory Diseases, "History of 1918 Flu Pandemic."

13 Sumner, "Sports in the 1920s."

14 Outdoor Media Buyers, "List."

15 "5,000,000 Attendance Record for 1923 Grid Season, Most Successful in History of Game," *Pittsburgh Gazette Times,* December 3, 1923, 13, https://www.proquest.com/historical-newspapers/december-3-1923-page-13-18/docview/1856144443/se-2.

16 NCAA, "2019 Football Attendance."

17 West Virginia Public Broadcasting, "October 8, 1921"; Old Radio, "October 28, 1922"; Federal Communications Commission, "History of Commercial Radio."

18 Sterling and Kittross, *Stay Tuned: A Concise History of American Broadcasting*, 62.

19 Covil, "Radio and Its Impact."

20 "Grange Leads Illinois to 36–0 Victory over Iowa," *Pittsburgh Gazette Times,* November 2, 1924, 64, https://www.proquest.com/historical-newspapers/november-2-1924-page-24-64/docview/1856178749/se-2.

21 NCAA, "Football Award Winners."

22 NCAA, "Football Bowl Subdivision Records," 115–16.

23 "Grid Notes on Illini," *DeKalb Daily Chronicle* 25, no. 240, September 17, 1925, 6.

24 UIHistories, "Men's New Gymnasium/Huff Hall."

25 "New Gymnasium to Seat 8,000 at Basket Contests," *Daily Illini* 55, no. 6, September 20, 1925, 9.

26 "Notre Dame–Illinois Game Would Be Best of Year, *Indianapolis Star,* November 4, 1924, 12, https://www.proquest.com/historical-newspapers/november-4-1924-page-12-20/docview/1889571689/se-2.

27 "Notre Dame Accepts Illinois Challenge for Game in 1925," *New York Herald Tribune,* December 6, 1924, 16, https://www.proquest.com/historical-newspapers/notre-dame-accepts-illinois-challenge-game-1925/docview/1113192472/se-2.

28 "Illinois Central to Run Specials to Illini Games," *Daily Illini* 55, no. 15, October 1, 1925, 1.

29 "Illinois Opens Football Season with Nebraska U," *Bureau County Tribune* 53, no. 38, September 18, 1925, 1.

30 Kostora, "25 Craziest Football Terms."

31 "Enrollment Is but 96 Short of Ten Thousand," *Daily Illini* 55, no. 12, September 27, 1925, 1.

32 "Illinois! Illinois! YOUR Alma Mater," *Daily Illini* 55, no. 1, September 15, 1925, 7.

33 "Young Men from This City Have Left for U. of I.," *DeKalb Daily Chronicle* 25, no. 243, September 21, 1925, 8.

34 "Wanted—a Cheer Leader," *Daily Illini* 55, no. 13, September 29, 1925, 4.

35 George A. Huff, "Sportsmanship at the Stadium," *Daily Illini* 55, no. 17, October 3, 1925, 4.

36 Frederic J. Frommer, "The Strange History of Beer—'That Wicked Brew'—and Washington Baseball," *Washington Post,* April 11, 2023, https://www.washingtonpost.com/sports/2023/04/11/mlb-beer-prohibition-clark-griffith/.

37 Thornton, "Alcohol Prohibition."

38 "Dedication of Stadium, Deaths, Rise of University Buildings, All Seen during Year of 1924," *Daily Illini* 54, no. 91, January 1, 1925, 1.

39 "Western Intercollegiate Football: An Effort to Remove Certain Objections," *Purdue Alumnus* 14, no. 1, October 1926, 7.

40 Gay, "George Huff."

41 George Huff, "Huff Tells Opinion on Stadium Location; Define Controversy," *Daily Illini* 51, no. 155, April 1, 1922, 1.

42 "Illinois Needs New Yells," *Daily Illini* 54, no. 9, September 25, 1924, 4.

43 "Illini Welcome Pow-Wow Set for Sept. 23," *Daily Illini* 55, no. 1, September 15, 1925, 1.

44 "Kinley Gives Ephebic Oath to Freshmen," *Daily Illini* 55, no. 16, October 2, 1925, 1.

45 "Boy Scouts of Illinois and Indiana Gather Here for Game," *Daily Illini* 55, no. 16, October 2, 1925, 8.

46 Noah Nelson, "Chief Illiniwek Remains Embedded in UI History," *Daily Illini,* April 21, 2020, https://dailyillini.com/opinions-stories/2020/04/21/opinion-chief-illiniwek-remains-embedded-in-ui-history/.

47 "Freshmen to Hold First Track Drill in Stadium Today," *Daily Illini* 54, no. 188, April 25, 1925, 6.

48 "May 3, 1925," *Indianapolis Star,* May 3, 1925, 26.

49 USA Track and Field, "Harry Gill."

50 "Eldorado Township, Danville Tie in State Title Prep Meet," *Chicago Daily Tribune,* May 17, 1925, 2.

51 "Interscholastic Circus," photo description, University of Illinois Archives, Urbana-Champaign, accessed August 12, 2023, https://archon.library.illinois.edu/archives/index.php?p=digitallibrary/digitalcontent&id=16336.

52 Jackson, "School Circus," 12.

53 "Attendance Mark Broken by 29,085," *Daily Illini* 54, no. 208, May 19, 1925, 8.

54 "Landscape Men Set Out Trees and Shrubbery," *Urbana Daily Courier* 48, no. 88, April 14, 1925, 8.

55 "Start 1925 with Your Stadium Payment!" *MSN* 4, no. 1, January 1925, 1.

56 James O'Donnell Bennett, "U. of I. Work Is Given Seal of Consecration," *Chicago Daily Tribune*, June 15, 1925, 4.

57 "Stadium Coffers Low—Collections Total but $4,757," *Daily Illini* 54, no. 177, April 12, 1925, 1.

58 "Start 1925 with Your Stadium Payment."

59 Ibid.

60 Bennett, "U. of I. Work."

61 Ibid.

62 "Ice Skating Rink," *MSN* 4, no. 4, August 1925, 4.

63 "Stadium Ledger," *MSN* 4, no. 4, August 1925, 3.

64 "Ice Skating Rink."

65 "Illinois Calls to You Stadium Builders," *MSN* 4, no. 5, October 1925, 1.

66 "The A.A. Family," *MSN* 5, no. 1, January 1926, 4.

67 "G. Huff Explains Where Athletic Receipts Will Go," *Urbana Daily Courier* 48, no. 276, December 29, 1925, 6.

68 Ibid.

69 "Prof. White Talks to Pan-Hellenic," *Daily Illini* 55, no. 130 February 16, 1926, 10.

70 "Concrete Used in Stadium Is of High Grade," *Daily Illini* 55, no. 174, April 9, 1926, 12.

71 "Stadium Pavements," *MSN* 5, no. 2, June 1926, 3.

72 "Stadium Ledger," *MSN* 5, no. 2, June 1926, 3; "Athletics," *MSN* 5, no. 2, June 1926, 2.

73 Rosebery, "University of Illinois Memorial Stadium." In *Directory of University of Illinois Men,* 1926, 47.

74 "Stadium Ledger," June 1926, 3.

75 "Tickets First to Paid-to-Daters," *MSN* 5, no. 2, June 1926, 4.

76 "Get Your Name on the Right Side," *MSN* 5, no. 2, June 1926, 3.

77 "Zupmen Open Football Drill for 1926 Campaign in the Morning," *Urbana Daily Courier* 49, no. 215, September 14, 1926, 6.

78 "Tobin Describes '26 Grid Profits in Alumni News," *Daily Illini* 56, no. 125, February 6, 1927, 2.

79 "Plans Being Made Now for Newest Feature for Fans," *Daily Illini* 56, no. 280, August 9, 1927, 6.

80 "Board Decides Stadium Can't Be Assessed," *Daily Illini* 56, no. 284, August 13, 1927, 3.

81 Illinois was selected by the Helms Athletic Foundation, the National Championship Foundation, and the College Football Researchers Association. See NCAA, "Championship History."

82 BOT, meeting minutes, August 19, 1927, 427.

83 BOT, meeting minutes, September 27, 1927, 439.

84 "Gate receipts," Courtesy of DIA Archives.

85 BOT, meeting minutes, April 12, 1928, 614.

86 BOT, meeting minutes, August 19, 1927, 427, and September 27, 1927, 439.

87 "Open Hospital Rooms," *Daily Illini* 58, no. 10, September 19, 1928, 12.

88 "Crackle Cares for University Athletic Plant," *Daily Illini* 58, no. 43, October 27, 1928, 9.

89 "I-M Sports Take Slice of Profits," *Daily Illini* 58, no. 125, February 3, 1929, 6.

90 "Dickinson Rating Awards National Title to Trojans," *Daily Illini* 58, no. 79, December 9, 1928, 8.

91 Ibid.

92 "Statement of Memorial Stadium Fund as of December 31, 1928," in BOT, meeting minutes, January 9, 1929, 108; "I-M Sports Take Slice."

93 "Memorial Edifice Houses Many Sports; Improvements Made This Summer," *Daily Illini* 59, no. 8, September 15, 1929, 9.

94 "Stadium to Seat Close to 68,000 for Army Game," *Daily Illini* 59, no. 5, September 12, 1929, 6.

95 Fighting Illini Football, "Illini Football Attendance Records."

96 Smiley, "U.S. Economy in the 1920s."

97 O'Neill, "Annual Growth of Real GDP."

98 University of Illinois, "Registrar's Report: Comparative Enrollment by Curricula, Winter Session, 1930–31 and 1931–32," University Enrollment File, https://digital.library.illinois.edu/items/4c9a7440-1469-0133-a7c8-0050569601ca-2.

99 University of Illinois, "Registrar's Report: Comparative Enrollment by Curricula, Winter Session, 1932–33 and 1933–34," University Enrollment File, https://digital.library.illinois.edu/items/4ccc8030-1469-0133-a7c8-0050569601ca-3.

100 Staples, "History of Recruiting."

101 Scott, *SEC Football*, 37.

102 Athletic Director Dies Following Long Illness; Funeral Is Tomorrow," *Daily Illini* 66, no. 19, October 2, 1936, 1.

103 "Boy, Girl Scouts Visit Twin Cities," *Daily Illini* 66, no. 21, October 4, 1936, 4.

104 "University's Last Tribute Paid 'G' Huff," *Daily Illini* 66, no. 21, October 4, 1936, 1.

105 Ibid.

106 "Dope of the Day," *Daily Illini* 50, no. 177, May 5, 1921, 3.

107 Letter from James M. White to H. S. Green, November 22, 1922, Facilities and Services Archive.

108 David Hoff, "But, Can They Take It?" *Daily Illini* 66, no. 35, October 21, 1936, 5.

109 "Huff Gets Leave," *Daily Illini* 66, no. 18, October 2, 1936, 1.

110 "Zuppke Answers Question of Future Course in Ringing Address at Rotary Dinner," *Daily Illini* 66, no. 63 November 24, 1936, 1.

111 Fighting Illini Football, "Illini Football Attendance Records."

112 National Football Foundation, "Bob Zuppke."

113 US Census Bureau, *1870 Census*, 3, 5.

114 Spivey and Jones, "Intercollegiate Athletic Servitude," 943.

115 "Ike Owens: Most Valuable Player," *St. Louis Post-Dispatch,* November 26, 1947, 14.

116 National Football Foundation, "NFF Salutes the Black History Trailblazers."

117 Solberg, "Early Years," 216.

118 Ibid., 222.

119 "Reverse English," *Hillel Bulletin* 3, no. 9 February 17, 1927, 4.

120 Hill, "1927 NCAA Men."

121 "Dramatists Lay Plans for New Hillel Society," *Hillel Bulletin* 4, no. 1, October 4, 1928, 1.

122 "Houses Plan Homecoming Decorations," *Daily Illini* 57, no. 39, October 25, 1927, 1.

123 Los Angeles Conservancy, "William Pereira."

From World War II to 1960

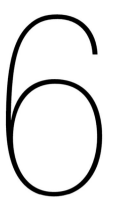

Introduction

On the morning of December 7, 1941, just before 8am Hawai'ian local time, an Imperial Japanese strike force that included six first-line airplane carriers launched a surprise air raid on the US Naval Base located in Pearl Harbor, Hawai'i. The next day, before a joint session of Congress, President Franklin D. Roosevelt obtained a joint congressional declaration of war. It had been just over 23 years, but the US was once more in a global conflict. Now a central part of campus life, Memorial Stadium would serve a vital role in the war effort, demonstrating remarkable robustness and flexibility to accommodate uses from temporary soldier housing to naval engine training workshops.

This era also marked the beginning of sustained integration on the football field, when Henry "Buddy" Young, a Black student, started the 1944 season and went on to become one of the most memorable players ever to wear the orange and blue. Once the war was over, millions of Americans who had served their country returned to the US, and approximately 2,300,000 veterans took advantage of the Serviceman's Readjustment Act of 1944, commonly known as the GI Bill, to attend college.[1] The University of Illinois at Urbana-Champaign greatly benefited from this program: through the war's end to 1960 "enrollment more than doubled."[2] Not surprisingly, student housing soon proved insufficient, and the Stadium became an effective short-term solution.

Like the postwar 1920s, the 1950s marked a period of economic stability and growth. And like the impact of radio during the Golden Age of Sports, the introduction of television broadcasting across American households in the 1950s would change the way fans approached football. Television also introduced the space age to American households, and images of Soviet satellites and cosmonauts, alongside American astronauts and spaceships, deeply influenced popular culture and locally affected the proposed design of Assembly Hall, the next anchor for the campus sports complex. Finally, the Fighting Illini football team would rack up multiple winning seasons under Coach Ray Eliot and confirmed Illinois' status as one of the premier athletic programs not only in the Midwest, not just in the Big Ten Conference, but in the country.

Memorial Stadium during World War II

The West Great Hall

When students returned for the spring 1942 semester after the attack on Pearl Harbor, preparations were already underway to address low enrollment. With the institution of Selective Service in 1940, civilian enrollment figures for the Urbana-Champaign campus fell from a high of 12,624 in 1938–1939 to a low of 5,824 in 1943–1944.[3] The *Illinois Alumni News* reported an even lower civilian enrollment of only 4,451 in its March 1944 issue.[4] Of these 5,824 students, 3,429 were women (Figure 6.1).

For most of 1941, Americans wondered if and when the US would enter the war. Letters to the *Daily Illini* revealed a student body concerned and engaged in public

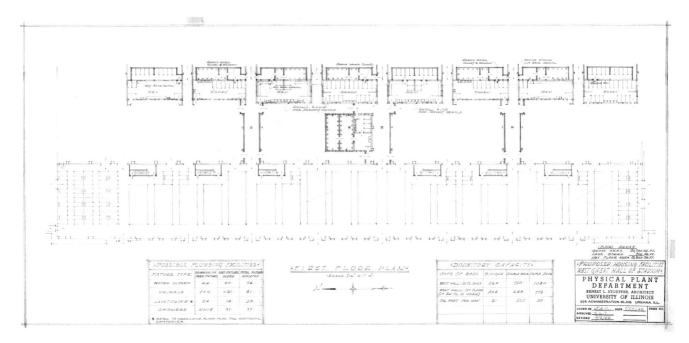

Figure 6.1
Memorial Stadium West Great Hall housing proposal, February 6, 1942. Courtesy of the University of Illinois Archives.

debate. But not only had the bombing of Pearl Harbor ended the country's neutrality, it had also claimed the first of 738 Illini lives lost during the war when William Schick, a flight surgeon with the medical corps, died.[5] To preserve the calm on campus, President Arthur Cutts Willard, who had replaced Acting President Arthur Hill Daniels in 1934, and other administrators held meetings and information sessions with students throughout December 1941.[6] At the same time, the University prepared for major logistical challenges. At its first meeting of 1942, the BOT approved a policy for sanctioned leaves of absence to ensure an orderly exit and eventual return of faculty, staff, and students.[7] For its part, the Athletic Association (AA) coordinated with leadership to review what facilities could be made available to support the war's needs and worked to transform them.

As early as January 1942, the University explored inserting a platform above the ground floor of the West Great Hall of Memorial Stadium to accommodate barracks-style housing that included single, double, and triple bunk arrangements. As a single-use space, it could accommodate a maximum of 1,080 people, but if a dining hall were added above as a mezzanine, it could be an additional 972 people.[8] While this dormitory project

was not executed, other plans were completed during the fall of 1941 and into the spring of 1942. In one improvement, the AA connected the Stadium to the University heating plant.[9] In late March 1942, the US Navy announced the need for a signal school. Almost immediately forty fraternities, the Old Gym (today Kenney Hall), and the Gymnasium Annex were converted into dormitories[10]; the Illini Union Ballroom became a mess hall; and ship masts were installed in Illinois Field, the football team's old playing field, so that navy trainees could receive "realistic instruction."[11]

While the great west hall did not initially become housing, early on it was considered for a space From December and into early January, the University of Illinois was in discussions with the Navy about providing a facility to train naval cadets to operate large diesel engines.[12] The military viewed the University as an ideal host institution because by request it had "increased the amount of physical education required of all male students as a means for conditioning them for military service."[13] By the second half of the summer, the navy was operating a diesel engine school on campus. Naval ships of the period utilized propellers, known as screws, powered by enormous diesel engines housed with fuel lines, high-pressure boilers,

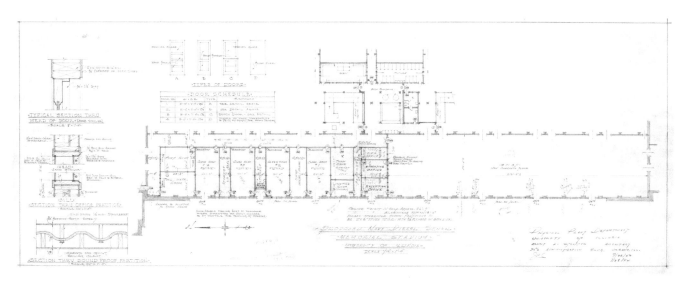

Figure 6.2
Naval Diesel School fit out, July 28, 1942. Courtesy of the University of Illinois Archives.

combustion chambers, cylinders, pistons, and crankshafts that transferred all the power to the water-immersed propellers. At that time, few buildings in the US possessed the size and accessibility necessary to hold these enormous diesel engines, much less transform them into instruction halls. For the navy, the "cavernous" Memorial Stadium was a natural choice for its Naval Diesel School (NDS) program.[14] Project drawings were implemented by September 14, 1942, the opening day of the fall semester (Figure 6.2), in time to welcome up to six hundred commissioned officers who would participate in the NDS.[15]

The northern half of the West Great Hall was used for offices, a reception area, classrooms, storage, a pump room, and a tool crib. The southern half was designated the shop space to take advantage of the room's largely unobstructed expanse. To deal with the constant vibration generated by the diesel engines and prevent the concrete slab from cracking, the shop area received a new concrete floor. As support for the war's needs continued, additional changes and improvements were carried out: a new cooling system and the installation of a separate, smaller, machine shop with a press, lathe, and worktables. Under time pressure, the University fronted the money to make these modifications, allocating just under $62,000.[16] The Department of Defense then reimbursed the University and proceeded to cover all expenses associated with fitting out the NDS.

Faced with limited naval recruits, Congress lowered the age of military service to 18 years in November 1942. Then in December, it enacted various incentive programs for the army and navy to get recent high school graduates with officer potential to enlist. For the navy, the V-12 program instituted across 131 colleges and universities—including at Illinois—allowed these graduates to enroll in college courses as they underwent military training.[17] Eventually, the V-12 program was rolled into the Naval Reserve Officers Training Corps, which would take a prominent role at football games.

Another example of the war's effect on the campus was the push to build an airport that would serve the region's transportation, research, and connectivity needs. At the end of August 1942, the BOT approved a funding proposal for facilities that according to the *New York Times* would "develop a research and educational program on the influence of atmospheric environment on humans, including problems relating to aviation, submarine and military medicine."[18] Despite unanimous consent of the legislature in late April 1943 to provide $250,000 to purchase 800 acres south of Champaign for the site,[19] a freeze on construction delayed the dedication until October 26, 1945.[20] The new airport, one of the few capable of handling airplanes up to 50,000 pounds in gross weight, tied University research directly with the NDS and other military programs across campus. Once in operation, the airport also played an instrumental role in expanding the football schedule to feature foes from further afield who had a new way to travel. Football was becoming a truly national game, and Illinois helped its rise to prominence.

In the Stadium's Shadow: Stadium Terrace and the Parade Ground Units

To show support for the country's role in the global conflict, in March 1943 the BOT approved making land available near the Stadium's terraces for victory gardens. The BOT estimated that 118 lots, each measuring 2,500 square feet, would be available for rent at $5 for the growing season.[21] In addition to the current student body, that food would be needed for more people. In August 1944, in response to a survey, 70% of the 4,000 respondents signaled a desire to return to school, and the Post-War Planning Commission, in coordination with the Building

Program Committee, would need to regroup to address the influx of returning members of the service.[22] It was resolved to ask the State of Illinois' General Assembly to fund the construction of new housing.

Until that could be built, the West Great Hall, terraces, and Illini Village were tapped for temporary housing to manage the shortage (Figure 6.3). With no more need for the NDS, the West Great Hall was cleaned and remodeled. From 1946 to 1947, about three hundred male students lived in a barracks-type arrangement. To provide further relief, the federal government shipped 270 prefabricated homes from nearby Charlestown, Indiana, and placed them on two sites (Figure 6.4): Stadium Terrace, just west of First Street and south of Gregory Avenue, and at Illini Village, located east of Mount Hope Cemetery between Pennsylvania Avenue and Florida Avenue (now occupied by the Pennsylvania and Florida Avenue Residence Halls). In addition, the

Figure 6.3
Unloading the prefabricated Stadium Terrace units. Courtesy of the University of Illinois Archives.

Figure 6.4
Stadium Terrace looking southeast toward Memorial
Stadium. Courtesy of the University of Illinois
Archives.

Figure 6.5
Parade Grounds Units west of the men's dormitories
and north of Memorial Stadium with Stadium Terrace
to the west. Courtesy of the University of Illinois
Archives.

Parade Grounds became the home of the aptly named
Parade Ground Units, makeshift constructions on the
site that later would be home to modern residence halls
(Figure 6.5). Though they were intended as a stopgap
measure, many of these temporary dormitories were in
use until the early 1960s.

The area south of the men's dormitories was scheduled for additional permanent housing; the first of four
dormitories constructed was Flagg Hall, which also
provided dining facilities for the Parade Ground Units.
The site between Euclid and Fourth Street was subsequently filled with Noble, Taft, and Van Doren Halls, as
funding became available. The land around the Stadium
that the AA had coveted for ballfields, courts, and fieldhouses would instead be urgently developed for housing
(Figure 6.6).

The Stadium as Patriotic Venue

In the second week of June 1942, with the West Great
Hall under renovation, the University prepared to
receive Illinois' Governor Dwight H. Green. Green's
attendance at Memorial Stadium was the culmination of
the Dedication to Victory campaign, a weeklong series

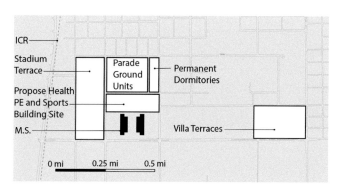

Figure 6.6
Post-war housing diagram. Diagram by Kevin J.
Hinders.

of events to energize support for the war.[23] Nearly 1,500
people from military and patriotic groups including the
Chanute field band, Reserve Officer Training Corps
members, and navy signal core trainees marched into
the Stadium.[24] Once the parade finished, Green spoke
about the January 1, 1942, joint declaration by leaders
from the US, the United Kingdom, the Union of Soviet
Socialist Republics, and China to establish the United
Nations. Thereafter, over the public address system
Associate Professor E. H. Reigner named all twenty-six
Allied nations while Girl Scouts presented their flags.

An estimated 10,000 people were expected to gather at the west stands to observe Flag Day, but more than 15,000 people attended the patriotic display, including former President Kinley in one of his final public appearances.[25]

Sports at the Stadium during World War II

After Zuppke's 1941 resignation on the heels of a devastating 27–0 loss to Northwestern, Raymond "Ray" Eliot (born Raymond Eliot Nusspickel) took the helm (Figure 6.7). Eliot had played under Zuppke between 1930 and 1931 and after graduation coached the Blueboys of Illinois College, the same college from which Jonathan Baldwin Turner had launched his push for land-grant universities that led directly to the founding of the University of Illinois. At Illinois College Eliot was an assistant coach during the 1932 and 1933 seasons and then became head coach for 1934–1936. After the 1936 season, Eliot was hired by Zuppke as the Illini line coach. On Zuppke's departure, Eliot's appointment as the head coach was approved by the BOT on February 14.[26]

The first time Eliot met the football team was on the first day of spring football practice, a cold March 1, 1942.[27] He ran basic drills under the east stands that would make up part of spring training for a full six weeks. That fall, for the first time the Big Ten Conference approved the option to schedule ten games per season. Instead of dropping football like fifty colleges and universities did in 1942, Illinois took advantage of the new rule to add a maximum of two games to the season. And what a season it was: the Fighting Illini played seven home games and were matched up with no less than five teams that were either ranked at some point or would end the season ranked by the Associated Press (AP) poll in the top 25.[28] Moreover, not only did Illinois play its traditional conference rivals like Ohio State, Michigan, and Northwestern, but the Fighting Irish of Notre Dame also came to Urbana-Champaign. The season additionally featured two military service teams: the Great Lakes Navy Bluejackets and the Camp Grant Warriors—slotted for those two extra games. Scheduling the games may have started as a show of support for the American armed forces, but these service teams were

highly ranked in the polls and were frequently superior to the college teams. This was because their rosters were often loaded with skilled college and professional football players serving in the military.

Eliot's ascent to head coach signaled a change in recruitment practices that more closely resembled those in the SEC. Now able to openly entice student athletes with scholarships and other NCAA approved incentives, Eliot coordinated with AA Director Douglas Mills to locate talented players. Almost immediately these efforts paid off. Just before the fall football season began, on September 5, 1942, Eliot oversaw a "[l]avishly acclaimed" group of returning and incoming football players during practices (Figure 6.7).[29]

Once the 1942 season began, Eliot's team fared better than Zuppke's last one, opening with a pounding victory over the University of South Dakota (46–0) and proceeding to win the next three games—including 12–7 over Iowa, then ranked 13 by the AP. However, the first loss of the season would come next at home against the Fighting Irish, 21–14. In the second to last game of the season, Illinois would lose at home 6–0 against the Great Lakes Navy Bluejackets. As a testament to their football prowess, the Bluejackets would finish the season by tying Notre Dame 8–8 at a game at Soldier

Figure 6.7
Coach Ray Eliot with players, 1946. *Left to right:* Paul Patterson, William Huber, Claude "Buddy" Young, Eliot, and Robert Cunz. Courtesy of the University of Illinois Department of Intercollegiate Athletics Archives.

Field in Chicago. In the end, however, Eliot's Illini finished with a 6–4 winning record, just outside of the AP top 25, but good enough to be ranked 11 under the criteria of Litkenhous Ratings.[30] Home attendance had totaled 96,302, including a single-game high of 43,476 against Notre Dame.[31] The burgeoning audience got a boost from the newly designated cheer section inside the Stadium. For all home games, 420 seats on the west side between the 35 and 45-yard lines were set aside for students to enthusiastically cheer on the home team.

Whereas the Fighting Illini had a winning record in 1942, the 1943 season ended miserably with a 3–7 tally. The Illini defeated conference foes Wisconsin and Iowa and logged one out-of-conference win against the University of Pittsburgh's Panthers. Losses included games against eventual national champion Notre Dame and two service teams. Most concerning, however, was that attendance for a home game never broke 16,000 people, and the total for the entire season was just 32,406. This was the lowest attendance recorded since the 1918 season when multiple games during the influenza pandemic were played with no audience.[32] For the 1944 season, the Illini eked out a winning record—led by Claude "Buddy" Young, whose 5′4″ stature and blazing speed earned him the moniker the Bronze Bullet plus records in track and field events. In 1944 alone, Young scored ten touchdowns.[33] Despite losses to Notre Dame, Ohio State, and Michigan, the Fighting Illini finished at 5–4–1, the tie coming with the vaunted Great Lakes Navy Bluejackets, and finished the year ranked 18 by the AP. His teammates would name Young the most valuable player. The outlook worsened in the 1945 season, however, when Illinois finished 2–6–1. At least some losses were close—seven points or less against four teams—to go with the tie to Wisconsin and wins against Iowa and the University of Pittsburgh.

A WWII Legacy That Still Resonates—Literally

To face the growing threat of Japan's military, the US Navy had ordered six Iowa-class battleships in 1939, but only four were built, and the planned *USS Illinois* (BB-65) was never completed. The *Illinois* would have been a 45,000-long-ton ship, with four screws, measuring

Figure 6.8
The bell cast for the *USS Illinois.* Courtesy of the University of Illinois Department of Intercollegiate Athletics Archives.

over 887 feet (270.4 meters) long, or approximately 2.5 football fields. To raise funds for the massive vessel, a pig from West Frankfort, Illinois, named King Neptune crossed the state from one fundraising event to another. In all, King Neptune helped collect over $19,000,000 toward construction of the *USS Illinois.*[34] On December 6, 1942, almost a year to the day of Pearl Harbor, the *Illinois'* keel was laid down. On August 11, 1945, three days before the official Japanese surrender, construction was indefinitely suspended. When the war ended, just over 20% of the ship had been completed.[35] By 1958 it had been completely scrapped, and its materials were scavenged for other naval projects. Although the *Illinois* was never completed, the US Navy saw fit to cast its bell and presented it as a gift to the University and the school's Naval Reserve Officer's Training Corps. Students in the program now haul it onto the field for Illini games and ring it after the Illini score points and clang the accumulated total points after each score (Figure 6.8).[36]

Memorial Stadium After WWII

Post-war Racial Integration

When George Dinsmore Stoddard took over as president in 1946, he had to steer the University through the adjustments of a post-war world. In all, 20,276 Illinois students, alumni, staff, and faculty had served, and thousands did return to their studies. The state population had dropped from 7,995,000 in 1941 to 7,601,000 by 1945 with so many Illinoisians serving abroad, but the 1946 census revealed a new record high population of 8,155,000 residents.[37] Bolstered by this base and the GI Bill, enrollment numbers at Illinois would swell. Whereas civilian enrollment for the fall 1944 semester was 7,344 students, total enrollment for fall 1945 more than doubled to 14,955.[38] Just like the post-WWI euphoria that permeated 1919, great enthusiasm and optimism prevailed for most, but not all, on campus at this time. Despite the post-war promises of greater opportunities, exclusion of Black students remained a significant problem.

Movements to end segregation and other discriminatory practices had begun to consolidate in the 1930s and led to the formation of the Congress for Racial Equality (CORE) by James Farber at the University of Chicago in 1942.[39] Soon thereafter, a chapter opened off campus to serve University of Illinois students. As WWII drew to a close in the spring of 1945, attention soon focused on addressing challenges closer to home. Amongst the thousands of veteran Illinois GIs, were a significant number of Black African Americans, who having served their country, returned to find a country, state, and local community that readily discriminated against them. Bolstered by the influx of African American veterans, students inspired by CORE formed the Student-Community Interracial Committee of Urbana-Champaign (S-CIC).

Central to S-CIC's mission was to desegregate restaurants, theaters, movie houses, and other public venues. After some success in integrating commercial establishments, the S-CIC shifted to a more educational role, which generated internal strife about its direction.[40] Eventually the S-CIC dissolved and reorganized as the Student Community Human Relations Council in 1951.[41] This new incarnation retained educational aspects from its predecessor but returned to street activism, engaging with commercial establishments like barber shops that continued to discriminate against African American students. Activism from such groups had a powerful influence on the University, which acknowledged in June 1946 that systemic problems with campus housing could lead to racial conflict.[42] After multiple meetings with student groups like the S-CIC, the BOT issued a statement opposing racial discrimination:

> The Board of Trustees of the University of Illinois has already expressed its general policy on the question of equal and fair treatment for all citizens of this country irrespective of race, creed, or color. In carrying out this policy the University fully appreciates the fact that it has certain responsibilities for action. In addition to the many specific actions it can take and does take as the need may arise, there are four large programs which would substantially modify the circumstances which now give rise to race tensions on and near the campus and to actions which might appear to be discriminatory.[43]

Although the University had taken a major, and public, step in the right direction and signaled that it would lead in the fight for integration, that same year Jean Knapp, an undergraduate at Illinois, noted that "Negroes are not allowed on baseball, basketball, tennis, and swimming teams." This ban persisted until 1957.[44]

Expansion to Midcentury

Although the war had ended, its effects reverberated in 1946. A total of twenty-eight athletes who had lettered in a sport had died during the war, and the AA planned to honor these students before the October 6 game against the Indiana Hoosiers. After the traditional flag ceremony, the names of the 28 student athletes were announced, and then the flags were lowered to half-mast.[45] That evening after the 0–6 loss, Illinois student athletes, coaches, boosters, and select members of the community gathered for a banquet at which Athletic Director Douglas R. Mills presented Coach Eliot with a bronze plaque inscribed with the names of the fallen.[46]

That year the Stadium also amplified its standing as a bulwark of community life not merely for sports but for regional culture as a whole. The venue got its first visit by the Illinois Farm Festival, and on the evening of August 29, Memorial Stadium hosted one of the most colorful and legendary events ever to take place within its confines: a hog-calling contest.[47] Meanwhile student veterans living in the temporary quarters in the West Great Hall—fittingly dubbed Stadium Hall—did not feel so welcome, and from their sense of isolation requested "immediate action in obtaining adequate transportation facilities to and from campus. Most of us are veterans and feel that we've done enough walking in service to last us for quite some time. During the winter months it will be especially difficult for most of us to attend classes."[48] In response bus service to and from the Stadium was instituted, and in this way, the Stadium catalyzed the public transportation system for the entire community.

With the energy from change in the air, the Fighting Illini would reach a new milestone. Led by Buddy Young on offense and Isaiah Owens on defense, the team amassed eight wins to finish the season at 8–2. The lone home loss of 26–6 against Notre Dame was played before one of the largest crowds ever: 75,119.[49] Though today this number is just outside of the top ten of the most attended home games, it would be the largest audience until 1982.[50] Though the 1946 season did not feature any service teams, the additional games meant that schools could schedule more in-conference games and boost the possibility of a conference championship—an increasingly necessary step toward an invitation to a bowl game and more revenue.

Success on the field naturally led to renewed student fervor. The Block I cheering club was revived in 1946 when the "War Whoops pep club launched a new Block I, numbering 884 students."[51] However, alumnus John Franch credits Barbara Shade, Block I's primary leader, with introducing in 1948 the distinctive card routines to the Block I repertoire, which she had learned at the University of Southern California. Unfortunately, decades later the Block I would once again cease to meet.

Having completed an impressive season, the Fighting Illini accepted an invitation to their first-ever postseason bowl game to battle the Pacific Coast Conference's champion, UCLA, at the Rose Bowl. On January 1, 1947,

in front of a crowd of 90,000, Illinois won 45–14. After rushing 103 yards and scoring a touchdown, Young was named the game's most valuable player along with teammate Julius Rykovich. When the Fighting Illini, a Big Nine conference team (the University of Chicago had withdrawn from the Big Ten in 1939), and Pacific Coast Conference member UCLA met at the Rose Bowl, it marked the start of an official interconference agreement that matched a top finisher from each league at the game for nearly 60 years.

But after the 1947 season the Illini would finish 5–3 and unranked by the AP. Among the losses was a 14–7 contest against the Michigan Wolverines, who would go on to an unblemished 10–0 record and be ranked second by the AP. Just two years removed from their Rose Bowl victory, Illinois would suffered a losing season, winning just three games and losing six. The Illini, however, were able to defeat Kansas State University, Purdue University, and the University of Iowa Hawkeyes at Memorial Stadium. Just like the year before, the Illini lost to a tough Wolverine team, 28–20, which would eventually claim the nation's number one AP ranking and the national championship. Among the Michigan players was All-American quarterback Pete Elliott, a future Illinois football coach. In 1949, his eighth season, Coach Ray Eliot's Illini managed just three wins, two ties, and four losses. That year the University of Missouri played its first game against Illinois since 1913. The Tigers would defeat the Illini 27–20 at Memorial Stadium.

Although that summer of 1950 the United States went to battle under the aegis of the United Nations, the Korean War did not have a discernable impact on the Illinois campus. With the usual activities in full swing, the football team returned to top shape, achieving a 7–2 record. In the season opener on September 30, the Illini defeated Ohio University (in Athens, Ohio), 28–2. At that first home game, spectators witnessed innovation when after 50 years of men only cheerleading teams, female students joined the squads. The next week, the Illini would lose by a single point to Wisconsin, 7–6. Thereafter, Eliot's team would pull off an impressive six-game winning streak that included victories over UCLA and Washington. But the last victory proved to be the most impressive. In one of the most memorable games of Illini football history, Illinois—ranked 8—upset #1 Ohio State at Memorial Stadium, 14–7. The next week, sporting an AP ranking of 6, the Illini were bested 14–7 by the Wildcats at Northwestern. The team would finish fourth place in the conference and ranked 13 by the AP.

The 1950 season ended with Illinois staying home during the postseason. The 1951 season, however, marked another high point. Led by the ferocious defensive play of All-American and All-Big Ten Charles M. Boerio, the Illini would finish the season undefeated, with the only blemish a scoreless tie at Ohio State. That year also saw the Illini snap a losing streak to its in-state rival when they eked out a 3–0 win at Northwestern. Players like Boerio established Illinois' national reputation for its defense, which generated interest from other top defensive recruits who would eventually join the program over the next decades. That January, in the first nationally televised bowl game, the Illini would handily defeat #7 Stanford by a whopping 40–7 in front of another enormous crowd of 98,825 people at the Rose Bowl. Illinois would be ranked fourth in the nation.

Though the Illini surprised Michigan at Ann Arbor 22–13, the Illini would finish the 1952 season with a losing record, tallying four wins and five losses. In that tumultuous year, one of the lowlights happened when a riot broke out at Iowa Stadium. Tensions built up throughout the game as referees called penalty after penalty, and players from both teams were ejected. Iowa students started throwing bottles and other objects at Illini players and referees on the field. All hell broke loose, however, when first-year Iowa coach Forest Evashevski entered the field to seek clarification on the latest penalty; referees then issued a penalty for unsportsmanlike conduct on Evashevski, effectively ending any possibility for Iowa to come back in the game. Illinois would go on to win, 33–13. Irate Iowa students hurled cans, bottles, fruit, and other objects at the exiting Illini players and referees. Fearing injury, the Illini were ordered to run to the locker room, which prompted Iowa students to rush the field, where violent melees ensued. The fallout from the incident resulted in no scheduled games between the teams for the next 14 years. Iowa,

a traditional Illini rival, would not set foot in Memorial Stadium again until 1968.[52]

As bad as the riot at Iowa had been, the 1954 season might have been worse: the Fighting Illini won only a single game—against out-of-conference Syracuse University—and racked up eight losses. The last one-win season, in 1940, at least had only seven losses. Despite going into the home game against Wisconsin with a 1–6 record, Memorial Stadium was sold out with a crowd of 71,119, which extended the streak begun in 1946 of at least one capacity crowd home game in a season.[53]

The next year, the Illini would finish with a positive won-loss ledger with five wins, three losses, and one tie. As the season was winding down, on November 5 the Illini welcomed the undefeated and nationally top-ranked University of Michigan to Memorial Stadium. Before a crowd of just under 60,000, the Illini would stun the visitors, 25–6. So impressive was the victory that sportswriters across the country could not help but compare it to the game that had already become football lore. Fred Young, writing for the *Pantagraph,* declared: "It was one of the worst lickings that a Michigan team has taken, in fact, since that bright autumn afternoon in 1924, when Harold E. (Red) Grange reached an all-time peak and made monkeys of the late Fielding Yost's club."[54] The loss to Illinois was truly painful since it knocked Michigan out of the running for the Rose Bowl. Instead, because Ohio State honored the conference agreement that no team would play at the Rose Bowl in two consecutive seasons, Michigan State would end up with the invitation.

The Television Era Begins

The Impact of Mass Media

Like radio before it, television had an enormous impact on college football, and Memorial Stadium was integral to both. Back in 1922, WRM (We Reach Millions) had begun to broadcast Illini football games across the country from its campus AM radio station. Twenty years later the station, now with the call sign WILL, became only the second FM broadcaster in the state. When it began

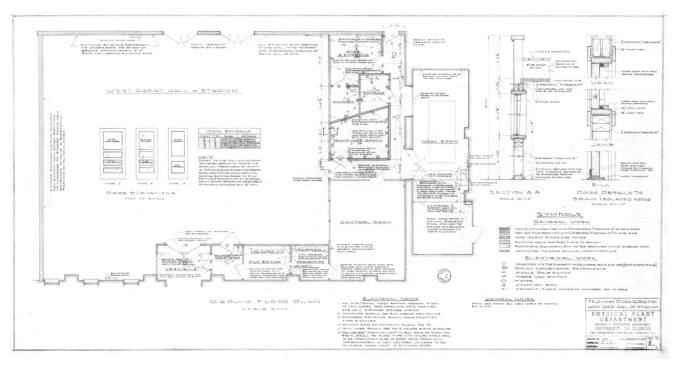

Figure 6.9
WILL broadcasting center at Memorial Stadium plan drawing. Courtesy of the University of Illinois Archives.

transmitting live University athletic events in 1946, it provided audiences with an opportunity to hear contests in basketball, baseball, and other sports and helped grow an Illini fanbase beyond the immediate region.[55] In 1952 the enterprise moved to the south end of the West Great Hall, where the diesel engine laboratories once stood. Three years later, the "makeshift studios" under the stands gained an antenna that soared high above the stadium and reached a brand new television audience at an estimated radius of 100 miles (160 kilometers) (Figure 6.9).[56]

By 1955, however, Illini football games had already been televised for at least seven years. A major milestone of the 1948 season was the first television broadcast from Memorial Stadium. Like radio, television broadcasting had small, exploratory spurts and then technology rapidly evolved as manufacturing capacity improved. And profitability made an enormous difference. In a first, the National Broadcasting Company televised a game between Waynesburg University and Fordham University in 1939, when the medium was still a rudimentary experiment. In 1950, with television broadcasts commercially viable, the American Broadcasting Company secured exclusive

rights to broadcast the University of Pennsylvania's football games for $150,000.[57] Other teams, like Notre Dame, entered into their own lucrative agreements. Television, however, soon proved to be a double-edged sword.

In the 1948 season the NCAA recorded an overall attendance of 19,134,159 fans at college football games, and the total increased slightly to 19,651,995 in 1949. But in 1950, the first year that television expanded its broadcasting reach, attendance fell to 18,961,688. For the next several years as television coverage spread, attendance dropped. The lowest point came in the 1953 season when only 16,681,731 visitors attended college football games.[58] Distressed by the impact television was having, the NCAA imposed regulations in 1951. At first, the NCAA denied networks and schools the opportunity to broadcast games live—only prerecorded games were allowed—but it later relented under pressure. In early September of that year, under the guidance of Ralph Furey, the athletic director of Columbia University and co-chair of the NCAA's television committee, the NCAA signed the first contract recognizing the rights and responsibilities of sponsors. Under the agreement, title sponsor Westinghouse Electric Corporation could request different programming later in the season if it felt that a particular team or game was no longer the best possible audience magnet.[59]

For Westinghouse, it meant that the broadcasting rights it had paid to the NCAA would not go to waste because of a team's lack of appeal. For the NCAA, it meant that it could continue comparing attendance with television viewership from a consistent framework. But schools across the country were unhappy with the NCAA's draconic regulations. After several years of back-and-forth between the schools, the NCAA, and the US government, a fragile détente was achieved. By 1955, the NCAA allowed schools that had sold out their stadiums to broadcast those games and also allowed them to broadcast regionally even if a game had not sold out. Under the tenuous agreement, the NCAA remained the ultimate authority regarding media rights and contract negotiations for regular season games. Bowl games, because of their sponsored nature, were from the outset free to negotiate media contracts without NCAA approval.

Money was never the only consideration in setting up televised football games. Just as radio had given college football a major boost in popularity, television had even larger effect 30 years later. Alumni, students, and community members could gather around a television set to watch their favorite team. The growing popularity of televised college football games also had an unintended, though not surprising, effect on professional football, which would have a reciprocal effect on college football. Unlike professional football in the 1920s, these teams were not playing second fiddle to their college counterparts. College football programs had always professed to be strictly amateur, and professional football from its inception paid players and coaches—even if the salaries were at a working-class level. Nevertheless, George Halas's move to recruit Red Grange in 1925 boosted attendance and fan loyalty to the Chicago Bears. Slowly, but steadily, professional football salaries, especially for players, rose. Joining the ranks of a professional team became an increasingly desirable goal—especially during the Great Depression.

By the start of the 1940s, professional football had developed a stable urban fan base. Like the NCAA, the National Football League (NFL) initially approached televised broadcasts with some hesitation. With eight NFL teams, about 1,275,000 people attended games in 1940.[60] By 1950, the number of teams had increased to thirteen, and attendance nearly doubled to just over 2,100,000.[61] Although televised broadcasts were blamed for low attendance at some games, in 1955, with televised broadcasts of professional games a staple of the American weekend, attendance jumped once again to just under 2,730,000.[62] While this is a far smaller number than even the low point of the 1953 college football season, over six hundred college and university football teams were members of the NCAA that year. In comparison, in 1955 the NFL had just twelve teams (the New York Yanks professional football team had ceased operations after 1951). With stadiums limited to just twelve locations, television broadcasting gave a home audience the ability to watch a local or regional NFL team compete against a rival from across the nation. While not all NFL owners immediately embraced television, most eventually did so with enthusiasm.[63] NFL broadcasts finally became competitive with Saturday college football programming, which prompted the NCAA to protest "vociferously."[64]

Today's blockbuster television and streaming-based conference realignments find their roots in this era. Lucrative television broadcasting contracts enabled professional players and coaches' salaries to surge. With potential college football recruits looking for an opportunity to join an NFL team after graduation, television coverage became a major subject at athletic departments across the nation. With the certainty of broadcasting agreements, football programs could use this exposure as a principal recruitment tool, which reinforced the chasm between schools in large conferences and those that were not and also failed to draw sports media's interest. Schools that could demonstrate regional or national television exposure could, and did, out recruit schools without similar agreements. Already by 1950 the importance of broadcasting Fighting Illini games at Memorial Stadium was exploited by Illinois when it joined

Michigan and Northwestern in a contract to show games on closed circuit television at local movie theaters.[65]

Public appetite for televised games generated a series of firsts the next year. On September 29, 1951, the National Broadcasting Company became the first media network to broadcast coast-to-coast a college football game with its coverage of Duke University versus the University of Pittsburgh. That same day, the Columbia Broadcasting System became the first network to broadcast a game in color while covering the California Golden Bears against the University of Pennsylvania's Quakers. For its part, Illini football continued to be at the forefront of sports television when it appeared at the January 1, 1952, Rose Bowl, the first nationally televised bowl game in history. Though Stanford led 7–6 at halftime, Illinois would cap its 1951 national championship season by scoring 34 unanswered points in the second half en route to a 40–7 victory.

Television—and its seemingly endless potential for income—was here to stay. Just four years later, the Big Ten "formulated a revenue-sharing model designed to pool all football television rights of its members and share those proceeds equally." The 1955 formula agreement insisted that teams would "continue to utilize a revenue-sharing model, dividing media rights, bowl payouts, and other profits among all conference institutions."[66]

Nearly immediately television vaulted to the top of the revenue streams for college football programs, and facility managers, including those at Memorial Stadium, were tasked with enabling broadcasting. Improvements ranged from strategically placed platforms for cameras and new production facilities to the installation of new sound and transmission equipment in specialized rooms, like the large antenna that was installed for WILL. The 1956 season was the first with regularly broadcast games. Though the Illini would finish with just two wins, one of those victories—like the 1955 win over Michigan—became part of college football mythology.

In a home game played before the largest season opener audience ever, the Illini beat the California Golden Bears, 32–20. The 54,833 fans witnessed the Illini rally from behind to overcome a 20-point deficit, scoring 32 unanswered points.[67] The victory over Cal

also served as the middle linebacker debut of future NFL Hall of Fame inductee Raymond "Ray" Nitshcke. Originally recruited as a quarterback, the scrappy Elmwood Park, Illinois, native was ferocious on the field. Playing iron man football—a system in which a single player is on both offense and defense during a game—Nitshcke developed a defensive acumen that would put him in the company of previous Illini greats like Isaiah Owens. He personified smashmouth football. In an example of the actions that make football players heroes—or, alternately, the content of parental nightmares—Nitshcke did not wear a face mask. These were not required in 1956, and helmets were not even mandated before the 1943 season. Before that roaring home crowd, Nitshcke's mouth encountered an Ohio State player's helmet during the starting kickoff. As a result of the collision, Nitschke lost two front teeth, and another two later fell out after dangling, from the roots, during the game.

However, the most historic game of 1956 came when Michigan State University arrived at Memorial Stadium boasting a #1 AP ranking. On October 27, playing in front of a capacity crowd, the Fighting Illini stunned the top team of the nation by a score of 20–13. Like in the season opener against California, the Illini would overcome a first-half deficit, racking up 20 unanswered points courtesy of Abe Woodson, the Big Ten indoor sprint champion. Woodson finished the game with a total of 198 yards, 116 of those coming from rushes.[68]

Illini Basketball's Impact on Memorial Stadium

Just as football was beginning an upward trend under Coach Eliot, another Illini team started a successful run under basketball coach Douglas R. Mills, who also served as the AA's director. In 1942 and again in 1943, the Illini basketball team, nicknamed the Whiz Kids, won the Big Ten Conference crown. With each home game, it became apparent that Huff Gym could not host the expanding number of basketball fans. Home games regularly sold out, easily filling all 7,000 seats.[69] A fieldhouse for basketball and other sports had been a dream of Huff and the AA for years. To garner support from other University departments, the AA proposed that the fieldhouse also be used for physical education and health classes. After the 1943 season, however, excitement over the basketball team and its facilities decreased. With multiple starters drafted into military service, success on the court ebbed.

The first formal attempt to fund the new fieldhouse came in 1945 as institutional construction budgets ballooned. In January the state's post-war planning commission requested that the General Assembly award the University of Illinois $14,699,000 ($247,326,500 in 2023)

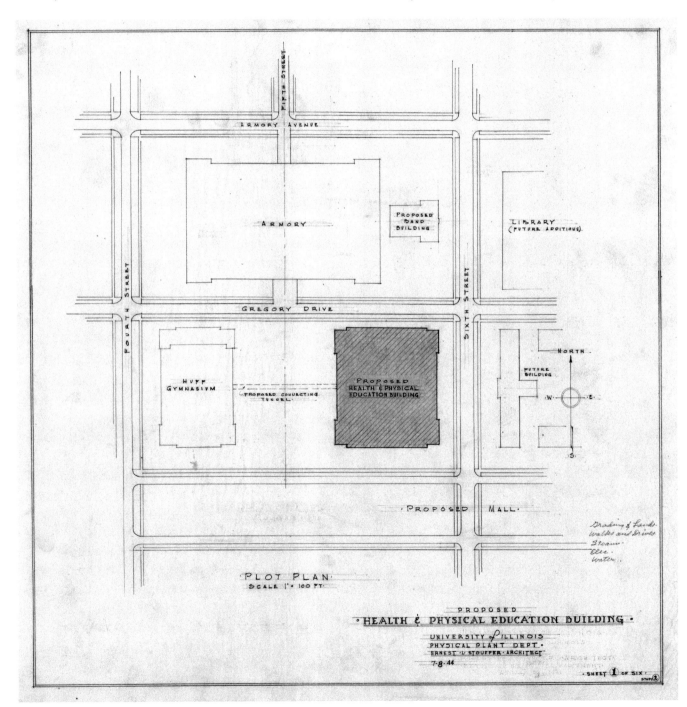

Figure 6.10
Initial site plan of fieldhouse proposal framing the Armory across from Huff Gym, February 1944. Courtesy of the University of Illinois Archives.

for new construction, deferred maintenance, and property purchases for all its campuses. At the Urbana-Champaign campus, funding requests included monies for residence halls ($1,500,000), land acquisitions ($250,000), and an assortment of other new research and teaching spaces such as structures for the chemical engineering, electrical engineering, and fine arts departments. Another request was $1,700,000 for the Betatron building, which using 1922 dollars would cost the same as Memorial Stadium.[70] Designed and built by Donald Kerst, the Betatron was the "world's first magnetic induction accelerator."[71] But, the most relevant request for the athletic programs was for a "sports building," valued at $2,300,000.

As early as 1941, the University had considered placing a fieldhouse east of Huff Gym to frame an axis from the Armory (Figure 6.10). By 1944, campus architect Ernest Stouffer had sited the fieldhouse on an axis with the

Armory to the south, across an implied quadrangle (Figure 6.11). By 1945, siting for the fieldhouse was proposed immediately north of the Stadium, south of the Parade Grounds, on the central north-south axis generated by Memorial Stadium (Figure 6.12).[72] Just one month after the funding request, schematic plans from Holabird and Root for the proposed structures were revealed. Drawings dated February 28, 1945, depict a large Georgian-style building directly north of the Stadium..

In a later iteration, a site plan placed a new Health and Physical Education Building directly north on an axis with Memorial Stadium and connected it underground via tunnels and above ground with terraces (Figure 6.13 and Figure 6.14).

This proposal was hotly debated on campus and across the state. Politicians including Governor Green and Senator E. R. Peters (representing St. Joseph) supported the

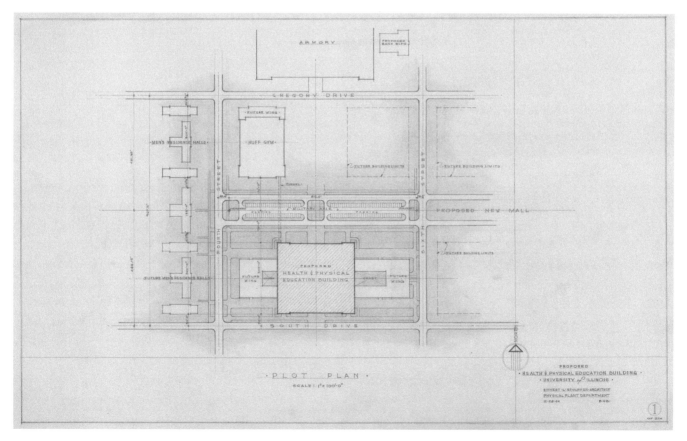

Figure 6.11
Site plan of fieldhouse proposal on an axis with the Armory south of the proposed military axis, December 1944. Note the dormitories to the west across Fourth Street and the proposed "New Mall" on the military axis. Courtesy of the University of Illinois Archives.

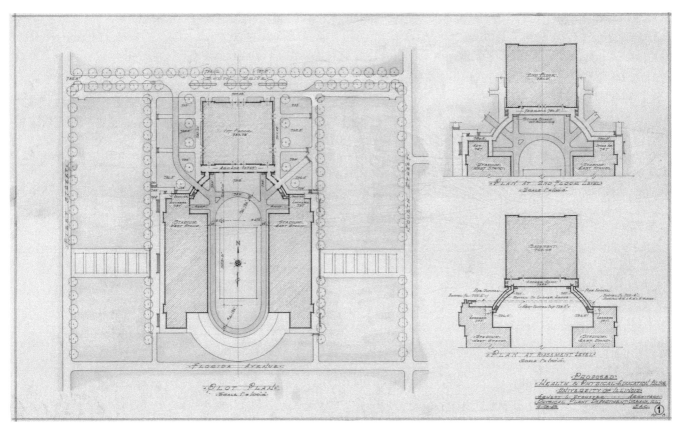

Figure 6.12
Site plan for a new Health and Physical Education Building north of Memorial Stadium. The structures were to be connected underground via tunnels and above ground with terraces (*right*). Courtesy of the University of Illinois Archives.

development of a fieldhouse that could serve the state as well as the University. But although the AA had sought funding of $2,300,000, estimates for the work soon ballooned to $4,500,000.[73] Students and faculty were divided, with some arguing that laboratories and dormitories were needed more than a "Sports Palace." Without a clear direction for the work, funding for capital projects went to other initiatives. Meanwhile, the state halted construction, and the so-called sports palace never gained funding. Faced with this reality, the BOT generated a list of priorities for new buildings. What had been envisioned as a health and physical education building would simply be a sports building, and it received the lowest prioritization for the 1947 budget expenditures—thus ensuring its demise. But as basketball's resurgence started packing Huff Gym again, the push for a new fieldhouse returned. To consolidate sports on campus, it needed to be directly

related to Memorial Stadium's overall location and axial characteristics. Several site plans were prepared that included not only the location of the new facility but also what programmatic elements it would house. By the late 1950s other schools had noted the rise of basketball and built new facilities, and Illinois began planning in earnest one of its own: this one would be south of Memorial Stadium and across Florida Avenue.

Decade's End

The 1957 Fighting Illini football team managed to improve to a four-win season, with all victories coming at home. These included upsets of #4 Minnesota and #11 Michigan. In addition, the Illini blanked the in-state rival Northwestern Wildcats 27–0 to close the season. While Coach Eliot was guiding the Illini in his

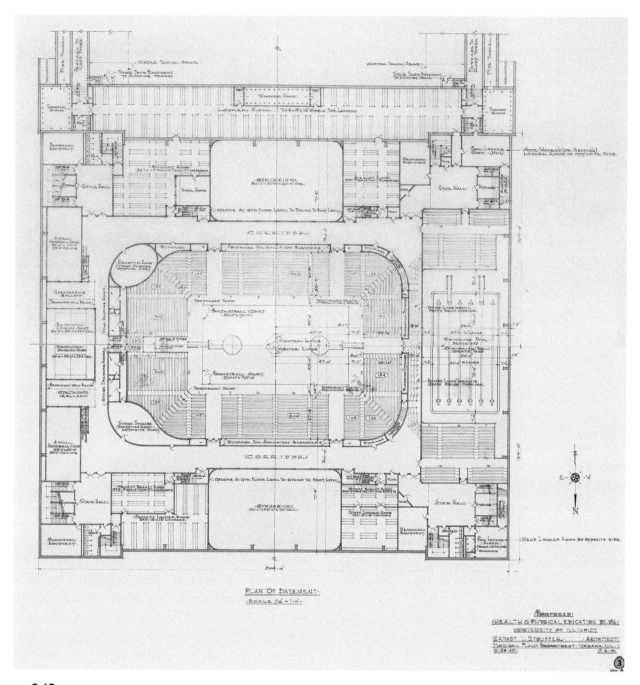

Figure 6.13
Basement in the proposed Health and Physical Education Building, 1945. Courtesy of the University of Illinois Archives.

sixteenth season in front of television cameras, another event generated national headlines—and major television coverage. On October 4, 1957, the Union of Soviet Socialist Republics successfully launched Sputnik, a small pulse-emitting satellite, into a low-Earth orbit.

One month later the Soviets launched a dog, Laika, into space. These events kickstarted the space race with the United States, and the Soviets had evidently taken the lead. Thanks to the wonders of television, on December 6 audiences witnessed an attempt to launch an American

Figure 6.14
Rendering for a new Health and Physical Education Building. Courtesy of the University of Illinois Archives.

satellite, Vanguard TV3, fail in spectacular fashion. But that setback did not deter efforts to send satellites and rockets out of the atmosphere, and it may have propelled the space race and all things related to it to the forefront of popular culture.

This infatuation with space exploration was directly manifested at the University in the 1957 plans for a field-house. Housing 18,000 to 20,000 seats, it was compared to a space "saucer come to rest" on the southern end of the campus.[74] The structure promised to Huff finally would be funded, but unlike Memorial Stadium, which relied on voluntary student and alumni donations and monies from the AA, the fieldhouse would be financed through student fees. This mechanism—a major capital project financing tool today—was possible because of a 1955 law that allowed schools to use student fees to pay off bonds issued to finance building construction or remodels.[75]

After several meetings throughout 1957 between the administration and the student building committee, the first proposed structures to fall under the new financing strategy were an addition to the Illini Student Union, a new student services building, and the new fieldhouse. To prevent funding from being redirected by the administration, bond legislation required that the University collect student fees to service and eliminate bond debt only after construction was completed. In July 1957 Governor William Stratton signed legislation clarifying bond finance measures, which prompted the University to issue bonds for a total of $12,000,000 ($131,389,750.89 in 2023) and $7,500,000 of that for the fieldhouse that would become Assembly Hall (now the State Farm Center).[76] In preparation to pay for these projects, the BOT raised the student fee to $20 ($200 in 2023) per semester starting that fall. With an enrollment of

Figure 6.15
Assembly Hall west entrance. Photograph by Kevin J. Hinders.

Figure 6.16
Assembly Hall interior. Photograph by Kevin J. Hinders.

23,519 that fall, this nominally represented $470,000 in revenue per school year.[77]

The firm Harrison and Abramovitz was selected to carry out the design. Max Abramovitz, an Illinois School of Architecture alumnus (class of 1930), conceived the venue as a circular form directly relating back to Memorial Stadium by punctuating the southern end of the playing field's north-south axis (Figure 6.15 and Figure 6.16). Today the building is centered in a mega-block with large parking lots surrounding it on all sides that can be used by both venues. On December 17, 1957, Abramovitz presented to an excited AA and BOT a model, plans, and renderings for Assembly Hall. After that meeting, he then presented the proposal to reporters at a press conference. During the presentation, referring to the 400-foot building, Abramovitz modestly said, "I know of no concrete structure like this: I think this is one of the largest bowls of its type." Drawing an explicit link to the space race and alluding to the lost capsule, Abramovitz added jokingly, "This is the Sputnik the Russians have been looking for—it came down here."[78]

Originally the venue was to not only hold athletic events like basketball games but also serve as an auditorium for musical and theatrical events. Park Livingston, president of the BOT, noted that Assembly Hall was a much-needed facility because it could cover everything from drama to athletics, was usable during the entire year, and could host almost any function. "The appearance of the building also impresses me," Livingston continued, "[i]t is one of the most significant landmarks that can be established on any campus anywhere. It is outstanding in its simplicity."[79] With Assembly Hall's construction beginning in 1958 and inaugurated on March 2, 1963, Huff's vision for a thriving sports campus was alive again. While State Farm Center (Assembly Hall) does periodically host musical concerts, and even game-shows, it became evident early on that its main function was to host sports events. A few years later, to address this discrepancy with the original design mandate, Harrison and Abramovitz, designers of performance halls at the Lincoln Center for the Performing Arts in New York, were retained to design the Krannert Center for Performing Arts.

Notes

1   National Archives, "Servicemen's Readjustment Act."

2   University of Illinois Library, "The GI Bill."

3   *University of Illinois Annual Register, 1943–44* (Urbana, 1944), 485.

4   *Illinois Alumni News,* March 1944, 3, col. 2.

5   John Franch, "The University of Illinois Goes to War," UI Archives' Student Life and Culture Archival Program, November 15, 2007, 1, https://archives.library.illinois.edu/slc/files/2014/09/WWIIHistory.pdf.

6   Idem., 2.

7   BOT, January 24, 1942, 748–49.

8   Cited in proposal drawings, courtesy of University of Illinois Archives, see Figure 6.1.

9   BOT, June 20, 1942, 931.

10 BOT, May 16, 1942, 887.

11 Franch, 11.

12 "Notre Dame and U. of I. Prepare to Train Navy Men: Check on Facilities to Set Up Schools," *Chicago Daily Tribune*, January 3, 1942, 11.

13 BOT, July 25, 1942, 17.

14 Franch, 12.

15 BOT, July 25, 1942, 17.

16 BOT, August 29, 1942, 63.

17 "The V-12 Officer Training Program," Naval History and Heritage Command, December 21, 2009, https://www.history.navy.mil/browse-by-topic/wars-conflicts-and-operations/world-war-ii/1942/manning-the-us-navy/v-12-program.html.

18 "Long Range Program on the Skyways Is Started by the University of Illinois," *New York Times,* August 30, 1942, 1.

19 "Approval Voted $250,000 U. of I. Airport Outlay: House Concurs, 118–0, in Senate Bills," *Chicago Daily Tribune,* April 29, 1943, 15.

20 Dorothea Kahn, "Illinois Airport Dedicated as University 'Classroom,'" *Christian Science Monitor,* 37, no. 282 October 16, 1945, 16.

21 BOT, March 20, 1943, 314.

22 BOT, January 20, 1945, 336.

23 "Green to Speak at Flag Day," *Daily Illini* 71, no. 210, June 10, 1942, 1.

24 Ed Orloff, "Thousands Hear Flag Day Talk by Governor," *Daily Illini* 72, no. 213, June 16, 1942, 1.

25 Ibid.

26 BOT, February 14, 1942, 771.

27 "80 Men Report for 1st Spring Grid Drill," *Daily Illini* 71, no. 138, March 3, 1942, 4.

28 "1942 Final AP Football Poll," College Poll Archive, accessed September 10, 2023, https://collegepollarchive.com/football/ap/seasons.cfm?appollid=55.

29 Fritz Jauch, "Brilliant Array 'Best Plebes in Decade,'" *Daily Illini* 72, no. 3, September 5, 1942, 4.

30 E. E. Litkenhous, "Ohio State Rated First by Expert: Litkenhous Announces Final Grid Standings," *Richmond News Leader,* January 21, 1943, 23.

31 "Notre Dame 21 Illinois 14," CougarStats, accessed September 12, 2023, https://cougarstats.com/games.php?show=details&game_id=2961.

32 "All-Time Attendance Figures," Fighting Illini Football, accessed September 17, 2023, https://fightingillini.com/sports/2016/8/18/football-attendance-records.

33 "Buddy Young," *BHA,* https://www.myblackhistory.net/ClaudeYoung.htm.

34 E. A. Kelloway, "Around the Farm and in the Feed Lot," *Wallace's Farmer*, June 3, 1956, 55.

35 Robert O. Dulin Jr. and William H. Garzke, *Battleships: United States Battleships in World War II* (Annapolis: Naval Institute Press), 137.

36 "Illinois in Focus." *University of Illinois, On Our Watch,* accessed October 6, 2023, http://oc.illinois.edu/OnOurWatch/infocus/102007.html.

37 "Illinois Population, 1900–2022," Macrotrends, accessed September 20, 2023, https://www.macrotrends.net/states/illinois/population.

38 "1944–45 and 1945–46 Civilian Enrollment by Curricula," University of Illinois Digital Collections, Accessed September 17, 2023, https://digital.library.illinois.edu/items/4d837340-1469-0133-a7c8-0050569601ca-2.

39 Deirdre Cobb-Roberts, "Interracial Cooperatives at the University of Illinois, 1940–1960," *American Educational History Journal* in eBlack Champaign-Urbana, item 913, 35, https://eblackcu.net/portal/items/show/913.

40 "Restaurant Ends Discrimination," *Daily Illini* 75, no. 10, October 2, 1946, 1.

41 Idem., 39–40.

42 BOT Meeting Notes, June 27, 1946, 1161.

43 BOT Meeting Notes, September 24, 1946, 54.

44 Donald Spivey and Thomas A. Jones, "Intercollegiate Athletic Servitude: A Case Study of the Black Illini Student-Athletes, 1931–1967," *Social Science Quarterly* 55, no. 4 (1975): 944.

45 "Letter Winners Who Gave Lives in World War II to Be Honored," *Daily Illini* 75, no. 2, October 4, 1945, 23.

46 Bob Doherty, "No Apologies for Team: Eliot," *Daily Illini* 75, no. 5, October 7, 1945, 7.

47 Jack Putman, "Campus Scout," *Daily Illini* 74, no. 209, August 30, 1946, 4.

48 "Stadium Hall Lodgers to Ask for 1-Mile Bus Ride to Class," *Daily Illini* 75, no. 9, September 29, 1946, 5.

49 "Capacity Crowds," Fighting Illini Football, accessed September 18, 2023, https://fightingillini.com/sports/2016/8/18/football-attendance-records.

50 Ibid.

51 John Franch, "Memory Lane: Building Blocks," UIUC Alumni, September 30, 2016, https://uiaa.org/2016/09/30/memory-lane-building-blocks/.

52 Scott Dochterman, "How Penalties, Apples, and a Punch Nearly Canned the Iowa-Illinois Football Rivalry," *Gazette,* November 14, 2014, https://www.thegazette.com/sports/how-penalties-apples-and-a-punch-nearly-canned-the-iowa-illinois-football-rivalry/.

53 "Capacity Crowds," Fighting Illini Football, accessed September 18, 2023, https://fightingillini.com/sports/2016/8/18/football-attendance-records.

54 Fred Young, "Illinois Stuns Michigan with 25–6 Upset Victory," *Pantagraph,* November 6, 1955, 33.

55 "The History of WILL," Illinois Public Media, accessed October 7, 2023, https://will.illinois.edu/about/history.

56 Ibid.

57 Frank, Matthew, "Flashback: The Time Penn challenged the NCAA's Ban on Televised College Football," https://www.thedp.com/article/2021/01/penn-football-ncaa-television-controversy-1951

58 "All-Time College Football Attendance," NCAA, accessed September 22, 2023, http://fs.ncaa.org/Docs/stats/football_records/2017/attend.pdf.

59 "TV Contract for College Football Lets the Sponsor Bar Poor Teams: TV FOOTBALL PACT BARS POOR TEAMS the Schedule for New York," *New York Times,* September 6, 1951, 1.

60 "1940 NFL Attendance," Pro Football Reference, accessed September 24, 2023, https://www.pro-football-reference.com/years/1940/attendance.htm.

61 "1950 NFL Attendance," Pro Football Reference, accessed September 24, 2023, https://www.pro-football-reference.com/years/1950/attendance.htm.

62 "1955 NFL Attendance," Pro Football Reference, accessed September 24, 2023, https://www.pro-football-reference.com/years/1955/attendance.htm.

63 David G. Surdam, "Television," in *Run to Glory and Profits: The Economic Rise of the NFL during the 1950s* (University of Nebraska Press, 2013), 225–54, 227, https://doi.org/10.2307/j.ctt1ddr7pc.16.

64 Ibid., 237.

65 Ronald A. Smith, *Play-by-Play: Radio, Television, and Big-Time College Sport* (Baltimore: Johns Hopkins University Press, 2001), 64.

66 "Big Ten History," https://bigten.org/sports/2018/6/6/trads-big10-trads-html.aspx.

67 David Condon, "High Voltage!" *Chicago Tribune,* September 30, 1956, 45.

68 Hal Middlesworth, "Illinois 20, Mich. State 13," *Detroit Free Press,* October 28, 1956, 1C.

69 Wilfrid Smith, "Illini Risk Lead against Badgers Tonight," *Chicago Daily Tribune,* February 20, 1943, 15.

70 "University Postwar Building Program Contains Request for Dormitory Financing," *Daily Illini* 74, no. 91, January 28, 1945, 1.

71 "Betatron," Physics, Grainger College of Engineering, accessed September 24, 2023, https://physics.illinois.edu/people/history/betatron.

72 Cited from drawings provided by the University of Illinois Archives, February 28, 1945.

73 "UI Sports Plans Revived," *Daily Illini* 75, no. 61, December 18, 1946, 1.

74 Cormie, "Approve 18,000 Seat Illini Arena," *Chicago Daily Tribune*, December 18, 1957, 1.

75 "Stratton Approves Using Fees for Building Debts," *Daily Illini* 84, no. 94, February 17, 1955, 7.

76 "University Will Issue Bonds for 3 Student Fee Buildings This Spring, Farber Predicts," *Summer Illini* 3, no. 4, July 11, 1957, 1.

77 "Frosh Enrollment Decreases; 23,519 Register for Classes," *Daily Illini* 87, no. 16, October 1, 1957, 4.

78 Tom Barber, "Plan Unique: Abramovitz," *Daily Illini* 87, no. 69, December 18, 1957, 1.

79 Pete Weitzel, "Approve Building Design," *Daily Illini* 87, no. 69, December 18, 1957, 1–2.

The Tumultuous Years, 1960 to 1975

CHAPTER

7

Introduction

The bright-eyed optimism and enthusiasm of the 1950s gave way to a fractured campus as the next decade began. As if to signal a more innocent age coming to an end, student water fights—unplanned events of reckless abandon that had started in 1957—abruptly led to violence and were harshly discouraged in 1961 after a journalist covering the fun literally lost an eye. That same year, the student-run University Committee on Student Affairs grew more impatient about necessary social change, demanding integration and support for minority civil rights by passing a "bill calling for end to racial discrimination in fraternities, sororities, and off campus housing."[1] Just two years later, President John F. Kennedy was assassinated while visiting Dallas, Texas, which sent a shocked nation into disbelief and mourning. A memorial service in his honor was held in the newly opened Assembly Hall, now part of the sports complex on the southwestern side of campus. That same year, the free speech movement led students—many of them children of those who had served in WWII—to protest the US's involvement in the Vietnam War. On campus, the first antiwar protest was held on December 18, 1964.

The second half of the decade would be more tumultuous still. Like most across the country, the Urbana-Champaign campus was a cauldron for activism. Not only did student protests against the Vietnam War become more frequent, but they also grew increasingly tense: students were confronting police officers and administrators, challenging the notion of state authority.

In 1965, the Student Committee on Political Expression (SCOPE) organized, and future film critic and alumnus Roger Ebert served as a leader. In one of its most influential actions, SCOPE successfully protested the reign of Dean of Students Fred Turner, which prompted his resignation one year later. Memorial Stadium would be the site for some of this political upheaval, and it would undergo its own changes—the first since the addition of the south-side horseshoe. As the decade ended in 1969, the US effectively "won the Space Race" when on July 21 of that year, Apollo 11's Eagle Lunar Module landed on the moon, enabling two American astronauts to walk on its surface. Three years later, faced with an increasingly unpopular war, President Richard M. Nixon began the gradual pullout from Vietnam. A year later, faced with the prospect of an impeachment trial in the US Senate, Nixon's resignation brought a close to an era.

The 1960s

The Stadium as Anchor of Campus Life

The turmoil of the 1960s compelled institutions like the University of Illinois to navigate between the stability of established rules and authority and the changing nature of students' views and politics. By this point televised sports—especially at the college level—was a cornerstone of American culture, and its domination left schools wrestling with their transformation into a sort of minor league for professional football and

DOI: 10.4324/9781032643885-7

193

basketball. Lucrative television contracts and increasing broadcast coverage, coupled with publicity about players, centered sports in an ongoing debate about the role of academia. In the 1930s, schools were framed as purveyors of education, not venues for sports. In the early 1960s, recruitment tactics divided views on the role of college athletes. In 1959, Coach Ray Eliot faced this two-pronged challenge directly: television and the allure of large paychecks had tempted Rich Kreitling, an All-American tight end, to skip his final year of eligibility and instead play for the Cleveland Browns. On another front, academic requirements took a toll on the roster when first-string halfback Dick McDade was ruled ineligible to play and up-and-coming star Bernie Clay left "due to scholastic difficulties."[2] The debates grew impassioned and divisive. In one *Daily Illini* article, B. Poe argued that

[t]he academic approach to college athletics lacks common sense. Worse, it is contradictory and harmful to the very persons and principles it would ostensibly protect and promote.

First, we must agree on basic issues: intercollegiate athletics are desirable.

Poe goes on to enumerate reasons for college sports' importance, but tellingly buttresses his case by noting that

college athletics provide the student body with a unifying interest, in short, a means to an esprit de universitatem [sic], so to speak. This point is perhaps most difficult to defend or substantiate, but any student who has felt the thrill of hearing the roars and groans of 60,000 fellow fans at an interception or fumble or of seeing the clever manipulations of the Block-I in the Stadium knows what I mean.[3]

After summarizing the points supporting widening recruitment efforts and reducing admission requirements for potential student athletes, Poe bluntly concludes that "[t]he academic persecution of athletes is a most grievous flaw in the system. Particularly in a state

university, or any college wholly or partially supported by public funds, democratic principles should prevail without question or exception."[4] Not all agreed. In his letter to the editor, Patrick Tuite, a law student, observed that

[w]hen in the law school, where I had hoped to study Saturday afternoon, I was confronted with a notice stating that the law library—arsenal of legal learning—would be closed at noon on days of home football games. The situation has reached the appalling point where an educational holiday is being called in honor of a gridiron battle.

Like Poe, Tuite highlighted the Stadium's role as a symbol, but in the opposite sense, concluding that it was a good time for the University to re-evaluate its scholastic program and start making the football fan subservient to a student's needs and not vice versa. Maybe then this University will no longer be 'a group of small buildings located around a football stadium.'"[5]

Despite Tuite's exhortation, the Stadium had already become the spatial landmark—if not the most important cultural site—associated with the University. Assembly Hall was going up on the south side, and WPGU, a student-run radio station broadcasting from its namesake location at the Parade Grounds Unit, announced that it was "looking forward to shortly moving into new studios in the residence halls being constructed north of Memorial Stadium."[6] *Daily Illini* authors situated another addition to the campus under construction at the time by its relationship to the Stadium: "MEMORIAL STADIUM stands across the street from the south window of the lounge connecting the new Fine and Applied Arts building proper and the Krannert Art Museum."[7]

It was perhaps fitting that, weather permitting, since its construction Memorial Stadium had served as the venue for the campus graduation ceremony. In a sense, it was an appropriate setting for a final milestone in which students were transformed into alumni and moved from a campus community to a larger and ever-growing network of alumni that together formed the backbone of athletic support. At the 1961 ceremony, nearly 2,500 students—an estimated 1,800 of them undergraduates—gathered at Memorial Stadium.[8]

Throughout the decade, the Stadium continued to consolidate its position as a social landmark. In early April 1964, the BOT approved a proposal to officially extend the Illioskee Spring Carnival to a three-day celebration. Students marked the beginning of spring by burning Old Man Winter as an effigy, and then snake dances led participants from the residence halls to the north end of Memorial Stadium for a 45-minute program that included cheerleaders and Chief Illiniwek.[9] And for the most notable statewide celebration of the period, the Stadium hosted "the 150 most representative living athletes who are natives of the state" during halftime of the home game against Iowa in a salute for the 150th anniversary of Illinois' founding.[10]

1960: The Coach Pete Elliott Era Begins

In 1960, the Fighting Illini would have their first new head coach in eighteen seasons. Ray Eliot stepped down with an 83–73–11 total record that included three conference titles, two Rose Bowl wins, and a share of a national championship.[11] For new coach Pete Elliott—a Bloomington, Illinois, native—this position was a homecoming of sorts (Figure 7.1). At the end of March, with the playing field in a "general poor condition," Elliott made a pitch in front of the Urbana-Champaign press for training facilities that would enable the team to practice despite inclement weather and less-than-ideal field conditions.[12] Ultimately practices were postponed until the first Saturday of April, which also drew over 40 high school coaches from across the state for the twelfth annual Illinois Spring Football Clinic.[13] By the end of April, the field's condition had improved enough for the team to practice until summer break, but the need for additional accommodations persisted.

Meanwhile, the Stadium continued to demonstrate its versatility, readily adapting for other uses. Small-scale renovations and modifications, like the addition of broadcasting facilities, made it possible to host logistic and staging activities for various athletic programs during the early 1960s. For example, the training room

Figure 7.1
Head Coach Pete Elliott. Courtesy of the University of Illinois Department of Intercollegiate Athletics Archives.

in the northeast tower was revamped so that student athletes could be medically examined and cleared to participate in sports.[14] Another alteration, this one for safety, involved installing a new "lightning protection system" that required rehabilitating and adding equipment.[15] Though lightning strikes are rare, the Stadium's contrasting height with the surrounding topography has made it an occasional target of midwestern electrical storms. As recently as 2015, a lightning strike in proximity to the Stadium delayed the season's opening game.[16]

During the summers, the Stadium remained a magnet for regional gatherings. Each July for 12 years in a row, on an ever-more magnificent scale, it served as the hub for July 4 festivities. The pinnacle came in 1962 when people from various communities, local residents, veterans, members of the armed services, marching bands, and students paraded from the intersection of Green Street and Coler Avenue in Urbana down to the Stadium for the County Freedom Celebration. The Fourth of July festivities continued with a concert and a gymnastics exhibition put on by Charlie Pond's Palaestrum Kids. Then the Stadium was the site of a "mammoth fireworks display, the climax of Champaign-Urbana's annual Fourth of July Freedom Celebration." Impressively for the period, the show would be themed:

> The firing on Fort Sumter, the first shots in the Civil War will be re-enacted in brilliant fireworks in one of the largest fireworks displays in the history of the Freedom Celebration. Throughout the evening 152 aerial bombs will explode as ground displays are being set off. At the end of the show 108 bombs shot off in rapid succession will turn the sky into a torrent of sound, color and motion.[17]

After the fireworks, community members could choose where to continue celebrating by listening to Bob Norman's orchestra perform on the west-side tennis courts or by square dancing on the east-side tennis courts. Overall, an estimated 40,000 filled the Stadium during the day and into the night.[18] This tradition of hosting Fourth of July celebratory fireworks would last until 1989.[19]

There would be not as much revelry during the early years of Pete Elliott's head coaching stint, however. In the first contest under Elliott, a home game at Memorial Stadium, the #4 AP-ranked Illini avenged the previous season's opening loss by defeating the University of Indiana Hoosiers, 17–6. After nabbing a victory from West Virginia, the three-game homestand culminated with a contest against the #5 Ohio State Buckeyes. On October 8, a capacity crowd celebrated the 50th anniversary of the establishment of homecoming—a tradition attributed to Illinois students. But the Illini lost to the Buckeyes, 7–34, and the team's top 25 ranking. After falling to #10 Minnesota, the Illini defeated Penn State at home (10–8) and stunned #15 Purdue University in an away game, 14–12. Then, in a first for the schools, the Elliott brothers—"Bump" at Michigan and Pete at

Illinois—faced each other at Ann Arbor. The Wolverines outlasted the Illini 7–8. Elliott's first season came to a finish with a victory at home against the Wisconsin Badgers and an away loss to Northwestern University. The 5–4 record placed Illinois fifth in the Big Ten.

As disappointing as the 1960 season was, 1961 would mark a nadir in Illinois football history. During the summer five football players, four of them lettermen, departed or were removed from the team.[20] With only 12 returnees on a roster of 55 and with the certainty that other players would be lost for the season as a result of injuries, the "smallest Illinois football squad since World War II" lost all games that season.[21] One of the few highlights was the recognition of Director of Bands Mark H. Hindsley for his service to the University since 1934 during halftime of the Illinois versus Northwestern game. As dire as the 1961 season had been, at least the foundations for a better future were put in place. At a time when NCAA rules mandated that college football players sit out their freshman year, the Fighting Illini managed to recruit one of the best incoming classes in the nation.[22] Among the student athletes was future Hall of Fame linebacker Dick Butkus, who held "an integral role in a program rebuild under coach Pete Elliott."[23]

Stadium attendance, already trending lower because of the disappointing 1960 season, plummeted in 1961. Taylor Bell, writing for the *Daily Illini,* summarized the feeling of dread:

> this season the Illini boast a young, inexperienced team—picked to finish near the bottom of the conference race—and many students are satisfied to stay home on Saturday afternoon to tend to their knitting . . . . It's an old story unfamiliar to this campus. Losing teams rarely draw crowds.[24]

Bell was not wrong. Whereas in 1959 home attendance over five games tallied 276,199, in 1961 the total dropped to 208,960. After the 1961 winless season, attendance for the four home games in 1962 tumbled to 143,701, its lowest nonwartime audience since 1941. Examined from a per-game average vantage point, the difference is even more stark. In 1959, the average home game attendance was 55,240. In 1962, that number had plunged over 36% to 35,295.[25] Such a steep drop not only represented a significant revenue decrease but also imperiled the value of broadcasting rights, as fewer fans tuning in to catch the Illini on the radio or television meant a smaller market for advertisers and fewer dollars for Illinois.

Turning these bleak numbers around was at the forefront of the agenda for Athletic Director Douglas Mills at the annual Big Ten athletic directors' meeting in Chicago. Among his goals was to urge rule changes like the popular return of free substitution during games and larger traveling rosters.[26] Other policy proposals, like renewing a Rose Bowl contract with the Athletic Association of Western Universities (formerly the Pacific Coast Conference), were favored by most. Changes to the recruitment rules, however, would be a true challenge. Back in 1956, the Big Ten had adopted directives that prioritized need-based scholarships for players. Parents who could afford their child's tuition were expected to contribute at least half the amount. Among those who had a strong opinion about this approach was a sophomore sportswriter, the future film critic Roger Ebert (class of 1964). Ebert argued that the rest of the NCAA should adhere to the Big Ten's recruitment practices, and not the other way around. Radical in his time, Ebert grasped that financial incentives were critical to college sports and argued that for "those high schools who do have need for help, of course, funds should be available—as they should be available for everyone. Like a Salary."[27]

The Big Ten athletic directors did not agree. Under the 1961 rule change, academic criteria established who got a scholarship offer. Student athletes were required to carry a grade point average of no less than 1.7, or C−, to be eligible to play football. At the time, the Big Ten athletic directors felt this policy made them more competitive with other conferences.[28] At the same Chicago meeting, it was also decided that the Big Ten would incorporate NCAA standards on student athlete stipends, except for the $15 per month allowed for laundry.[29]

In January 1962, in the shadow of the somber football season, a committee formed by three members of the College of Physical Education met with President David Henry with a proposal to change the intramural sports

program. The three main goals centered on increased participation in intramural sports by women, expanded staff involvement and supervision, and building new facilities.[30] According to the *Daily Illini,* Illinois had fallen to fifth among Big Ten schools in space allotted for students, and even more dramatically was behind all other conference schools in spending on intramural sports. To reach parity, the University needed updates that included facilities such as a 195,000-square-foot recreation center.[31] The winless season, however, had ravaged the AA's finances. To cut operations costs, the AA surrendered on September 1 the administration of intramural sports to the College of Physical Education.[32] As a result, no intramural building would be possible for several years.

That summer these conflicts between the role of sports, academic ability, and finances lurked below the surface at commencement held in the Stadium, when Governor Otto Kerner memorialized the centennial of the Morrill Act, which had established land-grant colleges. He specifically pointed to the link between the legislation and the University of Illinois:

[I]t is proper to pay a special tribute to this university and we as citizens of this state may take pride that it was Jonathan Baldwin Turner and Abraham Lincoln whose names are so intimately tied to the establishment of land-grant colleges. For it has been the land-grant pattern which has made it clear that intellectual ability is found among all our citizens. The tradition established must be guarded. No student who has the ability to profit from higher education should be denied the opportunity—and society denied his contribution—because of his race, his religion, or his financial wherewithal. We must, of course, recognize the special mission of a university like the University of Illinois and provide for the maintenance and expansion of its role.[33]

But higher education also had to provide more than just intellectual growth—or so was the sentiment on campus. Throughout the University, from school administrators to the student body, pressure was growing to field a winning football team. In a column written by Taylor Bell after interviewing Mills, the *Daily Illini* sports editor could not be clearer: a "winning football team capable of filling Memorial Stadium on Saturday afternoons is an absolute necessity. For football is the life's blood of the Athletic Association."[34] Stadium attendance was not just about school spirit or ticket sales. It was a proxy for the AA's financial health and could dramatically alter many aspects of everyday student life.

But with two victories, the 1962 season was only a slight improvement over the 1961 season. The first win came in an away game over Purdue, 14–10. A small home crowd witnessed the second during the final match of the season against the Michigan State Spartans, which ended 7–6. While the season may not have been a success from the win-loss viewpoint, it had at least offered the start of a new tradition. Dad's Day weekend had been inaugurated in 1920, and the title King for a Day was first bestowed on a father drawn randomly from nominees in 1948. For the 1962 season, Jean E. Siden, father of sophomore architecture student Gary Siden, was randomly picked to become King Dad. King Siden was paraded around the football field before kickoff and was crowned during halftime of the game against the Wisconsin Badgers.[35]

Finally in 1963, sports across the University had a good year. The newly established College of Physical Education's administration of the intramural program "provided a unified and cooperative program to satisfy the recreational needs of the University community."[36] Among the new initiatives was making Memorial Stadium more accessible to intramural track and field athletes. That spring an "outdoor meet held in Memorial Stadium" included "the 100-yard dash, 220-yard dash, 440-yard dash, 440-yard relay, high jump, broad jump and the shotput."[37]

After a five-month delay, Assembly Hall was finally inaugurated on March 2 to great fanfare, and the opening came just in time to host the final two games of the 1962–1963 season, when the Fighting Illini first beat Northwestern on March 4 and then Iowa on March 9.[38] Not to be left out, football hosted over 500 high school coaches from every Illinois county for a clinic that spring. After attending various lectures and networking

opportunities, the coaches were treated to an enormous fish fry dinner in the west great hall.[39]

Memorial Stadium marked the start of another tradition in June 1963 when the University Bands, the AA, the School of Music, and the Division of University Extension invited all uniformed high school bands across the state for clinics and a performance at the November 2 game between Illinois and Purdue.[40] In all, over eighty bands marched in the pregame and halftime shows.[41] This invitation is extended annually to this day.

Finally, the football team had a much-needed breakout season. Led by fierce defensive play by most valuable player Dick Butkus and explosive offense by running back James "Jim" Grabowski, the Fighting Illini would finish the season with a record of seven wins, one loss, and one tie. On September 28, over 42,000 fans witnessed a home win opener against the Marv Levy–coached California Golden Bears, 10–0. Thereafter, home attendance never dipped below 51,000 fans. The Illini drew even against #8 Ohio State, and their lone loss came against the #2 Michigan Wolverines. The Illini finished the regular season by playing a dominant defense to vanquish Michigan State, 13–0, in an away game. Having defeated the Spartans, who had been ranked second, the Illini captured the Big Ten title and were invited to play on January 1, 1964, in the Rose Bowl. Before a nationwide television audience and a sold-out Rose Bowl Stadium in Pasadena, California, the Fighting Illini defeated the University of Washington Huskies 17–7 and finished the season ranked 3 by the AP (Figure 7.2 and Figure 7.3).

The Stadium and Postmodern Reality

Images of Thich Quang Duc, a 73-year-old Buddhist monk, immolating himself in Saigon (today, Ho Chi Minh City) to draw attention to religious inequality in Vietnam were televised throughout the world in the summer of 1963. Those powerful moments encapsulated how television was influencing audiences in unpredictable ways. Among those who understood the impact of this young medium was Roger Ebert. Ebert, who had joined the *Daily Illini* as a sportswriter, attended multiple home games during the 1963 season. In early November, he utilized his regular column, "Ars Gratia,"

Figure 7.2
First Illinois touchdown at the 1964 Rose Bowl. Courtesy of the Division of Intercollegiate Archives.

to critique what he called the "pseudo-event." In an essay that preceded Marshall McLuhan's seminal 1967 book, *The Medium Is the Message*, and Jean Baudrillard's 1981 treatise, *Simulacra and Simulation,* Ebert criticized people's inability to focus on the immediacy of the moment, which combined with a lack of awareness of television messaging made viewers susceptible to manipulation. Ebert declared:

We live in the age of the pseudo-event.

It no longer matters whether anyone heard the tree fall in the forest. What matters is whether or not the fall of the tree was documented on television.

The vast majority of Americans are no longer capable of believing something on their own authority.

After describing several pseudo-event examples to make his point, he turned his attention to Memorial Stadium to illustrate the insipient, but real, social phenomenon in which people are more concerned about delivered content about an experience than the experience itself. He invited his readers to look for themselves:

You don't believe me? Look around you at the next Illinois home game and see how many people who are sitting in Memorial Stadium are, nevertheless,

Figure 7.3
Dick Butkus (#51) and Jim Grabowski (#33) when they played for the Chicago Bears. Courtesy of the Division of Intercollegiate Archives.

holding transistor radios to their ears so that Larry Stewart can TELL them what is going on before their very eyes. Or remember, if you will, how many Americans watched the solar eclipse on television when the real thing was going on in the heavens right outside their doors.[42]

On the one hand, perhaps every generation experiences the same phenomenon of inattention as technology evolves. On the other hand, perhaps Ebert was gifted with a clairvoyant vision of the unsettling effect that the media has on contemporary society's sense of spatial experience (Figure 7.4).

Zuppke Field

With a successful 1963 Illini football season in the books, the University began executing major improvements on campus. First, after 17 years of use, the housing units at the Stadium terrace would be dismantled in phases. The BOT awarded Shapland Construction Company a contract to demolish 136 units.[43] Two months later, at the November BOT meeting, several new capital projects were discussed including new sports venues and the expansion of the available facilities for sports and recreation. The building budget totaled $36,240,000, and $18,250,000 would come from state coffers and the rest would be from "non-state sources."[44] Among the listed proposed projects was a new center for performing arts. Originally Assembly Hall was conceived as a venue half dedicated to sports and half dedicated to performances. But it had become primarily a sports venue that occasionally hosted musical programs—and it got a prime workout from the fervent basketball fans. As a result, a separate, world-class facility for dance, music, and theater was essential. This project would be built and would open later that decade as Krannert Center for the Performing Arts—and was designed by Assembly Hall architect Max Abramovitz.

In the midst of campus updates, the College of Physical Education and the AA successfully lobbied the BOT to consider new facilities as part of the 1963 scheme:

Physical Education Building and Women's Gymnasium addition. Appropriations request, $1,480,000 (total project, $6,310,000—the remaining amount to come from non-state sources). Gross square feet, 251,240.

The main unit of this program is a new physical-education building, for the use of both men and women, to provide 223,690 gross square feet of space. The addition to the Women's Gymnasium (17,550 gross square feet) will include a swimming pool, and additional space as described below.

The present activity space assigned to the College of Physical Education. together with the west great hall of the Stadium and the Ice Rink, provide 249,078 net square feet of space. Based upon the University standards for such space, the present facilities are adequate for 19,768 students. This would indicate for the present student body of 27,020 students that there is a deficiency of

Figure 7.4
Zuppke Field's north wall and the scoreboard. Courtesy of the University of Illinois Archives.

91,374 net square feet of recreation space on the campus. The proposed Physical Education building and Women's Gymnasium addition will provide 139,912 additional net square feet of activity space, giving a total of 388,990 net square feet, which would give sufficient physical-education and recreation space for 30,872 students. The new building will be designed for use by both men and women, and will provide 17,200 net square feet for use by women alone, 36,600 net square feet for use by men alone, and 46,627 net square feet of play area for use by both men and women—plus a swimming pool of 21,525 net square feet and miscellaneous space (lounge, conference, and office) of 5,860 net square feet, for a total of 128,812 net square feet of indoor space.[45]

Across campus, the mood about sports had lifted. The once glum *Daily Illini* writers were now bragging about the Illini's "regained stature as a national football power."[46] Other articles praised coaches Elliott, Harry Combes (basketball), Charles Pond (gymnastics), and student athletes for their individual and team feats. In effect, football's Rose Bowl success and basketball's rise to the Elite Eight in the NCAA 1962–1963 postseason tournament had students feeling hopeful again.

Men's Track and Field at the Stadium

Under the guidance of track and field head coach Leo T. Johnson, the Fighting Illini earned three Big Ten outdoor championships and three top-ten NCAA finishes between 1958 and 1960 (Figure 7.5).

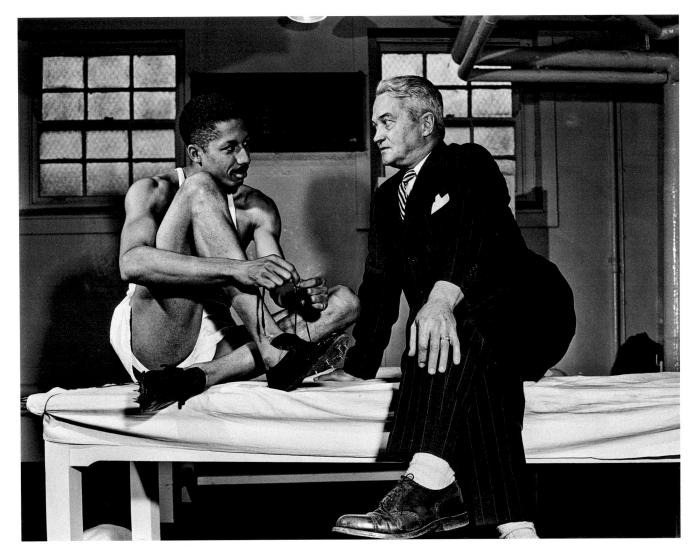

Figure 7.5
Athlete Bill McKeown and Head Coach Leo T. Johnson. Courtesy of the Division of Intercollegiate Athletics Archives.

The Illini were led by several stars, like dual-sport athlete Bill Brown (football and track) and Del Coleman. But without a doubt, Jamaican-born George Kerr, "the finest half miler in the world," was the "backbone of the track team."[47] Kerr capped his Illini career by setting a new course record and meet record for the 800 meters. Along with five other candidates, Kerr was nominated for the 1960 Illinois Athlete of the Year award. The year before, students had voted Kerr the runner-up, and he had been edged out by legendary gymnast and 1991 International Jewish Sports Hall of Fame inductee Abie Grossfeld (Figure 7.6).

Voting results were announced at the statewide high school track and field meet held over the May 20 weekend. Despite the stellar career, Kerr would once again be named runner-up, this time coming in second to William "Bill" Burrell, who had not only been a consensus All-American and 1959 Silver Big Ten Award Winner but also a fourth-place Heisman Trophy nominee. With this honor, Burrell joined the ranks of legendary Black Illini football players like Buddy Young—the Bronze Bullet—who won the award in 1944.

For Johnson's 23rd season, the first outdoor meet took place the weekend of April 22. The Illini were

Figure 7.6
George Kerr. Courtesy of the Division of Intercollegiate Athletics Archives.

joined by fellow Big Ten teams Iowa, Northwestern, and Wisconsin plus out-of-conference foe Marquette. Though the Illini were now without Kerr, they did have Big Ten champions Ken Brown, a distance runner; Bill Brown at shotput; and broad jumper Paul Foreman.[48] The Illini finished in third place in the Big Ten outdoor championships that year, beaten by Indiana and ceding the conference crown to Michigan.

In spring 1964, Trenton Jackson clocked in a record-setting, wind-aided 9.4-second 100-yard dash, and Bogie Redmon threw the discus a Memorial Stadium record of 161 feet and 6 inches.[49] Despite grabbing these two new records, the Illini could not claim a Big Ten title for some time. Johnson retired at the end of the 1965 season after winning "three NCAA championships in 1944, 1946 and 1947, and 17 Big Ten championships,

10 outdoors and seven indoors. His teams also finished as runners-up at the NCAA meets in 1953 and 1954."[50]

Women's Track and Field at the Stadium

Although women have been competing at the highest levels of international competition since the 1928 Olympic Games in Amsterdam, track and field meets at the college level were usually arranged on an as-needed basis, often years between competitions. Finally, under the aegis of the Association for Intercollegiate Athletics for Women, the first women's track national championships meet was held in May 1969 in San Marcos, Texas.

The second was held at Memorial Stadium and was hosted by the Department of Physical Education for Women on May 29, 1970. Over 250 participants from more than 20 colleges competed to qualify for the US Olympic team. Illini Cheryl Rogers, a freshman hurdler, had toured Europe in 1969 with the US team.[51] In what was considered a "minor upset," the Illini won the meet, beating second place Alcorn State, third place Texas Women's College, and 50 other teams for the title.[52] A year later, Nell Jackson—an associate professor in the Department of Physical Education for Women who had been the head coach of the US women's track and field team for the 1956 Olympic Games in Melbourne—was again named the coach for the Munich Olympics squad and also was selected as chair of the women's track and field committee for those games.[53] Perhaps indicative of the popularity of women's collegiate sports at the time, the *Daily Illini* posted the news on the last page of the day's issue. At least it was a start (Figure 7.7).

Huff's Ghost Haunts Illini Football

In a case of historic irony, one of the worst recruitment scandals in college sports came under the reign of Athletic Director Douglas Mills. After all, Mills had witnessed firsthand the animosity Huff and Zuppke held toward recruitment practices at other colleges, especially the many ethically questionable temptations these presented to coaches and administrators—at least in the context of

Figure 7.7
Head Coach Nell Jackson. Courtesy of the Division of Intercollegiate Athletics Archives.

that era. When Mills decided it was time to retire in 1966, almost immediately two candidates emerged as most likely to take his position: Assistant Athletic Director Mel Brewer and Pete Elliott. According to Murray Nelson, a sports scholar, by December 1966 it was apparent that Elliott would land the position. Certain he had been passed over, Brewer revealed to President David Henry the existence of a "slush fund" created from secret donations that were used for payoffs.[54] The University immediately acted, suspending multiple student athletes and launching an investigation in coordination with the Big Ten.

Initially, it did not seem like anyone on campus was worried about the fallout from the revelation of the irregular fund. Murray notes that University staff

> were hopeful that the penalties would not be severe and looked for some support from the athletic directors at the University of Iowa, Forrest Evashevski,

and Michigan State, "Biggie" Munn. In 1953 Munn and Michigan State had been accused of paying out approximately $20,000 through the Spartan Foundation to players, mostly football players, but "no written records were kept and part of the money went unaccounted for. MSU received a mild one-year probation for what was labeled 'improper aid to athletes.'"[55] Evashevski presided over a football scandal in 1961 which involved illegal aid, but there was even less of a punishment. Since they were both voting members of the panel deciding, it was quite surprising when a unanimous vote of the Big Ten Athletic Directors in the week of February 19, 1967, supported two-year penalties of Big Ten ineligibility for all the players involved on both teams, plus the demand for the immediate firing of Head Football Coach Pete Elliott, Head Basketball Coach Harry Combes and Assistant Basketball Coach Howard Braun.[56]

In retrospect, University administrators had probably erred in not asking Big Ten committee members with personal conflicts to recuse themselves from the adjudication. After all, not only had Evashevski been the coach when the riots broke out at the 1952 Illinois versus Iowa game but his son was now a quarterback at rival Michigan.

Still reeling from the imposed penalties, the University of Illinois appealed the decision but had limited success. Of the 30 student athletes initially implicated, fourteen lost their eligibility after the hearings.[57] After the appeals, of those fourteen student athletes who had been suspended, seven were eventually cleared of wrongdoing, although the scandal had affected the mental health of some. Of the remaining seven, five were permanently suspended, which effectively ended their college sports eligibility and in some cases any possibility of participating in professional sports.[58]

The Big Ten's demand that the three coaches be fired was at first met with defiance. From local business owners and politicians to public figures, including future Chicago Bears coach Mike Ditka, reactions were almost entirely against the Big Ten's decision. Murray writes that

[t]he Illinois High School Coaches Association (IHSCA) voted to support the retention of the three coaches, in the face of this demand by the Big Ten. Defying the ban would lead to the potential expulsion of the University of Illinois from the conference. The action of the IHSCA in supporting the retention of the coaches was also publicly reinforced by the Governor of Illinois, Otto Kerner, the football players of the university, the Illinois Alumni Association and the Board of the Illinois Athletic Association.[59]

Representative Henry Hyde (R-Chicago)—author of the Hyde Amendment that restricted federal funding for abortions—announced his intention to start a probe into the Big Ten's governing body and processes, while Ohio State football head coach Woody Hayes observed that the imposed penalty was excessive and more about setting an example for other schools.[60] Despite the public bravado, Illinois eventually relented, and the three coaches

resigned later in 1967. The BOT then appointed Gene Vance as athletic director, named James "Jim" Joseph Valek the football head coach, and made Harvard "Harv" Schmidt the basketball head coach. Nevertheless, the reputational and psychological damage had been done. For the next seven seasons—from 1967 to 1973—the Fighting Illini football team would not end with a positive tally. In the deepest humiliation, in 1968 the Illini would win only once, a home game against Northwestern.

Besides the trouncing of the rival Wildcats, there was at least one other major Stadium highlight that fall. At the September 28 home game against Missouri, the Marching Illini put on one of the most memorable performances in the venue's history. Under the direction of Everett Kisinger, the band delivered a big top theme, complete with formations that resembled a circus tent, two trapeze artists, and Disney's Jumbo being fed a peanut set to a musical medley with songs by Henry Mancini.[61] As memorable as the Marching Illini had been on that day, nothing could overcome the feeling of doom that swept over the football program. A year later in 1969, the Fighting Illini, "[d]ecimated by injury and the psychological aftermath of the slush fund scandal," finished the season with no wins at all for the second time in its history.[62] Adding insult to literal injury, the new scoreboard added in 1968 did not work for the season finale, a home loss to the Iowa Hawkeyes.[63] After four consecutive losing seasons, three of which were catastrophic, Valek was let go and was replaced in 1971 by Robert "Bob" Blackman, who would guide the Illini to their first winning season in almost a decade in 1974.

Stadium Changes through 1974

The Carillon

In the early 1920s, campus architect James White had prepared Stadium drawings that showed a carillon tower on the north side (Figure 3.14). Typically composed of at least 23 and as many as 48 tuned cup-shaped bells rung by striking the keys of an organ-like instrument called a clavier, a carillon is designed to broadcast sounds over vast distances as the bells clang and swing from a frame atop a tall structure like a bell tower. The proposed car-illon was intended to act as a visual and acoustic land-mark for those approaching the Stadium from afar. On November 24, 1962, 40 years after its design was final-ized, the Stadium finally got its carillon.

But this carillon, a gift of Mr. and Mrs. Rollin Staley, was unique. First, the console was installed not at the Sta-dium or even immediately near it but instead at the south end of what had become known as the Quad—the central grassy rectangular courtyard surrounded by buildings—at the Auditorium. Rather than rely on traditional hammers hitting the bells, the Schulmerich Carillon used electricity to magnify its sound. The Carillon Americana model

> consists of small bronze bell units which, when struck by metal hammers, produce pure bell tones barely audible to the ear. The resultant bell vibra-tions then are picked up electrostatically, ampli-fied to desired proportions, and reproduced from a lofty height in Memorial Stadium. The presence of the stentors in this great memorial structure is especially appropriate.[64]

After a key on the clavier is played at the Auditorium, "its impulses are carried by wires through campus tunnels to Memorial Stadium, where the stentors are located in the northeast tower."[65] After the dedication at the Auditorium, thousands traveled to the Stadium to listen to John Klein perform a dedication concert at 12:30. Later that day, dur-ing the season football finale in which the Fighting Illini defeated the Michigan State Spartans 7–6, Klein per-formed *Shadows,* the Michigan State University song, and Illinois' alma mater song, *Hail to the Orange* at halftime.[66]

Upgrades

Following the assassination of President Kennedy, stu-dent groups petitioned for Assembly Hall to be renamed in his memory. In a December vote, figures from foot-ball lore, including Zuppke and Grange, were nomi-nated also, and even Max Abramowitz, Assembly Hall's designer, earned student votes. But when the voting had ended, the original name of the venue was retained.[67] Evidently the voting had identified an overwhelming

desire to recognize Zup in some fashion for his service, and in mid-September of 1964, the BOT, resolved to name Memorial Stadium's playing field Zuppke Field.[68] While naming a playing field within a venue, as opposed to the entire stadium, is a common practice today, at the time the *Daily Illini* claimed this was "unheard of!" The BOT's decision elicited widespread derision, if not anger, and the editorial board of the *Daily Illini* outright deemed it an "insult."[69] Almost immediately confusion arose, as the entire venue was frequently referred to as Zuppke Memorial Stadium.

Nonetheless, on November 12, 1966, the field was dedicated to Zuppke, who had coached the Fighting Illini from 1913 to 1941 and had died nearly a decade earlier and buried just behind his old friend, George Huff. It was fitting that a concrete wall embossed with Zuppke's name was incorporated into the Stadium's north seating sec-tion. On that Dad's Day, the Fighting Illini defeated the University of Wisconsin Badgers, 49–14. This matchup had been specifically chosen for the dedication since Zup had graduated from Wisconsin back in 1905.

During this period, not since the south-side horse-shoe seating was added in 1929 had Memorial Stadium enjoyed so many structural and programmatic additions. The advent of television, and complaints from the press corps, next prompted the AA to add a new press facil-ity. In the early 1960s, the Football Writers Association of America regularly recognized Memorial Stadium's broadcasting facilities as one of the poorest in the entire country.[70] In October 1966, the BOT at last announced that it had approved just under $30,000 in "funds to cover the cost of preparing plans and specifications for the Addition to the Press Box at Memorial Stadium."[71] A week later, an ad in the *Daily Illini* listed a summarized scope: "The work includes demolition of the existing Press Box on the west stands of the Stadium and construction of a new three-level Press Box with steel frame, steel deck floors, exterior insulated siding and new elevator from ground level."[72] After drawings were prepared by Holabird and Associates (a new incarnation of Holabird and Roche)[73] and bids were received for the new facility in Decem-ber, the AA "awarded a contract for $508,298 to Kuhne-Simmons Co., Inc., Champaign, the lowest bidder, for the construction of a press box at Memorial Stadium."[74]

Preparation began in late December 1966 and work got underway in January 1967. The new press box would provide better vantage points from which to survey Zuppke Field. All told (Figures 7.8–7.12),

[t]he press box will have a frontage on the field of 135 feet at each level. The first deck will have two rows of seating for working press, the second, five booths for public address announcers, game timers and scoreboard operators, statisticians, and television, as well as 90 front feet for still and motion picture photographers and television cameras; the third, 15 booths for radio stations.

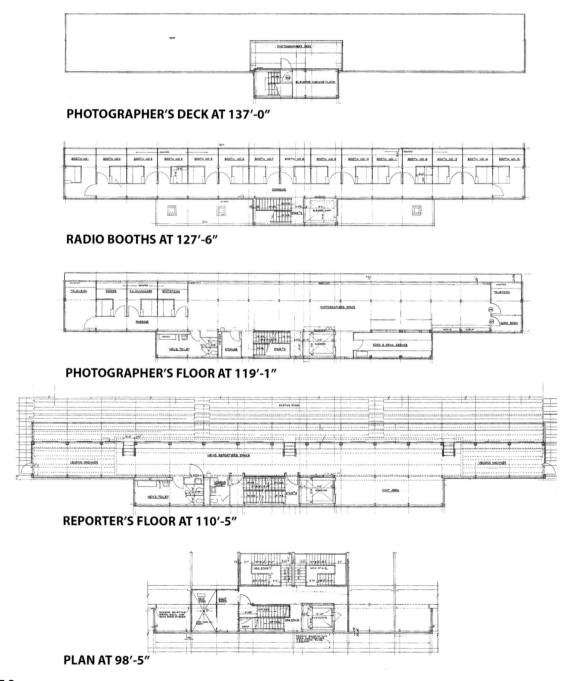

PHOTOGRAPHER'S DECK AT 137'-0"

RADIO BOOTHS AT 127'-6"

PHOTOGRAPHER'S FLOOR AT 119'-1"

REPORTER'S FLOOR AT 110'-5"

PLAN AT 98'-5"

Figure 7.8
1967 Press box. Image by Kevin J. Hinders from drawings in the University of Illinois Archives.

Figure 7.9
1967 Press box as seen from the field. Courtesy of the Division of Intercollegiate Athletics Archives.

At the rear of the first two levels will be a service area 9×80 feet.

This will house restrooms, a lunch counter, coat racks, work and storage space, stairways and elevator.

The elevator will rise from the west great hall. Stairs will begin at the level of west balcony tunnels.

Elevator machinery room and stairs will extend above the service area, with a width of 32 feet.

The front portion of the structure will be cantilever construction to reduce view-obstructing steel supports to a minimum. Windows of the first deck, will be canted, lending a futuristic appearance and, practically, keeping off the rain.

The press box will be heated and mechanical ventilation will be provided in enclosed areas. Maximum capacity of the press box will be approximately 330.[75]

The new facility allowed for the integration of cutting-edge broadcasting technology, but perhaps the most important alteration was financially driven. Though there was a net loss of seats because of the density of

Figure 7.10
1967 Press box photographer's floor. Courtesy of the Division of Intercollegiate Athletics Archives.

the modified section of the upper-tier deck, the new three-story structure included more luxurious suites. Because of their impact on the business model, integration of seating suites into stadiums had become a major priority for sports venues across the country. While college and professional sports teams often had continuous strings of sold-out games even when all games were televised, most athletics programs had reduced attendance, especially in down seasons. Like the financial model of airline business class seating, the calculus was easy: in exchange for a reduction in low-cost seating capacity, a limited number of more luxurious seats reduced maintenance costs and substantially augmented revenue.

To attract and retain these high-paying fans, stadium operators were obligated to provide more amenities like lounges, bars, and exclusive invitation-only clubs. These settings, by design, became sites for high-level networking. Wealthy alumni and boosters socialized not only together but also with high-ranking college and athletics administrators. This kind of in-person socialization had become central to successful fundraising, regardless of whether it was for sports or academic endeavors.

In May 1967, a steelmakers' strike generated the first delay in construction. Then in mid-July 1967, the cement finishers union went on strike to demand a wage increase of $1.25 per hour. Three buildings going

Figure 7.11
1967 Press box reporter's floor. Courtesy of the Division of Intercollegiate Athletics Archives.

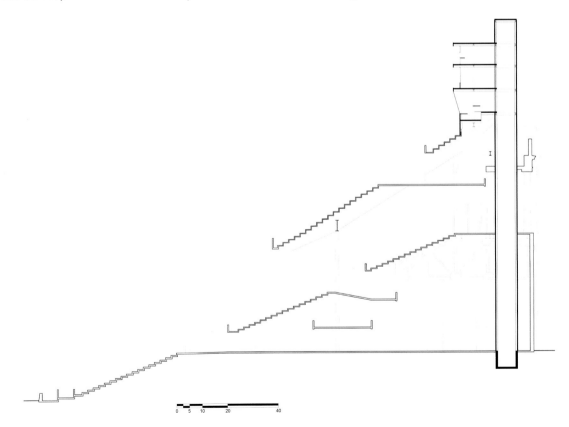

Figure 7.12
1967 Section through the west stands and press box. Drawing by Stephen Feronni.

Figure 7.13
New scoreboard, Ohio State game, Oct. 5, 1985. Courtesy of the Division of Intercollegiate Athletics Archives.

up—Krannert Center for the Performing Arts, the Psychology Building, and the press box—were now at risk of not meeting their scheduled openings.[76] By early August, accumulated delays pushed the press box's partial termination date from August 18 to September 15.[77] Despite that, the season opened at Memorial Stadium as originally planned and to a home game win, 34–6, against the University of Pittsburgh Panthers.

As the decade came to a close, one more significant modification was completed when the scoreboard was replaced after more than 30 years of use (Figure 7.13). The new scoreboard was situated 60 feet in front of the old one, and among its improvements was a numeric time readout rather than a traditional three-hand clock-face. The old scoreboard and its north wall were then scheduled for demolition to make way for the new intramural sports facility—yet ground would not be broken for that structure until October 1969.[78]

Despite the updates, Stadium attendance was still slumping, and the abysmal football records season after season did not encourage fans to show up. It was even harder to justify braving the cold weather that would set in toward the end of October and through November. Not surprisingly, in a *Daily Illini* column published in 1970, Terry Shepard half-jokingly suggested placing a dome over Memorial Stadium to help fill it for home football games.[79] Meant as nothing more than a pithy suggestion at the time, that dome would eventually be installed—strictly for practices—in the 1980s.

There might have been no dome, but the Stadium plus its location near Assembly Hall, were still driving major urban changes. In 1968, the Champaign Development Corporation (CDC), a taskforce set up by the Champaign City Council to study ways to activate the city's moribund core, proposed to elevate First Street at Washington Avenue above the ICR tracks north of downtown to "link with I-74 and I-57, providing direct cross-town access to Memorial Stadium and the Assembly Hall on First St."[80] Besides elevating the street, the CDC also proposed widening First Street into four full lanes and renaming it Illini Boulevard.[81] This proposal was meant to address traffic congestion on days that football, basketball, and major performances were held. Ultimately this proposal was rejected, but other transportation projects would have to address the traffic issues.

Stadium Upgrades in the Early 1970s

With a disastrous 1969 season only 18 months in the past, the University and the AA realized that recruitment needed a jumpstart. In February 1971, new football head coach Robert "Bob" Blackman announced "plans to spend over $500,000 to relocate and remodel the Illini dressing room and to refurbish the football training table in Memorial Stadium."[82] Of that amount, $130,000 had already been raised by alumni, while the rest would be financed through a combination of forward-looking ticket subscriptions and rising sales revenue. Blackman was unsparing in his comment that the existing "dressing rooms are adequate, but there hasn't been much change in them since Red Grange walked out. We plan to build new locker rooms in the south end of Memorial Stadium." He added, "We want wall to wall carpeting, sauna baths, and new training facilities" and then concluded by stating the goal: "[t]his will help morale of the players and benefit us in our recruiting program."[83] That spring, in an effort to signal a fresh start and win back the state's interest, the Illini debuted new orange uniforms during practices and then held scrimmages throughout Illinois.[84]

The 1971 season, however, had a dismal start. The Illini would open the fall with six consecutive losses, the first three without scoring a single point, and half of which came at home. Then, in the most dramatic fashion, the team would go on to win the final five games. This streak included an upset of #17 Purdue at home and two home victories, one against Northwestern and a shutout of Iowa to end the season 5–6.

Despite those encouraging results, talk of a 1972 Rose Bowl season was premature: the Illini would finish that season 3–8. Eliminating the nearly 64,000 wooden seats that had graced its tiers since opening day with aluminum planks apparently did nothing to help game play.[85] Even the first-ever, albeit unofficial, Pork Day was not conducive to a win. On September 29, 1973, amid a national beef shortage, members of the Sigma Chi fraternity handed out pork recipes and prepared pork burgers.[86] Though the food was good, the game was not, and Illinois lost to a visiting West Virginia team, 10–17. Though 1973 ended with the same record as in 1971, this time the Illini opened the season by winning five of the first seven games but then proceeded to lose the final four, including the last game of the season against Northwestern at Evanston.

With the 1973 football season over, Cecil Coleman, who had replaced Gene Vance the year before as athletics director, announced the formation of the Golden Anniversary Fund Committee to lead a $1,650,000 campaign to fund the remodel of the aging Memorial Stadium.[87] The proposed plan called for new artificial turf and a lighting system, which would mean that night games could be held. The rest of the funds would go toward renovating the shower and locker rooms, refurbishing the great west and great east halls, maintenance, landscaping, a new message board, and parking improvements.[88] Coleman claimed that these extensive upgrades would benefit everyone on campus, not just the football team: "you could hold intramurals, club sports, and physical education classes there" (Figure 7.14).[89]

Significantly, Coleman also made a keen observation. The NCAA was in search of stadiums that could host night games because that would expand viewing hours into the evening. Having a broader selection of games available to televise could provide a valuable new source of revenue for the team and the AA.[90] These modifications and additions were also viewed as crucial to recruitment efforts to land the best student athletes.

The new turf was supposed to be installed just in time for the Chicago Bears to play an early August preseason game against the St. Louis Cardinals in 1974. Though the Bears did meet the Cardinals at Memorial Stadium that summer, neither the lights nor the artificial turf had been installed.[91] Approval for those improvements, as well as much-needed structural repairs, was stalled until mid-October.[92] The game had at least demonstrated that Memorial Stadium

Figure 7.14
Aerial view of the stadium with new press box, 1972. Courtesy of the Division of Intercollegiate Athletics Archives.

could host a regular season NFL game even if only a disappointing 7,600 tickets were sold thanks to a lack of interest in watching mostly free agents and then a players' strike.[93]

The Stadium as Backdrop of Activism

Student Activism

In response to social changes and pushes for greater equality, the Special Educational Opportunities Program (SEOP) was instituted during the 1967–1968 school year to increase enrollment among "'disadvantaged' students—those with deprived economic and educational backgrounds—to the freshman class to enter in September 1968."[94] That same spring, the Interfraternity Council, the governing body for the campus Greek system, took an important step toward acknowledging that its houses perpetuated segregationist practices. It further announced that it would begin a process of promoting rapid and complete racial integration.[95]

As the new decade began, anger over the United States' actions in Vietnam and Cambodia was powering a constant wave of protests throughout the country.

On May 4, 1970, the Ohio National Guard was called to disperse student protesters on Kent State's campus. The soldiers assembled at the top of a ridge, where they ordered the protesting students to leave. Some students responded by throwing rocks at the soldiers, who opened fire, tragically killing four and wounding another nine.[96] The already volatile mood across college campuses boiled over. Four days later, over two hundred colleges and universities closed in solidarity with student protests and as an act of defiance against the Nixon administration.[97] Nearly two thousand Illinois students began protesting near the University Central Receiving Depot on South Oak Street in Champaign. After state, county, city, and campus police confronted the demonstrators, approximately half of the student group ran south toward the Stadium. Thereafter,

[a] crowd of nearly 1,000 quickly gathered on the west side of Memorial Stadium where the state police are housed during their stay on campus. A brief scuffle broke out when state police arrested two students and ushered them inside the stadium. Two students were reportedly injured when they were clubbed by police.

Several glass bottles and a few rocks were thrown at police. State and local police then charged students several times and made seven additional arrests, but the crowd failed to disperse entirely.

Several hundred Illinois National Guardsmen arrived at the stadium by convoy about 4:45 p.m. and the entire area was later cleared by police and guardsmen. Those students remaining in the area were pushed back to the Men's Residence Halls on Peabody Drive.[98]

Responding to the severity of the situation, the *Daily Illini* took the unusual step of publishing an extra issue to provide an almost blow-by-blow account of the day's events. In all, 102 students, 72 men and 30 women, were arrested.[99] Protests continued to erupt on campus, and before the end of the year two bomb threats targeted Memorial Stadium during football games, and four more threats were announced.[100]

Student and community activism of this period was not limited to protests, and information campaigns and fundraising for causes around the world were held at the Stadium. On Sunday, May 9, 1971, students and members of the Urbana-Champaign community gathered for the day's Walk for Development.[101] Then in its second year, the event was organized by the International Walk for Development, which sought to raise funds to "help feed hungry Biafrans, South Americans, ghetto dwellers, and American Indians."[102] While the Fighting Illini hosted the University of Michigan track team, walk participants followed a 25-mile route that started at the Stadium, crossed through Champaign and Urbana north to Crystal Lake Park, and then turned back to the Stadium. In all, "about 1,200 people walked in the Champaign-Urbana project" that day, and nearly 800 completed the full route.[103]

In a sign of the changing times and while debates over the appropriateness of funding Memorial Stadium's renovations proceeded, the Greater Champaign Area Chapter of the National Organization for Women (NOW) argued against any funding so long as women's sports were ignored. That year, as NOW pointed out, women's sports had been reduced from nine programs to five. The University and the AA had cited a lack of funding as the cause of the cutbacks.[104] Despite advances in gender equity, the campus and the NCAA were still far off from true parity. Title IX—which mandates that no person be excluded from participation in, denied the benefits of, or subjected to discrimination because of their sex under "any education program or activity receiving Federal financial assistance"—had been signed into law in June 1972 by President Nixon, but enforcement was still weak and unevenly applied.[105]

Nixon had signed the legislation just as he was pushing toward reelection. His landslide victory in 1972 disguised the fragile fabric of a nation still roiling with struggles for equality, antiwar protests, civil rights sit-ins, civil disobedience, and violence. Just over two years after Title IX became law, Nixon resigned from the Office of the President to avoid an impeachment trial, and in many ways helping to bring an end to an American season of discontent.

Notes

1 University Library Student Life and Culture Archives, "Student Life at Illinois."

2 "Kreitling Signs with Browns," *Summer Illini* 5, no. 2, June 25, 1959, 1.

3 B. Poe, "Academic Athletic Approach Harmful," *Daily Illini* 89, no. 121, March 26, 1960, 8.

4 Ibid.

5 "Readers Comment on Football Weekends, Queen Idea," *Daily Illini* 89, no. 37, November 4, 1959, 6.

6 "WPGU's Programming Revamped; New Features, Interviews Planned," *Daily Illini* 89, no. 94, February 18, 1960, 8.

7 Wade Freeman, "Arts Building Nearly Finished," *Daily Illini* 89, no. 96, February 20, 1960, 9.

8 "UI to Graduate 2,500 on June 17," *Farmer's Weekly Review* 40, no. 20, 2.

9 Dixie Cowan, "Illioskee to Run 3 Days," *Daily Illini* 93, no. 132, April 10, 1964, 6.

10 "To Honor State's Top 150 Athletes at UI Nov. 23," *Daily Illini* 98, no. 34, November 22, 1968, 28.

11 Boand, "Boand System Selection." At Wayback Machine. http://cfbdatawarehouse.com/data/national_championships/champ_results.php?selector=Boand%20System

12 Ed Lewis, "Elliott Wants Warm Weather," *Daily Illini* 89, no. 121, March 26, 1960, 15.

13 Ed Lewis, "Coaches Clinic This Saturday," *Daily Illini* 89, no. 124, March 31, 1960, 11.

14 "Baseball Physicals," *Daily Illini* 89, no. 119, March 24, 1960, 12.

15 BOT, meeting minutes, December 21, 1960, 260.

16 Shannon Ryan, "Lightning Strikes, Forces Postponement of Illinois Opener to Saturday," *Hartford Courant*, updated August 23, 2019, https://www.courant.com/2015/09/05/lightning-strikes-forces-postponement-of-illinois-opener-to-saturday/.

17 "Ready Noisy July 4," *Daily Illini* 7, no. 2, June 29, 1961, 1.

18 "County Freedom Celebration Draws 75,000 to See Parade," *Daily Illini* 7, no. 3, July 6, 1961, 1.

19 Christine Tirona, "Officials: July Fourth Festivities Will Be Different from Past Years," *Daily Illini* 118, no. 166, June 30, 1989, 3.

20 "Five Illini Gridders Gone," *Summer Illini* 7, no. 1, June 19, 1961, 23.

21 "Gridders' Outlook Brightens," *Daily Illini* 91, no. 1, September 12, 1961, 31.

22 John Smetana, "105 Illini Frosh Gridders Open Drill," *Daily Illini* 91, no. 6, September 19, 1961, 14.

23 Bardahl, "Illinois Football Recruiting Rewind."

24 Taylor Bell, "UI Student—Fair Weather Fan," *Daily Illini* 91, no. 11, September 26, 1961, 13.

25 Illini Football, "Illini Football Attendance Records."

26 "Big Ten Grid Coaches Favor Rule Changes at Convention," *Daily Illini* 91, no. 60, December 7, 1961, 10.

27 Roger Ebert, "Ars Gratia. . . ," *Daily Illini* 91 no. 12, September 27, 1961, 6.

28 "Big 10 Drops Need Factor from Policy," *Indianapolis Star,* December 8, 1961, https://www.proquest.com/historical-newspapers/december-8-1961-page-36-50/docview/1891703102/se-2.

29 "Big Ten Alters Aid Code," *Detroit Free Press,* December 8, 1961, general ed., https://www.proquest.com/historical-newspapers/december-8-1961-page-51-60/docview/1858780787/se-2.

30 "That New IM Program," *Daily Illini* 91, no. 73, January 9, 1962, 6.

31 Ibid.

32 "Mills Discusses UI Athletics, New Big 10 Rulings, Recruiting," *Daily Illini* 91, no. 114, March 17, 1962, 4.

33 "Kerner Cites Needs of Education," *Summer Illini* 7, no. 7, August 1, 1962, 29.

34 Ibid.

35 "Crown 'King Dad' during Rally Today," *Daily Illini* 92, no. 49, November 16, 1962, 2.

36 "Expanded IM Sports Program," *Daily Illini* 92, no. 100, February 23, 1963, 6.

37 "Enlarges Campus Participation," *Daily Illini* 92, no. 100, February 23, 1963, 7.

38 Frank Hughes, "Throngs See U. of I. Unveil 'Covered Dish,'" *Chicago Tribune,* March 3, 1963, 18.

39 "500 Coaches at UI Football Clinic," *Daily Illini* 92, no. 135, April 20, 1963, 12.

40 "Ask High Schools to Band Day," *Daily Illini* 92, no. 165, June 5, 1963, 10.

41 David Condon, "Boilermaker Squad Tries for Revenge," *Chicago Tribune,* November 2, 1963, B1.

42 Roger Ebert, "The Pseudo-Event," Ars Gratia . . . , *Daily Illini* 93, no. 42, November 6, 1963, 6.

43 BOT, meeting notes, September 16, 1964, 85.

44 BOT, meeting notes, November 24, 1964, 234–38.

45 Ibid., 236–37.

46 Larry Beaupre, "UI Sports Gain Stature, National Attention," *Daily Illini* 91, no. 84, January 18, 1964, 8.

47 Taylor Bell, "Six Nominated for Illini AOY," *Daily Illini* 89, no. 143, May 3, 1960, 11; Ed Lewis, "Spring Starts Teams Rolling," *Daily Illini* 89, no. 134, April 21, 1960, 11.

48 "Cindermen Open Outdoor Season in 5 Team Meet," *Daily Illini* 90, no. 135, April 22, 1961, 8.

49 Larry Beaupre, "Records Fall; Trackmen Top CTC," *Daily Illini* 93, no. 156, May 16, 1964, 10.

50 Fighting Illini, "Leo Johnson."

51 "Women's Track Set to Start Today," *Daily Illini* 99, no. 162, May 29, 1970, 17.

52 "UI Women Cop Track Title," *Daily Illini* 99, no. 164, June 2, 1970, 20.

53 "Coach Awaits Munich," *Daily Illini* 101, no. 79, January 19, 1972, 19.

54 Nelson, "Illinois Slush Fund Scandal."

55 Jenkins, "Fighting Illini," 90.

56 Nelson, "Illinois Slush Fund Scandal."

57 "Illini Appeal Rejected," *Chicago Tribune,* March 4, 1967, Pt. 1, 1.

58 Nelson, "Illinois Slush Fund Scandal."

59 Ibid.

60 "Illinois Trustees Back Henry's Stand," *Chicago Tribune,* March 10, 1967, Pt. 3, 1.

61 "Banb [*sic*] to Salute Circus," *Daily Illini* 98, no. 14, September 27, 1968, 23.

62 Thomas Rivera, "0–10 Campaign Is Dismal Prospect for Illini Team," *Chicago Tribune,* November 22, 1969.

63 Thomas Rivera, "Iowa Brings End to Illinois' Most Dismal Season, 40 to 0: Even Scoreboard Doesn't Work during Rout," *Chicago Tribune,* November 23, 1969.

64 UIHistories, "Dedication of the Schulmerich Carillon," 2.

65 Ibid.

66 Ibid., 3

67 "Trustees to Recieve [*sic*] Voting Results," *Daily Illini* 93, no. 92, February 7, 1964, 3.

68 BOT, meeting notes, September 16, 1964, 101–2.

69 Editorial Board, "An Insult," *Daily Illini* 94, no. 8, September 24, 1964, 10.

70 "New Press Box Slowed by Strikes; Completion Delayed," *Daily Illini,* August 1, 1967, freshman ed., G-3.

71 BOT, meeting notes, October 13, 1966, 177.

72 "Legal Notice," *Daily Illini* 96, no. 26, October 22, 1966, 9.

73 Sally Wagner, "New Facilities Construction Continues," *Daily Illini,* August 1, 1967, freshman ed., A-10.

74 BOT, meeting notes, December 8, 1966, 279.

75 "New Press Box Slowed by Strikes."

76 Sally Wagner, "Construction Comes to Halt as Cement Workers Strike," *Summer Illini* 13, no. 4, July 13, 1967, 2.

77 Wagner, "New Facilities."

78 "Scoreboard Nears Finish," *Daily Illini* 98, no. 2, September 11, 1968, 20.

79 Terry Shepard, "Ticket Proposal," *Daily Illini* 100, no. 65, December 12, 1970, 17.

80 Carl Schwartz, "CDC Presents Plans," *Daily Illini* 97, no. 111, March 8, 1968, 1–2.

81 Carl Schwartz, "CDC Traffic Plans Affect Entire Region," *Daily Illini* 97, no. 112, March 9, 1968, 1.

82 "Blackman Discloses Plan," *Daily Illini* 100, no. 99, February 24, 1971, 24.

83 Roy Damer, "Blackman Plans 'First Class' Grid Plant for Illinois," *Chicago Tribune*, February 24, 1971.

84 Roy Damer, "Illini Unveil New Look; Blues Win," *Chicago Tribune*, May 16, 1971.

85 "Iron Workers to Stop Picketing Stadium," *Daily Illini* 102, no. 3, September 15, 1972, 34.

86 David Condon, "In the Wake of the News: Beef Shortage Hits Illinois Grid, Too," *Chicago Tribune*, October 3, 1973.

87 Roy Damer, "Illini Seek $1,650,000 for Stadium," *Chicago Tribune,* December 15, 1973.

88 Ibid.

89 Ibid.

90 Ibid.

91 Artificial turf was often referred to as AstroTurf after it was installed in Houston's Astrodome, home of the Astros baseball team.

92 "Artificial Turf for Illinois Stadium," *Chicago Tribune,* October 17, 1974, C7.

93 Don Pierson, "Bears vs. Cards—No Bargain," *Chicago Tribune,* August 3, 1974.

94 Bruce A. Morrison, "The 'Incident' at the Illini Union," *Daily Illini* 100, no. 115, March 18, 1971, 12.

95 "Greeks Propose Autonomy, Non-Discrimination Pledge," *Daily Illini* 97, no. 111, March 8, 1968, 1.

96 Lewis and Hensley, "May 4 Shootings at Kent State University."

97 Robert D. McFadden, "Students Step Up Protests on War," *New York Times,* May 9, 1970.

98 "Confrontation Persists All Day; Students, Police Clash at Depot," *Daily Illini* 99, no. 148, May 9, 1970, 1.

99 "102 Arrested," *Daily Illini—Extra,* May 10, 1970, 2.

100 G. Robert Hillman, "UI Steers Clear of Firebombings," *Daily Illini* 100, no. 57, December 2, 1970, 1.

101 "Illini Notes," *Daily Illini* 100, no. 146, May 8, 1971, 12.

102 Rick Pope, "Hunger Walk Raises Money, Blisters," *Daily Illini* 100, no. 115, March 18, 1971, 19.

103 Judy Heurdejs, "The Walk Goes On and On," *Daily Illini* 100, no. 147, May 11, 1971, 3.

104 Judy Arter, "More Money for Women's Sports," Letter to the Editor, *Daily Illini* 103, no. 42, October 19, 1973, 17.

105 United States Courts, "14th Amendment."

A New Stadium Era

CHAPTER

8

Introduction

The week that President Richard M. Nixon resigned and Vice President Gerald Ford was sworn in as president in 1974, Roberta Flack's *Feel Like Makin' Love* dethroned John Denver's *Annie's Song* to become Billboard's number-one hit in the United States.[1] Ford, a Michigan native, had played football as a linebacker, backup center, and long snapper at the University of Michigan, traveling to Champaign to play the Fighting Illini in 1933. After graduating, he would earn his law degree at Yale, where he was also an assistant football coach. After finishing law school, he enlisted as an officer and served in the US Navy between 1942 and 1946.

On April 30, 1975, during Ford's presidency, the United States withdrew completely from Vietnam, ending an especially painful chapter in American history. As the country began to heal, attention turned to pressing domestic challenges. The 1973 oil crisis, sparked when the "Arab members of the Organization of Petroleum Exporting Countries (OPEC) imposed an embargo against the United States in retaliation for the U.S. decision to re-supply the Israeli military and to gain leverage in the post-war peace negotiations," had hamstrung economic options.[2] Financial uncertainty, low interest rates, and federal budget deficits incurred to boost military spending in Vietnam in the late 1960s and into the early 1970s, combined with OPEC's oil embargo, produced inflation rates not seen since the US entry into World War II in 1942. In 1974 inflation reached 11.05%, and in 1980 the rate peaked at 13.55%, while simultaneously the economy stagnated—a condition later dubbed "stagflation."[3] Adding to the general malaise in the region, the upper Midwest would mourn the loss of the Great Lakes freighter *Edmund Fitzgerald* and its crew of 29 when it sank off the coast of northern Michigan on November 10, 1975 A few months later, Gordon Lightfoot would compose a haunting song memorializing the events of that fall

After winning the presidential race in November 1976, James "Jimmy" E. Carter—who had no football career but also served in the US Navy—was forced to navigate complex global geopolitical and economic crises for the next four years. Civil war in Afghanistan erupted in 1978, and soon the new leftist government teetered toward collapse, which prompted the Soviet Union to invade in 1979. To protest the Soviet incursion, the United States announced a boycott of the Olympic Summer Games that were to be hosted by Moscow in 1980. Then in February 1979, following several years of increasing turmoil, Iran's ruler, Mohammad Reza Pahlavi, was overthrown by an Islamic revolution that brought Ayatollah Khomeini to power. The decade ended with 52 American diplomats being held hostage by the new Iranian government. Negative economic headwinds, and the inability of the United States to retrieve the hostages, would prove too much for Carter's reelection bid, and he lost to native Illinoisan, former actor, and governor of California Ronald W. Reagan. Coincidentally, Reagan had played football as a lineman while attending Illinois' Eureka College between 1930 and 1932.[4]

Throughout the 1980s inflation steadily decreased year on year as the economy stabilized. Yet at the

DOI: 10.4324/9781032643885-8

beginning of the decade college football was jolted by a seismic shift when the US Supreme Court in *National Collegiate Athletic Association v. Board of Regents of the University of Oklahoma* found that "the NCAA plan for televised football games impose[d] a restraint on the free market and thus violate[d] the Sherman Act."[5] Conferences and schools could now negotiate their contracts with media distribution companies individually. While television and radio broadcasting rights had become a central part of schools' revenue as far back as the 1930s, these institutions were now unshackled by the dictates of the NCAA. The impact was immediate, as programs that could secure better television coverage consolidated their football (and basketball) hegemony by recruiting stronger athlete classes that widened the gap between them and smaller, less successful—and therefore less visible—programs. In a nostalgic statement about the connections between sports and education, one of the two dissenting justices, Byron R. White,

> argued that the Court erred by treating the NCAA as a purely commercial and profit-oriented organization. Because the NCAA is uniquely linked to both amateur athletics and higher education, it has been allowed a great deal of leeway in regulation that would be condemned in a purely business environment. He further argued that the NCAA plan 'reflects the NCAA's fundamental policy of preserving amateurism and integrating athletics and education.'[6]

College sports, especially football, could take another step toward wielding their huge economic power and implementing their eventual self-governance.

With this backdrop, Memorial Stadium would rise to international prominence. In 1985 it hosted one of the most important events in farming and musical history: Farm Aid. It was especially fitting that the first-ever Farm Aid concert be held at the Colossus of the Prairie for Illinois had long been at the heart of American agricultural production, and its contributions to the American breadbasket, along with its industrial prowess, had birthed the land-grant university movement. Memorial Stadium's production of Farm Aid was so successful

that the event remains a fixture of the American music and agricultural landscape.

The football program would garner similar recognition on the national scene after struggling for most of the 1970s. A major upswing under Head Coach Mike White in the early 1980s continued through the end of the decade when in 1989 Head Coach John Mackovic lead the Fighting Illini to a 10–2 season record and an invitation to a bowl game. On the first day of the new decade, the Fighting Illini defeated the #16 Cavaliers of the University of Virginia 31–21 in Florida's Citrus Bowl, finishing the season ranked 10 in the nation and bursting with optimism.

Memorial Stadium Evolves, 1974–1989

Funding Renovations

In 1974, Memorial Stadium celebrated its first 50 years. This milestone provided the impetus for the Golden Anniversary campaign drive to raise funds and upgrade the aging facility. Though the anniversary was a festive occasion, the United States' mood had soured in an atmosphere of economic and political uncertainty. Like the rest of the country, the state of Illinois started showing the strain of the national downturn. In mid-January 1975, Governor Daniel Walker announced a plan to invest $2 billion across the state to spark economic growth and increased employment. Of that amount, $12,000,000 would be dedicated to upgrade, remodel, and construct new buildings on the University of Illinois Urbana-Champaign (UIUC) campus.[7] Memorial Stadium would benefit—which was only appropriate since a recent "engineering study determined that Memorial Stadium was falling apart and would have to be closed down unless it was extensively renovated."[8]

To pay for the immediate repairs and upgrades of the late 1960s—like the new press box and artificial turf—the University of Illinois Foundation had initially secured a $1 million loan for the Athletic Association (AA. The Foundation borrowed another $575,000, which meant the debt service on these loans alone was estimated at $130,000 a year.[9] Thanks to poor attendance at football games, the AA needed financial assistance to pay such a massive bill. In mid-February 1975, the University of Illinois' Board of Trustees (BOT) requested from the state an additional $9.5 million for remodeling projects that included $500,000 specifically for "the installation of lights in Memorial Stadium."[10] Ultimately, the Illinois Board of Higher Education denied the funding.[11]

Nevertheless, the BOT approved the construction budgets, contractors, and project management team to undertake the other improvements in September 1975. After reviewing the bids, the BOT contracted with Ralph J. Henneman and Associates to supervise three distinct activities. General construction and installation would be executed by C. A. Petry and Sons of Champaign, while Peoria's Unarco-Rohn was in charge of remodeling the ramp towers, and Anderson Electric Company, based in Danville, IL, would install cable and lighting equipment. To underscore that taxpayer money would not be used for this scope of work, the BOT further noted that all necessary "funds are available in the Foundation's Golden Anniversary Fund from gifts and pledges to provide Phase I of the lighting improvements" (Figure 8.1).[12]

Once the lighting system was installed, Memorial Stadium became the only venue in the Big Ten capable of hosting a night football game. Like radio broadcasting during the Great Depression, television broadcasting had become the major revenue source during the stagflation

Figure 8.1
Memorial Stadium with newly installed artificial turf and lighting. Courtesy of the Division of Intercollegiate Athletics Archive.

days of the 1970s. New lights would not only reinforce the University's reputation for innovation but would also expand the hours of Stadium use, which of course meant an upsurge in revenue-producing opportunities. At 100 footcandles, however, the lighting system produced more than enough illumination for a night game but only about half of the amount necessary to *televise* one.

Moreover, the University, and Athletic Director Cecil Coleman specifically, had not yet discussed the possibility of scheduling night games with Big Ten foes. Coleman was confident that the Big Ten would agree to night games, especially televised ones, because a single nighttime game could produce approximately half a million dollars in additional revenue from broadcasting rights alone.[13] Even so, it would take another 11 years before the AA and the BOT would approve $153,493 for the appropriate lighting system to broadcast nighttime games.[14]

Although it was stuck like the rest of the conference with daytime games only for the time being, the football team managed to end the 1974 season on a winning streak—but not with a bowl bid. The source of the program's struggles, including poor attendance at Memorial Stadium, were linked by *Daily Illini* sportswriter Jeff Metcalfe back to the slush fund scandal of 1966–1967.[15] Metcalfe was not alone in making this connection. Nearly two years later, *Chicago Sun-Times* sportswriter Bill Gleason would point to the fallout from the scandal as a major cause for the program's inability to vie for the conference crown.[16] The University needed to change the perception of its sports operations.

In January 1975, administrators from the College of Physical Education announced that three new tennis courts would be built, and several other tennis courts, including those adjacent to the Stadium, would be resurfaced. This initiative included moving tennis practice from the Stadium's great west hall —deemed unsuitable because of its deteriorating state— to the new indoor training facilities at the Armory. Previously, indoor tennis training had been housed at the Stadium's great west hall (GWH), but due to their deteriorated state, were considered unsuitable for continued use.[17]

The push for income to remodel more aging facilities also involved raising the cost of admission. By fall 1974, the typical football ticket price had climbed to $7 per home game, and a basketball ticket was $3. Not surprisingly, students began to grumble at these costs, with one writing to the *Daily Illini* not merely to complain about the price increase but also to attribute the low Stadium attendance to the tickets' high cost.[18] *Daily Illini* staff writer Gary Labedz was even more explicit about his displeasure at the rising cost of tickets and the Illini's less-than-stellar season results. He likened the combination to "just finishing a hot dog and realizing that it's an intestine stuffed with ground up tails and snouts. Yeach." Moreover, Labedz made clear his discontent that the AA was requesting

> a percentage of the money that students pay for swim meets in the IMPE [Intramural Physical Education] building. The AA owns Memorial Stadium, but students pay for IMPE. Charging students for meets there is like charging [head football coach] Bob Blackman to use the stadium men's john.[19]

Regardless of the criticisms, the Stadium needed to be updated if the Fighting Illini wanted to remain competitive in any sense. One plan was to install artificial turf on Zuppke Field—an idea that had been floated before the 1974 NFL preseason game between the Bears and Cardinals. The AA argued that new turf would have two main benefits: increased use by other athletic teams and insurance against cancellation of half-time performances because of poor field conditions. In October 1974, the BOT approved $500,000 for the turf—plus an additional $200,000 for renovations—but that decision was not unanimous. "At least one trustee expressed concern . . . about the possible effect the artificial turf would have on injuries to athletes."[20] Through the Golden Anniversary campaign drive, the Foundation received enough private donations to cover the full amount.[21] Installation began in May right after the football team held its annual Orange-Blue scrimmage and was finished before the 1975 season.[22]

The new turf was impressive, but unfortunately it had no discernible effect on the team's win-loss record over the next two seasons. Not even the installation of a First Nations totem pole in the summer of 1976 helped change the luck of the Illini. The pole set adjacent to Zuppke Field was a gift from alumnus Barton Cummins in commemoration of Chief Illiniwek's fiftieth anniversary. The 16-foot-tall pole had been "carved by Maurice Dennis, a chief of the Abenaki tribe of Canada whose Indian name is Mathawilasis. It was painted by his wife Juliette."[23] In August 1983, the pole made headlines when it was stolen apparently as a prank, found by Kevin Grice in a farm near the town of St. Joseph, repaired, and reinstalled before the September 17 home game against Stanford.[24]

After the 1976 season once again proved disappointing, Blackman requested an opportunity to address the BOT to allay concerns about the football program. The *Daily Illini* reported that among the arguments Blackman made to the BOT to keep his job was an outright criticism of Memorial Stadium:

"If they really want to have an improved football program there are some things that have to be faced" Blackman said. "I have written some of this out which may not be appropriate at this time but I have enough love for the University of Illinois that I think these are the things needed to improve the program whether I'm retained or not."

Blackman did not want to discuss specific areas of his presentation, but it appears that poor facilities will be one of the topics. Earlier this week the main water line to the Stadium was not working and the players could not take showers after practice. Blackman said this is what happens when you have a facility as old as Memorial Stadium.[25]

In addition, he chastised the BOT for not giving him an opportunity to directly address its members previously. With pressure mounting to field a winning team that would fill seats and attract television audiences, especially after raising fall 1976 ticket prices again by one dollar, Coleman confirmed a few days later that Blackman had been let go.[26]

With Blackman's tenure in the past, the BOT approved a $160,600 budget to remodel the northeastern locker rooms in the Stadium and then restricted the

Foundation's debt for the Stadium.[27] In February 1978, the BOT discussed authorizing a parity bond issue of $24,000,000 that would be repaid by raising the student fee to $15 per semester.[28] For Memorial Stadium, the bond measure would have set aside $1,278,073. After an initial discussion, BOT member Arthur R. Velasquez suggested that financing the work needed at the Stadium be postponed, and after further discussion the BOT approved the bond measure but not spending money on the Stadium.[29] Over the next weeks, a new plan was developed to issue series bond debts and sell other financial instruments to raise $43,865,000. At the May 15 BOT meeting, the new plan was announced: the BOT would use the money to carry out projects and make strategic purchases that included buying Memorial Stadium and IMPE.[30] Though not unanimously, the motion passed. Eventually in November 1982, the AA would agree to reimburse the BOT for use of the Stadium.[31]

Thanks to this infusion of cash, during the summer of 1978 the first major work of "concrete restoration and sealing of the east and west balconies" was completed.[32] Another phase of the project was approved in April 1979 when $1,913,111 was set aside "for concrete restoration, leveling, and sealing the remaining exposed concrete surfaces of the stands between the ramp towers." In addition, the BOT requested that various alternatives be considered to augment the basic work requested, and one option included accessible seating.[33] But other planned work would have to wait, as the bids for repairs presented in January 1979 were rejected. These bids "which included work for concrete restoration, sealing, electrical and mechanical upgrading, tuckpointing, painting of structural steel and masonry work, exceeded the funds available."[34]

Meanwhile new head coach Mike White had begun to reshape the football program. His first-year record of 3–7–1 does not seem impressive, but victories over Northwestern, Michigan State, and Iowa plus a tie with the Air Force Academy and a loss of just seven points to #7 Ohio State late in the season were true accomplishments for the squad. Confident of the team's new direction, the BOT began to take on other supporting projects. A new sound system costing $135,470 would be installed during the spring semester of 1982.[35] The discussion about a new scoreboard, however, centered on its cost-benefit analysis:

> Although the present scoreboard at Memorial Stadium continues to provide the necessary game information in readable form, it is believed by the director of athletics and the Athletic Association at the Urbana-Champaign campus to be obsolete in terms of contemporary spectator presentation. A modern electronic scoreboard, which would include a message section to provide a greater range of information during football games (and a timing device for track meets), is proposed as a part of the promotion and marketing plan of the Athletic Association. The assumption is made that an overall improvement of the stadium and attendant facilities will improve ticket sales.[36]

After significant pushback from other BOT members, Earl L. Neal suggested that the BOT request bids but with the explicit requirement that any contract would be subject to BOT funding approval.[37] Seeing no potential downside, the BOT approved a novel proposal: the company that won the design, installation, and maintenance bid would get paid over a ten-year period from sales of scoreboard-shown advertisements approved by the University and the AA. After the ten-year period, the scoreboard would become the property of the University. The University ultimately selected American Sign and Indicator Corporation from Spokane, Washington, for the job.[38]

Now the Stadium renovations were on a roll. In April 1981 not only was the scope of work that had been postponed in January 1979 finally approved, but Edward W. Iossi, Inc., from Davenport, Iowa, was contracted to restore

> the concrete deck above occupied areas of the stadium in the southeast, southwest, and northwest concourses and horseshoe walkway, major plaster on the exterior and minor plaster on the interior toilet walls, and four end colonnade ceiling areas, waterproofing the northwest basement mechanical room, and modifying the pressbox east trough drains.[39]

Next came the pouring of a new 4-inch-thick concrete floor in the great east hall. These projects were expected to be finished in August, well before the first football game of the season.[40]

A New Round of Sanctions

In April 1981, after finding quarterback Dave Wilson ineligible to play along with other violations, the Big Ten Board of Faculty Representatives sanctioned the AA.[41] Initially, the amount was set at $1,500,000, but later that was reduced to $500,000 with most of the monetary sanctions resulting from a smaller share of Big Ten television revenues.[42] The AA would also be held to a restructuring agreement: going forward, the AA's board would always have to be presided over by a faculty member. In response, besides considering exiting the Big Ten in protest, University supporters concocted creative financing mechanisms to fund work on the Stadium and other school facilities, including using proceeds from the Illinois State Lottery. In 1981, State Senator Stanley Weaver and State Representative Virgil Wikoff, both local Republicans, introduced legislation that directed the state lottery to earmark funds for campus buildings and maintenance.

After the legislation was introduced, University of Illinois President Stanley O. Ikenberry met Big Ten Commissioner Wayne Duke to ensure that no conference rules were being violated. Duke and the rest of the Big Ten commissioners were less than amused with the circumvention of the penalties but admitted that the Big Ten was powerless to stop the innovative funding scheme. Even though the legislation faced additional disapproval closer to home—especially from the other state universities—on September 3, Governor James R. Thompson traveled via helicopter from Springfield and landed inside Memorial Stadium. After exiting the aircraft, he signed the legislation and then proceeded to share a few thoughts with the cheering crowd. According to the *Daily Illini*, when asked by reporters if other state schools could benefit from a lottery bill, the governor rebuffed the idea. "U of I is our only public land grant school. It has a unique status in Illinois and possibly the world."[43]

Turf, Illumination, and Branching Out

Ironically, although the AA had justified the need for artificial turf on the new surface's promise to increase the Stadium's capacity to host additional sports, a report presented to the BOT noted that soccer and rugby teams could not use the field because the turf was painted with permanent football hashmarks.[44] Though it was not mentioned by name, by extension access to the newly resurfaced Zuppke Field was also denied to the men's lacrosse team, which had been established as a club sport squad in 1972 and played matches on the practice field just east of Memorial Stadium.[45]

Despite their ban from the new turf, the Illini rugby clubs did not actively lobby to use Memorial Stadium. Perhaps this was because Zuppke Field at 53.3 yards wide was much narrower than a typical rugby field, which can range between 74 and 76.5 yards in width. This difference was untenable for a standard match with fifteen-player teams. Instead, rugby shared the eastern playing field with lacrosse. In a case of what can be described as an attendance ecosystem, the rugby teams capitalized on their field's location across from the Stadium and occasionally scheduled matches to coincide with the end of a football game to attract students' attention as they departed.[46]

Soccer faced different tradeoffs: having a somewhat narrower field than usual—between 50 and 100 yards was the norm—but more visibility made it well worth the cramped space in the Stadium. During this period, soccer was still in its nascency although it had first been played at the University of Illinois as an organized sport in 1909.[47] It had become a varsity sport in 1927, but after the team was unable to play at least three Big Ten opponents to retain varsity status, it was disbanded after the 1935 season.[48] Yet, that an official report would mention soccer at all at this time reflected its reemergence on campus. Not coincidentally, right after the field was publicly deemed unusable for soccer, John Grochowski, a *Daily Illini* sports editor, complained about the decision, titling his column "Time for AA to Treat Soccer as a Growing Sport."[49] Grochowski, citing fellow *Daily Illini* writer and soccer-playing senior Bernie Schoenburg, noted that Zuppke Field could easily be modified

by painting soccer hashmarks and boundary lines in colors distinct from those for football. Despite these public recriminations and widespread support for soccer throughout later decades, Memorial Stadium's artificial turf would remain painted strictly for football.

Schoenburg and soccer club president Ken Klamm, however, continued to push for access to Memorial Stadium. As the fall semester began, Schoenburg and Klamm initiated a "letter-writing campaign to overcome the AA's stinginess despite complaints by Coleman."[50] Then Klamm publicly sought the opportunity to *rent* Memorial Stadium to get his incipient but well-trained soccer team inside the Stadium's confines. Coleman denied all requests, but after continued lobbying Klamm and Schoenburg convinced the AA. On October 28, 1975, the Fighting Illini club soccer team played two games at Memorial Stadium against in-state rivals Northwestern University and the College of DuPage.[51] In an interview for the *Daily Illini,* Schoenburg noted that he was "'looking forward to playing on the artificial surface. It's going to be a good field to play on. Astroturf is the best field except for well-kept grass.'" He also anticipated greater exposure for the club: "'I think a lot of people are reluctant to watch us play on our normal field (on the corner of First and Gregory streets), but they will come out and see us play at the stadium.'"[52] In front of the largest crowd to attend an Illinois soccer game to that point, the Fighting Illini lost the match to Northwestern 5–4, after relinquishing a first-half 2–0 lead. In the Sunday match against DuPage, the first half ended scoreless, and then sophomore goalkeeper David Jacobson and the Illini surrendered two unanswered goals to lose 2–0.[53] After a defeat in an away game a week later, the Illini beat Illinois State 4–2 in the season finale at Memorial Stadium.[54] Over the next few seasons, the men's soccer team would play several times at Memorial Stadium, with the first-ever night match held on October 16, 1976.[55] Those early games at Memorial Stadium were an important milestone in the development of soccer on campus and within intercollegiate sports in general. This higher profile would eventually bring a surprising outcome: while men's soccer has not yet become an NCAA-sanctioned sport at Illinois, women's soccer was officially recognized by the NCAA in 1997.

Besides the artificial turf for Zuppke Field, one other significant and controversial expense was incurred as the summer of 1975 came to an end. The AA purchased and installed 20 state-of-the-art Nautilus weightlifting machines at a cost of $60,000 (roughly $340,000 in 2023).[56] Five years before, these highly integrated and expensive weightlifting machines had been brought to the market by Arthur Jones. Their popularity snowballed when well-known athletes and coaches openly endorsed them. Among the company's biggest supporters was legendary Fighting Illini alumnus Dick Butkus, who not only used the machines but also toured the country with Jones to promote the equipment. As part of a promotional campaign, Butkus, Jones, and Don Shula, the head coach of the Miami Dolphins, collaborated with Dr. James A. Peterson from the United States Military Academy in West Point to carry out an eight-week study titled Project Total Conditioning.[57] The addition of these machines to the strength and conditioning routine of elite college student athletes would help prompt gymnasiums across the United States and Canada to follow suit. In this way, the University of Illinois, the AA, and Memorial Stadium played a crucial part in catalyzing the fitness craze that overtook the United States in the 1970s and 1980s.[58]

This broad attention to fitness across the country that helped integrate sports more into everyday life set the stage for a distinctive contest at the Stadium in April 1976. Started in Chicago in the 1950s, the Special Olympics were sporting events "where individuals with intellectual disabilities could learn what they could achieve in sports and not dwell on what they could not do."[59] Capturing the Olympic spirit that was sweeping the world with the upcoming 1976 Montreal summer games, competitors from Champaign and nearby counties descended on Memorial Stadium to hold their own grand meet. Families and friends gathered at the Stadium to cheer on the athletes, who had to qualify regionally and at the state level before attempting to make the team for the upcoming 1979 International Special Olympics that would be held in Brockport, New York.[60] Thanks to financial support from 4-H House, the Champaign Park District, and the Knights of Columbus, not only was the event well organized with 75 Knights acting as chaperones and Illini cheerleaders invigorating the crowd,[61]

but admission was free to all and all participants earned a ribbon for competing.[62] The regional Special Olympics meet would be held annually at Memorial Stadium until 1982.

Also jump-started during the decade was the movement to bring pro ball to town. When only 12,877 people attended the 1974 exhibition game between the Chicago Bears and the St. Louis Cardinals at Memorial Stadium, organizers were understandably disappointed that Memorial Stadium had not been as attractive a venue as they expected.[63] Among the challenges that preseason game faced was a ban by the University and the AA on the sale of alcohol, including beer, at the Stadium, and that prohibition was not be lifted to lure the NFL. Both teams, however, returned for an encore match in August 1975. Tickets cost $7 and were touted for sale via mail or at ticket offices in Chicago, St. Louis, and Urbana-Champaign. An entire year had passed since that last preseason game that the Bears, the Cardinals, and the University of Illinois had also heavily promoted, but all that advertising didn't matter. Game attendance was still far below expectations, increasing by only 6,250 people to reach a 19,127 total.[64] Spectators—and the fans who declined to attend—might have considered this another forgettable exhibition match. Nonetheless, the experience of hosting NFL teams would prove to be important when over 25 years later Memorial Stadium would act as the Chicago Bears' home field during the 2002 season.

Track and Field Takes Center Stage

Track and Field Emerges

In 1966, Gary Wieneke became the new head coach. Over the next five decades, the Illini under his direction, won 13 Big Ten indoor and outdoor Championships and coached four Olympians. His success and leadership were instrumental in bringing the NCAA Track and field championships to Memorial Stadium (Figure 8.2).

The 1975 season marked an upsurge in outdoor athletic events. At the close of the men's indoor track and field (T&F) competitions, the Fighting Illini had achieved second place in the Big Ten and a top 20

Figure 8.2
Head Coach Gary Wieneke. Courtesy of the Division
of Intercollegiate Athletics Archives.

national finish, raising expectations for the upcoming
outdoor season. During the first April weekend of 1975,
the men's T&F team, led by future Olympian Michael
Durkin, proved that the excitement was warranted. Tim
Smith, a freshman from Chicago, won the 440-yard race
and anchored the mile relay. Future Olympian Charlton
Ehizuelen came in first in the long and triple jumps and
with teammates Smith, Ray Estes, and Al Melton won
the 440-yard relay. Most impressively, Big Ten champion Mike Baietto set a varsity record for shot put and
discus, while Jim Coxworth set the varsity record for
hammer, surpassing the 1928 high mark by a whopping
17 feet and 2 inches (Figure 8.3).[65]

A month later during the United States Track and
Field Federation Classic, an event hosted at Memorial

Stadium, senior Ben App won three events, while Coxworth set a new record, tossing the hammer an additional 9 feet.[66] Having edged Big Ten indoor champion
Indiana, Illinois won its first Big Ten outdoor championship since 1964. Jubilant, the team carried first-year head
coach Gary Wieneke and assistant coach Tom Pagani
into the Memorial Stadium's steeplechase water hole.[67]
A few weeks later, the Illini men's team placed eleventh
at the NCAA outdoor national championships.[68] A year
later when Illinois defended the Big Ten outdoor T&F
crown, Tom Meyer of the University of Chicago Track
Club set yet another hammer throw record at Memorial
Stadium, reaching a distance of 191 feet and 9 inches.[69]
Also present at that meet was his teammate Rick Wohlhuter, a 1972 Munich Olympian and the 1976 800-meter
bronze medalist, who handily won the 880-yard run.[70]

The women's T&F team also inaugurated its season
that first weekend of April at Memorial Stadium by
taking first in four events on the way to placing third
overall. This admirable showing was bolstered by Bev
Washington, who won both the long jump and the high
jump, and Nancy Wertman, who finished first in the
60-yard dash.[71] Two weeks later, the Illini women hosted
a seven-way meet that included Michigan State, the Big
Ten's leading team now helmed by former Illinois coach
Nell Jackson. The Illini finished third, with the Spartans'
point total overwhelming a distant second-place Illinois
State.[72]

But this heavy use of the track over nine years had
taken its toll. The BOT noted that

[t]he present resilient track surface in Memorial
Stadium was installed in 1967. The surface is
uneven, and portions of the asphalt base need to
be replaced. In other areas the bond between the
surface and base has failed, permitting water to
infiltrate. Portions of the present surface are also
worn through to the base. The existing condition
does not provide an acceptable facility and could
result in injury.[73]

The BOT instructed the AA to set aside $200,000 and
then awarded $180,000 to the Monsanto Company out
of St. Louis, Missouri, to replace the surface.[74] Work

Figure 8.3
Big Ten champion men's track and field team. Courtesy of the Division of Intercollegiate Athletics Archive.

was finished before the end of September and included a switch to metric markings to align with international competition standards.

The Apex of Track and Field Competition

The new surface and measurement system were particularly important because Illinois had been named the host site for the NCAA men's outdoor championships in 1977. Arizona State won the meet with 64 points, while the Fighting Illini placed seventh with 30 points, first among all Big Ten teams and an improvement over tenth place in 1975. Individually, Illinois had several top-five performers. Craig Virgin finished second in the 10,000 meters and Charlton Ehizuelen was second in the long jump and third in the triple jump. In field competition, Doug Laz came in fourth in the pole vault (Figure 8.4).[75]

In 1979, the Illini hosted for the second and final time the men's NCAA outdoor championships. This time the Illini placed only 40th, while the University of Texas at El Paso nabbed 64 points to win. Gail Olson was the only athlete to finish in the top five for Illinois when he secured fifth place in the high jump. Those in attendance at Memorial Stadium, however, witnessed track and field history when Ronaldo Nehemia, competing for the University of Maryland, became the first person ever to run the 110-meter hurdles in under 13 seconds. As soon as the race was over, a voice came on the Memorial Stadium public broadcasting system announcing, "Ladies and gentlemen, you have just witnessed the fastest hurdles race in the history of track and field."[76] Unfortunately, a world record was not registered because Nehemia's 12.91-second run was technically aided by a 3.5-meter-per-second wind, which was above the 2.0-meter-per-second limit.

58th Annual Track & Field Championships
May 29-June 2 • University of Illinois • Champaign, Illinois

Figure 8.4
Program cover, 58th Annual NCAA Track and
Field Championships. Courtesy of the Division of
Intercollegiate Athletics Archive.

For high school T&F student athletes across the state
of Illinois, the 1977 and 1979 NCAA outdoor championships deeply impacted their lives. At the end of the
1970s and into the early 1980s, T&F student athletes
chose to attend the University of Illinois specifically
because of the lasting impression that had been made on
them while attending the NCAA outdoor championships
at Memorial Stadium. For some, the impact of attending the Stadium fueled dream to someday compete on
behalf of the Illini. For example, despite never being
recruited to be on the Illini T&F team, Arthur Georges,
a long-distance runner from St. Joseph High School
(in Champaign County), strove to first be admitted to
the University, and thereafter, seized the opportunity to
join as a "walk-on" the T&F team. Others, like Thomas

Stevens, Joseph Cullen, Gregory Reynolds, and Kerry
Dickson, were recruited by Wieneke and Durkin. They
felt For them, Memorial Stadium loomed large in their
recruitment, and felt it was a privilege to compete at
Memorial Stadium, even if collectively they agreed that
"it always felt like we were running against the wind,
no matter which way we were running."[77] By the early
1980s, the T&F began to experience a slide in seasonal
results. Still, these long-distance runners felt that moving the T&F events out of Memorial Stadium took some
wind out of the program's sails.

Perhaps the slide in the national standings impelled the
University to make changes to support the T&F program.
As the new decade rolled in, the AA began planning to
move the teams out of Memorial Stadium and into their
own venue. Before that, the Stadium would be the site of
a combined meet, one final first for T&F events. For Head
Coach Jessica Dragicevic, this 1981 event was the culmination of lengthy lobbying. Dragicevic confirmed that
combined meets were "beneficial for the athletes, more
exciting for the fans and more efficient for both administrators and officials."[78] Despite this confidence boost, the
T&F teams still had to accommodate more critical needs
on campus. When students filled the Armory during registration for spring classes each year, the teams' practices
were interrupted and the athletes were forced to use the
GWH of Memorial Stadium.[79] But that shuffling of venues would end in 1984. Before the 1985 football season,
the track and all other T&F facilities were permanently
removed from Memorial Stadium.[80]

Illini Football, 1975–1990

A Struggling Team

In 1975, Head Coach Bob Blackman started holding
practices on the newly installed artificial turf. Unlike
previous training sessions, as rain fell on an August
day, the field did not transform into a sloppy, muddy
mess. During an interview with the *Daily Illini,* Blackman praised the artificial turf's performance during the
downpour, as it permitted the players to continue prac-
ticing.[81] Among those returning that season was senior

Stuart "Stu" L. Levenick, who had moved from right guard to right tackle.[82] Levenick would become vice president at Caterpillar in Peoria and later through a generous gift in honor of his wife, Nancy, endowed the Levenick Institute for Sustainability, Energy, and Environment fellows program at Illinois. Also part of that team was record-setting placekicker Dan Beaver, who graduated owning most of the Illini's placekicking records and many of the Big Ten's. On October 18 in a game against the Purdue Boilermakers, Beaver kicked a 57-yard field goal, still the longest Illini field goal in Memorial Stadium history.[83]

After that heavy rain during practice, the players continued to prepare for the season opener against the Iowa Hawkeyes. The Illini beat Iowa in Iowa City for the first time in seven years (27–12) but would then proceed to lose the home opener against the #5 University of Missouri Tigers (30–20). The first home game win came against the Washington State Cougars during Dad's Day on October 4. Perhaps to address the ongoing discontent over ticket prices—and of course fill the stands—the AA announced that student tickets purchased in advance would cost just $5 rather than $7.[84] As the season ended, the Illini were unable to match the previous year's success, finishing 5–6. The last games had proved particularly challenging, especially when the #1 team in the nation, the Ohio State Buckeyes led by two-time Heisman Trophy winner Archie Griffin, steamrolled the Illini. The very next week the Illini matched up at home against the #4 Michigan Wolverines, marking a brutal back-to-back pair of Saturdays at Memorial Stadium. But then the Illini managed to upset #16 Michigan State in East Lansing and finished the season by defeating the Northwestern Wildcats at Evanston, 28–7. Though the 1975 season was subpar, sports fans across the state did not have to wait to be more pleasantly distracted by the burgeoning men's basketball team. Now under the guidance of first-year head coach Lou Henson, that Fighting Illini squad would steadily emerge as a perennial Big Ten contender.

Between Fighting Illini games that year, Memorial Stadium would twice function as the locus of community activities, both courtesy of football. On October 18, women from the intramural league played an "all-star football game" at Memorial Stadium.[85] Though this league of 850 players had been operating for quite some time, this was only the sixth all-star game and the first held at the Stadium. Two teams, each with a roster of 14 women, met on Zuppke Field.[86] A series of flag football games, starting on October 11 and lasting through the last Saturday of the season, brought together over 500-grade school boys and girls on the fields to the west of the Stadium, just across First Street.[87] According to the *Daily Illini,* the games were part of a larger community effort supervised by the Gra-Y, a program of the McKinley YMCA, with college students acting as coaches and referees. Because the flag football matches coincided with home games, participants could simply cross First Street to watch the Fighting Illini.[88]

In spring 1976 with the new lighting system installed, spring football practices were held for the first time at night.[89] After celebrating the US bicentennial in grand fashion on July 4—with "a giant birthday cake, baked by Eisner's"—at the Stadium, the fall football season had finally arrived.[90] Early victories against Iowa at home and an upset of #6 Missouri at Columbia would propel the Fighting Illini to their first national ranking since the 1974 season. But then the Illini were trounced by the visiting Baylor Bears, 34–19. Not even Dan Perrino and his Dixieland jazz band, Medicare 7, 8, or 9, could change the Illini faithful's disenchantment. Perrino, a longtime music instructor and regular fixture of campus life, often performed on the Stadium's west side, where his group used the venue's monumental facade as a backdrop. During football Saturdays, Perrino and his band would generate a festive atmosphere for those arriving. On the way out after a game's conclusion, Perrino's music uplifted downtrodden fans after a loss or energized a jubilant crowd after a win. Like halftime shows or flag ceremonies, this performing tradition perpetuated the Stadium's role as a community center and landmark. But Medicare 7, 8, or 9 could not help the Illini win the next two games, and the team would lose six of its last nine.

Like the year before, the Illini would finish the season by beating in-state rival Northwestern, this time 48–6 in front of a home audience. In a major highlight of the season, Illini placekicker Dan Beaver kicked the extra point after the first touchdown and broke Red Grange's college scoring record—one that had stood since 1925.[91]

Still, fans were not impressed with the team. During the entire season, only once did attendance at a home game surpass the 60,000 mark, and that was against Texas A&M. Sadly, the lowest attendance of the season came against the hapless Wildcats, who started and finished the day with only one victory in their season, so few fans saw Beaver make Illini history. Even with Beaver and the other talented players like quarterback Mike Wells and All-American center Larry McCarren that Coach Blackman had recruited, he could not lead the team to surpass or even match the high-water mark of the 1974 season. Faced with another losing tally, Blackman would not have his contract renewed.

Regardless of whether Blackman was right or wrong to point to the Stadium's aging condition as a cause for the less-than-stellar results on the field, he had at least made public the need for significant updates. With Blackman out, Athletic Director Cecil Coleman introduced Gary Moeller as the next head coach. Moeller, a former defensive coordinator under famed Michigan head coach Glenn Edward "Bo" Schembechler Jr., was tasked with returning the Illini football program to its former winning ways. Unfortunately, Moeller was not able to improve on Blackman's results and lasted just three seasons. In 1977, Moeller's first year, the Illini finished 3–8, with two of the wins coming at home; in 1978, the final tally was 1–8–2 with ties at home with Northwestern and Wisconsin. Before the 1979 season began, Coleman was fired. When Moeller failed to deliver any significant improvement in 1979, when the team finished 2–8–1, Neal Stoner, the new athletic director, made sure that was Moeller's final stint and hired a new head coach ready to make changes.

The Mike White Era

In 1975 the California Golden Bears, coached by Mike White, won a share of the Pac-8 Conference crown. After the 1977 season, White was let go and joined the San Francisco 49ers as the offensive line coach but did not stay long. When he returned to the college football ranks as the new Fighting Illini football head coach in 1979, he immediately embraced Memorial Stadium as

part of his recruitment strategy and took new players on tours.[92] Even though the Fighting Illini went 3–7–1 in his first season, the next year he guided the team to a 7–4 record and its first winning record since 1974. Due to Big Ten sanctions imposed earlier in the year, the Illini were ineligible to play in a bowl game.

Then, in 1982, the Illini, led by multicategory-leading quarterback Tony Eason, finished the regular season with an identical 7–4 record, earning an invitation to play in a bowl game for the first time since the 1964 Rose Bowl. On December 29, 1982, the Fighting Illini played against the last Alabama team to be coached by Paul William "Bear" Bryant at the Liberty Bowl in Memphis, Tennessee. Though Eason, a future NFL star quarterback, threw for 423 years on a frigid night, the Illini lost 21–15.[93] Despite the loss and the Big Ten's sanctions, two consecutive winning seasons marked an unmistakable trend.

With the arrival of Mike White and more wins in the books, a renewed enthusiasm for the Fighting Illini was felt across campus. Sensing the positive energy, AD Stoner and the AA began an all-out campaign to seize the moment. First came a slogan: "The '80s Belong to the Illini."[94] Next Tom Porter, a former Illini wrestling coach who had been entrusted with promoting AA programs, suggested a novel idea: TailGREAT (Figure 8.5). The concept was to promote tailgating at Memorial Stadium as a community-focused event as enjoyable as a football game. Among the strategies employed to attract attendees was a series of contests centered on four themes: Student, Most Spectacular, Most Unique Theme, and Most Illini. Over the season the AA would judge entries for the best pregame tailgate party in each category.[95] After the last game, the AA selected a grand prize winner, who received a trip for eight people to Hawaii. Runners-up got a trip to an Illini bowl game, and honorable mentions came with awards of trips to away games and special dinners.

The tailgating campaign was a major success. Partygoers responded with extravagant events, humorous skits, and ad hoc celebrations. Michael Pearson, writing for FightingIllini.com, reports that Kevin Cramer and Susan Ducey were married on the tennis courts and held their wedding reception just west of the Stadium. In another example of the lengths people went to, John Homeier, a Springfield resident, hosted a party for 3,000

Figure 8.5
TailGREAT at Memorial Stadium. Courtesy of the Division of Intercollegiate Athletics Archive.

people that included "flying up live alligators and grilling gator burgers."[96] Whereas TailGREAT in 1982 had drawn nearly 100 entries, the 1983 event was even bigger, generating over 150 entries.[97]

The most important component, however, was the tailgating parties. In spring 1982, Porter began planning for the first TailGREAT event for the opening home game of the season—a bout against in-state rival Northwestern University. The AA-sponsored tailgate party, the first of what is now a tradition, utilized the northwest terrace, just off the northwestern Stadium tower. That party catered to the Illini faithful, especially

major program boosters, who had the opportunity to socialize with Illini AA and the coaching staff.[98] Though TailGREAT proved to be enormously successful, it was initially discontinued after the 1988 season, introduced once again in 2019, only to be suspended in 2020 because of the COVID-19 Pandemic.

Concern over the Stadium's Structure

With the team experiencing season-on-season success, attendance was on the rise. In 1979, Moeller's last season as head coach, home attendance for football games averaged a mere 45,009 people—far below the Stadium's maximum capacity. In 1980, White's first season, the average jumped to 51,741; in 1981, the average grew again to 62,365. Once the Illini had a winning record, average attendance swelled once again, this time to 70,785 people—practically capacity crowds. From Moeller's last season to White's third year, attendance had grown over 57%. In fact, during White's tenure, the Stadium reached its highest average home attendance per game *ever*: a stunning 76,399 people per game in 1984.[99] For the first time since 1925, the Stadium had multiple capacity crowd home games in the same season. But the combination of a now nearly 60-year-old Stadium and a massive and energized crowd led to an unexpected phenomenon.

On September 11, 1982, with a throng of just a few 100 people short of full capacity for a home game against the Michigan State Spartans, "the upper east deck of Memorial Stadium shook."[100] The same day that the *Daily Illini* reported the shuddering, the BOT contracted Hanson Engineers, Inc., from Springfield to "determine the cause of movement of the east upper main stands experienced by spectators during the September 11, 1982, football game; (2) make recommendations for corrective work; and (3) assess its safety for occupancy."[101] While the full study would take about three weeks, the next home game would take place only two weeks later. Preliminary results disclosed by the engineering firm about 10 days after the initial incident suggested that the "movement of the main stands on the east side of Memorial Stadium was caused by the rhythmic and unified motion of fans in the east balcony."[102] This kind of structural vibration is what architects and structural engineers call mechanical resonance, which is when a building acts like a tuning fork. When a force is repeatedly applied in intervals to the structure—like a massive amount of people jumping in unison—vibrations can be produced. If the vibrations match the structure's natural period, or harmonized vibrations, then the entire building can move. Apparently, a full Stadium and an energized performance by the Marching Illini was enough to get the east stands to rock.[103]

Overshadowed by news of the vibrating Stadium was that Ralf Mojsiejenko, the placekicker for Michigan State, had used a 2-inch tee to kick a 61-yard field goal, longer than Beaver's record kick and still the longest ever at

Memorial Stadium.[104] Before the next contest, metal plates were welded to the columns to stiffen them, while Hanson Engineers placed sensors under the eastern seating tier to monitor structural movement during the upcoming game against the University of Pittsburgh, #3 in the nation.[105] With Illinois ranked 19, a capacity crowd of 71,547 people were treated to a quarterback duel between Eason and future Hall of Famer Dan Marino. Unfortunately for the home fans, Pitt's Panthers defeated the Illini without any tectonic incidents at Memorial Stadium, 20–3.[106]

About a week after the Pittsburgh game, Hanson Engineers presented the results of its structural analysis and then the BOT contracted with the firm "for the professional services required to define the scope of the work necessary for the structural design upgrade and rehabilitation work required for Memorial Stadium."[107] By December 1982, Hanson had

> identified four alternative schemes to strengthen and stiffen the existing structural steel frame and has recommended that a computer-modeled dynamic analysis be performed by a consultant to analyze the Stadium structure to determine the dynamic effects of the application of the most appropriate alternative corrective schemes.[108]

To execute this innovative computer-based analysis, Hanson recommended Agbabian Associates, a specialized consulting firm located in California.[109]

Complaints and reports of the Stadium's movement during games continued throughout the fall, especially with capacity crowds. The University and the AA were aware that the Stadium was showing its age. Although its original design had been on the cutting edge and modernizations and integrated technological changes over the previous decades had kept it functional, now it required multiple updates, upgrades, and additions to match the best facilities around the country. With two consecutive home games nearing and then surpassing the all-time single-game attendance record of 75,119 set against Notre Dame in 1946—the first in October against the Ohio State Buckeyes with 73,488 and the second in a November bout against the University of Michigan Wolverines with 75,256—the University and the AA were confident enough in the program's future to significantly invest in Stadium improvements.[110] In February 1983, with the structural studies and the season completed, the BOT received a proposal to reinforce the Stadium's structure estimated at $1,017,000.[111]

And the money kept pouring in for upgrades. Next the BOT approved an additional scope that included "a project of $1,165,000 for modifications to the steel structure of the east and west main stands and balconies, and rehabilitation of the east balcony walkways, restrooms, and concession facilities."[112] Since the steel reinforcement and construction would begin in early May, commencement was moved to Assembly Hall.[113] With structural upgrades to the east balcony walkways done, the BOT then followed up with a similar approval in October for "$650,030 for rehabilitation of the west balcony walkways, restrooms, and concession facility."[114]

During this time, the BOT began exploring master plans to place a new administration building next to the Stadium. Eventually, the AA decided that with the Stadium undergoing repairs and renovations, it would instead consider siting the new administration building to the south of Florida Avenue and east of Fourth Street.[115] As part of this new siting proposal, the BOT demonstrated its confidence in the football program by allotting nearly $270,000 to remove the tennis courts to the east, between the Stadium and Fourth Street, "to improve and enlarge the football practice area."[116] That move was significant for two reasons: first, it converted what had been a rather public space in the sports campus into one that was closed off; and second, it began executing a master plan that incorporated all lots between the Stadium's eastern side and Fourth Street and up to Peabody Drive into part of the football program's growing footprint. This transformation was visible when in mid-June of 1983 the BOT awarded a contract to English Brothers, the original Stadium contractor, to build a

> seven-foot-high enclosure, which consists of brick columns with decorative iron fencing, [to] enclose three sides (north, east, and south) of the football practice area. The approximately 1,830-linear-foot enclosure will have seven pedestrian gates, three vehicular openings, and a removable, all-weather vinyl privacy screen.[117]

Memorial Stadium at the Forefront of Accessibility

As soldiers returned from Vietnam throughout the early 1970s, the number of veterans injured and with disabilities increased dramatically, which generated a new level of awareness about the disability community's needs. In 1973, the US government passed the Rehabilitation Act, which stated that

> [n]o otherwise qualified handicapped individual in the United States . . . shall, solely by reason of his handicap, be excluded from the participation in, be denied the benefits of, or be subjected to discrimination under any program or activity receiving federal financial assistance.[118]

The legislation soon sparked a movement to make the built environment accessible to everyone. Over the next 17 years, activism, lawsuits, and growing consciousness about people with disabilities impelled the passage of the Americans with Disabilities Act (ADA) in 1990. During a period when many companies and institutions avoided or even ignored the law, the University and the AA were among the first to proactively address the needs of the disability community.

From the Stadium's inception, Holabird and Roche, the original architects, had utilized ramps, including vomitoria, to move tremendous numbers of people quickly and safely. Though the original ramps from the early 1920s do not have the mandated 1-foot rise for 12-foot run mandated by today's ADA, the 1983 modifications to Memorial Stadium epitomized an earnest effort to not only incorporate but also celebrate the inclusion of the disability community. In a powerful statement of support led by Timothy J. Nugent, Professor of Rehabilitation Education and Director of the Rehabilitation Education Center and the Division of Rehabilitation Education Services, the University sought to host the World Wheelchair Games in 1984. Nugent "was a leader in the development of architectural accessibility standards, public transportation, adaptive equipment, and recreation activities for people with disabilities" and had founded the National Wheelchair Basketball Association.[119]

In preparation for this event, the BOT approved the "construction of a concrete ramp for wheelchairs on the west side of Memorial Stadium."[120] Recognizing the importance of accessibility, Chancellor John Cribbet remarked to the *Daily Illini* that the ramp had "been a long time coming, and should have been done a long time ago."[121] The ramp was completed in time for the fall football season, but the University canceled the World Wheelchair Games because of a lack of funding.[122] Had the event gone forward, Memorial Stadium would have been host to over 2,500 athletes from 80 countries.[123]

The Euphoria of Winning Seasons

With most of the structural concerns resolved by fall 1983, the football season began with high hopes. But a surprise opening loss at Missouri, 28–18, made for a shaky start. One week later, the Fighting Illini hosted the first home game of the season, beating the Stanford Cardinal, 17–7. After winning against Michigan State in East Lansing, the Illini came home to host #4 Iowa. Before a full house, the Fighting Illini crushed the visiting Hawkeyes, 33–0. Now ranked, the #19 Illini bested the Wisconsin Badgers at another away game, setting up the first of two epic matches that season. On October 15, the Illini hosted the #6 Ohio State Buckeyes, a game in which 73,414 people witnessed a resurgent Illinois team beat the Buckeyes, 17–13.[124] The elated home crowd rushed the field and for the first time in Stadium history took down the goal posts.[125]

Two weeks later, the Illini, now ranked 9, faced the #8 Wolverines. With each successful week, the team drew larger and larger home crowds. To address the need for more seating, organizers placed temporary bleachers in the Stadium's south horseshoe. Setting yet another new record for Memorial Stadium attendance, an energized 76,127 people watched the Illini snap a 16-game losing streak against the Wolverines with a 16–6 clobbering. After finishing the regular season 10–1, the 1983 Fighting Illini became the first team in Big Ten history to win nine conference games. As conference champions, the Illini traveled to the Rose Bowl for the first time in 20 years. Ranked #4, the

Illini were matched up against UCLA's Bruins, the Pac-10 leaders. Despite being favored in Pasadena, the Illini were stunned by the Bruins 45–9 and ended the season ranked #10. Back home the success of the team, combined with community-focused programs like TailGREAT, had resulted in record crowds. Not surprisingly, 1983's average home game attendance climbed to 73,871.[126]

On the heels of a Rose Bowl trip, the Illini were set for a banner 1984 season. Instead, an ominous cloud hung over the program. In July, the NCAA had notified the University and the AA that it was investigating the football program's recruitment practices.[127] At the end of the summer, the NCAA levied sanctions that included two years of probation, forced firings of coaches, salary freezes, and other punitive measures.[128] Before the season began, the AA installed bleachers in the southern horseshoe to accommodate hoped-for ample crowds.[129] The first game was a rare season opener—that ended in a win—against the Northwestern Wildcats on September 1. A week later, the Illini beat Missouri, 30–24. For that game, Memorial Stadium hosted 78,297, its largest crowd ever for a sporting event. Next, Illinois traveled to Palo Alto but fell to Stanford. The next week, the Illini returned home to crush the visiting Michigan State Spartans, 40–7. True to the season's pattern, the Illini won at home and lost all games away to finish 7–4. Despite the winning record, sanctions prevented an invitation to a bowl game.

Even with the losses, the final tally was good enough for a second-place tie in the Big Ten that year. In addition, the home-game winning streak helped establish the still-standing attendance record of 76,399 people per game.[130] With tickets at $12 for general admission and $7 for students, this meant that gate receipts, even accounting for courtesy passes, were producing over $500,000 in gross revenue per game. In 1983 alone, the AA finished with a positive balance of $500,000, which was partially used to pay for the removal of the tennis courts to the east of the Stadium.[131] Thanks to a healthy financial ledger, the product of a record-setting year-over-year growth in attendance, the University and the AA began to heavily invest in new facilities and upgrades.

Celebrating the Roots of Memorial Stadium: Farm Aid 1985

In the first half of the 1980s, the American economy left behind the stagflation of the 1970s, but the residual effects still stretched across the nation. In an effort to arrest and then reverse the steep inflation rates, the Federal Reserve System raised the prime lending rate multiple times. Farming was hit particularly hard by this two-directional crunch: inflation, which drove farm product prices up, also inflated real estate values. Farmers sought to maximize profits and rushed to increase production to meet domestic and global demand. To achieve this higher output, farmers usually relied on credit, paying off the loans after selling their products. Moreover, farmers used their land as the guaranteeing asset for seemingly cheap but adjustable-rate loans. Unfortunately for farmers, the government's approach to controlling inflation was so successful that land values—and especially farmland prices—sank. In just four years, the average value fell a harsh 29%.[132]

On one hand, this dramatic drop generated a gap between the land's value and the value of the farming credit—what in real estate is colloquially called an underwater asset. On the other hand, domestic and global agricultural demand also fell, especially after the US government applied an embargo policy on grain sales to the Soviet Union in 1979 because of its invasion of Afghanistan. With grain and other farm products in surplus, demand had not only been met but also easily surpassed, which dragged down commodity costs and cut into expected revenues. This meant that farmers could no longer pay their debts. Even worse, surrendering their land in payment was not enough to cover their outstanding loans, as the assets were underwater.

As farms failed financially, they often took down with them the banks that had issued the loans. Charles W. Calomiris, R. Glenn Hubbard, and James H. Stock note that

> [i]n 1983, seven insured commercial agricultural banks failed; in 1984 and 1985, the figure rose to thirty-two and sixty-eight, respectively. Agricultural banks accounted for 41 percent of the insured commercial banks that failed in 1984; in every quarter since, they have accounted for more than half of total bank failures. Agricultural banking in general has become substantially more fragile. In 1984, more than 20 percent of total agricultural loans outstanding at banks were to borrowers with a debt-equity ratio in excess of 70 percent and a negative cash flow.[133]

With the US government slow to aid hurting farmers, the music community took the lead. In the summer of 1985 at Live Aid organized by Bob Geldof, musicians played to audiences across the world to generate funds to help end the famine that had struck Ethiopia. When Bob Dylan took the stage, he made a comment about helping farmers pay off their loans in the US. Inspired by Dylan's idea, Willie Nelson began organizing a benefit for American farmers and farms, met with Illinois Governor Jim Thompson, and kicked off Farm Aid (Figure 8.6 and Figure 8.7).

Scheduled between two home games (against Southern Illinois and Ohio State) on September 22, 1985, the event brought together musicians from across the country to play music and raise money for farmers. At Memorial Stadium over the course of a full day, Willie Nelson was joined by 53 other musical acts, encompassing all genres, including John Mellencamp, Bob Dylan, Neil Young, Bonnie Raitt, B. B. King, Billy Joel, Roy Orbison, Tom Petty and the Heartbreakers, Carole King, Sammy Hagar, the Beach Boys, Charlie Daniels Band, and Lou Reed. In all, an estimated record crowd of 80,000 people watched Farm Aid inside the Stadium.[134] Over a 12-hour period, the inaugural concert raised $7,000,000.[135] Still an annual event, Farm Aid concerts and programs have "raised more than $78 million to promote a strong and resilient family farm system of agriculture."[136]

Eventually, the US government did enact legislation to stop further farm bankruptcies before they affected the overall economy. In 1985, Congress passed the Farm Bill; one year later, it enacted the Family Farmer Bankruptcy Act of 1986, which offered a debt-restructuring plan for farms under Chapter 12 bankruptcy regulations.[137] Nonetheless, the damage to

Figure 8.6
Farm Aid 1985, Looking toward the stage to the north. Courtesy of Memory Lane Photography, Photograph by Scott Christenson.

Figure 8.7
Farm Aid 1985, Looking south from the stage. Courtesy of Memory Lane Photography, Photograph by Scott Christenson.

farming communities was overwhelming. In 1935, amid the Great Depression, the number of farms in the US had reached 6.8 million; in 1990, the number had plummeted to 2.1 million.[138] Rural communities and small towns across the country had been decimated.

New Practice Facilities to End the Decade

Before Memorial Stadium had even been constructed, George Huff had a vision for an ever-growing sports campus that would include multiple facilities. Once the Stadium was completed in 1924, Huff's vision would gradually be realized over the next decades. In 1984, full of optimism because of full coffers and outstanding attendance, the BOT and the AA decided it was time to add a new training facility directly adjacent to the Stadium. In October 1984, the AA requested

a football facilities addition to Memorial Stadium. It consists of a weight-training room, additional training-room facilities, meeting rooms,

equipment distribution and storage areas, and office and conference room space for the football coaches' staff, and will contain 18,000 gross square feet. The total project is estimated to cost $2.2 million.

On October 6, 1984, the Board of Directors of the Athletic Association authorized an allocation of $220,000 for the cost of professional architectural and engineering services through the receipt of bids for the addition. The source of this allocation is from private gift funds held by the University for the benefit of the Athletic Association.[139]

Thereafter,

[d]uring the initial planning phase, the Athletic Association completed its program requirements, resulting in an increase in the size of the addition to 27,000 gross square feet, and confirmed the need for the total renovation of the football facilities area in the northeast ramp tower.[140]

Most significant was that funding had been obtained from private gifts to the program (Figure 8.8).

At the same October 6 meeting, the trustees also "authorized a special appropriation of $390,000 in planning funds for a track stadium, artificial playing surface replacement, and for football facilities renovation and an addition."[141] The decision had been made to move the T&F teams out of the Stadium by 1985. Realizing that it would take time to design, obtain permits, and build the new training facility, the BOT "authorized an additional special appropriation of up to $156,150 in planning funds for an air-supported structure, and the remodeling of the locker room in the northwest ramp tower of Memorial Stadium."[142] Nearly 25 years had passed since Head Coach Pete Elliott had pitched the idea of covering the Stadium field, but the air-supported structure, later dubbed "the Bubble,"[143] would span the field to provide the necessary isolation from inclement weather. With

the Bubble approved, major renovations, including new foundation work, were critical. In light of the damage that this construction would inflict, the BOT and AA decided to carry out a full resurfacing of Zuppke Field. For just under $1,700,000, contractors were to completely remove the older artificial turf, demolish the existing base, and install new artificial turf (Figures 8.9–8.11).[144]

In April, the BOT approved nearly $200,000 to remodel locker rooms in the northwest tower, which had not been significantly upgraded during the 1977 renovation of the home locker rooms in response to Coach Blackman's complaints.[145] Meanwhile, the Bubble and other additions required modifications to the structural foundation. To avoid relying on student fees or a loan from the Foundation to pay for the structural work and $1,500,000 for the Bubble, the University issued a series auxiliary facilities revenue bond debt of $4,200,000 that was later expanded an additional $188,000 to match

Figure 8.8
Rendering of the football offices. Courtesy of the Division of Intercollegiate Athletics Archive.

Figure 8.9
The Bubble exterior. Courtesy of the Division of Intercollegiate Athletics Archive.

Figure 8.10
The Bubble exterior. Courtesy of the Division of Intercollegiate Athletics Archive.

Figure 8.11
The Bubble interior. Courtesy of the Division of Intercollegiate Athletics Archive.

the Stadium's projected costs.[146] Once foundation work was finished in mid-July 1985, the Air-Tech Division of Iwin Industries, Inc., which was located in East Rutherford, New Jersey, would begin installing the specialized air-supported structure for $698,000.[147] The BOT awarded Kuhne-Petry Associates a $1,770,650 contract to execute the general construction for the new football training facility, while three local subcontracting companies—A and R Mechanical Contractors, Hart and Schroeder Mechanical Contractors, Inc., and Modern Electric Company of Illinois—were retained for electrical and other specialized work for $436,800.[148] But these months-long projects would not be completed by the first home game of 1985.

Despite starting with a rank of 11, the Fighting Illini finished the season with an overall record of 6–5–1. The only home loss was the season opener against the #6 University of Southern California, 20–10. White's Illini were able to defeat #5 Ohio State 31–28 and battle to a 3–3 tie with #4 Michigan. With a third-place finish in the Big Ten and the bowl ban concluded after the 1984 season, the Fighting Illini were invited to the Peach Bowl in Atlanta, where they succumbed to Army, 31–29, on the last day of the year on a slippery, soupy field courtesy of the Georgia rain. Almost immediately after the regular season was over, construction of the Bubble resumed. Up by January 1986, it immediately became the talk of the University and eventually of the state. Even Mike Ditka, head coach of the Chicago Bears during their Super Bowl championship season, leased Memorial Stadium and the Bubble for practices.[149] From newspaper articles to flyers to advertisements, the Bubble was the star attraction during the winter and through spring.

Unfortunately, the additional comfort provided by the Bubble during spring practices was not enough to deliver a winning football season.[150] The Illini finished 4–7, with one of the worst losses ever at Memorial Stadium coming at the hands of #6 Nebraska, 59–14. The

Figure 8.12
Fire damage to the artificial turf at Memorial Stadium.
Courtesy of the Division of Intercollegiate Athletics
Archive.

Figure 8.13
Fire damage to the artificial turf at Memorial Stadium.
Courtesy of the Division of Intercollegiate Athletics
Archive.

next season the Illini continued to decline, finishing
3–7–1 with the three wins coming at home against East
Carolina, Wisconsin, and Minnesota. Saddled with debt
and staring at a precipitous drop in attendance, the AA
began debating whether it should retain or fire White. In
mid-January with the NCAA initiating an investigation
into new recruiting violations, White resigned. Three
weeks later at a Memorial Stadium press conference,
AD Stoner introduced former Kansas City Chiefs head
coach John Mackovic as the new leader for Illinois.[151]

By the end of his first season, Mackovic had steered
the Illini back on track. The 6–5–1 won-loss record
would earn Mackovic and the Illini a date with the University of Florida Gators at the All-American Bowl in
Birmingham, Alabama. But Florida would win 14–10.
At the close of the final season of the 1980s, Mackovic's
turnaround of the team was evident. The Illini went 9–2,
losing only to the #8 Buffalos of the University of Colorado in an away game, 38–7, and at home against the #3
Wolverines, 24–10.

But vandalism marred that season. On September 24,
three students intended to brand the turf using lighter fuel

and charcoal but instead caused a fire that spread over a
40-by-10-yard swath of Zuppke Field (Figure 8.12 and
Figure 8.13). The University scrambled to replace the
entire playing field's surface at a cost of $589,000 just in
time for the home game victory on October 7 against the
Ohio State Buckeyes.[152] The Illini finished the regular season ranked #11, and as runners-up to the Wolverines were
invited to a New Year's Day bowl. On January 1, 1990,
the Illini defeated the University of Virginia Cavaliers in
the Florida Citrus Bowl, 31–21—the first bowl game victory in decades—and earned a #10 national ranking.

Notes

1 Billboard, "Billboard Hot 100."
2 US Department of State, "Oil Embargo."
3 Macrotrends, "U.S. Inflation Rate 1960–2023."
4 The Fighting Illini have played the Eureka Red Devils
  only once for a home win, 40–0, in 1891.
5 Oyez, "National Collegiate Athletic Association v. Board
  of Regents of the University of Oklahoma."

6 Ibid; BOT, meeting minutes, October 16, 1974, 92.

7 "Extra Money Proposed for University Building Renovations," *Daily Illini* 104, no. 84, January 18, 1975, 1.

8 Bob Consentino, "Where Will the Money Come From?" *Daily Illini* 104, no. 137, April 10, 1975, 5.

9 Ibid.

10 Bob Consentino, "Trustees Seek Extra Project Funds," *Daily Illini* 104, no. 108, February 20, 1975, 1.

11 Consentino, "Where Will the Money Come From?"

12 BOT, meeting minutes, September 17, 1975, 398.

13 Randy Kulat, "Coleman Plans Big Things for 'New' Stadium," *Daily Illini* 105, no. 62, November 14, 1975, 39.

14 BOT, meeting minutes, May 8, 1985, 576.

15 Jeff Metcalfe, "Slush Fund Scandal Still Affects Illinois' Football, Basketball Programs," *Daily Illini* 104, no. 87, January 22, 1975, 24.

16 Bill Gleason, "Illinois Football Problems Go Back to Slush Fund Revelations in 1966," *Chicago Sun-Times,* in *Daily Illini* 106, no.50, November 3, 1976, 21.

17 Jeff Metcalfe, "3 New Tennis Courts to Be Built," *Daily Illini* 104, no. 87, January 22, 1975, 24.

18 "Thank You, Cecil," letter to the editor, *Daily Illini* 104, no. 91, January 28, 1975, 14.

19 Gerry Labedz, "The AA Will Soak You If You Don't Watch Out," *Daily Illini* 104, no. 101, February 11, 1975, 17.

20 Ibid.

21 Bob Consentino, "Artificial Turf Benefits Stressed," *Daily Illini* 104, no. 109, February 21, 1975, 1.

22 Tom Burket, "Spring Football, 'Grass Era' End," *Daily Illini* 104, no. 154, May 6, 1975, 32.

23 Ira Pilchen, "Illini Totem Pole Reported Stolen, Valued at $5,000," *Daily Illini* 113, no. 2, August 25, 1983, 5.

24 "It's Back!" *Daily Illini* 113, no. 18, September 15, 1983, 3.

25 Don Friske, "Bob Blackman to Plead His Case," *Daily Illini* 106, no. 62, November 19, 1976, 40.

26 Don Friske, "Cecil Coleman, Illinois Athletic Director Likes to Stick to Policy," *Daily Illini* 105, no. 139, April 14, 1976, 29.

27 BOT, meeting minutes, April 20, 1977, 260; BOT, meeting minutes, March 15, 1978, 566.

28 BOT, meeting minutes, March 15, 1978, 568–70.

29 Ibid, 569.

30 BOT, meeting minutes, May 15, 1978, 606–8.

31 BOT, meeting minutes, June 16, 1983, 262.

32 BOT, meeting minutes, April 20, 1979, 251.

33 Ibid., 250–51.

34 Ibid., 251.

35 BOT, meeting minutes, April 15, 1982, 527.

36 BOT, meeting minutes, February 19, 1981, 169–70.

37 Ibid., 170.

38 BOT, meeting minutes, March 19, 1981, 212–13.

39 BOT, meeting minutes, April 16, 1981, 237–38.

40 BOT, meeting minutes, May 21, 1981, 266–67.

41 John Hillburg, "Illinois Faces Probable Probation," *Daily Illini* 110, no. 149, April 30, 1981, 1.

42 "Governor's Present Carries State Stigma," *Daily Illini* 111, no. 9, September 3, 1981, 18; Linda Kay, "State Lottery Enriches Illini, Stirs Resentment," *Chicago Tribune,* February 28, 1982, C1.

43 Paola Boivin and Zack Nauth, "Thompson OKs Bill to Create UI Lottery," *Daily Illini* 111, no. 10, September 4, 1981, 1.

44 Consentino, "Artificial Turf Benefits Stressed."

45 Tom Gordon, "LaCrosse Team Gains Split in Tourney," *Daily Illini* 101, no. 116, March 21, 1972, 22.

46 Joe Orris, "Winning Streak on the Line as Ruggers Face Wisconsin," *Daily Illini* 106, no. 48, October 30, 1976, 47.

47 "Foreigners to Play Curtainraiser Today," *Daily Illini* 39, no. 40, November 6, 1909, 1.

48 Nails Florio, "No Big 10 Games, No Soccer in '36! Team Is Warned," *Daily Illini* 65, no. 81, December 11, 1935, 5.

49 John Grochowski, "Time for AA to Treat Soccer as a Growing Sport," *Daily Illini* 104, no. 110, February 22, 1975, 19.

50 Fred Speck, "Soccer Club Has Biggest Win," *Daily Illini* 105, no. 45, October 22, 1975, 27.

51 Alan Fredman, "Hustling Co-captain Schoenburg Active in Weekend Soccer Play," *Daily Illini* 105, no. 44, October 21, 1975, 27.

52 Ibid.

53 Alan Fredman, "Soccer Club Fails to Achieve Goals in Losses at Memorial Stadium," *Daily Illini* 105, no. 49, October 28, 1975, 26, 28.

54 Alan Fredman, "Soccer Club Pleases Coach with Closing Victory," *Daily Illini* 105, no. 59, November 11, 1975, 30.

55 Wally Haas, "Soccer Club Wants Support for First Night Game," *Daily Illini* 106, no. 36, October 14, 1976, 32.

56 Jeff Donnelly, "Nautilus—Building Bodies a New and Better Way," *Daily Illini* 105, no. 110, February 25, 1976, 22.

57 Peterson, "Total Conditioning."

58 Stern, "Fitness Movement."

59 Northwestern University Special Olympics, "About Us."

60 Special Olympics, "A Joyful New Movement Gains Momentum."

61 Wally Haas, "Everyone's a Winner at Special Olympics," *Daily Illini* 105, no. 149, April 28, 1976, 27.

62 "Mom's Day Weekend," *Daily Illini* 105, no. 45, April 22, 1976, 5.

63 Randy Kulat, "Bears Take on Cardinals Today," *Daily Illini* 105, no. 4, August 23, 1975, 40.

64 Pro Football Archives, "1975 Chicago Bears (NFL)."

65 Randy Kulat, "Smith 'Unbelievably Strong' in Outdoor Track Opener," *Daily Illini* 104, no. 134, April 8, 1975, 32.

66 Randy Kulat, "Coxworth Breaks Hammer Throw Record in Classic," *Daily Illini* 104, no. 153, May 3, 1975, 20.

67 Pierson, Don, "Illini Capture Big Ten Track Title," Chicago Tribune (1963-1996), May 18, 1975, B6.

68 Jeff Drumtra, "Star Track," photographs by Shiela Reaves, University of Illinois Urbana-Champaign, *Illio 76* (Urbana-Champaign: Illini Publishing), 1976, 195.

69 Wally Haas, "Coxworth Makes Comeback in Hammer Throw," *Daily Illini* 105, no. 134, April 7, 1976, 28.

70 Wally Haas, "Quality Workouts Help Prepare Rick Wohlhuter for Olympic Trials," *Daily Illini* 105, no. 135, April 8, 1976, 40.

71 Judi Antonicic, "Women's Track Team 3rd in Meet behind Trio of 1st-Place Finishes," *Daily Illini* 104, no. 134, April 8, 1975, 32.

72 Judi Antonicic, "Illini Women Finish Third in Track Meet," *Daily Illini* 104, April 22, 1975, 31.

73 BOT, meeting minutes, June 16, 1976, 685.

74 Ibid.

75 Milesplit Illinois, "NCAA Division 1 Track and Field Championships 1977."

76 Maloney, "Renaldo Nehemiah."

77 Interviews: Arthur Georges, Thomas Stevens, Joseph Cullen, Gregory Reynolds and Kerry Dickson, January 26, 2024.

78 Zack Nauth, "Women to Run alongside Men's Team at Track Outing," *Daily Illini* 110, no. 130, April 3, 1981, 24.

79 Molly Bolger, "Registration Evicts Track Team," *Daily Illini* 112, no. 77, January 12, 1983, 1.

80 BOT, meeting minutes, March 21, 1985, 214.

81 Wally Haas, "Blackman Juggles Illini Starting Offensive Line," *Daily Illini* 105, no. 10, September 3, 1975, 32.

82 Ibid.

83 Fighting Illini Football, "Memorial Stadium Records."

84 "Special Football Announcement to U of I Students," *Daily Illini* 105, no. 18, September 13, 1975, 19.

85 "Women All-Stars to Play in Stadium," *Daily Illini* 105, no. 43, October 18, 1975, 18.

86 Ibid.

87 Randy Kulat, "The Small Battles before the Big War," photographs by Shiela Reaves, *Daily Illini* 105, no. 60, November 12, 1975, 24.

88 Ibid.

89 "Football Team to Scrimmage under Lights," *Daily Illini* 105, no. 146, April 23, 1976, 38.

90 Carol Mencke, "Fourth of July Events Expand for Bicentennial," *Daily Illini* 105, no. 171, June 24, 1976, 13.

91 Robert Markus, "Blackman's Closing Act Leaves Illinois Cheering," *Chicago Tribune,* November 21, 1976, B1.

92 Mike Bass, "White's Name Helps Sell Illinois to Potential Recruits," *Daily Illini* 109, no. 103, February 20, 1980, 28.

93 John Husar, "Bryant Goes Out a Winner," *Chicago Tribune,* December 30, 1982, 23, https://www.newspapers.com/article/chicago-tribune-dec-30-1982-trib-1/20049474/.

94 David Condon, "Illini Certain '80s Belong to Them," In the Wake of the News, *Chicago Tribune,* March 31, 1982, G3.

95 Scott Heiberger, "All Cordially Invited to Illini 'Tailgreat,'" *Daily Illini* 112, no. 1, August 25, 1982, 64.

96 Pearson, "'People Got Crazy.'"

97 Ibid.

98 Ibid.

99 Fighting Illini Football, "Illini Football Attendance Records."

100 Marilyn Idelman, "Stadium Movement Prompts Safety Study," *Daily Illini* 112, no. 14, September 14, 1982, 1.

101 BOT, meeting minutes, November 18, 1982, 102.

102 Glenora Croucher, "Engineers Suggest Stadium Measures," *Daily Illini* 112, no. 19, September 21, 1982, 32.

103 Doug Lee, "Spectators Rock Big Ten Stadia—Literally," *Daily Illini* 112, no. 23, September 25, 1982, 3.

104 Lucky's Amazing Sports Lists, "Field Goals 60 Yards or More."

105 Tom Osran, "Fans Say the Stadium Moved, while Officials Deny Event," *Daily Illini* 112, no. 44, October 12, 1982, 1.

106 Fighting Illini Football, "Illini Football Attendance Records."

107 BOT, Meeting Minutes, November 18, 1982, 102.

108 BOT, Meeting Minutes, January 20, 1983, 144–45.

109 Ibid.

110 Fighting Illini Football, "Illini Football Attendance Records."

111 BOT, Meeting Minutes, February 17, 1983, 164.

112 BOT, Meeting Minutes, April 21, 1983, 215.

113 Lucy Piton, "UI Trustees Pick Assembly Hall as Site of '83 Commencement," *Daily Illini* 112, no. 104, February 18, 1983, 1.

114 BOT, Meeting Minutes, October 20, 1983, 400.

115 Valli Herman, "Sports Complex Future Depends on Funding," *Daily Illini* 112, no. 87, January 26, 1983, 7.

116 BOT, Meeting Minutes, March 17, 1983, 190.

117 BOT, Meeting Minutes, June 16, 1983, 269.

118 US Equal Employment Opportunity Commission, "Rehabilitation Act of 1973."

119 Grigg and Prom, "Finding Aid."

120 BOT, Meeting Minutes, June 16, 1983, 270–71.

121 Lisa Collins, "University Trustees Pass Building Plans," *Daily Illini* 112, no. 159, June 17, 1983, 20.

122 Brian Nadig, "Wheelchair Games Axed by University," *Daily Illini* 113, no. 83, January 17, 1984, 1.

123 Collins, "University Trustees Pass Building Plans."

124 Fighting Illini Football, "Football History vs Ohio State University."

125 John Husar, "College Football: Illinois' Late TD 'Upsets' the Plan," *Chicago Tribune,* October 16, 1983, C4.

126 Fighting Illini Football, "Illini Football Attendance Records."

127 Joe Zenkel, "Illinois Stays Silent on Letter of Inquiry," *Daily Illini* 113, no. 173, July 12, 1984, 16.

128 "Newspaper Report Says Illini Hit with Sanctions," *Daily Illini* 113, no. 177, July 19, 1984, 20.

129 Jeff Legwold, "Illini Offense Sputters, Gains Win over 'Cats," *Daily Illini* 114, no. 12, September 5, 1984, 40.

130 Fighting Illini Football, "Illini Football Attendance Records."

131 Lucy Piton, "Trustees OK New Practice Field," *Daily Illini* 112, no. 124, March 18, 1983, 5.

132 Calomiris, Hubbard, and Stock, "Farm Debt Crisis," 441.

133 Ibid, 441–42.

134 Farm Aid History Harvest, "Share Your Memories of Farm Aid!

135 Farm Aid, "Farm Aid: A Concert for America."

136 Farm Aid, "About Us."

137 Dinterman, Katchova, and Harris, "Financial Stress," 1.

138 Iowa Pathways, "The Farm Crisis of the 1980s."

139 BOT, Meeting Minutes, October 18, 1984, 101.

140 BOT, Meeting Minutes, March 21, 1985, 215–16.

141 Ibid., 214.

142 Ibid.

143 Michael Lufrano, "Bubble over Field Considered by AA," *Daily Illini* 114, no. 126, March 22, 1985, 28.

144 BOT, Meeting Minutes, March 21, 1985, 214–15.

145 BOT, Meeting Minutes, April 18, 1985, 247.

146 BOT, Meeting Minutes, April 10, 1986, 550.

147 BOT, Meeting Minutes, July 18, 1985, 352.

148 Ibid., 358.

149 Brian Nadig, "Police Call Criminal Activity 'Very, Very Quiet' Over Break," *Daily Illini* 115, no. 76, January 20, 1986, 3.

150 David Campbell, "'No-Names' Battling to Win First-String Quarterback Job," *Daily Illini* 115, no. 129, April 14, 1986, 36.

151 Tony Garcia, "Mackovic Next Illini Mentor," *Daily Illini* 117, no. 90, February 3, 1988, 36.

152 "Arson Fire Destroys Field at U. Illinois Stadium," *Chronicle of Higher Education,* October 4, 1989, A2.

The New Millennium

Introduction

In January 1989, former vice president George H. W. Bush was sworn in as president of the United States. Across the world, an economically and politically weak Soviet Union saw itself obligated to undergo change. The traditional Cold War divisions were slowly evaporating—so much so that the University of Illinois Urbana-Champaign (UIUC) and the University of Southern California (USC) flirted with opening their 1989 seasons by playing each other in the Glasnost Bowl in Moscow.[1] Throughout 1989, East Germans had been traveling through Czechoslovakia, into Hungary, and across Hungary's western border into Austria. Without fear of Soviet reprisal, the Hungarian government refused East Germany's request to stop border crossings into Austria. For East Germany, the accelerating mass exodus of residents eventually caused the Berlin Wall to come down in 1989, and West and East Germany officially unified on October 3, 1990.

In the summer of 1990, Iraq invaded Kuwait. In January 1991, a United Nations-endorsed and US-led coalition of 42 countries began Operation Desert Storm, introducing the world to "shock and awe," as CNN and other cable news services broadcast the war live on television. In response, UIUC students marched from downtown Champaign to the campus Quad in opposition. And in another dramatic political episode, a few months later the Student Government Association voted to end support for Chief Illiniwek.[2] This marked the beginning of the gradual elimination of the once-beloved figure at the University. Before the

year closed, on December 26, 1991, the Soviet Union officially dissolved, which marked not only the end of communism across most of Europe but most significantly the Cold War.

Back in the US, new wave music, which had emerged in the 1980s in Europe, gave way to the Seattle-centered grunge sound. Led by groups like Nirvana and its lead singer Kurt Cobain, the music critiqued a deep consumerist culture. With a goal of increasing corporate profits, the Canadian, Mexican, and US governments negotiated a trilateral free trade agreement. After William "Bill" J. Clinton took office, he signed into law the North American Free Trade Agreement, which would alter the approach to American labor and agricultural practices. A highly popular Clinton easily won reelection in November 1996 but spent the better part of the last years of his presidency mired in controversies.

Then in April 1999, the intimate fabric of American life was shredded when two teenagers walked into a Colorado high school and opened fire, killing 13 people and wounding 20 others. To close 1999, fear swept across the world as technology experts questioned how computers and other complex systems would adjust to the change of millennia in internal clocks when technology built to manage only twentieth-century dates switched to the year 2000. Ultimately—after much planning, consternation, and patching—few systems were affected, and a relieved populace went on with their lives on January 1, 2000.

Toward the middle of 2000, a once robust economy sputtered and stalled when technology companies' stocks tumbled sharply, dragging the US into what would later be dubbed the "dot-com bubble." After a brief recession,

DOI: 10.4324/9781032643885-10   245

that November Bush was elected president after a highly controversial recount and Supreme Court decision.

For the first time since the attack on Pearl Harbor, the US faced a foreign threat within its borders when on September 11, 2001, terrorists flew airplanes into the World Trade Center in New York City and the Pentagon, while another airplane went down in Somerset County, Pennsylvania. In all, nearly 3,000 people died as a result. Three days later, the government of a wounded nation voted in favor of authorizing force and initiated an invasion of Afghanistan. Still reeling from the events of 9/11, in March 2003 the Bush administration received congressional approval to invade Iraq. US armed forces would remain in active combat there until 2011 and still maintain a strong military presence. In Afghanistan, US military action formally would not end until August 2021—nearly 20 years later. Like the Vietnam War, military casualties, costs, and civilian suffering eventually made these military actions highly unpopular.

Despite the tumultuous political climate and emotional turmoil of the period, Fighting Illini teams were performing well. During Head Coach William "Bill" Self's first season, the men's basketball team won the Big Ten Conference. After losing to Arizona in the Elite Eight, the Illini finished the 2001–2002 season ranked #4 in the country. Not to be outdone, the Fighting Illini football team would also win the Big Ten Conference in 2001 as well. In 2003, the men's tennis team went 32–0, nabbing the NCAA National Championship. As the fall semester began, the University announced that with 6,801 students, the school had enrolled the largest freshman class ever.[3] And in major academic news, three faculty members were awarded 2003 Nobel Prizes: Paul C. Lauterbur shared with Sir Peter Mansfield the Nobel Prize in Medicine, while Anthony J. Leggett earned the Nobel Prize in Physics (with Alexei A. Abrikosov and Vitaly L. Ginzburg).

With conflict still running high between supporters and detractors, the community found a sports-related reprieve when twenty-eight past and present student athletes competed in the Athens Olympic Games, winning 20 medals. The following winter during the 2004–2005 season, the Fighting Illini basketball team, under second-year head coach Bruce Weber, would lose only two games—unfortunately, the second one was the

NCAA National Championship defeat to the University of North Carolina Tar Heels, 75–70.

In fall 2007, an overheated US economy began to wither, especially as commodity prices, like those for wheat and corn, climbed unabated. The next year a badly managed mortgage derivatives market triggered an implosion that ushered in the great recession. Between 2008 and 2009, US households lost nearly $19 trillion in net worth.[4] As it did during the Great Depression of the 1930s, the US government passed controversial legislation to shore up businesses and stimulate economic growth, which prompted a new phrase to enter the American lexicon: "too big to fail." Despite the stabilizing financial outlook of 2012 bolstered by the policies of Barack Obama —the first African American president of the nation—racially charged events like Trayvon Martin's murder in 2013 and the trial of his killer or the 2014 police shooting and death of Michael Brown in Ferguson, Missouri, unleashed social unrest, mass protests, activism, and the founding of the Black Lives Matter movement.

In this setting, one of the most acrimonious elections since the pre–Civil War era sent Donald J. Trump—a real estate developer and television personality—to the White House. For the second time in three elections, the Republican candidate had tallied the required number of electoral votes but had failed to win the popular vote. The next four years would be even more turbulent, as fictitious and real accusations plagued all branches of the federal government. Despite the incessant scandals, tax cuts helped strengthen the economy until the COVID-19 pandemic changed everything.

On the last day of December 2019, the World Health Organization (WHO) called attention to an alarming spike in pneumonia cases.[5] On January 21, 2020, the first confirmed case of COVID-19, an illness caused by infection with a novel coronavirus, was reported in the United States.[6] Nine days later, WHO declared a global health emergency. Amid scandals and accusations, the US Centers for Disease Control and Prevention (CDC) began an aggressive program of social distancing and lockdowns intended to "flatten the curve" of infections and deaths and pushed to develop an mRNA vaccine. With restrictions on dining and shopping and other socially based strategies being enforced in many parts of the world and the Olympic Games in Japan postponed, the US economy shrank dramatically by 2.8% in 2020.[7]

Adding to the country's growing woes, in May 2020 police in Minneapolis, Minnesota, murdered George Floyd, an African American, during his arrest. Despite strict policies to shelter in place, race-focused protests and then riots spread throughout major US cities, with groups firebombing federal buildings or looting urban core commercial establishments. Channeling widespread frustration with police policies and tactics and alleging systemic racism, the Black Lives Matter movement grew into a national sociopolitical force. That November, Trump lost his reelection bid to Obama's vice president, Joseph R. Biden, but on January 6, 2021, rioters inspired by Trump's claims of a "rigged election" broke into the US Capitol Building in a failed attempt to disrupt the certification of electors.[8]

Into early 2022, restrictive COVID-19 policies were slowly easing, but the combination of pent-up demand, government cash disbursements, and broken supply chains sourced abroad generated inflation not seen since the late 1970s. But these financial pressures did not halt military aggression, as Russia invaded Ukraine to occupy and secure eastern Russian-speaking provinces in 2022. Nineteen months later, Hamas terrorists crossed the border from Gaza into Israel, killing nearly 1200 people and taking over 250 hostages.[9] In response, Israel's government declared war and invaded Gaza in a brutal air and ground offensive that has claimed tens of thousands of Palestinian lives. Both conflicts have spurred protests across the United States and calls for peace. Now in 2024, with an upcoming and surely contentious presidential election, the US is bracing with the rest of the world for a challenging year. But the Urbana-Champaign community can see at least one celebratory time ahead: Memorial Stadium's first centennial.

Memorial Stadium in the 1990s

The Transformation of the Athletic Association

After the resignations of football coach Mike White and Athletic Director Neale Stoner for rule violations,

the Athletic Association (AA) was staring at a debt of nearly $1.5 million and needed the football and basketball programs to be successful.[10] But in October 1988, the Illinois General Assembly's Legislative Audit Commission argued that the AA needed to be dissolved so that a new administrative unit could be incorporated directly under the supervision of the University. Not only would all assets owned by the AA be absorbed but all employees would be held to the same rules as other state employees.[11]

Faced with the threat of these forced changes, in January 1989 the University and the AA agreed that a new administrative department would be established that would be directly supervised by the Office of the Chancellor and named John Mackovic, the former football head coach, as the athletic director.[12] Although internal audits revealed that the AA's debt was closer to $2,000,000,[13] the 1988 All-American Bowl appearance and the Fighting Illini basketball team landing in the Final Four led Vice President for Business and Finance Craig Bazzanni to estimate that the budget would nevertheless be about $200,000 "in the black."[14] Just seven months short of celebrating 100 years, the AA ceased to exist, and the Department of Intercollegiate Athletics (DIA) started operations on July 1, 1989.

Football and Stadium Highs and Lows

On January 1, 1990, after finishing the regular season 9–2, the Fighting Illini proceeded to defeat the #16 University of Virginia Cavaliers in the Florida Citrus Bowl. The following fall and a starting rank of 11 kicked off the "100 Years of Football Centennial Celebration."[15] The team opened with an away loss to the University of Arizona Wildcats, 28–16, but rebounded the next game at home to squeak past the eventual 1990 national champions, the University of Colorado Buffaloes, 23–22. The next week at another home game against the Southern Illinois Salukis, Illinois running back Howard Griffith set the still-standing NCAA record for most touchdowns by one player in a single game with his tally of eight (Figure 9.1).[16] Behind Griffith's running and Jason Verduzco's passing, the Illini would finish the regular season 8–3, with the lone home loss coming against

Figure 9.1
Howard Griffith running against the Southern Illinois Salukis. Courtesy of the Division of Intercollegiate Athletics Archives

the #13 Iowa Hawkeyes, 54–28. Despite a 30–0 loss to the Clemson Tigers in the Hall of Fame Bowl, the Illini finished ranke d 25 in the nation. With 31 touchdowns, Griffith would graduate with the record total and took a moment before ending his college career to honor another legendary player.[17] After the bowl game, Griffith visited Red Grange and "gave Grange a ball autographed by the team."[18] Just a few days later, the Illini family grieved when Grange died on January 28, 1991, at the age of 87.

The next season started in August—a first—with a home win against the East Carolina Pirates. Once again, the Illini lost only one home game, a setback against the #4 Michigan Wolverines, yet this time ended with a 6–5 record. Almost immediately after the season was

over, Mackovic resigned, and Lou Tepper, the team's defensive coordinator, was selected as the interim head coach. In the postseason John Hancock Bowl, the Illini defense was superb, but unfortunately, the offense sputtered in a 6–3 loss to the Pac-10's Bruins.

After a national search, Ronald "Ron" Guenther was named the DIA's new athletic director to support Tepper, now the official head coach.[19] With administrators and football staff in place, the Illini seemed ready for success. At first, it did not seem that Tepper's Illini had lost too much momentum, finishing the regular season 5–4–1 fortified by Simeon Rice, a fierce four-year starting linebacker who would graduate as the Big Ten's all-time sack leader.[20] Among the season's highlights, the Illini pulled off an 18–16 upset against #21 Ohio State in Columbus—extending the winning streak against the Buckeyes to five. With the season on the line, the Illini stunned the #3 Wolverines in Ann Arbor, drawing even at 22–22, and then beat Michigan State at home 14–10 to salvage the season and earn a bowl bid. On December 30 in the Holiday Bowl, the University of Hawai'i Rainbow Warriors defeated the Illini 27–17, bringing Tepper's first season at the helm to a close.

Tepper's second season was the first losing season in five years. One high point of the 1993 season was an upset of the #13 Michigan Wolverines at Ann Arbor, 24–21. Among the losses was a defeat to the #16 Penn State Nittany Lions who played host. Though not the first time these foes had met, when the Illini played against Penn State, it was the first time as a Big Ten Conference rivals, since Penn State had joined the conference in 1993.

When the Illini logged a winning 1994 season, attendance jumped from a 51,018 average per home game in 1993 to 60,294 in 1994—an increase of almost 20%.[21] To help further enlarge the fanbase and increase revenues, the DIA tried new initiatives. Among them was playing a season opener at Chicago's Soldier Field against the Washington State Cougars. Despite the 10–9 loss, the game was still considered a success among Chicago-based alumni, but concession stand operators back at Memorial Stadium complained about the lost income. Another plan was for a 35-foot-long blimp to fly over Zuppke Field with advertisements.[22] The most important event back

on campus, however, was the commemoration of the seventieth anniversary of Memorial Stadium's official dedication. On October 22, with the Illini hosting the Wolverines, Margaret Grange, Red Grange's widow, attended the unveiling of Grange Rock (Figure 9.2), a commemorative plaque inset into a stone block located on Zuppke Field's north end. Adding to the weight of the moment, the "rock came from the same Indiana Stone quarry that produced the granite [*sic, limestone*] columns of the stadium."[23] The 1994 season was capped by trouncing the East Carolina Pirates 30–0 in the Liberty Bowl.

Figure 9.2
Grange Rock. Courtesy of the Division of Intercollegiate Athletics Archives.

Of particular note that season was the contest against Penn State. Down by three points, the Nittany Lions stormed 95 yards in the final minutes against the Illini's nationally top-rated defense. In what Penn State fans call "The Drive," the Lions' fullback, Brian Milne, plunged forward for the go-ahead touchdown. With only 57 seconds left on the clock, the Illini were unable to answer. The implications of that game for college football were soon apparent. Due to contractual obligations, an undefeated Penn State played in the Rose Bowl, overwhelming the #12 Pac-10's Oregon Ducks 38–20. Meanwhile, the Nebraska Cornhuskers—the Big Eight Conference champions—also went undefeated and faced the University of Miami, ranked #3, in the Orange Bowl. While a push for a selection process that would place the top two teams in a championship game had been gaining momentum, the controversy that ensued from these unsatisfying matchups became a major catalyst to create the Bowl Championship Series (BCS).

For fall 1995, in Simeon Rice's final college season, the Illini finished 5–5–1. As a testament to assembled talent, Illinois' Kevin Hardy was selected second and Simeon Rice third overall in the NFL draft in the spring of 1996. Notably, this was the final season in which *any* college football game could end in a tie thanks to new rules. Fittingly, in the final game of the season, in the last football season that college teams could tie, the Illini tied the Wisconsin Badgers 3–3 in an away game. After that, college football teams would play an overtime period, exchanging possessions for an allotted time until the high scorer claimed the victory.

Although the Illini won their first-ever overtime game at Memorial Stadium, beating the Indiana Hoosiers 46–43, most of the second half of the 1990s were not kind to the team. In Tepper's fifth and final season, the Illini finished dead last in the conference with an overall record of 2–9. Among the low points was a pummeling November 9 loss against Ohio State—the worst loss ever to the Buckeyes—49–0.[24] With Tepper out, the DIA hired Ron Turner, the Chicago Bears' defensive coordinator, to be the next head coach.[25] But the Illini hit rock bottom, losing all eleven games of the 1997 campaign. Though winless seasons had happened twice before, first under Pete Elliott (1961) and then under Jim Valek (1969), eleven

losses in a single season set a new, albeit sad, record. With the Illini struggling, just over 30,000 people at the Stadium watched the last game of the season against the Michigan State Spartans, the smallest crowd since 1970.[26]

The next season was brighter: running back Robert Holcombe set the still-standing Illini record of most rushing yards with 4,105.[27] At the same time, Josh Whitman—the current athletic director, who has been in the role since 2016—began his college football career as an offensive tight end. With Penn State now part of the rotation, it would be the first time since the 1923 season that the Illini would not face the Wolverines—a span of 74 years.

But before the 1998 games could commence, a familiar problem originating with the Stadium's sitting literally surfaced once again. Much like Pete Elliott had done in the spring of 1960, Turner complained about the "terrible" condition of the practice fields to the east.[28] Late August rains had made the fields soggy and too unstable for football practices, which forced Turner to change plans just five days before the first game of the season.

After an opening loss that extended the losing streak to eighteen games, Turner's Illini finally achieved a victory by defeating Middle Tennessee State at home, 48–20. In total, the Illini nabbed three victories, including an away game in early October against in-state rival Northwestern University. Then in the last football season of the decade, century, and millennium, under the guidance of Coach Turner, the Fighting Illini earned an 8–4 record. Despite three home losses to Michigan State, Minnesota, and Penn State, upsets against the #9 Michigan Wolverines (35–29) and the #25 Ohio State Buckeyes (46–20), and a skillful victory over the Virginia Cavaliers at the MicronPC.com Bowl (63–21) garnered the team a rank of 24. More importantly, it marked the beginning of a remarkable run to start the new decade, century, and millennium.

Restoration and Practice Facilities

When the Stadium received an air-supported structure, aka the Bubble, in January 1986, one main purpose was to provide an isolating zone for practices, especially when the weather outside was less than ideal. Another was that the Bubble could increase Stadium usage—particularly for campus and community events. By February 1990, events with titles like Bubble Bash were being hosted regularly in the dead of winter.[29] Featuring activities ranging from the Co-Rec Wiffle Ball Tournament and the team-based Competition Craze to the Goshin Jitsu Self-Defense Workshop, these functions were geared toward the student and community populations.[30] The Bubble also enabled winter and spring varsity teams, like men's baseball and golf and women's soccer, to practice and occasionally host games.[31] At other times, intramural teams benefited from the enclosure. In one example, the Illini women's rugby team held practices in the Bubble during the winter.[32]

During the 1980s, millions of dollars had been spent on structural and functional improvements, like the Bubble, to the Stadium. To be sure, these upgrades—including new locker rooms and structural stabilization of the seating decks—played a vital role in the turnaround for the now surging Fighting Illini football team. While the squad was having a successful 1990 season, that October the BOT addressed a plan to refurbish the Stadium: "the complete stadium restoration program was estimated to cost $39 million, if completed in three years."[33] Ed Sherman, writing for the *Chicago Tribune,* summarized the dire condition: the "67-year old stadium has deteriorated to the point where if major repairs aren't undertaken, it will end up being as functional as a pile of bricks."[34] Needed overhauls included replacing all the concrete in the seating upper decks, plumbing work, and resolving the ongoing problems with water drainage.[35] Though concerned about funding, the BOT committed to saving and bringing up-to-date Memorial Stadium. Trustee Don Grabowski—brother of famed Illini All-American running back and broadcaster Jim—captured the mood of the University's community when he asked, "what's the alternative?" He laid out the stark choices: "The reality is, if we don't do something, do we just watch the stadium crumble? Do you wait until it's unusable?" He concluded, "The reality is we do have a stadium, and if it means as much as $40 million to fix it, you try to come up with a plan to get it done."[36]

In January 1991, the BOT approved hiring project architects, set aside $100,000 for payment, and retained several firms:

Subsequently, the firm of Desman Parking Associates, Chicago, and the firm of Severns, Reid &

Associates, Inc., Champaign, were employed for the professional services required through the design development phase of the parking structure project on a fixed fee basis of $73,000 plus reimbursables estimated to be $16,000, and for the development of priorities for the initial restoration program at Memorial Stadium on an hourly basis not to exceed $90,000, plus reimbursable expenses authorized by the University, respectively. The firm of Severns, Reid & Associates, Inc., has employed the firms of Hanson Engineers, Springfield; Henneman, Raufeisen and Associates, Inc., Champaign; and Turner Construction Company, Chicago, to provide the professional engineering and construction management services required for the initial planning phase of the Memorial Stadium restoration project.[37]

To cover the first $100,000, the BOT used funds from the Auxiliary Facilities System, but, as before, the University turned to bond debt to finance the bulk of the initial phase of major projects that included "concrete replacement, toilet improvements, new storm drainage system, masonry reconstruction and repair, roof resurfacing, structural steel painting, and other code/life safety improvements."[38]

During summer 1991, in a Stadium first, precast concrete was used during the restoration process.[39] In October, with that project completed, the BOT moved to assign a nearly $9,400,000 general contract to Petry-Kuhne and Jones-Blythe.[40] After an initial struggle to contract a masonry specialist, the BOT engaged Hansen and Hempel to execute work on a contract just shy of $2,430,000.[41] Improvements to the seating decks were to be completed by August 1992.[42] During these extensive and lengthy refurbishments, construction workers frequently encountered hazardous weather conditions. In one close call, a 63 mph gust in June 1992 blew two painters off their scaffolding. Fortunately, both workers fully recovered (Figure 9.3).[43]

Worse than funding the enormous—and occasionally dangerous—renovations and managing the perpetual debt was that the football program was once again experiencing dwindling crowds. In 1992, attendance dipped to the smallest numbers since 1980.[44] As Andrew Bagnato pointed out in the *Chicago Tribune,*

This much seems certain: When a program is unsettled, ripples will almost always be felt in recruiting, in fundraising and in attendance at the money sports, football and men's basketball. Illinois, which believes it should be among the nation's athletic elite, has experienced trouble in each area. Average football attendance has dropped the last three seasons, and the Fighting Illini have managed only four Memorial Stadium sellouts since 1988.[45]

Figure 9.3
East Balcony Renovation. Courtesy of the Division of Intercollegiate Athletics Archives.

Others, like *Daily Illini* columnist Dennis Bronstein, chose a more optimistic view: "Memorial Stadium symbolized Illinois athletics 1991–1992. The stadium underwent a major reconstruction in the spring, just as most of the various Illini teams were in a rebuilding period last year."[46]

Although repairs to the seating decks and masonry were finished by late summer 1992, during the first game of the season, in what can be called a case of déjà vu, Stadium spectators reported vibrations. Hanson Engineers, who had worked on strengthening the structure ten years before, inspected the east grandstand and declared that the "stadium is very safe."[47] Robert Cusick, the vice president of Hanson, was present at the game, heard about the vibrations during half time, stood up from his seat in the east lower deck, traveled up to the east upper deck, and sat down to experience firsthand what other fans were reporting. He told the *Chicago Tribune,* "I did detect some small movement of a seating section where I was sitting," and then added, "[t]he movements were quite small. They were of no concern to me."[48] Ultimately, no additional work was necessary, as the Stadium was inspected and certified safe. The season continued without incident—at least in terms of structural integrity.

Later that season, one chapter in Stadium history came to a close when Reuben C. Carlson, a key student leader for the funding drive in the 1920s, died on October 15.[49] Carlson, class of 1921, chaired the Student Executive Committee, which had coaxed pledges of $700,000 from undergraduates for the Stadium's construction. He was so dedicated to the cause that he and Anna Coolley, his future wife and the women's chair, "became known as Mr. and Mrs. Stadium."[50] Carlson's death, nearly seven decades since the campaign to build the Stadium got underway, was a powerful reminder of the links between the Stadium and generations of students at UIUC. The Stadium and the DIA could have used Reuben and Anna's fundraising magic, since the downward attendance trend continued to drain the sport's coffers. The grim situation compelled the DIA to discontinue "men's swimming, men's and women's diving, and men fencing to save more than $300,000."[51] Despite the financial woes, the football team's poor record, and low attendance, the DIA extended Tepper's contract another three years.

During these lean years—much like it had done since its inception—the Stadium anchored statewide events. In July 1993, the University hosted the Prairie State Games, which featured amateur teams in events like bowling, soccer, and basketball. In all, nearly 3,000 people from across the state participated.[52] With track and field relocated out of Memorial Stadium in 1985, the Stadium itself was no longer an event venue. Instead, the west terrace was the site for an athlete's village and corporate sponsor tents.[53] Unfortunately, with state and private funding dwindling, the Prairie State Games were discontinued after the summer of 1995.[54]

In February 1994, another piece of Huff's sports complex was approved at long last. A series of new buildings would be constructed around Memorial Stadium and Assembly Hall. First, the BOT recommended "the employment of Woolpert Consultants, Belleville, for the professional consulting services required for the campus recreation fields at the Urbana campus."[55] The BOT specified that

> The $2.2 million project consists of developing play fields at two locations. The first area is on the west side of campus bounded by Oak Street, First Street, Gregory Drive, and a line extending west from Peabody Drive. This area is to be developed into athletic fields including intramural football fields, soccer fields, basketball courts, sand volleyball, and a roller blade hockey court. Fields will be fenced, lit, and irrigated. The site is also to include a service and storage facility (6,000 gsf). The second area is on the southwest corner of Lincoln Avenue and Florida Avenue. The site will contain a fenced and lit soccer field.[56]

Second, the BOT approved another sports complex that had been requested by the DIA in June 1993.[57] For this project, the BOT recommended that O'Donnell, Wicklund, Pigozzi, and Peterson of Deerfield handle the architectural and engineering services.[58] The BOT outlined the scope: "The $6.7 million project consists of a 39,900 gsf facility which will house the administrative offices for the Division of Intercollegiate Athletics (DIA) and offices for the majority of men's and women's athletic programs, as well as the ticket office functions."[59] The building, later christened Bielfeldt Athletics Administration Building, was formally dedicated in 1996.[60] In addition to making a few changes to the initial plans, the DIA worked with the architectural firm to relate the new structure back to other campus buildings and Memorial Stadium (Figure 9.4):

The $7.2 million, 43,000-square-foot Bielfeldt Building, located on the east-west axis between the Atkins Tennis Center and State Farm Center, land which used to be the University Golf Course, was endowed by Gary and Carlotta Bielfeldt, and their family, of Peoria, Illinois.

The building incorporates facets of other DIA and university buildings throughout campus. The roof is arched similarly to that of the Armory. Columns are imbedded in the wall of the Hall of Fame

Room subtly reminding visitors of the columns found at Memorial Stadium. Window sills look like those found at Huff Hall. The red brick and limestone materials are similar to those used on most campus buildings. While the glass found on the exterior of the building is a light blue echoing the University's colors of orange and blue.

The Bielfeldt Athletics Administration Building unites the University of Illinois Division of Intercollegiate Athletics (DIA) administration, coaching (except men's and women's basketball, football, and men's tennis), corporate relations, I-FUND, marketing, sports information, and video staffs under one roof instead of throughout campus as was previously the case.

Also included in the Bielfeldt Building is a professional development and seminar room equipped with state of the art audio/visual equipment. A large lounge used to greet recruits and entertain potential donors. Locker rooms used by both the DIA staff and women's soccer team, a training room, exercise room, and the University of Illinois Division of Intercollegiate Athletics Library.[61]

Two years later, the BOT approved an "indoor practice space for the men's football team, as well as multipurpose space for other sports and intramural programs. The proposed site for the facility is at the southwest corner of Fourth Street and Peabody Drive adjacent to Memorial Stadium and the Intramural Physical Education Building, which is in proximity to the existing football offices, locker rooms, and outdoor practice field east of Memorial Stadium."[62] Among its special features were an "80-yard football field with one end zone, storage, and restrooms. The field would be an Astro-Turf 'E' system composed of stone fill below a rubber cushion system under the pad and turf."[63] The construction of this facility would prompt the phasing out of the much beloved Bubble.

These plans could not be executed quickly enough. Just a month later, Coach Ron Turner complained about the "terrible" conditions of the practice fields immediately to the east of the Stadium —another criticism in the decades-long lament about the facilities.[64] At the

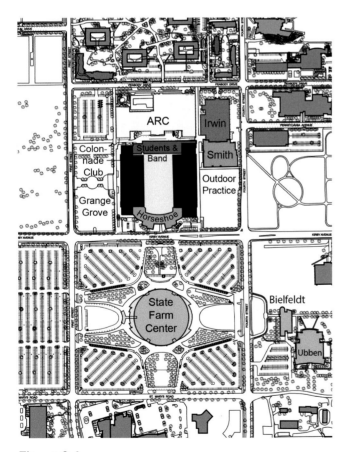

Figure 9.4
Memorial Stadium Campus Plan. Image by Kevin J. Hinders.

November BOT meeting, the project's $12,000,000 budget was approved. Designed by Ratio Architects, based in Indianapolis, the new facility featured a "red brick exterior and a slanted roof that reaches an internal height of 50 feet."[65] The brick cladding was an effort to provide material continuity with the Georgian style of campus. Moreover, to preserve the scale of the buildings near that location, the 50-foot height was evident only at the center of the practice structure, and steeply curved sides provided a much lower slung roof to match the other roof heights along Fourth Street. To provide as much free space as possible below the roof, large trusses running parallel to the long side of the building provide support. As a result, the structure has an atypical slope with one high end, so while Illini players can practice running and throwing and can kick field goals in one direction toward the high point, "[p]unting is strictly forbidden."[66]

As Gary Reinmuth noted in the *Chicago Tribune,* "Illinois is the only Big Ten school without its own permanent indoor practice building" and then detailed the project: "[c]onstruction of the $12.5-million structure, partly financed with a $7.5-million gift from the Irwin Family Foundation, could begin as early as June. Completion of the building, just east of the Intramural Physical Education building, is scheduled for October 2000. It is the first step in the planned replacement of the AstroTurf in Memorial Stadium with grass."[67] For his part, Coach Turner immediately implicitly linked the new training facility with student athlete recruiting: "I guarantee that's something that has been pointed out by every school that has one." He then added that undertaking such a project "shows the commitment of the administration to the football program to do whatever it takes to be successful" (Figure 9.5 and Figure 9.6).[68]

Figure 9.5
Irwin Indoor Practice Facility under construction. Courtesy of the Division of Intercollegiate Athletics Archives.

Figure 9.6
Irwin Interior Practice Facility interior looking southeast. Image by Kevin J. Hinders.

Once the Irwin Indoor Practice Facility was completed, it would be 19 years before the next part of the massive sports training complex would open. Located immediately east of the Stadium, the Henry Dale and Betty Smith Football Performance Center—an impressive 107,650 square feet—houses "expanded strength and conditioning and sports medicine space, coaches' offices, position meeting rooms, player development areas, locker rooms, and other areas for recruiting and prospect hosting."[69] Once it was ready for use in 2019, Illini football players could walk west from that $79.2 million facility directly to the Stadium before a game instead of across Grange Grove—a designated lane for tailgating. Interestingly, whereas the west side of the Stadium features Grange Grove, named in part after arguably Illinois' most famous *offensive* player, the Smith Center features to its east, just off Fourth Street, a sculpture of Dick Butkus, arguably Illinois' most famous *defensive* player (Figure 9.7).

Sources of Revenue

In 2002, "the stadium got a new video scoreboard, improvements in the press box, heated bathrooms and updated football locker rooms., before it became the home field of the [Chicago] Bears."[70] Even with a piecemeal approach that had also included a new kind of artificial turf, scoreboards, and new concrete seating decks, "[b]y the dawn of the new millennium, the stadium was beginning to show its age. To modernize and structurally stabilize the aging structure, the University began soliciting proposals for upgrading the stadium in

Figure 9.7
Henry Dale and Betty Smith Football Performance Center. Courtesy of the Division of Intercollegiate Athletics Archives.

late 2004. One of the most pressing renovations [was] to replace the concrete in the horseshoe and structurally stabilize that section of the stadium. To generate revenue to cover the costs of construction, one of the renovations proposed [was] to add luxury VIP stadium boxes" (Figure 9.8).[71]

This action was part of a recurring pattern: Illini coaches struggling to produce winning seasons would, rightly or wrongly, identify Memorial Stadium as a contributor to the lack of results. To Pete Elliott's practice facilities, Bob Blackman's outdated locker rooms, and Mike White's lack of indoor practice space was added a renewed call for improved practice fields by Ron Turner. And, just as in the past, the DIA responded with upgrades. This time the DIA announced that it was studying a major overhaul of the Stadium that would entail demolition and even more new construction. In 2004, the University requested proposals from consultants to produce a "feasibility study to evaluate the stadium and develop a plan for improvements. The work will include an analysis of the building's physical condition and conformity to life-safety codes, an analysis of event operations, and a market analysis of the demand for premium seating at the stadium, and of potential sponsors and advertisers for Illinois football."[72] The primary objective was revenue: "Suites would be separate, enclosed areas that would be available for small groups, with 12 to 16 seats, food service, restrooms and television monitors. Club seats could be indoors or outdoors, and fans sitting there would have access to an indoor

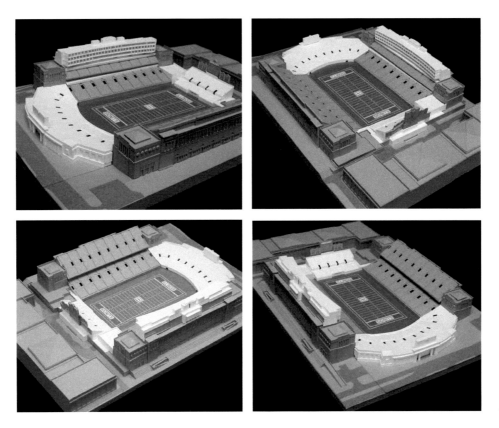

Figure 9.8
Memorial Stadium 2008 addition proposals study model. Courtesy of the Division of Intercollegiate Athletics Archives.

area similar to the suites."[73] Exclusive suites, luxury service, clubs, and party facilities would not only make the Stadium competitive with other Big Ten programs in recruitment allure but would also produce a handsome return on investment.

The pressure to field a consistently winning sports team is overwhelming when radio, network television, cable, and digital streaming contracts are at stake. The $100,000,000 contract for television and cable broadcast rights that the Big Ten had signed in 1995 with ESPN for ten years was soon going to expire.[74] The implications of having another down year and a reduced share of the total national audience would certainly complicate internal and external revenue-sharing negotiations. It was clear that the DIA needed to invest through a major overhaul of the Stadium, and since 2004 had been another losing football season, coaching changes were necessary to invigorate the program. As Matthew Dixon

recounts, the importance the DIA placed on television contracts was not misplaced:

Things changed in 2007 when they split the package between ESPN and Fox for another 10 years but this time it was worth $1 billion from ESPN and $1.5 billion from Fox. There was also this small detail in the Fox deal in which the Big Ten launched its very own network called the Big Ten Network. At the time, no other conference had done something like this but it worked out well for the conference because it will bring in nearly $3 billion over the original 20-year agreement with Fox. It was a visionary move by the Big Ten and one that was copied by every other conference as a way to generate additional TV revenue.[75]

Most recently, the Big Ten signed a seven-year, $7 billion television contract in July 2023. Vincent Pensabene, a sportswriter, noted, "The Big Ten TV deal does a lot for the future of the conference. With a floor of $80 million per team, that is going to be able to attract almost every non-Southeastern Conference (SEC) program in the country to join. With the ability to start on three different networks as well, the reach the conference will have is second to none."[76] Since the entire recruitment model of the student athlete is now all but a quaint concept, athletic departments across the country are competing in a real cash sweepstakes to recruit athletes who will bring spectators to stadiums and viewers to broadcast media.

Today digital media is crucial for ongoing revenue. Not restricted to the outgoing streaming coverage of games and events taking place inside a venue, digital media brings in dollars through the sale of advertisements. The DIA is working with the University to get extensive wireless fidelity (WiFi) coverage to the Stadium at the steep price of nearly $2,000,000. For Athletic Director Josh Whitman, adding WiFi is not simply a matter of keeping up with technology but also about providing services that spectators crave. WiFi advertisements, in the form of banners, will produce an entirely new source of revenue for the DIA. As of December 2023, installing a robust WiFi network will cost nearly $2,000,000 dollars. But, as Whitman notes, "fans' tastes continue to evolve," and what the Stadium offers must change to match expectations.[77]

With the 2021 Supreme Court's unanimous decision in *NCAA v. Alston* to support "college student-athletes in an antitrust challenge to the college-sports association's rules against compensating athletes,"[78] student athletes still cannot be paid by their schools, but in effect, they can, like college football players, sell their name, image, and likeness (NIL) so that they "can profit off themselves."[79] As James Park summarizes, "NIL gives players the right to publicity that ordinary citizens already have, but that the NCAA previously didn't allow. Players can accept money from businesses in exchange for using them in products or advertisements, and can also promote themselves or other companies in public appearances."[80] In essence, the ruling has completely changed the landscape of recruitment, because

now schools, through a network of boosters, are competing for students who are viewed as viable market commodities capable of selling their endorsements to an enormous sports industry ranging from clothing to gear and beyond. This new perspective has made television and digital media coverage all the more important to any sports program, as highly regarded and highly desirable recruits seek constant exposure in a bid to position themselves in the marketplace. While installing WiFi in a stadium may seem trivial—merely a way to entertain fans—it is crucial to remain competitive at the highest echelons of college sports.

Chief Illiniwek

No topic proved to be more contentious within the University of Illinois community—and eventually became the source of fierce debate across the nation—than the figure of Chief Illiniwek. Since the 1960s, scholars and activists have been calling for an end to the use of Native American imagery, mascots, and names in sports, and some in Urbana-Champaign had voiced similar concerns over the decades about the portrayal of the Chief.[81] In 1989, Robert Honig, a UIUC student, and two First Nations representatives, James Yellowbank, coordinator of the Indian Rights Committee, and Faith Smith, president of the Native American Educational Services in Chicago, met with UIUC administrators to request that the school retire Chief Illiniwek.[82] Senator Paul Simon signed a petition to retire Chief Illiniwek a month later, and Alan Dixon, also a senator from Illinois, defended the University's attachment to the Chief.[83] Meanwhile, Governor Jim Thompson sided with those who wanted to keep the Chief at school events.[84] Though the University offered to consider the petition, administrators initially decided to keep the Chief but police its image. Efforts to retire the Chief, however, were only beginning. Small protests were held throughout that fall. In March 1990, on the day of student tryouts to become the next Chief Illiniwek, protesters gathered outside Memorial Stadium. Campus police were called, and though tensions ran high, no arrests were recorded that evening.[85]

After the BOT voted in 1990 to retain Chief Illiniwek, the friction seemed to lessen for a brief period. Three years later, the Homecoming Planning Committee decided that for the first time since 1926, Chief Illiniwek would not participate in events outside the Stadium, particularly the parade.[86] This action drove the conflict back into the open, with many students attending the 1993 homecoming game against the Northwestern Wildcats wearing "orange stickers proclaiming their support for Chief Illiniwek."[87] Although many still wanted the Chief, the tide was slowly turning against the symbol. A *Daily Illini* editorial stated the issue succinctly: "The main point is that there are better ways to honor Native Americans and show University pride that do not offend anyone."[88]

Just before a home game on September 26, 1998, against the Iowa Hawkeyes, 100 students from the Progressive Resource/Action Cooperative, a group opposed to the Chief, met in front of Foellinger Auditorium. Dressed in all black clothing while chanting "Win the game, lose the Chief," the group marched to the Stadium with a campus police escort. Along the route, those in favor of retaining the Chief shouted back, "Safe the Chief, and get a life!"[89] Whereas some saw the Chief as a racist caricature, others saw him as a symbol of respect. Adding to the debate was the perspective of "members of the Peoria tribe of Miami, Oklahoma—the only legal descendants of the Illini Indians." In an interview conducted by local television station WICD they stated that they felt proud that the University of Illinois honored them with this symbol.[90] Opponents dismissed Peoria tribal support by stating that they did not speak for or represent all Native Americans. Without consensus, the controversial symbol remained a fixture at Illinois sports events, albeit with less prominence, steadily becoming less popular.

With the University community still divided about Chief Illiniwek, the NCAA decided the matter by announcing in August 2005 that schools that continued to utilize Native American imagery would be banned from participating in postseason events. Two years later, the University announced that Chief Illiniwek would no longer form part of the school's imagery. The Chief made his last official appearance on February 21, 2007, performing at halftime of the home basketball game between the Illini and Michigan.

The Stadium and Campus Life

Few events have made so dramatic an impact on American life as the terrorist attacks of September 11, 2001. Along with alterations to many daily activities, just about all college and professional sporting events were postponed to the weekend of September 21–23 and, true to its name, Memorial Stadium became the site of an emotional "memorial and unity" ceremony on September 15.[91] Over "10,000 students, faculty and community members gathered at the stadium, where the Marching Illini began by playing 'The Star-Spangled Banner.'"[92] After holding a moment of silence, Chancellor Nancy Cantor addressed the crowd and tried to offer comfort and time for reflection. Organized by students, the ceremony also featured comments by President James Stukel and Kenneth Schmidt, a trustee, plus performances.

In another sign of unity, a new event later that decade brought the Midwest community together: the Illinois Marathon. The first race was run on April 11, 2009, from Assembly Hall to its stirring finale at the "newly remodeled Memorial Stadium for a finish at the fifty yard line."[93] In all, nearly 9,500 people participated in six categories[94]: 5K, full marathon, half marathon, marathon relay, wheelchair, and Clydesdale/Athena.[95] Since its inception, the marathon has only become more popular, with 2020 the only year that it was not run due to the COVID-19 pandemic. Over the last 15 years, new categories have been added, like the 1K youth category and a 10K, while others have been discontinued, like the Clydesdale/Athena option. In 2010, the event's local roots grew when it was bought by six locals and Christie Clinic.[96] Today as many as 14,000 people take to the streets and, just as they did in the marathon's first year, participants regardless of category finish at the Stadium's 50-yard line. Individuals who achieve a new personal record are also encouraged to ring a bell located near the south end zone (Figure 9.9).

Figure 9.9
Christie Clinic Illinois Race Weekend, 2016 finish line heading south. Courtesy Christie Clinic Illinois Race Weekend.

In one of the most important contributions to community spirit, the University and the DIA unveiled plans in 2015 to reconceptualize Lot 36, the space between the western facade of Memorial Stadium and First Street to its west, as Grange Grove. The idea, as pitched by Athletic Director Mike Thomas, was to borrow the welcoming area near the football stadium on the Ole Miss campus affectionately called "the Grove" for an esplanade leading up to Memorial Stadium's main west entrances.[97] At the center of the path, a statue of Red Grange would welcome people on their way to a game or, in the spirit of TailGREAT of nearly 30 years before, those who want to stroll by tents, kiosks, and organized activities designed to enrich the tailgating experience. Grange Grove was inaugurated on September 5 for the season-opening home game against Kent State. As part of the festivities, Fighting Illini football players would walk through Grange Grove on their way to the locker rooms before the game to tunes from the Marching Illini and spirited yells from cheerleaders. Although this tradition was discontinued once the Henry Dale and Betty Smith Football Performance Center opened in August 2019, Grange Grove is still the place for Illini tailgating and private events, including wedding receptions and bar and bat-mitzvahs dinners (Figures 9.10–9.12).

Figure 9.10
Red Grange
Statue, Courtesy
of the Division
of Intercollegiate
Athletics Archives.

Figure 9.11
Grange Grove
Entry. Courtesy
of the Division
of Intercollegiate
Athletics Archives.

Figure 9.12
Grange Grove.
Courtesy of
the Division of
Intercollegiate
Athletics Archives.

New Decade, New Century, and New Millennium

Football in the 2000s

Between 1997 and 1999, Memorial Stadium hosted three NFL preseason scrimmages, with the 1999 version featuring the St. Louis Rams and the Indianapolis Colts. This usage by NFL teams was significant for several reasons. First, the clubs brought national exposure to UIUC and Memorial Stadium. Second, these exhibition games were part of a larger strategy to increase revenue. Third, they were proof that the Stadium could function as an NFL venue—a virtue that would soon come in exceptionally handy. In May 2002 after more than a year of negotiations, the DIA stressed a shared history in announcing that the Chicago Bears would "play their 2002 season and 2003 preseason at Memorial Stadium during Soldier Field's $500 million renovation."[98] As part of the agreement, the Bears would pay the "University 10 percent rent, based on gross ticket sales. The University and Bears also [would] equally split parking and concessions profits."[99] As part of the deal, only minor renovations of restrooms and concessions were carried out. Of all the

possible pitfalls that could have scuttled the agreement, the toughest to overcome was the request by the Chicago Bears that beer be sold at the games. State law would have to be changed. Acting on the University's behalf, State Representatives Rick Winkel (R-Champaign), and Tom Berns (R-Urbana) introduced a bill to allow the sale of alcohol at the Stadium, but a House subcommittee rejected any changes.[100] After much lobbying, Governor George Ryan signed a law in January 2002 that allowed specific vendors to sell beer at Bears games played at Memorial Stadium.[101] Despite this outcome, uncertainty surrounding the legislation had spurred local politicians to consider revising their own alcohol sales laws.

The Stadium had been conceived, built, and dedicated during Prohibition and had never been the site of alcohol sales. On the one hand, the ability to sell beer would have certainly resulted in higher revenues for the Bears and the University under their revenue-sharing agreement; but on the other hand, it would have almost certainly prompted fans to expect alcohol sales at Illini games. Not surprisingly, the debate about alcohol sales at the Stadium quickly spilled over to Champaign County and its incorporated towns and cities. From the 1850s to the mid-1930s,

Illinois had been a "Sunday Law" state, prohibiting the sale of alcohol on Sundays. After the repeal of Prohibition, each county, city, and town enacted its own alcohol laws or ordinances. Champaign County and the cities of Champaign and Urbana had introduced ordinances that steadily increased the hours that alcohol could be sold on Sundays.

Once the Illinois House of Representatives had denied the University's petition to permit the sale of alcohol at Memorial Stadium on Sundays, local establishments sensed an opportunity and pushed for earlier start times for alcohol sales. In Champaign, the "Liquor Advisory Commission suggested allowing Sunday morning alcohol sales when the Chicago Bears play at Memorial Stadium."[102] Local businesses soon argued that they should be able to sell on any Sunday, starting at 9:00 a.m.[103] Eventually, Champaign, Urbana, and Savoy passed ordinances that prohibited the sale of alcohol on any day between midnight and 6:00 a.m. for off-premises consumption and from 2:00 a.m. to 6:00 a.m. for on-premises consumption.

Even without alcohol offered in the stands, fans greeted the 2000 season with great enthusiasm. For the first three games, the Illini delivered: three victories and a #17 national ranking. In week four, the #10 Michigan Wolverines traveled to Champaign for a rare match-up between the two teams while nationally ranked. In front of a capacity crowd, the first since 1995, the Wolverines beat the Illini 35–31.[104] The Illini would go on to lose five of the last seven games to end the season with an overall record of 5–6.

With expectations much lower for the following fall, the Illini stunned fans by opening the 2001 season with three straight wins. In week four, the team, newly ranked 22, traveled to Ann Arbor, ultimately losing to #17 Michigan. Unlike the previous year, the Fighting Illini would then win the next seven games. Quarterback Kurt Kittner delivered an Illini record twenty-seven touchdowns in one season, and road victories included two over ranked opponents, Purdue and Ohio State.[105] As the season progressed, enthusiasm was evident among the Illini faithful, with tickets for two home games selling out. Thanks to a regular season record of 10–1, the Illini secured the Big Ten championship and played in the Sugar Bowl against #12 Louisiana State University. In what was basically a home game for the Tigers in New Orleans, the #7 Illini were defeated 47–34.

In 2002, for the first time since the World War II years, the Illini played twelve regular season games, but the extra contest didn't help garner a winning record, and the final tally was 5–7, leaving the Illini out of the postseason. Over the next few years, the Illini would continue to struggle. In what became Turner's last two seasons, the Illini would go a demoralizing 1–11 and 3–8. Two days after the final game of the 2004 season, an overtime loss to the Northwestern Wildcats, Ron Guenther made the call and sent Turner to the showers for good.

The Zook Era and a Major Overhaul

Only seven days after Turner had been let go, Ronald "Ron" A. Zook, former head coach of the University of Florida Gators, was seen on campus.[106] Zook had an NFL pedigree and had just led Florida to three straight winning seasons. With these credentials, Zook generated a great deal of excitement, increasing ticket sales, when he was named head coach. Unfortunately, with an overall record of 2–9 in 2005, Zook's first season was worse than Turner's last. Maybe a new atmosphere would change the team's fortunes.

In May 2006, a major overhaul of Memorial Stadium was announced:

> The UI Board of Trustees approved the first phase of the $116-million renovation of Memorial Stadium at its meeting May 11 in Chicago.
>
> The first phase of the project is slated to begin after the 2006 season comes to a close and should last about two years, said Athletic Director Ron Guenther.
>
> The design of the new stadium will preserve the historical aspects of the architecture while modernizing the 83-year-old stadium that needs new concessions areas and bathrooms and improved seating. . . .
>
> University officials have argued that the stadium must be renovated in order to remain competitive with other Big Ten schools.[107]

This round of renovations, later named the Renaissance project, was the result of the DIA's 2004 request for proposals. The mammoth project included forty suites, clubs, party rooms, and other luxury facilities. HNTB, a large national architectural firm out of Kansas City, Missouri, was slated to design the new addition, while Hunt Construction Managers was hired as general contractors. Under pressure because of his underwhelming first year,

Coach Zook compared the 2005 Illini season with the Stadium's renovations: "We are in a construction zone right now, building a foundation for bigger things in the future."[108] Apparently, that base needed reinforcement since during the 2006 season the Illini managed to defeat

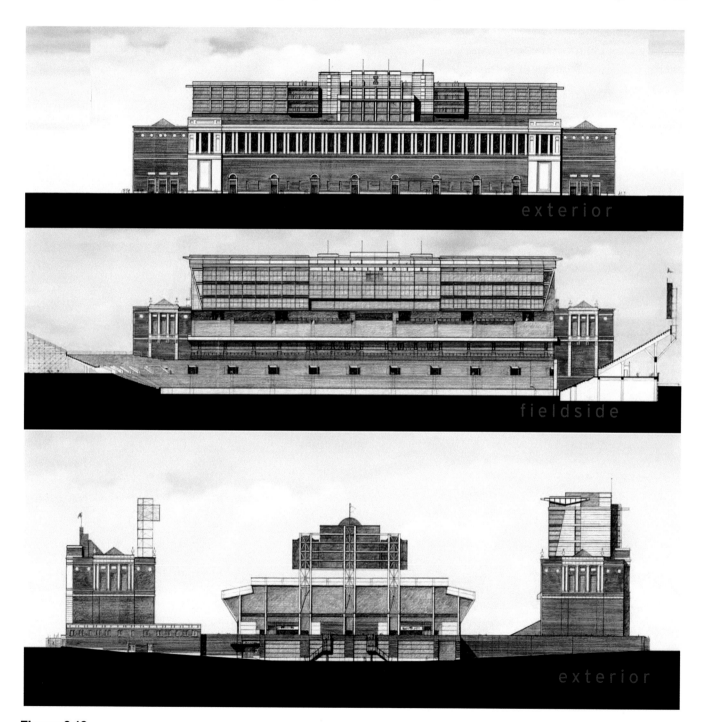

Figure 9.13
HNTB proposed alterations to Memorial Stadium. Courtesy of the Division of Intercollegiate Athletics Archives.

only one out-of-conference opponent plus Michigan State. And that fall marked the end of one tradition: in the last home game of the season, a Veterans' Day tilt against Purdue University, Chief Illiniwek danced for the last time on Zuppke Field (Figure 9.13).

Finally, the breakout season occurred in 2007. Although the Illini lost the season opener against Missouri by a touchdown, the first home game ended in a victory against Western Illinois, 21–0. Key to that success was the new student section on the north end. Holding 6,200 students and the Marching Illini Band, the design enabled cheers and jeers to travel throughout the Stadium and reverberate loudly, which provided a highly desirable advantage when opposing offensive players were on the field (Figure 9.14 and Figure 9.15).[109]

And there was a lot to cheer about with Rashard Mendenhall scoring a record seventeen touchdowns in a single season to help Illinois win nine of the next eleven games. In addition, one of those victories was a major first: on November 10, the Fighting Illini traveled to Columbus and defeated on the road a #1 team by edging Ohio State 28–21. In a tie with Michigan for second place in the Big Ten, the #13 Illini were invited to play in the 2008 Rose Bowl against USC's Trojans.

Although the Illini were dealt a crushing 49–17 loss, making a bowl game, especially the Rose Bowl, meant a generous payout, in this case $2.1 million.[110] Moreover, increased merchandise sales from shirts, mugs, hats, and other items emblazoned with its Rose Bowl appearance handed to the Illini and the DIA significant additional revenue. Getting a bowl game invitation also elevated

Figure 9.14
Students and band section at the north end of Memorial Stadium. Courtesy of the Division of Intercollegiate Athletics Archives.

the status of the program by setting it before a national audience, and that publicity would attract top players, recruiters, and the NFL.

To top off this upward trajectory, the University celebrated a milestone (Figure 9.16):

a completed Memorial Stadium 'Renaissance' project that encompassed two years of work and over $121 million. The renovations to the north end zone were completed in August 2007. . . . Among the renovations on the west side was the addition of luxury suites, indoor and outdoor club areas, and a refurbishment of the concourses. An outdoor club space, the Colonnades Club, was added under the west balcony and allows for indoor game-day hospitality, as well as outdoor chair-back seats for game viewing. In the west balcony, a three-level structure

was built to house two floors of suites and an indoor club space, as well as a new press box for media seating and game day operations. The indoor club, which seats 200, has been named the "77 Club" to honor the retired number of Illinois gridiron legend Harold "Red" Grange. The premium seating areas also serve as Champaign[-]Urbana's premier event space, and have hosted weddings, banquets, receptions and meetings since their opening.

Also added underneath the newly enclosed north bleachers during the Illinois Renaissance project, the Illinois football complex got an expansion and refurbishing of the weight room, training facilities and meeting space. The entire project was conducted while keeping the stadium in a functioning capacity for the Illinois football team during the time of construction.[111]

Figure 9.15
Student Cheering Section. Courtesy of the Division of Intercollegiate Athletics Archives.

Figure 9.16
Weight room facility. Courtesy of the Division of Intercollegiate Athletics Archives.

It is a testament to the vision of the University and the DIA that the "original architecture of Memorial Stadium [was] being carefully preserved throughout renovation."[112] At the same time, it is a testament to the strength of Memorial Stadium's original design that 84 years after its dedication, it still had its sense of spatial identity, even when a new press box, luxury suites, and other facilities were added. As Assistant Athletic Director Kent Brown pointed out, "[t]he stadium is a campus icon and really an icon for the state of Illinois" (Figure 9.17).[113]

Besides the Colonnade Club with its imposing suites, press boxes and club space, the stadium's north endzone was capped with a new student section. Below the student seating concessions and restrooms. At the ground level are weight rooms and facilities. While some decried the relocation of students as a plan to allow for higher ticket prices in the more premium seats, the move to the end zone proved a popular endeavor. Students and band seating sections now terminate the north side of the field.

Sitting atop the Zuppke wall, the Marching Illini Band is seated just below the students, where throughout the games, their brassy tunes continue a long-standing tradition of rousing the students to cheer on the Illini.

The Marching Illini and football have been linked for well over a century. In 1907 the band performed the first halftime show during the University of Chicago game. By the first Homecoming at the University of Illinois, they had established themselves as a regular attraction. Starting with the Stadium's dedication, the famous "Three-in-One" has been highlighted at each football game's halftime. Today, the band is an integral aspect of the game-day experience, from the pregame march into the Stadium to the musical interludes between plays. When the Stadium was modified in 2014, the student section and the band were permanently relocated to the north-end zone seating. The band was placed in a crucial location, just below the student section, to maximize the Illini home-field

Figure 9.17
Colonnade Club under construction, April 2008. Courtesy of the Division of Intercollegiate Athletics Archives.

advantage. This is because acoustically, this new placement capped the north end zone creating a boisterous atmosphere much appreciated by the athletes on the field. The band's placement has become so cherished, that its placement has fostered a new tradition in which the players join their fellow students at the north end zone following emotional victories while the band plays *Alma Mater* for loyal Illini (Figure 9.18).

On at least one occasion, the band upstaged the game. In 2004, two of the country's finest college marching bands, the Florida Agriculture and Mining University (FAMU) and the Illinois Marching Illini, joined forces to perform a thrilling musical arrangement that highlighted their contrasting styles. This performance was led by James F. Keene, Illinois Director of Bands (1985–2008)

and Dr. Shelby Chipman, Director of Bands for FAMU. Dr. Chipman had been a graduate student at Illinois where he completed his master's degree in music education (Figure 9.19).[114]

With the Renaissance project fully implemented, Memorial Stadium's new capacity crowd was set at 62,870 spectators, a drop of nearly 16,000 people from the all-time high in 1984.[115] The Illini began the 2008 season ranked #20 in the nation but lost the opening game to #6 Missouri, 52–42. Although the Illini would recover and win the next two games at home, they finished with a 5–7 record. The 2009 season continued that downward slide into a 3–9 final tally. One of the few highlights happened on Halloween when the Illini upset the visiting Michigan Wolverines 38–13.

Figure 9.18
North endzone
following the
Ball State game,
September 2, 2017.
Photograph by
Kevin J. Hinders.

Figure 9.19
Florida Agriculture
and Mining
University band,
September 4,
2004. Courtesy
of the Division
of Intercollegiate
Athletics Archives.

From 2010 to the Redbox Bowl

After two consecutive losing seasons, Zook's Illini finally reversed course, finishing the 2010 regular season 6–6, good enough to be invited to a postseason bowl game. In a Big Ten versus Big 12 match-up, the Illini traveled to Houston to give the Baylor Bears a 38–14 battering. Considered a lower-tier bowl game, the Texas Bowl paid out $612,500 to each team.[116] The win and the relatively small purse seemed inconsequential on the national stage, precipitating a still unresolved debate regarding a college team's cost-benefit for participating in these bowl games. Regardless, the Texas Bowl brought an end to another era. When Ron Guenther announced his retirement after 19 years at the helm of the DIA, John Supinie, writing for Springfield's *State Journal-Register* encapsulated Guenther's tenure: "Athletics director Ron Guenther kept his department out of the red ink and Illinois out of the NCAA penalty box for the bulk of his 19 years on the job. But during the last few years, his coaches and teams didn't win enough games to keep everyone happy."[117]

In 2011, attracted to the Big Ten's lucrative television contract, the Nebraska Cornhuskers joined the conference and left behind the Big 12. Now with an even number of teams, the conference was reorganized into the Legends Division and the Leaders Division, each with six teams. The two division leaders would play one another to crown the new conference champion. The Illini, playing in the Leaders Division, started off strong, winning six straight games, but then dropped the last six. Sensing a team in disarray, the DIA fired Coach Ron Zook and most of his staff after the regular season. But the Illini were invited to the Kraft Fight Hunger Bowl in San Francisco, California, and bested the UCLA Bruins, 20–14. Since the bowl payout was just $750,000, some sports analysts questioned whether the Illini would make money by traveling all the way to the Bay Area. Associate Athletic Director Kent Brown stressed that money was not the sole object: "when the college football season kicks off every fall, all 128 teams in the NCAA's Football Bowl Subdivision are gearing themselves up for and want to go to a bowl game." He added, "[t]hat's part of the great tradition of college football," finally

concluding that "[t]here's the pride factor of being in a bowl game."[118]

This sense of achievement and confidence in the team were bolstered by more additions to the Stadium. Before the 2012 season, the University installed (Figures 9.20–9.22)

a new FieldTurf Revolution surface and banners commemorating Illinois' national championships, Big Ten championships and bowl appearances were installed. The turf features the Block I logo inside an outline of the state of Illinois at midfield, similar to the design at center court of the State Farm Center floor, and alternating shades of green every five yards. For the 2013 season, a new high-definition video display measuring 36 feet tall by 96 feet wide was installed in the south horseshoe. In addition, two LED ribbon displays measuring more than 420 feet in length were added to the fascia between the seating decks on each side of the field, and additional video displays measuring 17 feet by 10 feet were mounted to the northeast and southeast towers.[119]

In 2012 new head coach Timothy "Tim" Beckman, who had previously coached the Toledo Rockets, had an underwhelming year, losing all conference games and logging just two victories for a 2–10 record.[120] The 2013 season showed marginal improvement with two additional wins, including an away game against Purdue. When the University of Maryland Terrapins and the Rutgers Scarlet Knights joined the Big Ten for 2014, the conference was once again reorganized into two new divisions: East and West. The geographic boundary was defined by the Indiana-Ohio state lines, which made scheduling games somewhat easier in terms of time zones and travel times. Another major change in 2014 was the addition of playoffs. Football Bowl Subdivision teams discarded the BCS and adopted the College Football Playoff. Under the new format, four teams selected by a committee would play in semifinal games. The winners from each game would then face each other in a national championship game.

That fall, the Illini managed to continue the positive trend, achieving a 6–6 record. After defeating

Figure 9.20
Band halftime show October 6, 2023. Courtesy of the Division of Intercollegiate Athletics Archives. Photograph by Kevin Snyder.

Northwestern University at Evanston 47–33, the Illini headed to the Zaxby's Heart of Dallas Bowl, where they were trounced 35–18 by Louisiana Tech. Amid troubling allegations of influencing medical decisions, Athletic Director Mike Thomas and Beckman were fired just weeks before the 2015 season.[121] Rising to the occasion, former offensive coordinator William "Bill" J. Cubit stepped in but managed to get the team only to 5–7.

Josh Whitman—a Former Illinois tight end (1997–2000), an assistant coach under Guenther, and the athletic director at Washington University—took over the role as the athletic director and signaled a new direction for the squad:

"I appreciate the leadership that Bill Cubit provided our football program during what has been, unquestionably, a very tumultuous time," Whitman said. "He accepted the challenge on an interim basis under incredibly difficult and unusual circumstances, and he has continued to work diligently for the betterment of our student-athletes. Through his efforts, he has kept the program moving forward. Bill is a good man and a good football coach. All of us in the Illini Nation owe him a debt of gratitude for his work leading our team these last months. At this juncture, however, I think it is most important that we position our program for long-term success by creating a more stable environment for the coaches, players, and prospective student-athletes."[122]

On March 7, Whitman announced that Lovie Smith, the one-time Chicago Bears head coach, would lead the football program. From the first Black football players during the World War II years, like half back Buddy

Figure 9.21
West Stands with Colonnade Club. Courtesy of the Division of Intercollegiate Athletics Archives.

Young to Mel Meyers, the first Black quarterback in 1959, the Fighting Illini had finally filled one of the most glaring gaps in the long march toward inclusion. It was not lost on the UIUC campus, the state of Illinois, or the nation as a whole that the Fighting Illini had hired their first Black head coach.[123]

In a vote of confidence in Smith and the future of the football program, the "University of Illinois submitted a Request for Professional Services Qualifications to start plans to renovate Memorial Stadium. The plan's biggest request is specifically for changes in the horseshoe seating in the south end zone. The form says a new football operations addition will be added to the horseshoe. It will be the first major renovation to the south end zone since 1929."[124] But Smith could not turn the team around despite this boost. In 2016, the team finished second to last in the West Division with a 3–9 record.

The next year the Illini fared worse, losing all but two games. Finally, a glimmer of hope shone in 2018 with four wins. Unfortunately, the Illini also matched their worst defeat ever and set the record for the worst defeat at Memorial Stadium, when the Iowa Hawkeyes delivered a 63–0 loss. Also notable about that season was that for the first time since 1913, Illinois did not play either Michigan or Ohio State, which broke a streak of 105 years of matchups. Smith's fourth season in 2019 ended with a 6–6 record, including an upset by the slightest of margins, 24–23, in a homecoming game against the #6 Wisconsin Badgers. With an invitation to the Redbox Bowl, the Illini traveled to Santa Clara and faced a 35–20 drubbing by the California Golden Bears. After this more successful campaign, expectations for Smith's squad climbed for the 2020 season. Then in January 2020 the world changed.

Figure 9.22
Scoreboard and end zone seating. Courtesy of the Division of Intercollegiate Athletics Archives

The COVID-19 Pandemic and Beyond

The day after the Redbox Bowl was played, the WHO office in the People's Republic of China was alerted to an outbreak of pneumonia cases. On January 20, 2020, the CDC announced the first case of infection with SARS-CoV-2, a novel coronavirus, in the United States.[125] Four days later, the second case of SARS-CoV-2 in the US was reported in Illinois. By the second week of March, the WHO had declared a worldwide pandemic.[126] With news of the virus spreading across the Midwest, on March 13 the Big Ten suspended all sports activities.[127] Just two days after that, on March 15, the first state governments begin to implement shutdowns and lockdowns, to "flatten the curve." From that moment onward, multiple policies,

including "social distancing," where people were to keep apart no less than 6 feet (roughly 2 meters), and mask-wearing mandates were issued by Governor J.B. Pritzker.

While the virus infected and killed millions across the world that spring, uncertainty about the future of everything, including college football, was unsettling, and planning was difficult. As the summer of 2020 approached, questions arose about the safety of holding football practices and launching the season. Conference reactions varied: The Pac-12 canceled the entire season. Initially, the Big Ten considered that approach as well and postponed "all regular-season contests and Big Ten Championships and Tournaments, due to ongoing health and safety concerns related to the COVID-19 pandemic."[128] Other divisions, like the

Figure 9.23
Social distancing and cutout images in Memorial Stadium during the 2020 Covid-19 season.

SEC, instead pondered when training sessions would begin. In late July, the SEC announced that practices would begin on August 17.[129] Moreover, the SEC had decided that teams would play ten games that season with in-conference foes.

Faced with complaints from players, coaches, and fans that pointed to the SEC's actions, the Big Ten reversed course and announced a start date of October 23 for a truncated season.[130] Following the SEC model, the Big Ten would also play only in-conference games. Begrudgingly, the Pac-12 finally followed suit and initiated a shortened season of seven intraconference games without spectators present.[131] That delayed and shortened season was crucial to negotiations when USC and UCLA—the teams in the Pac-12's largest television market—bolted out of the conference to join the Big Ten in 2024. A hit to the Pac-12's reputation from

that reversal, cuts to revenue and television exposure, and the departure of its biggest teams were instrumental to the conference's implosion.[132] With football back on for 2020, the Illini played all the conference tilts except for one home game against the Ohio State Buckeyes that was canceled due to COVID-19 concerns. Neither spectators, cheerleaders nor the Marching Illini Band, however, were permitted to attend the games during the fall of 2020 (Figure 9.23). The Illini finished with a 2–6 record, beating Rutgers and Nebraska on the road. After the Illini lost to Northwestern at Evanston 28–10, Lovie Smith was fired.

Bret Bielema, a native of Prophetstown, Illinois, took over in 2021. Though Bielema's first season was also a losing season, the team did manage to upset #7 Penn State, 20–18, and #20 Minnesota, 14–6, on the road. In 2022, the team finished second in the West

Division. That fall started with wins in the first seven games, pushing the Illini as high as #16 in the rankings before stalling and going into a three-game losing streak. After a pounding victory over Northwestern on the road, 41–3, the Illini set off for the ReliaQuest Bowl in Tampa Bay, Florida. There they were defeated by the Mississippi State Bulldogs, 19–10. In 2023, the Illini finished 5–7, but four of those losses were by four or less points. With a bowl berth on the line, the Illini could not get the job done and dropped the last game at home to Northwestern, 45–43.

Now the 2024 season is upon the Illini football team, and the 100-year anniversary of Memorial Stadium's grand dedication will be celebrated, rightfully so, in a game on October 19, 2024, against the Michigan Wolverines, the defending national champions. Only time will tell if the spirit of Red Grange, the Galloping Ghost, will return to form and help his teammates stun the reigning national champion Wolverines once again.

Notes

1 Chicago Tribune wires, "College Football Notes," *Chicago Tribune,* November 16, 1988, E3.

2 University Library Student Life and Culture Archives, "Student Life at Illinois: 1990–1999."

3 University Library Student Life and Culture Archives, "Student Life at Illinois: 2000–2009."

4 Investopedia Team, "2008 Recession."

5 Schumaker, "Timeline."

6 Ibid.

7 World Bank, "GDP Growth."

8 Naylor, "Read Trump's Jan. 6 Speech."

9 Bureau of Counterterrorism, "Foreign Terrorist Organizations."

10 John Pletz, "Mackovic Prepared for Double Challenge," *Daily Illini* 118, no. 88, February 1, 1989, 38.

11 Kate Coughlin, "State Warns AA: Restructure Soon," *Daily Illini* 118, no. 37, October 13, 1988, 1.

12 Catherine Spellman, "Task Force: Give UI Direct Control of AA," *Daily Illini* 118, no. 74, December 7, 1988, 1.

13 John Pletz, "State Report Says AA Deeper in Debt," *Daily Illini* 118, no. 103, February 22, 1989, 1.

14 Ed Sherman, "Cash and Credibility Woes Still Plague Illini Sports," *Chicago Tribune,* April 13, 1989, 1.

15 Melissa Isaacson, "Women Catch a Break—Albeit a Little One," *Chicago Tribune,* December 25, 1990, A7.

16 Ken Green, "Illini Cheers Continue for RB Griffith," *Chicago Defender,* September 26, 1990.

17 Fighting Illini Football, "Individual Records."

18 Andrew Bagnato, "Remembering Red," *Chicago Tribune,* October 20, 1994, https://www.chicagotribune.com/news/ct-xpm-1994-10-20-9410200017-story.html.

19 Ron Tillery, "Guenther Named New Illinois Athletic Director," *Daily Illini* 121, no. 156, June 11, 1992, 16.

20 Fighting Illini, "Simeon Rice."

21 Fighting Illini Football, "Illini Football Attendance Records."

22 Andrew Bagnato, "Pay-for-Play Idea Making a Comeback," *Chicago Tribune,* August 16, 1994, F5.

23 Fighting Illini, "The Return of the Galloping Ghost."

24 Fighting Illini Football, "Football History vs Ohio State University."

25 Steve Hanf, "Bear's Turner Named UI Coach," *Daily Illini* 126, no. 65, December 3, 1996, 1.

26 Gary Reinmuth, "Illini Go Out Fighting, but without a Win: Long, Painful Season Ends with 0–11 Record," *Chicago Tribune,* November 23, 1997, A8.

27 Ibid.

28 Gary Reinmuth, "Lumpy Field Makes for Grumpy Coach," *Chicago Tribune,* September 1, 1998, 5.

29 "Bubble Bash," *Daily Illini* 119, no. 103, February 12, 1990, 12.

30 Ibid.

31 Julie Novak, "Damage to 'Bubble' Repaired," *Daily Illini* 128, no. 84, January 28, 1999, 7.

32 "Illinois Women's Rugby Club," *Daily Illini* 119, no. 94, January 30, 1990, 7.

33 BOT, Meeting Minutes, January 11, 1991, 161.

34 Ed Sherman, "Illini Stadium Needs Major Repair Work: Trustees May Face $40 Million Bill," *Chicago Tribune,* February 14, 1991, A1.

35 Ibid.

36 Ibid.

37 "Report of Action by the President of the University: Parking Structure, Chicago; Memorial Stadium Restoration, Urbana," BOT, Meeting Minutes, March 14, 1991, 219.

38 BOT, Meeting Minutes, April 11, 1991, 251–52.

39 BOT, Meeting Minutes, July 11, 1991, 329–30.

40 BOT, Meeting Minutes, October 10, 1991, 386–87.

41 BOT, Meeting Minutes, January 16, 1992, 447–48.

42 Ed Sherman, "Hall of Fame Finds an Appropriate Home," *Chicago Tribune*, July 19, 1992.

43 Cattleya Pinyo, "Fall from 20 Feet Hurts Two Workers," *Daily Illini* 121, no. 160, June 18, 1992, 3.

44 Andrew Bagnato, "Illinois Sees Future with Binge-Free Bowls," *Chicago Tribune,* December 28, 1992, A3.

45 Andrew Bagnato, "Illinois Needs More of the Same Old Thing," *Chicago Tribune,* September 2, 1992, B1.

46 Dennis Bronstein, "Reconstruction Will Push Teams to Top," *Daily Illini,* August 17–23, 1992, 16.

47 Andrew Bagnato, "Memorial Stadium Vibrations Good and Safe," *Chicago Tribune,* September 9, 1992, B7.

48 Ibid.

49 Janita Poe, "Reuben Carlson, 94; Real Estate Executive and U. of I. Fundraiser," *Chicago Tribune,* October 26, 1992, N_A6.

50 ATO Gamma Zeta Chapter, "Gamma Zeta's Campus Impact."

51 Andrew Bagnato, "Attendance Drop Hits Illini Budget," *Chicago Tribune,* December 16, 1993, B9.

52 Gary Reinmuth, "Despite Money, Other Problems, Prairie State Games Still Work," *Chicago Tribune,* July 12, 1993, A7.

53 Ibid.

54 Ann P., "Prairie State Games."

55 BOT, Meeting Minutes, February 11, 1994, 450.

56 Ibid.

57 BOT, Meeting Minutes, June 11, 1993, 284–85.

58 BOT, Meeting Minutes, February 11, 1994, 451–52.

59 Ibid.

60 Fighting Illini, "Bielfeldt Athletics Administration Building."

61 Ibid.

62 BOT, Meeting Minutes, July 9, 1998, 21.

63 Ibid., 22.

64 Reinmuth, Gary, "LUMPY FIELD MAKES FOR GRUMPY COACH: [NORTH SPORTS FINAL EDITION]," *Chicago Tribune*, Sep 01, 1998,5.

65 Gary Reinmuth, "Illinois Unveils Practice Facility Plans," *Chicago Tribune,* November 24, 1998, B2.

66 Will Brumieve and Breda Murphy, "Football Team Looking Forward to New Facility," *Daily Illini* 129, no. 108, March 1, 2000, 1.

67 Ibid.

68 Ibid.

69 Fighting Illini, "Henry Dale and Betty Smith Football Performance Center."

70 Jodi Heckel, "UI Begins Study of Its Stadium," *Champaign-Urbana News-Gazette,* August 21, 2004, https://www.news-gazette.com/news/ui-begins-study-of-its-stadium/article_a6297c92-4a3d-5603-9ae4-283fead1dc27.html.

71 UIHistories, "Memorial Stadium."

72 Heckel, "UI Begins Study of Its Stadium."

73 Ibid.

74 Dixon, "College Football TV Contracts."

75 Ibid.

76 Pensabene, "How Much Does Big Ten TV Deal Pay."

77 Interview with Athletic Director Josh Whitman, November 15, 2023.

78 Matt Ford, "The One Thing the Supreme Court Got Right: Blowing Up College Sports," *New Republic,* August 25, 2023, https://newrepublic.com/article/175193/supreme-court-alston-college-sports.

79 Parks, "NIL in College Football."

80 Ibid.

81 David Walker, Andrew J. Rausch, and Chris Watson, *The Native American Mascot Controversy: A Handbook* (Scarecrow Press, 2009).

82 "Indians Seek to Oust Chief Illiniwek, Mascot," *Chicago Defender,* October 9, 1989.

83 Robert Davis, "Senators Split on Illini Mascot," *Chicago Tribune,* November 8, 1989, S2.

84 Robert Davis, "Thompson Lauds Chief Illiniwek," *Chicago Tribune,* November 17, 1989, D3.

85 "Cops, Illiniwek Protesters Record Each Other," *Chicago Defender,* March 14, 1990.

86 Andrew Bagnato, "Chiefly, Illini Mascot Issue Back on the Front Burner," *Chicago Tribune,* November 3, 1993, B2.

87 Ibid.

88 "Education Key in Chief Debate," *Daily Illini* 123, no. 49, October 29, 1993, 16.

89 Matt Hanley, "A Campus Divided," *Daily Illini* 128, no. 90, February 5, 1999, 1.

90 Ibid.

91 Adam Jadhav, "Memorial Stadium to Hold Service," *Daily Illini* 131, no. 18, September 14, 2001, 6.

92 Joan Wagner, "Coming Together," *Daily Illini* 131, no. 19, September 17, 2001, 1.

93 Zielinski, "Illinois Marathon."

94 Jacob Hurwith, "In First Year, Illinois Marathon Exceeds Most Expectations," *Daily Illini,* vol. 138, no. 134, April 13, 2009, 1A.

95 "Illinois Marathon," *Online Race Results,* https://www.onlineraceresults.com/race/view_race.php?race_id=10170#racetop

96 Debra Pressey, "Christie, Local Buyers Take Over Illinois Marathon," *Champaign-Urbana News-Gazette,* September 27, 2010, https://www.news-gazette.com/news/christie-local-buyers-take-over-illinois-marathon/article_3303c8c8-47be-519f-8e83-2f3b70c9af35.html.

97 Cain, "Illinois Athletic Director Mike Thomas."

98 Joan Wagner, "Illini, Bears Together Again," *Daily Illini* 131, no. 151, May 6, 2002, 8.

99 Ibid.

100 Kate Clements, "Illinois Lawmakers Consider Allowing Beer Sales at Champaign-Urbana," *Champaign-Urbana News-Gazette,* March 1, 2001.

101 Tiffany Arnold, "Bears and Beers Now Go Hand in Hand," *Daily Illini* 131, no. 75, January 11, 2002, 5.

102 Leslie Hague, "Sunday Sales a 'Bear' of a Controversy," *Daily Illini* 131, no. 154, June 13, 2002, 1.

103 Ibid.

104 Fighting Illini Football, "Year-by-Year Records."

105 Fighting Illini Football, "Individual Records."

106 Bobby La Gesse, "Zook at Illinois?" *Daily Illini,* vol. 134, no. 68, December 1, 2004, 1.

107 Sabryna Cornish, "Trustees Approve First Phase of Memorial Stadium Renovation," University of Illinois News Bureau, May 18, 2006, https://news.illinois.edu/view/6367/211583.

108 Neil Milbert, "Zook Expects Improvement," *Chicago Tribune,* August 21, 2006.

109 Nick Fawell, "Stadium Prepares for Makeover," *Daily Illini,* vol. 135, no. 97, February 10, 2006, 1.

110 Christine Des Garennes, "Bowl Breakdown: Is It Worth the Trip?" *Champaign-Urbana News-Gazette,* December 21, 2014, https://www.news-gazette.com/news/bowl-breakdown-is-it-worth-the-trip/article_1cc64a29-dd72-5bb3-a4ef-4ee02ac30623.html.

111 Fighting Illini, "Memorial Stadium."

112 Lisa Chung, "Projects Pave Way for Green Campus," *Daily Illini* 137, no. 5, August 23, 2007, 6.

113 Ibid.

114 "DR. SHELBY R. CHIPMAN, DIRECTOR OF BANDS," *FAMU,* https://cssah.famu.edu/departments-and-centers/marching-100/shelby-chipman-biography.php

115 The record was 78,297 for the September 8, 1984, game against Missouri (Fighting Illini Football, "Illini Football Attendance Records").

116 Welin, "Texas Bowl 2010."

117 John Supinie, "U of I Athletic Director Guenther Retiring June 30," *Springfield State Journal-Register,* May 17, 2011, https://www.sj-r.com/story/sports/college/fighting-illini/2011/05/17/u-i-athletic-director-guenther/44245544007/.

118 Des Garennes, "Bowl Breakdown."

119 Fighting Illini, "Memorial Stadium."

120 Associated Press and *Los Angeles Times,* "Illinois Hires Tim Beckman, Previously at Toledo, as Coach," *Seattle Times,* December 10, 2011, https://www.seattletimes.com/sports/college/Illinois-hires-tim-beckman-previously-at-toledo-as-coach-college-football/.

121 Bennett, "Illinois Fires Tim Beckman."

122 Werner, "Breaking: Whitman Dismisses Cubit."

123 ESPN.com News Services, "Illinois Hires Lovie Smith as Coach."

124 Cole Henke, "University Progresses on Memorial Stadium Renovations," *Daily Illini,* September 21, 2016, https://dailyillini.com/showcase/2016/09/21/university-submits-plans-possible-memorial-stadium-renovations/.

125 David J. Sencer CDC Museum, "CDC Museum COVID-19 Timeline."

126 Ibid.

127 Stevens, "Big Ten Conference Halts All Organized Team Activities."

128 Big Ten Conference, "Big Ten Statement on 2020–21 Fall Season."

129 Blake Toppmeyer, "SEC Pushes Back Start Date for Preseason Football Practice," *Knoxville News Sentinel,* August 5, 2020, https://www.news-press.com/story/sports/college/football/2020/08/04/sec-football-practice-start-delay-2020/3292238001/.

130 Anderson, "Big Ten Reverses Course."

131 Pac-12 Conference, "Pac-12 Announces Resumption."

132 Cobb, "Pac-12 on Brink of Collapse."

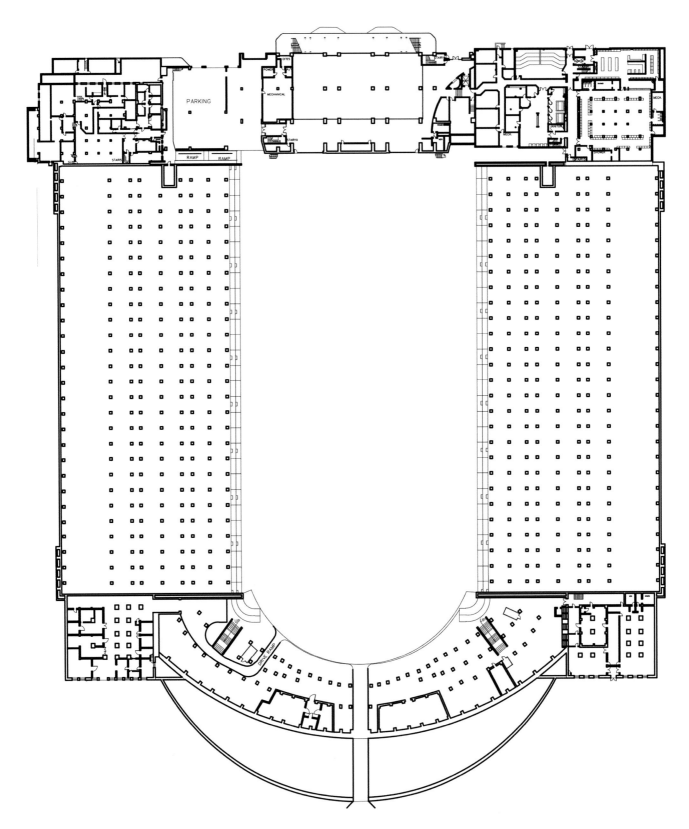

Figure C-2.1
Field Level Plan. Image by Kevin J. Hinders.

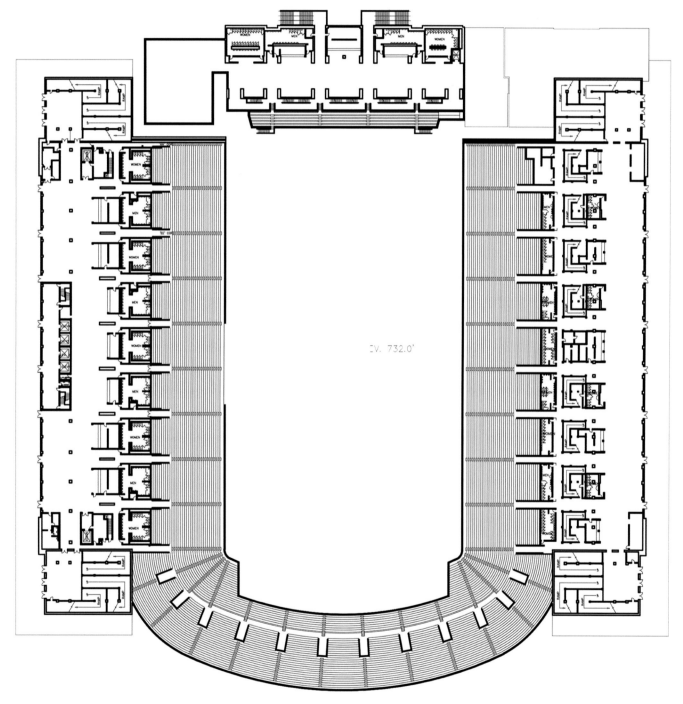

Figure C-2.2
Entry Level Plan. Image by Kevin J. Hinders.

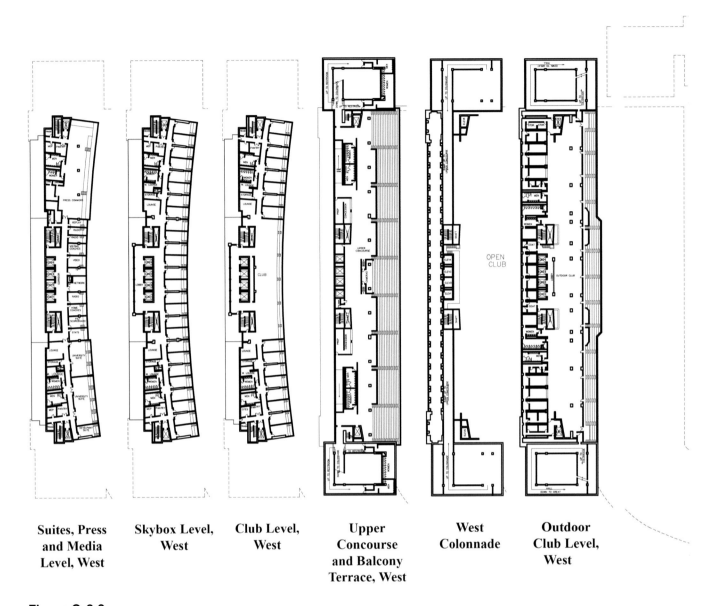

| Suites, Press and Media Level, West | Skybox Level, West | Club Level, West | Upper Concourse and Balcony Terrace, West | West Colonnade | Outdoor Club Level, West |

Figure C-2.3
Upper level Plans. Image by Kevin J. Hinders.

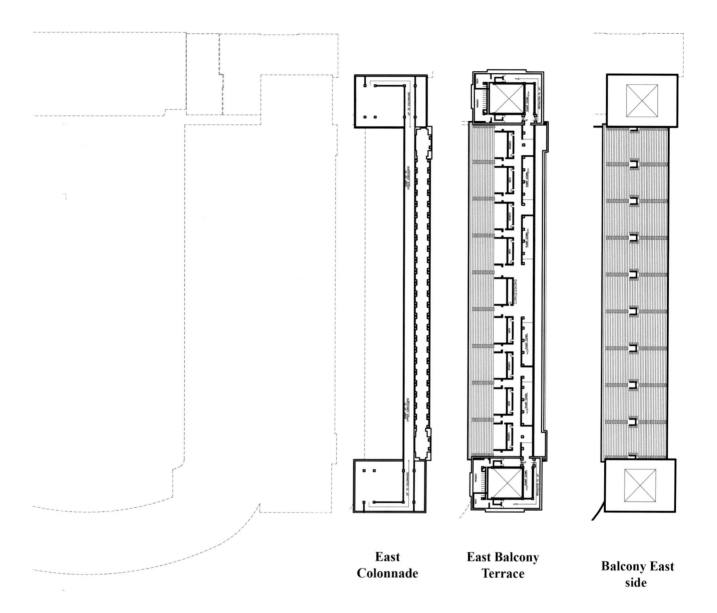

**East
Colonnade**

**East Balcony
Terrace**

**Balcony East
side**

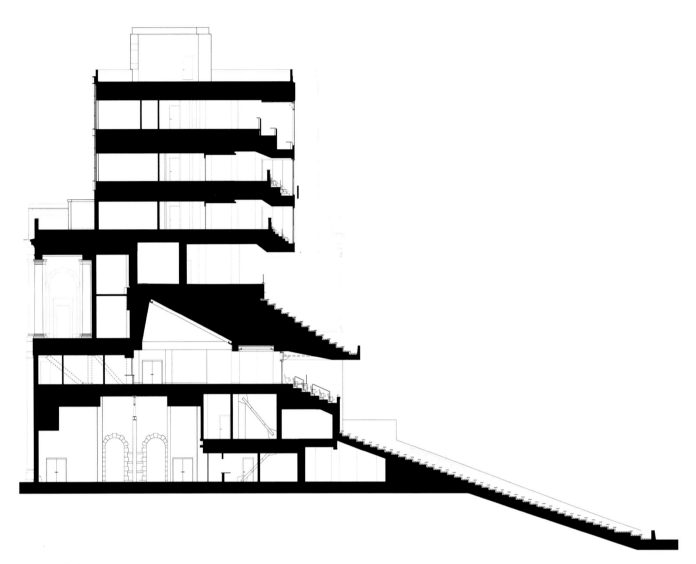

Figure C-2.4
West Stadium at the 10 Yard Line. Image by Kevin J. Hinders and Stephen Ferroni.

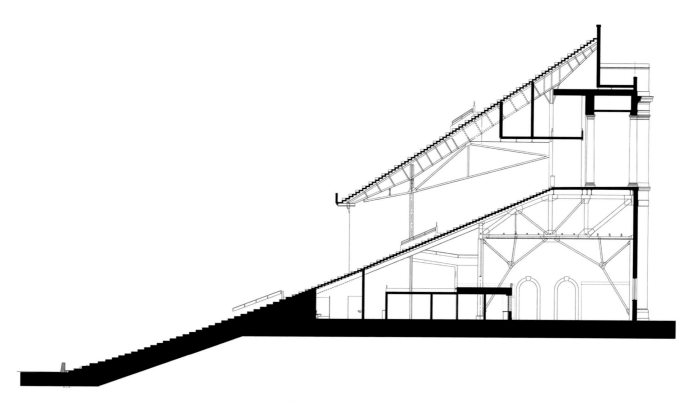

Figure C-2.5
East Stadium Section. Image by Kevin J. Hinders and Stephen Ferroni.

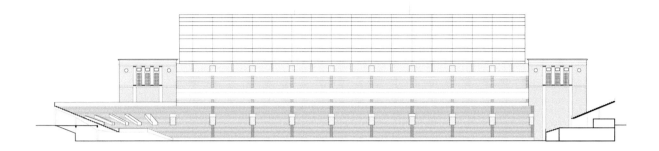

Figure C-2.6
Longitudinal Section. Image by Stephen Ferroni.

Figure C-2.7
West Stadium image: Courtesy of the Division of Intercollegiate Athletics Archive.

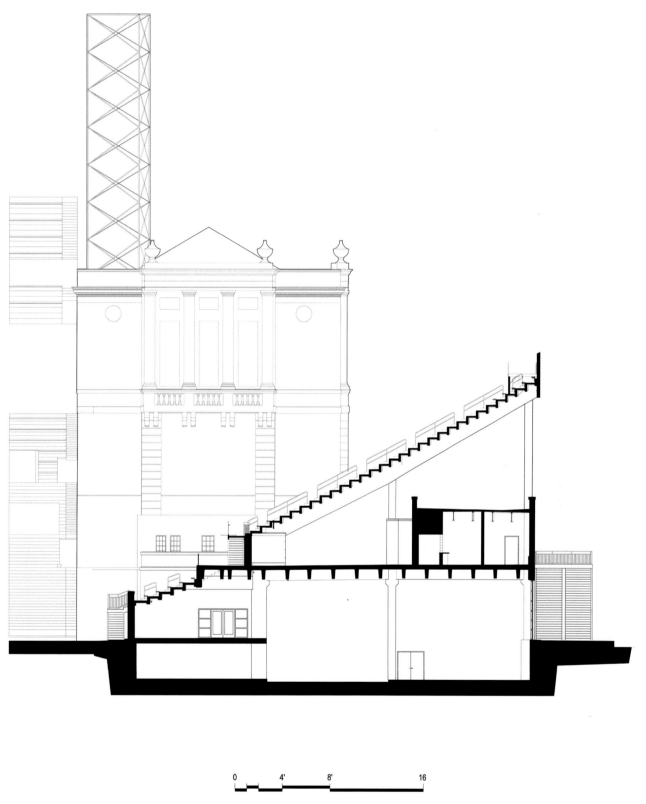

0   4'   8'   16

Figure C-2.8
North Endzone Section. Image by Kevin J. Hinders.

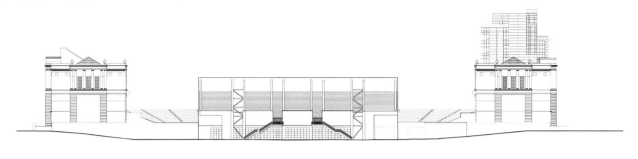

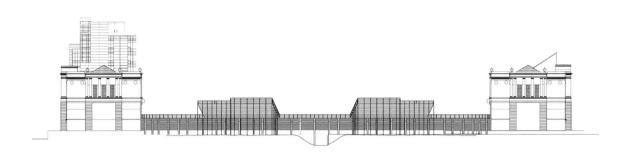

Figure C-2.9 and C-2.10
North Elevation and South Elevation. Images by Kevin J. Hinders.

Figure C-2.11
Photograph of the Stadium from the south endzone. Courtesy of the Division of Intercollegiate Athletics Archives.

Figure C-2.12
Photograph of the West Colonnade Club. Courtesy of the Division of Intercollegiate Athletics Archives.

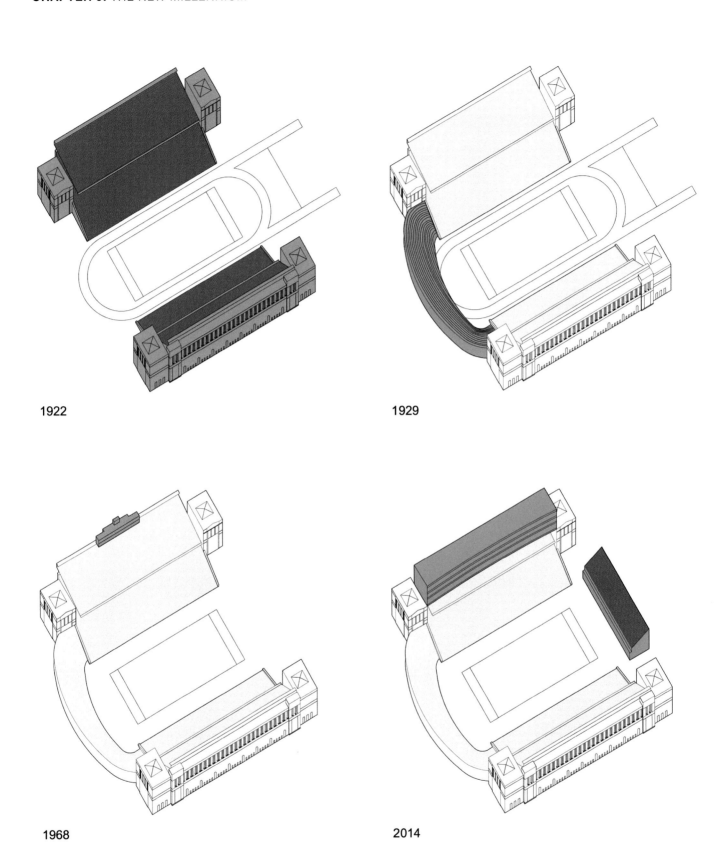

1922

1929

1968

2014

Figure C-2.13
Stadium progression 1924-2014. Image by Stephen Ferroni.

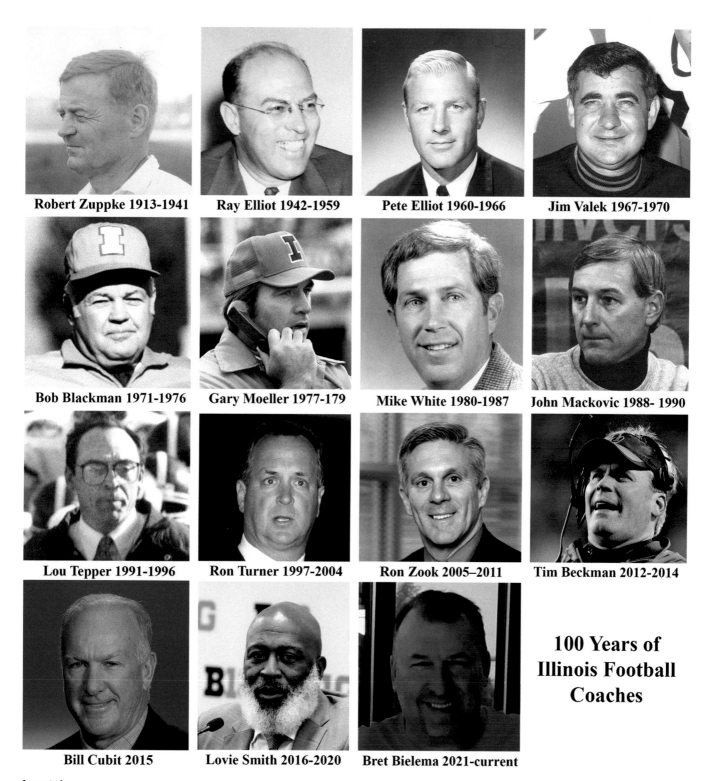

Robert Zuppke 1913-1941   Ray Elliot 1942-1959   Pete Elliot 1960-1966   Jim Valek 1967-1970

Bob Blackman 1971-1976   Gary Moeller 1977-179   Mike White 1980-1987   John Mackovic 1988- 1990

Lou Tepper 1991-1996   Ron Turner 1997-2004   Ron Zook 2005–2011   Tim Beckman 2012-2014

Bill Cubit 2015   Lovie Smith 2016-2020   Bret Bielema 2021-current

100 Years of Illinois Football Coaches

Inset 4
One Hundred Years of Illinois Football Coaches. Images courtesy of the University of Illinois Division of Intercollegiate Athletics Archives.

The Point After

One Hundred Years of Sports and Innovations

Since its conception, and throughout its long history, the University of Illinois Memorial Stadium has embodied the geographic, historical, socioeconomic, and political factors present in its contextual environment. From the student-led funding campaign that gave life to the venue, to the recent development of digital streaming, the Stadium has continued to adapt and evolve, its robust and flexible design a testament to its innovative spirit and a hallmark of long-term sustainability. Significantly, from its construction onward the "Colossus of the Prairie" has had, over its first 100 years, a tangible impact on the University of Illinois Urbana-Champaign (UIUC), as well as on the wider local, regional, and national community.

Blessed with a generous watershed feeding various regional streams and river systems, rich fertile agricultural soil formed by previous geological eras, and enormous coal reserves and various other minerals, like galena (lead), what would become the State of Illinois first attracted some of the earliest Paleoindian inhabitants and later European traders and settlers. Throughout the nineteenth century, the state of Illinois consolidated its economic and political power as its burgeoning agriculture and industry spurring geometric population growth. By the late 1850s and into the early 1860s, Illinois politicians, which included President Abraham Lincoln and the state's congressional delegation, were able to deliver the Morrill Act, which sparked the development of Land Grant Universities. Among the first

schools to be founded under this legislation was the University of Illinois, then called the Illinois Industrial University, which was conceived to educate and train the much-needed future leaders of industry and agriculture. After the Champaign delegation successfully lobbied state legislators, the University was founded in 1867 in Champaign County. Over the next decades, as the state's population continued to grow, so did the school's student enrollment.

In response, the University increased its academic programs, added physical education, and expanded intercollegiate sports. These sports, like American football, became central to the academic and social life of not only the school, local community, and state, but the country as a whole. From the end of the nineteenth century, American football continued to evolve, spurring on its popularity across the country. Meanwhile, in the first decades of the twentieth century, Illini football teams claimed multiple national championships, establishing the Fighting Illini as one of the most storied programs in college football. Recognizing the importance of effectively guiding the growth of participation in sporting events, the University and its first Athletic Director, George Huff, utilized the Athletic Association (AA) to not only guide the University's campus-wide athletic programs but also support its thriving intercollegiate sports teams.

With the United States' (US) entry into the Great War in 1917, over 4.7 million Americans directly participated in the war effort. Of these, over 63,000 individuals sacrificed their lives to help bring hostilities to an end

DOI: 10.4324/9781032643885-11

293

in 1918. Once the war was over, millions returned to the US to start or continue their everyday lives, ushering in the "Golden Age," a period of economic, social, and political stability in the 1920s. The Fighting Illini football team continued to dominate college football, and with an expanding fan base established by a growing University student enrollment and consequent alumni family, demand for access to college football games exploded. New traditions, some established in the last years of the 1910s, like Homecoming, provided community-making events. Recognizing a tipping point, AD Huff and football Head Coach Robert "Zup" Zuppke, successfully lobbied for a new, state-of-the-art, stadium as a memorial to honor those who had perished during the Great War, while also providing a sports venue that would enable the Illini to compete against the well-established northeast football and Track & Field (T&F) programs.

The desire for, and eventual construction of, Memorial Stadium embodies as all built environments the social, political, economic, and aesthetic values and aspirations of its time. The Stadium was built in the first third of what would eventually be dubbed the "Roaring Twenties." Remarkably, even though the Stadium is a state facility, and hence a public facility, its construction was funded, at times torturously, by students, alumni, and sales revenue from its own operations, embodying the "can do" spirit of a then 50-year-old University of Illinois eager to compete with the premiere educational and sports institutions of its time. After contracting the architecture firm of Holabird & Roche to execute the design, the University and AA worked together to define the spatial qualities of the new Stadium: from its siting and spectator-friendly innovative two-tiered seating decks to the use of majestic Tuscan Columns, inscribed with the names of the Great War's fallen, and Georgian-style dark red brick facades, the Stadium emerged as a visible landmark. A landmark which Huff envisioned would anchor a new sports campus that enriched students' everyday lives.

Though construction started on September 11, 1922, the "soft opening" took place when the Fighting Illini defeated the University of Chicago Maroons, 3-0, on November 3, 1923. Less than a year later, on

October 18, 1924, the Stadium was officially dedicated in a history-making game where millions of Americans heard on the radio how the legendary Harold E. "Red" Grange and the Fighting Illini defeated the University of Michigan Wolverines, 39-14. For the rest of the decade, Stadium ticket sales not only helped the AA pay off construction balances, but also sponsor the Stadium's second-phased horseshoe seating, and other sports facilities on campus. Among these were the Ice Arena, which today still houses the ice rink across the street from UIUC's armory. The regional impact was so dramatic that new highways were built, including an extension that connected Kankakee to Champaign, to provide the rapidly expanding automotive-bound spectator a faster route to Illini football games. With a new Stadium, the Illini track and field (T&F) team competed at the highest levels, frequently hosting state-wide and regional events. Eventually, Memorial Stadium would have its time in the national spotlight as a T&F venue, when it hosted twice, 1977 and 1979, the NCAA outdoor national championships.

In what is one of the most important factors in the evolution of college sports, mass media communications arrived in the early part of the 1920s via radio broadcasts. By the late 1920s, radio broadcasting had become a profitable mass medium, largely due to its capacity to bring audiences the performance of legendary sports figures like that of the Galloping Ghost, as Grantland Rice had dubbed Red Grange, combined with on-air paid advertisements. As the prosperity of the 1920s gave way to the Depression of the 1930s, securing revenue from any and all possible sources became a central concern for college sports programs throughout the country. Not surprisingly, with pressure to field successful, e.g., victorious, football teams needed to drive ticket sale revenues, recruiting the best student athletes, often with suspect tactics, emerged as a central topic of debate and controversy -one that that continues to this day. With Huff's passing in 1936, and Zuppke's long coaching tenure coming to an end in 1941 after a string of losing seasons, the Illini football program struggled to attract spectators to the Stadium at the end of the 1930s and into the 1940s. Then, on December 7, 1941, the United States was attacked by the Empire of Japan, forcing the country to enter World War II (WWII).

During WWII, the Stadium showed its versatility, first becoming a Navy educational and training facility, where sailors learned to maintain and operate the large diesel engines used for propulsion by American battleships. Then, after WWII ended, the GI Bill enabled millions of veterans to start or continue their education. The University, facing a housing shortage, readily transformed the Stadium into a dormitory to accommodate the surge. Later, student housing was built surrounding the Stadium.

Following WWII, post-war enrollment continued to grow, prompting campus expansion that included new housing, classrooms, research space, and new sports facilities. As the 1950s arrived, and the Stadium playing a central role, the Fighting Illini football program claimed its last national championship (1951). As visualized by Huff and architects at the time of its conception, Memorial Stadium provided the spatial anchor for the University's expanding intramural and intercollegiate athletics campus. An axis running north to south through the Stadium's goalposts organizes Assembly Hall (currently known as State Farm Center) to the south and the Intramural Physical Education (IMPE) building to the north (now referred to as the Activities and Recreation Center or ARC), which exemplify the University's commitment to sports and physical fitness. Then, in the mid-1950s, television, with its ability to bring sports into the family room, catalyzed the next evolution of college sports. Like radio before, television now has become a crucial source of revenue for sports programs, especially college football teams. Conferences, like the Big Ten, established revenue-sharing schemes that proved vital for member teams to compete at the national level. Regional loyalties, traditionally driven by regional alumni bases, gave way to national viewership, reflecting changes in American society as a whole.

Arguably, nothing drives revenue up more than a successful football season. Successful football programs are at the confluence of the best possible athletes, great coaching, and the latest in fitness and practice facilities. To recruit and develop the best possible student athletes, it was crucial that the University built new training and practice facilities, like the Irwin indoor practice facility and later the Smith Center. Just as in the past, UIUC was one of the first schools in the country to adopt a Nautilus Fitness system at an enormous cost. It is also key that schools maximize the student athletes mass media exposure since many—though not all—of these athletes aim for a career in the NFL (with the accompanying NFL salaries). This is why college athletic programs view their facilities, especially their homefield, as fundamental to ensure recruiting success. UIUC has wisely deemed that Memorial Stadium is an asset worth maintaining.

As the Stadium aged and college football evolved, new amenities and facilities were necessary. Frequently, building upgrades were directly correlated to meeting the demands of the market as the AA sought to increase sources of revenue. Not only did the Stadium undergo periodic maintenance to assure its continued structural stability performance capabilities, and prevent the loss of one of the most important assets of the state, but the venue also needed updates to keep technologically up to date. To address the Stadium's location on marshlands by reducing difficulties generated by a muddy field and support multiple sporting activities, the AA replaced the field's grass with artificial turf in the early 1970s. The installation of a new lighting system roughly at the same time signaled the expansion of the Stadium's operational schedule. Televised night games, however, would have to wait until the last half of the 1980s. Throughout the 1980s and 1990s, the steel structure was reinforced and the concrete seating decks were replaced. Updated restrooms and concession kiosks improved the spectator experience.

When Soldier Field in Chicago underwent an enormous transformation in 2002, Memorial Stadium, as its sister stadium, served as the temporary home of the Chicago Bears. This ushered in another wave of alterations, including a new digital scoreboard capable of showing replays, which revealed the expectations of sport spectators on campus and across a wider swath of society.

Yet, this necessary upgrade was nothing new. The Stadium's history is full of examples of the facilities being updated to address the constant changes in technology: from the introduction of radio, and then television broadcasting, to the current prevalence of digital streaming. In fact, the installation of new scoreboards, not only reflected the spectators' expectations for up-to-date informational technology but was key factor in introducing innovative AA financing mechanisms, especially when the AA was confronted with a lack of enthusiasm for student fees, state funds, or additional debt. Once-innovative financing mechanisms, e.g., selling advertisements to finance the scoreboard, have now become an industry standard for college (and professional) sports. Schools are constantly faced with developing strategies or identifying market trends, to produce the revenue needed to maintain assets like Memorial Stadium. At each step, whether installing a radio station and corresponding broadcast antenna and the later addition in the 1960s of a television-friendly press box, to the current ambitious project of installing a robust WiFi system, the Stadium and its stewards have labored to keep the facility, and by extension UIUC, relevant and competitive in the Big Ten conference.

In fact, mass media broadcasting rights have proven to be so fundamental to a successful program, it has supercharged the migration of football programs from conference to conference. The inability of a team to be successful over the long haul, on the one hand reduces future fanbases. In turn, this smaller fan base means less people viewing the team on any mediatic platform. Thus, affecting the overall conference's competitivity against other conferences, especially in recruiting. With the introduction of each new media, the money involved has changed the business model, and now digital media, like streaming services, means that people have more choices of entertainment than ever before in history. When radio was introduced, the popularity of college football spread quickly across the country establishing the "Golden Age of Sports." That explosive spread, in turn, drove the construction of venues that embodied this market expansion: stadiums, like the Illinois Memorial Stadium, captured the growing demand for sports entertainment. Today, the impact of digital technology is equally powerful. The inability to adapt to mediatic changes can lead to internal tensions, often generated by revenue-sharing agreements that must balance market size and share with the needs of all league members.

In one salient case, the unresolved conflict led to the collapse of a Power Five conference, the Pac-12. Unable to find a formula that worked for them, in December of 2022, the University of Southern California (USC) and the University of California at Los Angeles (UCLA) announced that they were leaving the Pac-12 and joining the Big Ten. In May of 2023, the University of Oregon and the University of Washington followed suit. Over the next months, the Pac-12 imploded, with all but four programs abandoning the conference.

Illinois Memorial Stadium is a Community Anchor

That 100 years later Illinois Memorial Stadium is still the home of the Fighting Illini football team, is a testament to the vision of the University and recent Department of Intercollegiate Athletics (DIA) directors, which understands that the Stadium is more than just a football facility. To simply see the Stadium as a sports venue is to miss perhaps its most important aspect, which is to understand what it *does.* From the beginning, the Stadium was to be a home for all of the State of Illinois. The Colossus of the Prairie was to become a beacon to attract all Illinoisans, and beyond, to become UIUC students. From the very beginning, whether it was a regional Boy Scout jamboree, marching band day, or Dad's Day, the Stadium has functioned as a wider space for socialization and community-building. It has been the site of massive July 4th celebrations, King Neptune's fundraising efforts, marathon finish lines, high school football championships, and even student-run performing circuses. As needed to fulfill its social role, the Stadium has repeatedly been modified to increase accessibility, including leading the way by adding wheelchair access ramps. So that as many people as possible can enjoy Illinois Memorial Stadium. As Arthur "Art" Georges, a steeple chaser and long-distance runner between 1980 and 1984 shared,

I was just a high school senior from nearby St. Joseph, but in the spring of 1979, I watched from Memorial's stands the NCAA outdoor championships; and I knew then, nothing would be more wonderful than to make Illinois' track and field team. The Stadium just made me dream.[1]

The Stadium had done exactly what the University had hoped it would do.

Not only are Grange Grove and the Colonnade Club the most notable and recent Stadium additions, but they also reflect the changing nature of collegiate sports and spectator experience. Accessible from the street without paying the fee, Grange Grove formalizes the west Stadium entry and provides a "front yard" atmosphere to game day's immense tailgating activities. Family and friends, sometimes with divided loyalties with the visiting school, socialize and remiss about times past. Other spaces within the Stadium, like Colonnade Club, allow for a luxurious spectator experience or hosting events.

From game day seating boxes, and press and broadcast accommodations, to elegant reception and meeting spaces, the Colonnade Club reflects a versatile Stadium addressing market needs.

At times, the Stadium was also the backdrop to painful events in history, including the use of the Stadium to jail Black UIUC students. It has been the dancing stage on which Chief Illiniwek, a still-divisive icon associated with UIUC history, first symbolically smoked a peace pipe at mid-field with UPenn's visiting Quaker back in October of 1926. To be sure, true racial de-segregation took longer than it should have, but the University continues to expand the diversity of its student body. Yet, these difficult events have also helped shape our present consciousness and strengthen our sense of community. From turbulent sociopolitical times in the 1960s and economic hardships which gave birth to FarmAid 1985, to a memorial service

Figure 10.1
Nebraska Game, Sept. 21, 2019. Courtesy of the Division of Intercollegiate Athletics Archives. Photograph by Craig Pessman.

with 10,000 participants four days after September 11, 2001, the Stadium has always been an integral component of not only campus life, but at times, the entire world. Its role in various historic moments proffering valuable lessons for us today.

In the future, Memorial Stadium Campus will continue to adapt and change with the times and its users' values. Already, the DIA is exploring ways to make the stadium more digitally accessible. Enhancing the spectator experience is seen as the most pressing factor in maintaining and upgrading the stadium. Spaces not imagined 100 years ago are now commonplace. In 1924, the stadium was heralded for its innovations and hospitality. Today, there is a unique balance between traditions, the Stadium's history, and the ever-changing way in which we experience sports and gathering socially. Over the next 100 years, the Stadium will continue to evolve to address athletic needs and just as importantly, the needs of its local, regional, national, and even international community.

Here is a cheer to the next 100 years of Memorial Stadium and its momentous impact on the University of Illinois, the state of Illinois, and the United States! (Figure 10.1)

I-L-L! I-N-I!

Note

1 Interview Arthur Georges, January 26, 2024.

Bibliography

Anderson, Greta. "Big Ten Reverses Course." Inside Higher Ed, September 16, 2020. https://www.insidehighered.com/news/2020/09/17/big-ten-reverses-decision-and-will-play-fall-football.

Angel, Jim. "Averages and Records for Champaign-Urbana, Illinois." State Climatologist Office for Illinois, Accessed December 14, 2023. https://www.isws.illinois.edu/statecli/cuweather/cu-averages.htm.

Antiquities and Monument Office. "Three Historic Buildings Declared Monuments." October 23, 2015. https://www.amo.gov.hk/en/news/index_id_40.html.

Arevalo, Wendy. "The V-12 Officer Training Program." Naval History and Heritage Command, December 21, 2022. https://www.history.navy.mil/browse-by-topic/wars-conflicts-and-operations/world-war-ii/1942/manning-the-us-navy/v-12-program.html.

ATO Gamma Zeta Chapter. "Gamma Zeta's Campus Impact." Accessed January 15, 2024. https://atoillinois.com/history/gamma-zeta-atos-impact-on-u-of-i-campus/.

Bardahl, Jayna. "Illinois Football Recruiting Rewind: Best Signee, Biggest Bust, the One Who Got Away, and More." *Athletic,* June 15, 2023. https://theathletic.com/4610626/2023/06/15/illinois-recruiting-history-best-worst-signings/.

Behle, J. Gregory. "Educating the Sons of Toil: Student Life at the University of Illinois, The Early Years." University Archives Sesquicentennial Speaker Series presentation, March 2, 2017. University of Illinois Archives, Urbana-Champaign.

Bennett, Brian. "Illinois Fires Tim Beckman One Week before Season Amid External Review." ESPN.com, August 28, 2015. https://www.espn.com/college-football/story/_/id/13533196/tim-beckman-fired-coach-illinois-fighting-illini.

Big Ten Conference. "Big Ten History." Accessed December 2, 2023. https://bigten.org/sports/2018/6/6/trads-big10-trads-html.aspx.

——. "Big Ten Membership History." June 11, 2010. https://bigten.org/news/2010/6/11/big_ten_membership_history.aspx.

——. "Big Ten Statement on 2020–21 Fall Season." August 11, 2020. https://bigten.org/news/2020/8/11/general-big-ten-statement-on-2020-21-fall-season.aspx#:.

Billboard. "Billboard Hot 100." Billboard, August 10, 1974. https://www.billboard.com/charts/hot-100/1974-08-10/.

Black History in America. "Buddy Young," myblackhistory.net. Accessed February 14, 2024. https://www.myblackhistory.net/ClaudeYoung.htm

Blum, David A., and Nese F. DeBruyne. *American War and Military Operations Casualties: Lists and Statistics.* Report RL32492, version 25. Washington, DC: Congressional Research Service, 2018.

Boand, William. "Boand System Selection." College Football Data Warehouse, February 11, 2010. http://cfbdatawarehouse.com/data/national_championships/champ_results.php?selector=Boand%20System.

Board of Trustees of the University of Illinois. "Historical Leadership." Accessed December 24, 2023. https://www.bot.uillinois.edu/UserFiles/Servers/Server_694865/File/UI-trustees-chronological.pdf.

——. Meetings Minutes Archive. University of Illinois, Urbana-Champaign. https://www.bot.uillinois.edu/meetings/minutes/minutes_archive.

——. *Tenth Annual Report.* Springfield: H. W. Rokker, 1881.

——. *Third Annual Report.* Springfield: State Journal Printing Office, 1870.

Bogue, Margaret Beattie. "The Swamp Land Act and Wet Land Utilization in Illinois, 1850–1890." *Agricultural History* 25, no. 4 (1951): 169–80.

Bruegmann, Robert. *Holabird and Roche, Holabird and Root: An Illustrated Catalog of Works.* Chicago: Garland in cooperation with the Chicago Historical Society, 1991.

Bureau of Counterterrorism. "Foreign Terrorist Organizations." U.S. Department of State. Accessed January 16, 2024. https://www.state.gov/foreign-terrorist-organizations/.

Burt, H. J. "Stadium Design." *Western Society of Engineers* 28, no. 3 (March 1923): 69–83.

Cain, Brandon M. "Illinois Athletic Director Mike Thomas Calls New Tailgate Area 'Grange Grove.'" Champaign Room, April 11, 2015. https://www.thechampaignroom.com/2015/4/11/8390033/illinois-athletic-director-mike-thomas-calls-new-tailgate-area-grange-grove.

Calomiris, Charles W., R. Glenn Hubbard, and James H. Stock. "The Farm Debt Crisis and Public Policy." *Brookings Papers on Economic Activity* 2 (1986): 441–85.

Carlson, Kurt A. "Backing the Boys in the Civil War: Chicago's Home Front Supports the Troops—And Grows in the Process." *Journal of the Illinois State Historical Society* 104, nos. 1–2 (2011): 140–65.

Chicago Public Library. "1924 Grant Park Stadium (Soldier Field) Completed." November 12, 2013. https://www.chipublib.org/blogs/post/1924-grant-park-stadium-soldier-field-completed/.

Cobb, David. "Pac-12 on Brink of Collapse: How College Football's Premier West Coast Conference Fell Behind in Realignment." CBS Sports, August 11, 2023. https://www.cbssports.com/college-football/news/pac-12-on-brink-of-collapse-how-college-footballs-premier-west-coast-conference-fell-behind-in-realignment/.

Cobb-Roberts, Deirdre. "Interracial Cooperatives at the University of Illinois, 1940–1960." *American Educational History Journal* 29 (2002): 35–42. eBlack Champaign-Urbana, item 913, https://eblackcu.net/portal/items/show/913.

Cole, Arthur Charles. *The Era of the Civil War, 1848–1870.* Urbana: University of Illinois Press, 1987.

College Poll Archive. "1942 Final AP Football Poll." Accessed September 10, 2023. https://collegepollarchive.com/football/ap/seasons.cfm?appollid=55.

Congress of the Confederation. "Northwest Ordinance; July 13, 1787." Avalon Project. Accessed December 24, 2023. https://avalon.law.yale.edu/18th_century/nworder.asp#.

CougarStats. "Notre Dame 21 Illinois 14." Accessed September 12, 2023. https://cougarstats.com/games.php?show=details&game_id=2961.

Cormie, Robert. "Approve 18,000 Seat Illini Arena: HALL TO COST $7,500,000, BE READY IN 1960 Will be Site of State Prep Meet ILLINOIS PLANS BASKET ARENA; TO SEAT 18,000." Chicago Daily Tribune (1923-1963), Dec 18, 1957.

Covil, Eric C. "Radio and Its Impact on the Sports World." American Sportscasters Online. Accessed November 30, 2023. http://www.americansportscastersonline.com/radiohistory.html.

David J. Sencer CDC Museum. "CDC Museum COVID-19 Timeline." David J. Sencer CDC Museum in Association with the Smithsonian Institution. Accessed January 22, 2024. https://www.cdc.gov/museum/timeline/covid19.html#:.

Davis, James Edward. *Frontier Illinois.* Bloomington: Indiana University Press, 1998.

Department of Physics. "Betatron." Accessed September 24, 2023. https://physics.illinois.edu/people/history/betatron.

Dinsmoor, William Bell. *The Architecture of Ancient Greece: An Account of Its Historic Development.* London: Biblo and Tannen, 1973.

Dinterman, Robert Ani L. Katchova, and James Michael Harris. "Financial Stress and Farm Bankruptcies in U.S. Agriculture" *Agricultural Finance Review* 78, no. 4 (2018): 441–56 https://doi.org/10.1108/AFR-05-2017-0030.

Directory of University of Illinois Men, in Chicago and Vicinity. George E. Owen, ed. Illini Club of Chicago, c.1926-1927.

Dixon, Matthew. "College Football TV Contracts since 1984: How Much Higher Can They Go?" *Sports Enthusiasts,* July 8, 2023. https://sportsenthusiasts.net/2023/07/08/a-comprehensive-history-of-college-football-tv-contracts-since-1984-how-much-higher-can-they-go/.

Dulin, Robert O., Jr., and William H. Garzke. *Battleships: United States Battleships in World War II.* Annapolis: Naval Institute Press, 1976.

Durand, Jean-Nicolas-Louis, *Recueil et parallèle des édifices de tout genre anciens et modernes: Remarquables par leur beauté par leur grandeur ou par leur singularité et dessinés sur une même echelle.* Paris: Vincent Fréal, 1801.

Ellis, David Maldwyn. "Railroad Land Grant Rates, 1850–1945." *Journal of Land and Public Utility Economics* 21, no. 3 (1945): 207–22.

English Brothers Company. "A History of Excellence." Accessed December 24, 2023. https://www.englishbrothers.com/about.

ESPN.com News Services. "Illinois Hires Lovie Smith as Coach." March 7, 2016. https://www.espn.com/college-football/story/_/id/14919209/illinois-fighting-illini-hire-lovie-smith-new-coach.

Federal Communications Commission. "History of Commercial Radio." October 17, 2023. https://www.fcc.gov/media/radio/history-of-commercial-radio.

Farm Aid. "About Us." Accessed January 3, 2024. https://www.farmaid.org/about-us/.

———. "Farm Aid: A Concert for America." Accessed January 3, 2024. https://www.farmaid.org/issues/industrial-agriculture/farm-aid-nearly-40-years-of-action-for-family-farmers/.

Farm Aid History Harvest. "Share Your Memories of Farm Aid! Accessed January 6, 2024. https://publish.illinois.edu/farmaidhistoryharvest/.

Fighting Illini. "Bielfeldt Athletics Administration Building." Accessed January 18, 2024. https://fightingillini.com/sports/2015/6/30/GEN_0630154135.aspx.

———. "Claude 'Buddy' Young." Hall of Fame. Accessed September 16, 2023. https://fightingillini.com/honors/hall-of-fame/claude-buddy-young/81.

———. "Henry Dale and Betty Smith Football Performance Center." Accessed January 24, 2024. https://fightingillini.com/facilities/henry-dale-and-betty-smith-football-performance-center/38.

———. "Leo Johnson." Hall of Fame. Accessed October 31, 2023. https://fightingillini.com/honors/hall-of-fame/leo-johnson/46.

———. "Memorial Stadium." Accessed January 21, 2024. https://fightingillini.com/facilities/memorial-stadium/64.

———. "The Return of the Galloping Ghost to Memorial Stadium." October 30, 2015. https://fightingillini.com/news/2015/10/30/Football_1030152550.aspx.

———. "Simeon Rice." Hall of Fame. Accessed January 16, 2024. https://fightingillini.com/honors/hall-of-fame/simeon-rice/61.

Fighting Illini Football. "Football History vs Ohio State University from Nov 15, 1902–Nov 18, 2017." Accessed January 1, 2024. https://fightingillini.com/sports/football/opponent-history/ohio-state-university/25.

———. "Illini Football Attendance Records." December 2017. https://fightingillini.com/sports/2016/8/18/football-attendance-records.

———. "Illinois Homecoming History." October 10, 2018. https://fightingillini.com/news/2018/10/10/football-illinois-homecoming-history.

———. "Individual Records." December 2023. https://fightingillini.com/sports/2016/2/27/football-individual-records.aspx.

———. "Memorial Stadium Records." December 2017. https://fightingillini.com/sports/2016/8/31/football-memorial-stadium-records.aspx.

———. "Year-by-Year Records." December 2023. https://fightingillini.com/sports/2016/8/9/football-year-by-year-records.aspx.

Franch, John. "Memory Lane: Building Blocks." University of Illinois Alumni Association, September 30, 2016. https://uiaa.org/2016/09/30/memory-lane-building-blocks/.

———. "The University of Illinois Goes to War." UI Archives' Student Life and Culture Archival Program, November 15, 2007. https://archives.library.illinois.edu/slc/files/2014/09/WWIIHistory.pdf.

Frankie, Wayne. "Building the Bedrock." *Guide to Rocks and Minerals,* 3–5. Geoscience Education Series 16. Champaign: Illinois State Geological Survey, 2004. https://www.ideals.illinois.edu/items/50380.

Gay, Timothy. "George Huff." Society for American Baseball Research. Accessed August 16, 2023. https://sabr.org/bioproj/person/george-huff/.

Goldberger, Paul. *Ballpark: Baseball in the American City.* New York: Alfred A. Knopf, 2019.

Grennan, Rory. "The Life and Death of the Elephant: The Secret History of the First University Building." University of Illinois Archives, November 9, 2012. https://archives.library.illinois.edu/blog/life-and-death-of-the-elephant/.

Grigg, Laura, and Christopher J. Prom. "Finding Aid for Timothy J. Nugent Papers, 1939–2007." Division of Disability Resources and Educational Services (DRES), University of Illinois Archives. Accessed December 30, 2023. https://archon.library.illinois.edu/archives/index.php?p=collections/findingaid&id=5724&q=&rootcontentid=24861.

Hankey, John P. "Illinois Central Railroad." *Encyclopedia of Chicago.* Accessed December 24, 2023. http://www.encyclopedia.chicagohistory.org/pages/627.html.

Hansel, Ardith K., and W. Hilton Johnson. *Wedron and Mason Groups: Lithostratigraphic Reclassification of Deposits of the Wisconsin Episode, Lake Michigan Lobe Area.* Bulletin 104. Champaign: Illinois State Geological Survey, 1996.

Hill, E. Garry. "1927 NCAA Men." *Track and Field News.* Accessed August 26, 2023. https://trackandfieldnews.com/wp-content/uploads/2018/05/1927.pdf.

Hill, Jemele. "Personal Seat Licenses, Rising Ticket Prices Spell Doom." *ESPN Page 2,* August 4, 2008. https://www.espn.com/espn/page2/story?page=hill/080801&sportCat=nfl.

Horseshoe Crab. "Pleistocene." Accessed December 24, 2023. https://www.horseshoecrab.org/evo/ceno/pleisto.html.

Hunt, William C. "Population of Illinois by Counties and Minor Civil Divisions." *Census Bulletin* 21. December 15, 1900.

Illinois Public Media. "The History of WILL." Accessed October 7, 2023. https://will.illinois.edu/about/history.

Illinois State Museum. "Illinois Agriculture Begins." A History of Illinois Agriculture. Accessed December 24, 2023. http://www.museum.state.il.us/OHIA/htmls/people/native/peo_na.html.

Investopedia Team. "2008 Recession: What It Was and What Caused It." Investopedia, December 18, 2023. https://www.investopedia.com/terms/g/great-recession.asp#.

Iowa Pathways. "The Farm Crisis of the 1980s." Iowa PBS. Accessed January 3, 2024. https://www.iowapbs.org/iowapathways/mypath/2422/farm-crisis-1980s.

Jackson, C. O. "The School Circus." *Journal of Health and Physical Education* 5, no. 3 (1934): 12. https://doi.org/10.1080/23267240.1934.10620698.

Jenkins, Dan. "The Fighting Illini." *Sports Illustrated,* March 6, 1967.

Kennedy, David, and Lizabeth Cohen. *The American Pageant: A History of the American People.* 15th ed. Stamford, CT: Cengage Learning, 2013.

Kenny, Jenny. "Illinois Memorial Stadium: An Architectural Gem, American World War I Monument, and Home of Fighting Illini Football." Local Architecture Chicago, August 31, 2023. https://www.localarchitecturechicago.com/university-of-illinois-memorial-stadium-an-architectural-history/.

Klein, Christopher. "How Military Service Teams Dominated College Football during World War II." History.com, November 10, 2021. https://www.history.com/news/world-war-ii-college-football-military-teams.

Klinkenberg, Dean. "The 70 Million-Year-Old History of the Mississippi River." *Science,* September 2020. https://www.smithsonianmag.com/science-nature/geological-history-mississippi-river-180975509/#.

Kostora, Nick. "25 Craziest Football Terms and Where They Come From." *Bleacher Report,* May 16, 2012. https://bleacherreport.com/articles/1184750-25.

LeBar, John, and Allen Paul. *College Sports on the Brink of Disaster: The Rise of Pay-for-Play and the Fall of the Scholar Athlete.* New York: Sport Publishing, 2022.

Lewis, Jerry M., and Thomas R. Hensley, "The May 4 Shootings at Kent State University: The Search for Historical Accuracy." Kent State University. Accessed December 4, 2023. https://www.kent.edu/may-4-historical-accuracy.

Los Angeles Conservancy. "William Pereira." Accessed August 17, 2023. https://www.laconservancy.org/learn/architect-biographies/william-pereira/.

Lucky's Amazing Sports Lists. "Field Goals 60 Yards or More." November 5, 2023. http://www.luckyshow.org/football/field%20goals%20of%2060%20yards%20or%20more.htm.

Macrotrends. "Illinois Population, 1900–2022." Accessed September 20, 2023. https://www.macrotrends.net/states/illinois/population.

———. "U.S. Inflation Rate 1960–2023." Accessed November 15, 2023. https://www.macrotrends.net/countries/USA/united-states/inflation-rate-cpi.

Maisel, Ivan. "Living Memorials for Those Who Served." ESPN.com, November 11, 2009. https://www.espn.com/college-football/columns/story?columnist=maisel_ivan&id=4643874.

Maloney, Ray. "Renaldo Nehemiah Owned The Track & Field World." *College Sports Journal,* May 20, 2021. https://www.college-sports-journal.com/renaldo-nehemiah-owned-the-track-field-world/.

Marching Illini. "Tradition." Accessed December 24, 2023. https://www.marchingillini.com/history-tradition/timeline.

Mee, Christopher, and Antony Spawforth. *Greece: An Oxford Archaeological Guide.* New York: Oxford University Press, 2001.

Milesplit Illinois. "NCAA Division 1 Track and Field Championships 1977." Accessed December 16, 2023. https://il.milesplit.com/meets/189330-ncaa-division-1-track-and-field-championships-1977/results/342319/formatted.

Miller, Ross. "The Great Fire and the Myth of Chicago." *Chicago History* 19, no. 1 (1990): 4–31. https://www.proquest.com/magazines/great-fire-myth-chicago/docview/1416368046/se-2.

Museum Link of Illinois. "American Indian Tribes of Illinois." Last updated October 2, 2002. http://www.museum.state.il.us/muslink/nat_amer/post/.

National Archives. "Servicemen's Readjustment Act (1944)." May 3, 2022. https://www.archives.gov/milestone-documents/servicemens-readjustment-act.

National Center for Immunization and Respiratory Diseases. "History of 1918 Flu Pandemic." Centers for Disease Control and Prevention. Accessed December 24, 2023. https://www.cdc.gov/flu/pandemic-resources/1918-commemoration/1918-pandemic-history.htm.

National Football Foundation. "Bob Zuppke." Hall of Fame. Accessed September 12, 2023. https://footballfoundation.org/hof_search.aspx?hof=1412.

———. "NFF Salutes the Black History Trailblazers." February 1, 2016. https://footballfoundation.org/news/2016/2/1/_55549.aspx.

National WWI Museum and Memorial. "Coming Home." Accessed December 24, 2023. https://www.theworldwar.org/exhibitions/coming-home.

National Collegiate Athletic Association. "Attendance Records." Accessed September 22, 2023. http://fs.ncaa.org/Docs/stats/football_records/2017/attend.pdf.

———. "Championship History." Accessed September 5, 2023. https://www.ncaa.com/history/football/fbs.

———. "Football Award Winners." Accessed December 24, 2023. http://fs.ncaa.org/Docs/stats/football_records/2016/awards.pdf.

———. "Football Bowl Subdivision Records." Accessed December 24, 2023. http://fs.ncaa.org/Docs/stats/football_records/2020/FBS.pdf.

———. "2019 Football Attendance." Accessed December 24, 2023. http://fs.ncaa.org/Docs/stats/football_records/Attendance/2019.pdf.

Naylor, Brian. "Read Trump's Jan. 6 Speech, a Key Part of Impeachment Trial." NPR, February 10, 2021. https://www.npr.org/2021/02/10/966396848/read-trumps-jan-6-speech-a-key-part-of-impeachment-trial.

Nelson, Murry. "The Illinois Slush Fund Scandal of 1966–67." *Sport in American History,* October 20, 2014. https://ussporthistory.com/2014/10/20/the-illinois-slush-fund-scandal-of-1966-67/.

Northwestern University Special Olympics. "About Us." Accessed December 12, 2023. https://studentorgs.northwestern.edu/specialo/.

O'Neill, Aaron. "Annual Growth of Real GDP in the United States of America from 1930 to 2021." Statista, January 12, 2023. https://www.statista.com/statistics/996758/rea-gdp-growth-united-states-1930-2019/.

Old Radio. "October 28, 1922: The First National Radio Broadcast of College Football." October 8, 2012. https://www.oldradio.org/2012/10/october-28-1922-first-national-radio.html;

Oldrey, Kathleen. "Historical Census Data: Champaign County since 1900." Champaign County Regional Planning Commission, October 5, 2018. https://ccrpc.org/news/2018/historical-census-data-champaign-county-since-1900/.

Outdoor Media Buyers. "List: Arenas and Stadiums in the United States." Accessed November 30, 2023. https://outdoormediabuyers.com/list-of-stadiums-in-united-states/.

Oyez. "National Collegiate Athletic Association v. Board of Regents of the University of Oklahoma." Accessed November 29, 2023. https://www.oyez.org/cases/1983/83-271.

P., Ann. "Prairie State Games: A Display of Athletic Talent." Urbana Free Library, January 10, 2020. https://urbanafreelibrary.org/local-history/blog/prairie-state-games-display-athletic-talent#.

Pac-12 Conference. "Pac-12 Announces Resumption of Football, Basketball, and Winter Sports Seasons." September 24, 2020. https://pac-12.com/article/2020/09/24/pac-12-announcement.

Parks, James. "College Football National Champions by Year from 1869 to Today." College Football HQ. January 9, 2023. https://www.si.com/fannation/college/cfb-hq/ncaa-football-rankings/college-football-national-championship-teams-since-1869.

———. "NIL in College Football: Here's What You Need to Know, and What's Next." College Football HQ. January 17, 2024. https://www.si.com/fannation/college/cfb-hq/ncaa-football/college-football-nil-rule-changes-what-you-need-to-know.

Pearson, Mike. "'I Will Give, Sir': Capital Campaign of 1921 Still Inspires." Fighting Illini Football, University of Illinois Athletics, April 25, 2018.

https://fightingillini.com/news/2018/4/25/football-i-will-give-sir-fighting-illini-capital-campaign-of-1921-still-inspires-today.aspx.

———. "'People Got Crazy'—80's TailGREAT Created Epic Atmosphere." August 7, 2019. https://fightingillini.com/news/2019/8/7/football-people-got-crazy-80s-tailgreat-created-epic-atmosphere.aspx.

Pensabene, Vincent. "How Much Does Big Ten TV Deal Pay per School? Exploring Tony Petitti's Exclusive Agreements with CBS, NBC, and FOX." Sportskeeda, August 3, 2023. https://www.sportskeeda.com/college-football/how-much-big-ten-tv-deal-pay-per-school-exploring-tony-petitti-s-exclusive-agreements-cbs-nbc-fox.

Pester, Patrick, and Kim Ann Zimmermann. "Pleistocene Epoch: The Last Ice Age." *LiveScience,* February 28, 2022. https://www.livescience.com/40311-pleistocene-epoch.html.

Peterson, James A. "Total Conditioning: A Case Study." *Athletic Journal* 56 (September 1975): 40–55.

Peterson, Jason. "Indigenous Illinois: The History of American Indian Tribes in and around Champaign County." Champaign County History Museum. Accessed December 24, 2023. https://www.champaigncountyhistory.org/single-post/indigenous-illinois-the-history-of-american-indian-tribes-in-and-around-champaign-county.

Powell, Burt Eardley. *The Movement for Industrial Education and the Establishment of the University, 1840–1870.* Urbana: University of Illinois, 1918.

Pro Football Archives. "1975 Chicago Bears (NFL)." Accessed January 15, 2024. https://web.archive.org/web/20220810230724/https://www.profootballarchives.com/1975nflchib.html.

Pro Football Reference. "1940 NFL Attendance." Accessed September 24, 2023. https://www.pro-football-reference.com/years/1940/attendance.htm.

———. "1950 NFL Attendance." Accessed September 24, 2023. https://www.pro-football-reference.com/years/1950/attendance.htm.

———. "1955 NFL Attendance." Accessed September 24, 2023. https://www.pro-football-reference.com/years/1955/attendance.htm.

Prom, Christopher. "Fighting Illini Name." Illinois Library, October 10, 2012. https://archives.library.illinois.edu/2012/10/10/fighting-illini-name/.

Rose, Peter. "Spectators and Spectator Comfort in Roman Entertainment Buildings: A Study in Functional Design." *Papers of the British School at Rome* 73 (2005): 99–130. http://www.jstor.org/stable/40311093.

Rosebery, C. J. "University of Illinois Memorial Stadium." In *Directory of Illinois Men in Chicago and Vicinity,* edited by George E. Owen. Chicago: Illini Club of Chicago, 1926, 442 pgs.

Schumaker, Erin. "Timeline: How Coronavirus Got Started." ABC News, September 22, 2020. https://abcnews.go.com/Health/timeline-coronavirus-started/story?id=69435165.

Scott, Richard. *SEC Football: 75 Years of Pride and Passion.* Minneapolis: Voyageur Press, 2008.

Scott, Sam. "The Big Game Disaster of 1900." *Stanford Magazine,* November–December 2015. https://stanfordmag.org/contents/the-big-game-disaster-of-1900.

Smiley, Gene. "The U.S. Economy in the 1920s." *EH.net Encyclopedia,* June 9, 2004. https://eh.net/encyclopedia/the-u-s-economy-in-the-1920s/.

Smith, Ronald A. *Play-by-Play: Radio, Television, and Big-Time College Sport.* Baltimore, md: Johns Hopkins University Press, 2001.

SmithGroup JJR. "The Impact of Place: University of Illinois at Urbana-Champaign Campus Master Plan." November 2017. University Office of Capital Programs, Real Estate, and Utility Services, University of Illinois System. https://www.uocpres.uillinois.edu/UserFiles/Servers/Server_7758/file/UIUC/mastrpln/uiucmp-tech-rpt-201711.pdf.

Solberg, Winton U. "The Early Years of the Jewish Presence at the University of Illinois." *Religion and American Culture: A Journal of Interpretation* 2, no. 2 (1992): 215–45.

Special Olympics. "A Joyful New Movement Gains Momentum." Accessed December 12, 2023. https://www.specialolympics.org/about/history/a-joyful-new-movement-gains-momentum.

Spivey, Donald, and Thomas A. Jones. "Intercollegiate Athletic Servitude: A Case Study of the Black Illini Student-Athletes, 1931–1967." *Social Science Quarterly* 55, no. 4 (1975): 939–49. http://www.jstor.org/stable/42859422.

Stadiumguide.com. "Rose Bowl Stadium." May 2, 2020. https://www.stadiumguide.com/rose-bowl-stadium/.

Staples, Andy. "A History of Recruiting; How Coaches Have Stayed a Step Ahead." *Sports Illustrated,* June 23, 2008. https://www.si.com/more-sports/2008/06/23/recruiting-main.

Sterling, Christopher H., and John Michael Kittross. *Stay Tuned: A History of American Broadcasting.* 3rd ed. Mahwah, NJ: Lawrence Erlbaum Associates, 2002.

Stern, Marc. "The Fitness Movement and the Fitness Center Industry, 1960–2000." *Business and Economic History On-Line* 6 (2008):1–26. https://thebhc.org/sites/default/files/stern_0.pdf.

Stevens, Matthews. "Big Ten Conference Halts All Organized Team Activities until April 6." Illini Now, March 13, 2020. https://www.si.com/college/illinois/football/big-ten-conference-statement-halt-team-activities-march-13-2020.

Stewart, Alva W. *College Football Stadiums: An Illustrated Guide to NCAA Division I-A.* Jefferson, NC: McFarland, 2000.

The Story of the Stadium. Urbana: University of Illinois, 1921.

Sumner, Jim. "Sports in the 1920s: The Golden Ages of Sports." *NCPedia,* January 1, 2004. https://www.ncpedia.org/sports/golden-age-sports.

Surdam, David G. *Run to Glory and Profits: The Economic Rise of the NFL during the 1950s.* Lincoln: University of Nebraska Press, 2013. https://doi.org/10.2307/j.ctt1ddr7pc.16.

Swann, David H. "A Summary Geologic History of the Illinois Basin." *Geology and Petroleum Production of the Illinois Basin: A Symposium,* vol. 1, edited by Daniel N. Miller Jr., 3–21. Evansville, IN: Schultz, 1968.

Thornton, Mark. "Alcohol Prohibition Was a Failure." *Cato Institute Policy Analysis,* no. 157 (July 17, 1991): 12.

Tilton, Leon Deming, and Thomas Edward O'Donnell. *History of the Growth and Development of the Campus of the University of Illinois.* Urbana: University of Illinois Press, 1930.

Turner, J. B. *Industrial Universities for the People.* Jacksonville, IL: Morgan Journal Book and Job Office, 1853.

UIHistories. "Dedication of the Schulmerich Carillon Americana at the University of Illinois." Accessed October 10, 2023. https://uihistories.library.illinois.edu/REPOSITORYCACHE/22/dpVzXf708O3JGr6C0qx3D8ai873sq4snhI5t44VTU42aHg0B5hYRh36EstoSNe8F0l29I84U1c8rJji7vF64T4UP6u25V2DMISXPj7p80b5_29112.pdf.

———. "Memorial Stadium." Accessed January 29, 2024. https://uihistories.library.illinois.edu/cgi-bin/cview?SITEID=1&ID=169.

———. "Men's New Gymnasium/Huff Hall." Accessed August 22, 2023. https://uihistories.library.illinois.edu/cgi-bin/cview?SITEID=1&ID=127.

United States Courts. "The 14th Amendment and the Evolution of Title IX." Accessed November 21, 2023. https://www.uscourts.gov/educational-resources/educational-activities/14th-amendment-and-evolution-title-ix.

University Library Student Life and Culture Archives. "Student Life at Illinois: 1960–1969." Archives Research Center, Horticulture Field Laboratory, University of Illinois Urbana-Champaign. Accessed October 4, 2023. https://www.library.illinois.edu/slc/research-education/timeline/1960-1969/.

———. "Student Life at Illinois: 1990–1999." Archives Research Center, Horticulture Field Laboratory, University of Illinois Urbana-Champaign. Accessed January 10, 2024. https://archives.library.illinois.edu/slc/research-education/timeline/1990-1999/.

———. "Student Life at Illinois: 2000–2009." Archives Research Center, Horticulture Field Laboratory, University of Illinois Urbana-Champaign. Accessed January 12, 2024. https://archives.library.illinois.edu/slc/research-education/timeline/2000-2009/.

University of Illinois. University Enrollment File. University of Illinois Archives Digital Collections. https://digital.library.illinois.edu/collections/26217450-a185-0131-4a3f-0050569601ca-c.

University of Illinois Alumni Association. "Lauren Corning Shull." Accessed December 24, 2023. https://uiaa.org/veterans/laurens-corning-shull/.

University of Illinois Annual Register, 1943–44. Urbana: University of Illinois, 1944.

University of Illinois Archives. "Fighting Illini FAQ." Accessed December 24, 2023. https://archives.library.illinois.edu/features/illini.php#3.

University of Illinois Division of Intercollegiate Athletics. "Historical Note." Accessed December 24, 2023. https://archon.library.illinois.edu/archives/index.php?p=creators/creator&id=29.

University of Illinois Library. "The GI Bill and the U of I." *The University of Illinois in the Cold War Era, 1945–1975.* LibGuide, March 17, 2022. https://guides.library.illinois.edu/c.php?g=348250&p=2350884.

University of Illinois Office of the Chancellor. "Illinois in Focus." *University of Illinois, On Our Watch.* Accessed October 6, 2023. http://oc.illinois.edu/OnOurWatch/infocus/102007.html.

University of Michigan Facilities. "Michigan Stadium." Accessed February 12, 2023. https://mgoblue.com/sports/2017/6/16/facilities-michigan-stadium-html.aspx.

USA Track and Field. "Harry Gill." Accessed August 10, 2023. https://www.usatf.org/athlete-bios/harry-gill.

US Census Bureau. *1870 Census: Volume 1: The Statistics of the Population of the United States.* Washington, DC: Government Printing Office, 1872. https://www2.census.gov/library/publications/decennial/1870/population/1870a-04.pdf.

———. *Twelfth Census of the United States.* Census Bulletin 21. Washington, DC: US Census Bureau, 1900.

US Climate Data. "Climate Champaign – Illinois." Accessed December 24, 2023. https://www.usclimatedata.com/climate/champaign/illinois/united-states/usil2051.

US Department of Labor. Bureau of Labor Statistics. *Wholesale Prices 1890 to 1926.* Bulletin 440. Washington, DC: Government Printing Office, 1927.

US Department of State. Office of the Historian. "Oil Embargo, 1973–1974." Accessed November 15, 2023. https://history.state.gov/milestones/1969-1976/oil-embargo.

US Energy Information Administration. "Coal Explained." Last updated October 19, 2021. https://www.eia.gov/energyexplained/coal/.

US Equal Employment Opportunity Commission. "Rehabilitation Act of 1973 (Original Text)." Accessed December 30, 2023. https://www.eeoc.gov/rehabilitation-act-1973-original-text.

US House of Representatives. "Representatives Apportioned to Each State (1st to 23rd . . .)." Accessed December 24, 2023. https://www.house.gov/the-house-explained.

Vaiden, Robert C. "Build Illinois: The Last 500 Million Years." *GeoNote* 4. Champaign: Illinois State Geological Survey. https://www.ideals.illinois.edu/items/110677.

VandeCreek, Drew E. "Economic Development and Labor in Civil War Illinois." *Illinois during the Civil War.* https://digital.lib.niu.edu/illinois/civilwar/economic.

Walker, Francis A. "Report of the Superintendent of the Ninth Census." *1870 Census: Volume 1: The Statistics of the Population of the United States.* Washington, DC: Government Printing Office, 1872.

Watterson, John Sayle. *College Football: History, Spectacle, Controversy.* Baltimore, MD: Johns Hopkins University Press, 2000.

———. "Political Football: Theodore Roosevelt, Woodrow Wilson, and the Gridiron Reform Movement." *Presidential Studies Quarterly* 25, no. 3 (1995): 555–64. http://www.jstor.org/stable/27551467.

Welin, Dan. "Texas Bowl 2010: Illinois vs. Baylor: A Complete Viewer's Guide." BleacherReport, December 21, 2010. https://bleacherreport.com/articles/548991-illinois-vs-baylor-in-texas-bowl-a-complete-viewers-guide.

Werner, Jeremy. "Breaking: Whitman Dismisses Cubit." 247Sports, March 5, 2016. https://247sports.com/college/illinois/Article/BREAKING-Whitman-dismisses-Cubit-75005541/.

West Virginia Public Broadcasting. "October 8, 1921: WVU vs. Pitt Marks First Live Football Radio Broadcast." October 8, 2019. https://wvpublic.org/october-8-1921-wvu-vs-pitt-marks-first-live-football-radio-broadcast/#stream/0.

Wickham, Jerry T. *Glacial Geology of North-Central and Western Champaign County, Illinois.* Circular 506. Urbana: Illinois State Geological Survey, 1979. https://www.ideals.illinois.edu/items/43048.

Williams, Carter. "How the Rose Bowl Became 'the Granddaddy of Them All.'" KSL.com, December 31, 2021. https://www.ksl.com/article/50320215/how-the-rose-bowl-became-the-granddaddy-of-them-all.

World Bank. "GDP Growth (Annual %)—United States." Accessed January 16, 2024. https://data.worldbank.org/indicator/NY.GDP.MKTP.KD.ZG?locations=US.

Zielinski, Michael. "The Illinois Marathon." Illinois Marathon, February 5, 2009. https://web.archive.org/web/20090419053758/http://www.illinoismarathon.com/Illinois%20Marathon%20course%20description.pdf.

Index

Note: **Bold** page numbers refer to tables and *italic* page numbers refer to figures.

Abbott, William L. 6, 40, 53, 77
Abramovitz, Max 3, 166, 190, 200
activism 178, 213–214
Adams, Alvin J. 120
African Americans 23, 164–165, 178, 246, 247
Age of the Spectator 139, 147–148
A. H. Barth Electric Co. 82, 100
Air Force Academy 223
alcohol 263; consumption 151; problem on campus 151; prohibition 151
Algonquian-speaking tribes 10
All-American Bowl appearance (1988) 247
all-star football game 230
American Broadcasting Company 181
Americans with Disabilities Act (ADA) 234
Anders, Alphonse 165
Anderson, Charles P. *121*
Aquilar, J. C. 32
Archaic period 10
Army game 147
artificial turf 212, 220, 222, 226; fire damage *241;* installation *221,* 222, 229; Zuppke Field 226
assemblage of orders 47
Assembly Hall 3, 193, 206, 234; inauguration 198; interior *189;* west entrance *189*
Association for Intercollegiate Athletics for Women 203
Astro-Turf 'E' system 254
Athens Olympic Games 246

Athletic Association (AA) 6, 24, 28, 31, 220, 293; autonomy questioned 37–38; financial assistance 221; financial health 198; football ticket receipts 43; funding 25; land acquisitions 32; land purchase from 77; leadership 172; revenue 32, 75; temporary grandstands 139; transformation of 247
Athletic Board of Control (ABC) 32, 35
Atlanta Constitution 101
Atticus, Herodes 45
Auburn University 2

Babcock, Kendric C. 152
Bagnato, Andrew 251
Baietto, Mike 227
Ballpark 48
band halftime *272*
Barrett, Edward E. 75
bas-relief sculptures *71, 72*
Battle of Château-Thierry, France 64
Baudrillard, Jean 199
Bazzanni, Craig 247
Beaver, Dan 230
Beaver Wars 11
Beckman, Timothy 271
Bedford limestone colonnades 68
Beer and Whiskey League 151
Bell, Jack 64
Bell, Taylor 196
Bergen, G. I. 17
Berns, Tom 263
Biden, Joseph R. 247

Bielema, Bret 275
Bielfeldt Athletics Administration Building 254
Big Nine conference team 179
Big Ten 26, 28, 43; all-time sack leader 248; athletic directors 197; champion men's track and field team *228;* championship 29; ESPN 258; governing body and processes 205; horseshoe stadiums 48; indoor championships 227; indoor sprint champion 183; night football game 221; outdoor championships 203; radio broadcast rights 148; recruitment practices 197; 1961 rule change 197; sanctions 231; stadium typologies **50**; television revenues 224
Big Ten Conference 26, 49, 104, 159, 163, 171, 246
Bing, Benjamin 165
Black Africans 12
Blackall, C. H. 31, *31*
Black Lives Matter movement 246, 247
Blackman, Bob 229, 238, 257
Blackman, Robert 205, 212, 223
Black students 164–165
Blake, Margaret Day 6, 77
Block I cheering club 179
Board of Trustees (BOT) 5, 6, 19, 25, 29, 35, 59, 72, 75; approval 25, 43; Auxiliary Facilities System 251; Campus Plan Commission 6; Chief Illiniwek 260; construction budgets 221; contractors 221; Ellis property

149; funding approval 224; funding proposal 173; indoor practice space, men's football team 254; master plans 31, 32; Mount Hope Cemetery 38; project management team 221; remodeling projects 221; selection official 53; Shapland Construction Company 200; stadium's siting and design 31

Boerio, Charles M. 180

Bogue, Margaret Beattie 9

Boneyard Creek 9, 89

BOT see Board of Trustees (BOT)

Bowl Championship Series (BCS) 250

Boy Scouts 152

Bradford, J. A. 39

Bradley Polytechnic Institute 159

Braun, Howard 204

Breeze, Sydney 12

Brewer, Mel 204

British Geological Survey time chart 7, 7

Bross, Benjamin A. 2

Brown, Bill 202

Brown, Ken 203

Brown, Kent 271

Brown, Maudelle 165

Brown, Michael 246

Brundage, Avery 52, 53, 162

Bubble 250; exterior 239; interior 240; winter and spring varsity teams 251

Buffalos of the University of Colorado 241

Building Program Committee 174

Buildings and Grounds Committee 25

Bureau County Tribune 150

Burrell, William 202

Busey, Mary Elizabeth Bowen 6, 38, 77

Bush, George H. W. 245, 246

Butkus, Dick 2, 196, 198, 200, 226, 256

Cahokia 11

California Golden Bears 183, 198, 231, 273

Calomiris, Charles W. 236

campus land acquisitions: 1867–1925 36, 36–37; 1900–1919 37; 1920–1925 37–40

Campus Plan Commission 6

Canina, Luigi 69

Cantor, Nancy 260

Carby, Eliza 19

Carby, Merrit 19

Carillon Americana model 206

carillon tower 52, 205–206

Carlson, Kurt A. 14

Carlson, Reuben C. 78, 253

Carnegie Report (1929) 153

Carr, Robert F. 5, 6, 35, 52, 53, 75

Carter, James E. 219

carved medallions, ramp towers 72

Cavelier, R.-R. 11

Cenozoic era 7

Champaign 155, 264

Champaign Chamber of Commerce 38

Champaign City Council 211

Champaign County 7, 9, 9–10, 17–19, 38, 75, 263, 293; assessment 19; proposal 19; temperature 10

Champaign Development Corporation (CDC) 211

Champaign Legion 30

Champaign Moraine 9, 9

Champaign-Urbana 1; see also Urbana-Champaign

Chicago Bears 30, 150, 182, 205, 212, 226, 240, 250, 263

Chicago Fire (1871) 23

Chicago's Soldier Field 248

Chicago Sun-Times 222

Chicago Tribune 104, 124, 156, 251

Chief Illiniwek 10, 152, 152, 245, 259–260

Chipman, Shelby 269

Christie Clinic 260, 261

circulation diagram 66

Circus Maximus 45, 45, 48

City Beautiful movement 57

City of Champaign 158

Civil War, Afghanistan 219

Clarke, Thomas Arkle 165

Clark, George Rogers 11

Clemson Tigers in the Hall of Fame Bowl 248

Cleveland Browns 194

Clinton, William J. 245

coal mines, Illinois 12, 13, 12–14

Cobain, Kurt 245

Co, Fabry 54

Cold War 245

Coleman, Cecil 212, 222, 225, 231

College Football: History, Spectacle, Controversy 28

College Football Stadiums 50

College of Physical Education 197, 222

College Place 77–78

Colonnade Club 268, 297; under construction 269; west stands with 273, 289

Colosseum 45, 46; bay elevation of 47; cross-section and elevation drawings 69; Flavian Amphitheater 46; Roman 48

Columbia Broadcasting System 183

Combes, Harry 201, 204

community anchor 296–298, 297

competition drawing 53

Complete That Stadium For Fighting Illini 35

Congress, Land-Grant College Act (1862) 16

Congress for Racial Equality (CORE) 178

Congressional Act (1818) 14

Coolley, Anna 78

Co-Rec Wiffle Ball Tournament 251

Corrugated Bar Company 82

cost-benefit analysis 224

County Freedom Celebration 196

COVID-19 pandemic 232, 246, 260, 274–276, 275

Coxworth, Jim 227

Crackle, Ben 160

Cramer, Kevin 231

Cribbet, John 235

Cubit, William J. 272

Cullen, Joseph 229

Cummins, Barton 223

Cusick, Robert 253

Daily Illini 29, 34, 39, 40, 150, 151, 163, 222

Dale, Henry 257

Daniels, Arthur Hill 172

Danville 26, 102, 122, 153, 221

Decatur Staleys 30

dedication ceremony 124–125, *125, 126*

DeKalb Daily Chronicle 150

Delphi 44, 45

Dennis, Maurice 223

Denver, John 219

Department of Intercollegiate Athletics (DIA) 28, 247, 253, 259, 296

Department of Physical Education 38

Department of Physical Training 26

DePauw University 149

design/construction, Memorial Stadium 43–73; commission 50–54, *51–56;* composition and function 66–71, *66–71;* conceived 43; considerations 59–64; contemporary typologies 48–50, *49,* **50**; early depiction of *60;* early drawing of *60;* ready to begin construction 72–73; site selection 54–57, *57–58;* Stadium as a memorial 64–66; Stadium ramp tower, interior *63;* three-tiered *61;* track facilities 72; typologies 44–47, *44–47*

Dickson, Kerry 229

digital media 259

Dillenback, Lemuel C. 50

Ditka, Mike 205, 240

diversity: Black students 164–165; Jewish students 165–166

Division I-A college football programs 50

Dixon, Alan 259

Dixon, Matthew 258

Dodona 44

Donor Committee (DC) 52

Doric colonnades 56

Dorsey Jr., Arvell *49*

double-decked football stadiums 49

Douglas, Stephen A. 12

Dragicevic, Jessica 229

Draper, Andrew Sloan 25

Dubuque, Julien 11

Ducey, Susan 231

Duke University 183

Duke, Wayne 224

Dunlap, Mathias L. 10

Durkin, Michael 227

Durm, Josef *47*

Dvorak, Bands Ray 152

Dyche Stadium 50

Dylan, Bob 236

Eason, Tony 2, 231

east balcony steel erection *90*

East Carolina Pirates 248, 249

east stands *87, 89, 92, 93, 95, 97, 109, 110, 112–119*

Ebbets Field, New York 49

Ebert, Roger 193, 197–199

Eckersall, Walter 104

economy 139; ascendancy 23; coal *12, 12–14;* COVID-19 pandemic 246

Ehizuelen, Charlton 227, 228

Eliot, Charles 28, 29

Eliot, Ray 171, 176, *176,* 178, 179, 183, 194, 195

Elite Eight 246

Elliott, Pete 194–198, *195,* 201, 204, 238, 250, 257

Ellis, David Maldwyn 12

Elmer Ekblaw, W. 27, 34, 75

Embarras River 9

Emperor Domitian 46

Emperor Titus 46

Emperor Vespasian 46

English Brothers 75, 82, 83, 149

English, Edward H. 82

engraved column inscription *121*

Enoch, A. I. 19

enthusiasm 2, 29, 159, 193

entry level plan *281*

Epidaurus 44

ESPN 258

Europeans 10–11

Evans, H. E. 153

Evans, Laura B. 75–77

Evashevski, Forest 180

facade diagram *71*

fall football training 104

Family Farmer Bankruptcy Act (1986) 236

Farber, James 178

Farm Aid (1985) 236–237, *237,* 297

Farrell, Henry L. 106

Federal Reserve System 236

Fenway Park, Boston 2, 49

Ferroni, Stephen: circulation diagram *66;* colonnade level *131;* east Stadium section *285;* elevation detail *136;* entry level plan *130;* entry level plan with horseshoe *132;* facade diagram *71;* land acquisition records, 1867–1925 *36;* longitudinal plan *134;* longitudinal section *286;* Memorial Stadium *58;* press box *210;* ramp tower elevation *135;* Soldier Field *58;* Stadium longitudinal section *68;* Stadium progression, 1924–2014 *290;* Stadium section diagram *67;* stair tower ramps *67;* west Stadium section *284*

field level plan *280*

Fighting Illini 1, 2, 6, 125, 139–147, *141, 144, 145,* 198, 219, 226, 235, 294; battle progression, Telegraph instruments *146;* Big Ten outdoor championships 201; crowds, approaching game *142;* crowds came early to Homecoming *140;* decorated, for occasion *143;* four-win season 186; vs. Iowa Hawkeyes 248; milestone 179; *vs.* Ohio State 240; overall record 240; succeed 149; *vs.* University of Southern California 240; *vs.* University of Virginia Cavaliers in the Florida Citrus Bowl 247; *vs.* University of Washington Huskies *199, 200;* winning record 177

Fighting Irish 176

Finance Committee 35

financial uncertainty 219

fire damage, artificial turf *241*

First Nations peoples 10–12

Flack, Roberta 219

Flagg Hall 175

Flavian Amphitheater (Colosseum) 46, *46*

Fleischman, G. 165

Florida Agriculture and Mining University (FAMU) 269, *270*

Floyd, George 247

Foellinger Auditorium 31, 32

Football Bowl Subdivision 271
Football Writers Association of
    America 206
Ford, Gerald 219
Fort Crèvecoeur 11
Fort Pitt Bridge Co. 82
"the Four Horsemen" 147
Fox Drive 9
Frankel, Rabbi Benjamin M. 165
Franklin Field in Philadelphia 148
French Wars 11
funding 6, 14, 25; challenge 33, 78–81,
    79, 80; renovations 220–224, *221*
Furey, Ralph 181

Galloping Ghost 2, 147, 159, 294
Gaza 247
Geldof, Bob 236
geographic context *7, 7–9, 8*
Georges, Arthur 229, 296
GI Bill 171, 295
Gibson City in Ford County 9
Gill, Harry 152, 153
Gilpatrick, Gladys 64
Girl Scouts 175
Glacial Drift Zone 11
Gleason, Bill 222
Glenn Hubbard, R. 236
Goldberger, Paul 48
Golden Age of Sport 147–148, 171;
    Age of the Spectator 147–148; era's
    zeitgeist 147
Golden Anniversary Fund Committee
    212
Grabowski, Don 251
Grabowski, James 198, *200*
grandstand 48
Grange Grove 261, *262, 263*, 297
Grange, Harold E. *see* "Red" Grange,
    Harold E.
Grant Park Stadium: competition
    drawing *53;* section of *62*
Granville's plan 16
Great Depression 139, 148, 182, 246
Great Hall 63, 68; completion of 107;
    early steel work *85;* formworks for
    84; ramps under construction *96;*
    steel columns erected *86*

Great Lakes 5, 11, 12, 219
Great Lakes Navy Bluejackets 176
Great War (1914–1918) 5, 27–29, 293
Great West Hall 139, 171–174; housing
    proposal *172;* interior image of *156;*
    looking north *96;* northern half 173;
    southern half 173
Greek theater *52*
Greek U-shaped stadiums 46
Green, Dwight H. 175
Gregory, John Milton 23
Grice, Kevin 223
Griffin, Archie 230
Griffith, Howard 247, *248*
Griffiths, John 163
Griggs, Clark Robinson 18, 19
Griggs, Silvonia 19
Grochowski, John 225
Grossfeld, Abie 202
groundbreaking 75, *76, 81*
Guenther, Ron 248, 271
gym *34*
Gymnasium Annex 172

Hagar, Sammy 236
Halas, George 30, 182
Hall, Arthur Raymond 26
Hamas terrorists 247
Hansel, Ardith K. *8*
Happy Valley Racecourse 63
Hardy, Kevin 250
Harvard: circus-style stadium 48;
    football stadium 48, *70*
Harvard Stadium *70*
Harvard's U-shaped stadium 48
Health and Physical Education
    Building: basement *187;* rendering
    for *188;* site plan *186*
Heath, W. A. 35
Henneman, Ralph J. 221
Henry, David 197, 204
Henson, Lou 230, 233
Highway 25 122
Hinders, Kevin J. 2, *121;* Assembly
    Hall interior *189;* Assembly Hall
    west entrance *189;* bas-relief
    sculptures *71, 72;* Campus Moraine
    9; carved medallions *72;* circulation

diagram *66;* east Stadium section
    285; entry level plan *281;* facade
    diagram *71;* field level plan *280;*
    Huff and Zuppke grave sites *164;*
    land acquisition records, 1867–1925
    36; north elevation *288;* north
    endzone section *287;* post-war
    housing diagram *175;* press box
    206, *207;* ramp tower elevation
    135; south elevation *288;* Stadium
    longitudinal section *68;* Stadium
    section diagram *67;* stair tower
    ramps *67;* three Memorial Stadium
    site proposals *40;* upper level plans
    282–283; west Stadium section *284*
Hinders, Kevin Michael 2
Hindsley, Mark H. 196
HNTB *265*
Holabird and Roche (H&R) 2, 6, 52,
    53, 59, 72, 73, 234, 294; competition
    drawing *53;* Donor Committee 52;
    early drawing of Memorial Stadium
    60; master plan, 1920 *33;* pragmatic
    approach 66; three-tiered stadium *61*
Holabird and Root 160, *162*
Holabird, William 51
Holcombe, Robert 250
Holocene 9, 10
Homecoming Committee 166
homecoming game 1; crowd photo *98;*
    Illini Field, 1910 *27;* panorama *105*
Homecoming Planning Committee 260
Homeier, John 231
Honig, Robert 259
honor court: carillon *52;* faculty
    rendering *52*
Hopkins, M. E. *13*
Horse Railroad 36
House legislature 17
House of Representatives 23
Hubbard, Ralph 152
Huff, George A. 2, 6, *25, 26,* 28, 29,
    31, 32, 35, 37, 38–40, 75, 81, 84, 89,
    99, 104, 107, 125, 149, 150, 151,
    152, 160, 203–205, 237, 293–295;
    basic needs now *vs.* future demands
    and continued 156; bookkeeping
    37; budgeting 37; death 163–164,
    164; donations 32; groundbreaking

76; hodgepodge approach 37;
leadership 26; legacy 163;
physical fitness 52–53; Prohibition
enforcement efforts 154; University
politics 43
Huff Gym 183, *184*
100 Years of Football Centennial
Celebration 247
Hunt, Myron 48
Hyde Amendment 205
Hyde, Henry 205

Ice Age 7, 9, 10
Ikenberry Commons Residence (ICR)
25
Ikenberry, Stanley O. 224
Illini basketball 183–186, *184–186*
Illini Football 229–241; euphoria
of winning seasons 235; Farm
Aid (1985) 236–237; forefront of
accessibility 234–235; new practice
facilities 237–241, *238–241;*
Stadium's structure 232–234;
struggling team 229–231; White,
Mike 231–232
Illini Pow-Wow 152
Illini Student Union 104, 106
Illini Union Ballroom 172
Illini Village 174
Illiniwek 10, 11, 152, 195
Illinois 5, 7, 124; agricultural fields 9;
coal mines 12, *13;* population of 12,
12, 23; railroad map *15*
Illinois Alumni News 171
Illinois Basin 7, 11
Illinois Central Railroad (ICR) 9, 14,
16, 54
Illinois College 16
Illinois Country 11, 12
Illinois Fields 27, 106, 149;
demolishing 29; Homecoming
game, 1910 *27*
Illinois General Assembly's Legislative
Audit Commission 247
Illinois High School Coaches
Association (IHSCA) 205
Illinois House of Representatives 18,
264

Illinois Industrial University 18; early
map of *20;* establishment 23
Illinois Marching Band Championships
153
Illinois School of Architecture (ISoA)
1–3, 50
Illinois Spring Football Clinic 195
Illinois State Lottery 224
Illinois Weekly Journal 16
inauguration 139–147, 198
Indiana Hoosiers 178, 250
Indiana Territory 12
Indian War 11
Industrial Revolution 5, 12
institutional football team 24, *24*
Intercollegiate Conference of Faculty
Representatives 26
International Jewish Sports Hall of
Fame 202
International Olympic Committee
(1940–1962) 53
Interscholastic Circus (IC) 154, *154*
Intramural Physical Education Building
254
Iowa Hawkeyes 149, 205, 230, 248,
260, 273
Iowa's Kinnick Stadium 48
Iowa State Cyclones 159
Iroquois Confederation 11
Iroquois Wars 11
Irwin Family Foundation 255
Irwin Indoor Practice Facility *255*
Irwin Interior Practice Facility *256*

Jackson, C. O. 154
Jackson, Nell 203, *204,* 227
Jackson, Trenton 203
Jacobson, David 225
James, Edmund J. 6, 28, 31
Jameson, Earl A. 165
Jewish students 165–166
Joel, Billy 236
John Hancock Bowl 248
Johnson, Leo T. 201, *202*
Johnson, Lewis Jerome 48
Johnson, W. Hilton *8*
Jolliet, Louis 11
Jones, Arthur 226

Kallimarmaro Stadium, Athens,
Greece *44,* 45
Kansas State University 179
Kaskaskia River 9
Kaufman, Chuck 166
KDKA (Pittsburg) 148
Keene, James F. 269
Kennedy, A. C. *20*
Kennedy, John F. 193, 206
Kenney Gymnasium Annex 25
Kennicott, Jonathan 17
Kerner, Otto 197
Kerr, George 202, *203*
Kerst, Donald 185
Khomeini, Ayatollah 219
King, B. B. 236
King, Carole 236
Kinley, David 5, 6, 28, 29, 34, 38, 40,
50, 75, 81, 101, *125,* 152, 160
Kiram, Tirhata 32
Klamm, Ken 225
Knox County 17
Korean War 179
Koronaio, George E. *44*
Krannert Art Museum 194
Krannert Center for Performing Arts
190
Kreitling, Rich 194

Labedz, Gary 222
Laika 187
Lake Michigan 5, 56, 151
Lake Zuppke 100
Land Grant Act (1850) 12, 14
Land-Grant College Act (1862) 16
La Salle, Sieur de 11
Lauterbur, Paul C. 246
Laz, Doug 228, *229*
Leaders Division 271
Legends Division 271
Leggett, Anthony J. 246
legislation 17, 28, 197, 224, 234; bond
finance measures 188; fund public
education 16; Nixon, Richard M.
214; Students' Army Training Corps
program 28; Yates, Richard 16
Leutwiler, Lester 152
Levenick, Stuart L. 230

Levy, Marv 198
"life ticket" granting 75
lightning protection system 195
Lincoln, Abraham 15, 16, 293
Lincoln Avenue 52, 158
Lindgren, Justa 26
Liquor Advisory Commission 264
Liscom, William M. 147
Litkenhous Ratings 177
Little, George 147
Little Wabash 9
Livingston, Park 190
Los Angeles Memorial Coliseum 48
Lowenthal, Fred 26
lucrative television contracts 194
Ludi Romani (Roman Games) 45
Lumberyard 27, 29

MacIntire, H. J. 156
Mackovic, John 220, 241, 247
Major League Baseball 151
Mansfield, Peter 246
Manspeaker, Emma 75
Marching Illini 1, 205, 260, 268
Margolis, Ralph 165, 166
Marquette, Jacques 11
Martin, Trayvon 246
Mason, A. C. 17
mass media impact of 180–183, 181
Mathawilasis 223
Matthews, Clyde 26
McCarren, Larry 231
McConn, C. M. 64
McCourt, James 2
McDade, Dick 194
McKeown, Bill 202
McKinley Field 30
McKinley Hospital 25
McLean County 18, 19
McLuhan, Marshall 199
McMillen, J. W. 104
The Medium Is the Message 199
Mellencamp, John 236
Memorial Stadium, 1924–1941
139–166; continues to evolve
154–164; diversity, impact on
164–166; Golden Age of Sport
147–148; inauguration 139–147;

from 1924 to Pearl Harbor 149–151;
new projects 154–158, 155, 156;
peak of the era 160, 161, 162;
Stadium improvements 158–160; as
venue 152–154
Memorial Stadium, 1990s 247–261;
Athletic Association, transformation
of 247; Chief Illiniwek 259–260;
east balcony renovation 252;
football and Stadium highs and
lows 247–250, 248, 249; restoration
and practice facilities 250–256,
252, 254–257; sources of revenue
256–259; Stadium and campus life
260–261
Memorial Stadium, building of
75–137; aerial photograph
of Stadium construction 93;
Athletic Association 77; College
Place 77–78; colonnade level
131; construction begins 83–89;
dedication ceremony 124–125,
125, 126, 133; derricks erecting,
steel frame 88; early grading and
foundation digging 83; early steel
work, Great Hall 85; east balcony
steel erection 90; east stands 87, 89,
92, 93, 95, 97; elevation detail 136;
entry level plan 130; entry level
plan with horseshoe, 1929 132; fast
track design and construction 75–78;
field and east stands 91; foundation
work completion 85; fulfilling
pledges 99–104, 100; funding
challenge 78–81, 79, 80; Great Hall
and ramp towers, formworks 84;
Great Hall steel columns erected 86;
homecoming action photograph 99;
homecoming game crowd photo 98;
longitudinal plan 134; October 17,
1924 124–125, 125, 126; purchasing
construction services and materials
81–83, 82; ramp tower elevation
135; soft opening 104–124;
stadium seating plan 103; Stoolman
property 76–77; structural steel
shop drawings 82; team photograph
(1924) 137; west stands 88, 91, 92,
94, 95, 97, 98

Memorial Stadium News 43
Memorial Stadium Notes (MSN) 64, 78,
80, 81, 86
Menorah Society 165
men's track and field 201–203, 202, 203
Meso-America 44
Metcalfe, Jeff 222
Meyers, Mel 273
Miami Dolphins 226
Michigan Canals 12
Michigan State kicker, longest field
goal 233
Michigan State Spartans 233, 235
Michigan Wolverines 6, 49, 120,
139–147, 149, 160, 179, 230, 248,
269, 294
Miletus 44
Mills, Douglas R. 176, 178, 183, 197,
203, 204
Milne, Brian 250
Mississippian period 10
Mississippi River 5, 7, 9, 11, 12
Mississippi State Bulldogs 106
Mittelman, B. 165
Moctezuma, Carlos 23
Moeller, Gary 231–233
Mojsiejenko, Ralf 233
Monument to Victor Emmanuelle II
56, 57
Morgan County 18
Morrill Act (1862) 14–16, 197, 293
Morrill, Justin 16
Mount Hope Cemetery 33, 54, 158, 163
Mount Zion in Macon County 9
The Movement for Industrial Education
and the Establishment of the
University, 1840–1870 16
Moynihan, C. J. 105
Mulberry, Dorothy 152
Municipal Grant Park Stadium 53

name, image, and likeness (NIL) 259
National Broadcasting Company 181
national championship season (1923)
106–107
National Collegiate Athletics
Association (NCAA) 26, 29, 162,
164, 181, 197, 203, 220, 259;

broadcasting rights 182; Elite Eight 201; Football Bowl Subdivision 271; incentives 176; media rights and contract negotiations 182; men's outdoor championships 228; new recruiting violations 241; regulations 181; sanctions 235; sponsors, rights and responsibilities 181; Track and Field Championships 226, *229*
National Football League (NFL) 182, 183, 213, 222, 226, 250, 263, 264, 295
National Organization for Women (NOW) 214
National Wheelchair Basketball Association 234
Nautilus Fitness system 295
Naval Diesel School (NDS) program *173*
Naval Reserve Officers Training Corps 173
NCAA *see* National Collegiate Athletics Association (NCAA)
NCAA National Championship 246
Neal, Earl L. 224
Nebraska 124, 150, 152, 240, *297*
Nebraska Cornhuskers 250, 271
Nehemia, Ronaldo 228
Neil-Duncan US Route 45 corridor 9
Neil Street and Stadium Drive *124*
Nelson, Murray 204
Nelson, Willie 236
new scoreboard, Ohio State game *211*
new stadium era 219–241; evolution, 1974–1989 220–226; funding renovations 220–224, *221;* Illini Football, 1975–1990 229–241; sanctions 224; track and field 226–229; turf, illumination, and branching out 225–226
New Year's Day postseason games 48
Nitshcke, Raymond 183
Nittany Lions 250
Nixon, Richard M. 193, 214, 219
Noble 77, *144*
non-Southeastern Conference (SEC) program 259
Norman, Bob 196
North American Free Trade Agreement 245

north endzone section *287*
Northwestern University 26
Northwestern Wildcats 180, 231, 235
North West Ordinance (1787) 14
Notre Dame 147, 150, 153, *153,* 177, 179
Nugent, Timothy J. 234

Obama, Barack 246, 247
O'Brien, John A. 78
O'Donnell Bennet, James 156
O'Donnell, Thomas Edward 29, *30*
Ohio National Guard 214
Ohio River Valley 11
Ohio State Buckeyes 163, 196, 230, 241
Ohio State in Columbus 248
Ohio State University 29
oil crisis (1973) 219
Old Annex Gym 32
Old Gym 149, 154, 172
Ole Miss campus 261
Olmec civilization 44
Olson, Gail 228
Olson, Ollie 163
Olympia 44, 45
Olympic Games 44, 162; Amsterdam 203; Athens 246; Melbourne 203; Japan 247
Olympic Summer Games 219
One Hundred Years of Illinois Football coaches *291*
Operation Desert Storm 245
optimism 89, 100, 103, 193, 220, 237
Orange Bowl 250
Orbison, Roy 236
Organization of Petroleum Exporting Countries (OPEC) 219
origins, of Memorial Stadium 23–41; dawn of organized intercollegiate sports 25–27, *25–27;* expanding boundaries 23–25; Great War (1914–1918) 27–29; impetus for 27–36; land acquisitions 36–40; land assembling 35–36; map of campus *41;* planning for 29–35, *30, 31, 33, 34*
Ottoman Empire 75

Owens, Hudson 165
Owens, Isaiah 179

Pac-8 Conference crown 231
Pac-10 235, 248, 250
Pac-12 274, 296; intraconference games 275; television market 275
Pagani, Tom 227
Pahlavi, Mohammad Reza 219
Paleo-Indian groups 10
Paleozoic era 7
Pan-Hellenic Council 158
Parade Ground Units 76, 174–175, *175,* 194
Park, James 259
Peabody Drive 234
Pearl Harbor 149–151, 172, 246
Pearson, Michael 231
Pearson, Mike 32
Peloponnese 44
Peng, Eliza *70*
Pennington, Gladys 144
Penn State vs. Illinois (1994) 248–250
Pennsylvanian period 7
Pensabene, Vincent 258
Pereira, William 166
Perrino, Dan 230
Perry, Lawrence 107, 120
Peters, E. R. 185
Peterson, James A. 226, 253
Petry, C. A. 221
Petty, Tom 236
Phoenix 27
physical education 6
physical fitness 52–53
Pittsburgh's Panthers 177
Platt, Charles 1, 2, 35, 54, 63, 102, 149
pledge payments 99, 101, 102, 107, 158
Pleistocene epoch 7, 9
Poe, B. 194
Polk, James 16
Pond, Charles 201
postmodern reality 198–200
post-war housing diagram *175*
Post-War Planning Commission 174
post-war racial integration 177–178
Powell, Burt E. 16, 18
Prairie State Games 253

press box 206, *207, 220;* aerial view of *213;* photographer's floor *209;* reporter's floor *210;* seen from the field *208;* west stands and *210*
Priene 44
Princeton's Palmer Stadium 48
Princeton University 148
Pritzker, J. B. 274
Project Total Conditioning 226
property values 38–40, *40, 41*
proposed stadium, faculty sketch 50, *51*
Provine, L. H. 28, 50, 53
Purdue's Ross Aide Stadium 48
Purdue University 26

Quad 206
Quakers 150
Quebecois native 11

radio 171; broadcasting 6, 72, 139, 194, 220, 221, 294; play-by-play calls 122; technology 148
railroad map of Illinois *15*
Raitt, Bonnie 236
Reagan, Ronald W. 219
realistic instruction 172
recruitment tactics 194
Redbox Bowl 271–273, *272–274*
Redden, Curtis G. 64
"Red" Grange, Harold E. 1, 2, 6, *6,* 104, 106, *145,* 147, 149, 150, 159, 182, 206, 212, 249, 261, *262*
Redmon, Bogie 203
regional newspapers 150
Rehabilitation Act (1973) 234
Reigner, E. H. 175
Reinmuth, Gary 255
ReliaQuest Bowl 276
religious rituals 44
Renaissance project 269
Reserved Officers Training Core (ROTC) program 28
Revolutionary War (1783) 5, 11
Reynolds, Gregory 229
Reynolds, John 17
Rhodes, J. W. *20*
Rice, Grantland 147
Rice, Simeon 2, 248, 250

Richards, C. R. 6, 82
Richart, F. E. 158
Ricker, Nathan 50
Roaring Twenties 139, 149–150, 160
Roche, Martin 52
Rock Island 14
Rodríguez-Suárez, Francisco J. 3, *3*
Rogan, Jonathan 23, 165
Rogers, Cheryl 203
Rokusek, Frank E. 104, 147
Roman Colosseum 48
Roman U-shaped stadiums 45, 46
Roosevelt, Franklin D. 171
Roosevelt, Theodore 28, 64
Roots, B. G. 18
Rosebery, Clarence J. 35, 75, 99, 100, 104
Rose Bowl 48, 106, *199,* 235, 266
Roselawn Cemetery *164*
Rotary Club 152
Rutgers Scarlet Knights 271
Rutherford, C. J. 104
Ryan, George 263
Rykovich, Julius 179

Sacconi, Giuseppe 56, *57*
Salt Fork Vermilion River 9
Salt River 9
Sarett, Lew 66, 125
SARS-CoV-2 274
Schell, Jacob Kinzer 26
Schembechler Jr., Glenn Edward 231
Schick, William 172
Schmidt, Harvard 205
Schoenburg, Bernie 225
School of Architecture *70*
scoreboard and end zone seating *274*
Senate-confirmed commission 18
Serviceman's Readjustment Act (1944) 171
Seymour, Bliss 64
Shade, Barbara 179
Shapland Construction Company 200
Shepard, Terry 211
Sherfy, Fanny B. 77
Sherman, Ed 251
Shull, Laurens 64
Siden, Jean E. 198

Simon, Paul 259
Simulacra and Simulation 199
slush fund scandal 205, 222
Small, Lennington 75, *144*
Smiley, Gene 160
Smith, Betty *257*
social distancing 274, *275*
socializing space 150–151
soft opening 104–124; after the 106–120, *108–120;* national championship season (1923) 106–107; Stadium completion 120–124, *121–124;* working toward 104–106, *105*
Soldier Field 53, *56, 58,* 295; colonnade *55, 65;* competition drawing *53;* compositional scheme 56; Dempsey Tunney fight *54;* neoclassical vocabulary 56; north side of 61
Southeastern Conference (SEC) 162
Southern Illinois Salukis 247, *248*
Soviet incursion 219
Special Educational Opportunities Program (SEOP) 213
Sputnik 187
stadium: longitudinal section *68;* section diagram *67;* section diagram *67;* three site proposals 40; *see also* Memorial Stadium
Stadium Captain's Handbook 78
Stadium Executive Committee 76, 120, 158
Stadium fund flyer *79*
stadium ramp tower: bas-relief sculptures *71, 72;* carved medallions *72;* elevation *135;* interior *63;* north and south 69
Stadium Terrace Units *174,* 174–175, *175*
Stagg, Amos A. 104
Stagg Field 149
stair tower ramps *67*
Staley, Rollin 206
Stanley Halas Sr., George 150
Stanton, William M. 50
State Farm Center 2, 3, 166
State of Illinois 12, 19
Steger, Herb 147

Sterling, Fred E. 101
Stevens, Thomas 229
Stewart, Alva W. 50
Stewart, Stanley P. 50
Stock, James H. 236
Stoddard, George Dinsmore 177
Stoner, Neale 247
Stoolman, A. W. 77
Stoolman property 40, 76–77
The Story of the Stadium 50, *61*
Stouffer, Ernest 185
Stratton, William 188
student activism 213–214
student cheering section *267*
Student Committee on Political
     Expression (SCOPE) 193
Student Community Human Relations
     Council 178
Student-Community Interracial
     Committee of Urbana-Champaign
     (S-CIC) 178
students: and band section *266;*
     convocations 152, *152;* protests 193,
     214
Students' Army Training Corps (SATC)
     program 28
subsidization 164
Sumner, Jim 147
Super Bowl championship 240
Swamp Land Act (1850) 9

TailGREAT 231, *232,* 261
taxation law 19
television: broadcasting 148, 171;
     contract 258; decade's end 186–190;
     Illini basketball's impact 183–186,
     184–186; mass media impact of
     180–183, *181;* public appetite 183;
     revenues 224
Tepper, Lou 248, 250, 253
Thomas, Mike 261, 272
Thompson, James R. 224
Thompson, Jim 259
Thornton, Mark 151
Tilton, Leon Deming 29, *30*
Tobin, L. M. 104
Toledo Rockets 271
Tonty, Henry de 11

track and field (T&F) 152–153, *153,*
     226–229; apex of 228–229, *229;*
     emerging 226–228, *227*
Treaty of Paris 11
Trowbridge, Raymond *55, 65*
Trump, Donald J. 246, 247
Tuite, Patrick 194
tumultuous years, 1960 to 1975
     193–214; activism 213–214;
     anchor of campus life 193–195;
     carillon 205–206; Elliott, Pete *195,*
     195–198; Huff's ghost haunts Illini
     football 203–205; men's track and
     field 201–203, *202, 203;* Stadium
     and postmodern reality 198–200;
     upgrades 206–213, *207–210;*
     women's track and field 203, *204;*
     Zuppke Field 200–201
Turner, Fred 193
Turner, Jonathan Baldwin 16, 18, 176
Turner, Ron 250, 254, 255, 257

Ukraine 247
Union of Soviet Socialist Republics 187
United States 43; college football's
     popularity 147; economy 147, 160;
     Great War (1914–1918) 27–29;
     sports and entertainment facilities
     159
United States Naval Academy 106
University of California, Los Angeles
     (UCLA) 165
University of Chicago 26, 104, 148
University of Chicago Maroons 104,
     149
University of Colorado Buffaloes 247
University of Hawai'i Rainbow
     Warriors 248
University of Illinois 23, 26, 106, 139;
     Athletic Association 43; established
     rules and authority 193; first football
     team, 1890 *24;* football radio
     broadcasts 148; grounds of *30;*
     legislation 197; masterplan of *31*
University of Illinois Foundation 220
University of Illinois Memorial
     Stadium: after World War II
     177–180; beginning of an era *6,*

6–7; Champaign County *9,* 9–10;
     coal, economy *12,* 12–14; conceived
     5–6; delivering on the promise
     19–20; geographic context *7,* 7–9, *8;*
     memories 1–3, *3;* Morrill Act (1862)
     14–16; origins of 23–41; prelude
     to 10–14; situation 16–19; during
     World War II 171–177
University of Illinois
     Urbana-Champaign (UIUC) 1, 220,
     245, 293
University of Indiana Hoosiers 196
University of Maryland Terrapins 271
University of Michigan 1, 26, 139, 219
University of Michigan's "Big House" 48
University of Minnesota 26, 63
University of Minnesota Golden
     Gophers 149
University of Nebraska's Memorial
     Stadium 49
University of Pittsburgh 148, 177, 183,
     233
University of Pittsburgh Panthers 211
University of South Dakota 176
University of Southern California
     (USC) 245
University of Washington Huskies *199,*
     200
University of Wisconsin 2, 26, 63
University of Wisconsin Badgers 106,
     149, 206
University's War Committee 28
upper level plans *282–283*
Upper Sangamon ridge 9
Urbana 1, 264
Urbana and Champaign Institute 18
Urbana-Champaign 122, *123,* 140, 150,
     171, 185, 193, 214
Urbana Daily Courier 159
US Centers for Disease Control and
     Prevention (CDC) 246
US Civil War (1861–1865) 14
US Navy 172, 177, 219
USS Illinois 177
US Steel Company 82

Valek, Jim 205, 250
Vance, Gene 205, 212

Velasquez, Arthur R. 223
Verduzco, Jason 247
Vermilion River 89
Vietnam War 193, 219; student protests 193; US's involvement 193
Virgin, Craig 228
V-12 program 173

Wabash Rivers 9
Walker, Daniel 220
Washington Evening Star 107
Washington State Cougars 248
Waters, Ethel 75
Watterson, John Sayle 28
Weber, Bruce 246
weight room facility *268*
Wells, Mike 231
Wertman, Nancy 227
Western Brick Company 102
Western Conference 151
Western Union Telegraph 122
West Great Hall 171–174; housing proposal *172;* northern half of 173; southern half of 173
west stands *88, 91, 92, 94, 95, 98, 108, 110–112, 114, 117;* casting balcony seating *97;* colonnade *113, 118, 119;* with steel and seating underway *91*
Wheeler, Hiram Hannibal 165
while football 139
White, Byron R. 220

White, James M. 38, 39, 50, 54, 139, 149, 158, 205
White, James S. 75
White, Mike 220, 223, 231–232, 247, 257
Whitman, Josh 250, 259, 272
Whiz Kids 183
Wieneke, Gary 226, *227*
WiFi network 259
WILL 180, *181*
Willard, Arthur Cutts 172
William, Paul 231
Williams, C. F. 27
Willis, G. C. 150
Wilson, Wendell S. 164
Wilson, Wilfred 147
Wilson, Woodrow 28
Winkel, Rick 263
Wisconsin Badgers 163, 196, 250, 273
Wisconsin Glacial Episode Illinois moraines *8*
women's track and field 203, *204*
Woods, John 9
Woodson, Abe 183
World Health Organization (WHO) 246
World Trade Center 246
World War I 43, 64
World War II (WWII) 3, 139, 171–190, 219, 295; expansion to midcentury 178–180; legacy 177, *177;* Parade Ground Units 174–175, *175;*

patriotic venue 175–176; post-war racial integration 177–178; sports at the Stadium during *176,* 176–177; Stadium Terrace Units *174,* 174–175, *175;* television era 180–190; West Great Hall 171–174, *172, 173*
World Wheelchair Games (1984) 234
Wrigley Field, Chicago 2, 49, *49*

Yale's football stadium 48
Yates, Richard 16, 17
Yellow-bank, James 259
Young, Claude Henry 2, 165, 171, *176,* 177, 179, 202, 272–273
Young, Fred 180
Young, Neil 236
Young, Roy Mercer 165

Zaxby's Heart of Dallas Bowl 272
Zeta Beta Tau 166
Zeus 44
Zook, Ronald A. 264, 271
Zuppke Field 200–201, 225, 266; artificial turf 222, 226; north wall *201;* resurfacing 238; scoreboard *201*
Zuppkeisms 164
Zuppke, Robert C. "Zup" 6, 26, *26,* 32, 39, 40, 52, 53, 139, 147, 150, 161, 163, *164,* 176, 203, 206, 294